Practical
Language
Testing

Glenn Fulcher

HODDER
EDUCATION
AN HACHETTE UK COMPANY

For all the inspiring teachers
I have been lucky enough to have
and especially
Revd Ian Robins
Who knows where the ripples end?

First published in Great Britain in 2010 by
Hodder Education, An Hachette UK Company,
338 Euston Road, London NW1 3BH

Hachette UK's policy is to use papers that are natural, renewable and
recyclable products and made from wood grown in sustainable forests.
The logging and manufacturing processes are expected to conform to the
environmental regulations of the country of origin.

The advice and information in this book are believed to be true and
accurate at the date of going to press, but neither the author nor the publisher
can accept any legal responsibility or liability for any errors or omissions.

British Library Cataloguing in Publication Data
A catalogue record for this book is available from the British Library

Library of Congress Cataloging-in-Publication Data
A catalog record for this book is available from the Library of Congress

ISBN: 978 0 340 984482

1 2 3 4 5 6 7 8 9 10

Cover Image © Anthony Bradshaw/Photographer's Choice RF/Getty Images
Typeset in 10 on 13pt Minion by Phoenix Photosetting, Chatham, Kent
Printed and bound in Great Britain by Antony Rowe, Chippenham, Wilts

What do you think about this book? Or any other Hodder Education
title? Please send your comments to educationenquiries@hodder.co.uk

http://www.hoddereducation.com

Contents

3 Classroom assessment

4 Deciding what to test

5 Designing test specifications

6 Evaluating, prototyping and piloting

7 Scoring language tests

Acknowledgements

I am deeply indebted to the Leverhulme Trust (www.leverhulme.ac.uk), which awarded me a Research Fellowship in 2009 in order to carry out the research required for this book, and funded study leave to write it. The generosity of the Trust provided the time and space for clear thinking that work on a text like this requires.

The University of Leicester was extremely supportive of this project, granting me six months' study leave to work entirely on the book. I would also like to thank staff in the School of Education for help and advice received while drafting proposals and work schedules.

I am grateful to the people, and the institutions, who have given me permission to use materials for the book.

Special thanks are due to Professor Yin Jan of Shanghai Jiao Tong University, and Chair of the National College English Testing Committee of the China Higher Education Department. Her kindness in providing information about language testing in China, as well as samples of released tests, has enriched this book.

I have always been inspired by my students. While I was working on the development of Performance Decision Trees (see Chapter 7), Samantha Mills was working on a dissertation in which she developed and prototyped a task for use in assessing service encounter communication in the tourist industry. In this book the two come together to illustrate how specifications, tasks and scoring systems, can be designed for specific purpose assessment. I am very grateful to Samantha for permission to reproduce sections of her work, particularly in Chapters 5 and 6.

Test design workshops can be great fun; and they are essential when brainstorming new item types. I have run many workshops of this kind, and the material used to illustrate the process of item evaluation in Chapter 6 is taken from a workshop conducted for Oxford University Press (OUP). I am grateful to OUP, particularly Simon Beeston and Alexandra Miller, for permission to use what is normally considered to be confidential data.

The book presents a number of statistical tools that the reader can use when designing or evaluating tests. All of the statistics can be calculated using packages such as SPSS, or online web-based calculators. However, I believe that it is important for people who are involved in language testing to understand how the basic statistics can be calculated by hand. My own initial statistical training was provided by Charles Owen at the University of Birmingham, and I have always been grateful that he made us do calculations by hand so that we could 'see' what the machine was doing. However, calculation by hand can always lead to errors. After a while, the examples in the text became so familiar that I would not have been able to spot any errors, no matter how glaring. I am therefore extremely grateful to Sun Joo Chung of the University of Illinois at Urbana-Champaign for the care with which she checked and corrected these parts of the book.

The content of the book evolved over the period during which it was written. This is because it is based on a research project to discover the language testing needs of teachers and students of language testing on applied linguistics programmes. A survey instrument was designed and piloted, and then used in the main study. It was delivered through the Language Testing Resources website (http://languagetesting.info), and announced on the language testing and applied linguistics discussion lists. It was also supported by the United Kingdom's Subject Centre for Languages, Linguistics and Area Studies. The respondents came from all over the world, and from many different backgrounds. Each had a particular need, but common themes emerged in what they wished to see in a book on practical language testing. The information and advice that they provided has shaped the text in many ways, as my writing responded to incoming data. My thanks, therefore, to all the people who visited my website and spent time completing the survey.

My thanks are also due to Fred Davidson, for a continued conversation on language testing that never fails to inspire. To Alan Davies and Bernard Spolsky, for their help and support; and for the constant reminder that historical context is more important than ever to understanding the 'big picture'. And to all my other friends and colleagues in the International Language Testing Association (ILTA), who are dedicated to improving language testing practice, and language testing literacy.

Every effort has been made to obtain the necessary permission with reference to copyright material. The publishers apologise if inadvertently any sources remain unacknowledged and will be glad to make the necessary arrangements at the earliest opportunity.

Finally, acknowledgements are never complete with recognition for people who have to suffer the inevitable lack of attention that writing a book generates. Not to mention the narrowing of conversational topics. My enduring thanks to Jenny and Greg for their tolerance and encouragement.

Figures

Tables

Preface

This book is about building and using language tests and assessments. It does what it says on the tin: it is a *practical* approach. However, it does not provide ready-made solutions. Language testing is a complex social phenomenon, and its practice changes lives. The book therefore assumes that you will wish to think carefully about testing and its impact in your own context.

The term 'practical' therefore needs some definition. The book is 'practical' in the sense that it gives guidance on how to do things to build a test. It is also 'practical' in that each chapter will be useful to you when you come to making decisions about when, why and how to conduct assessments. The book is designed to provide the *knowledge* you will need to apply, and the *skills* you will need to practise. However, if we are to build good language tests, we have to be aware of the larger social, ethical, and historical context, within which we work. If language testing and assessment are not guided by *principles*, we could end up doing more harm than good. Davies (2008a) has cogently argued that testing and assessment texts that do not embed knowledge and skills in principles ignore the increasing demand of professionalism and social responsibility.

Language professionals, applied linguists and educational policy makers need an expanded 'assessment literacy' in order to make the right decisions for language learners and institutions (Taylor, 2009). This literacy will be about learning the nuts and bolts of writing better test items (Coniam, 2008), and establishing a core knowledge base (Inbar, 2008); but it is also about appreciating the reasons why we test, why we test the way we do and how test use can enrich or destroy people's hopes, ambitions and lives.

Although I am far from being in the 'postmodern' school of language testing and assessment, the view that language testing is a social activity cannot be denied (McNamara, 2001). Nor can the fact that our practices are thoroughly grounded in a long history that has brought us to where we are (Spolsky, 1995). It is partly because of this history that many texts published 'for teachers' focus almost entirely upon the technologies of normative large-scale standardised testing. While it is important that teachers are familiar with these, they are not always directly relevant to the classroom. This book therefore tries to introduce a balance between standardised testing and classroom assessment.

The structure reflects a conscious decision to place language testing and assessment within context, *and* to provide the 'practical' guidance on the nuts and bolts of test building. Broadly, the first three chapters survey the language testing landscape upon which we can build. Chapter 4 is about the material that we can use in construction, and the rest of the book takes the reader through the process of building and implementing a language test.

Chapter 1 considers the purpose of testing in the broadest sense of why societies use tests, and in the narrow sense of how we define the purpose of a particular test. It looks at how tests are used, for good and ill; and the unintended consequences that testing can have on people who are caught up in the need to succeed. Chapters 2 and 3 deal in turn with large-scale standardised testing, and then with classroom assessment. The stories of both paradigms are set within a historical framework so that you can see where the theories and practices originate.

In Chapter 4 we begin the journey through the process of test design, starting with deciding what to test, and why. Chapter 5 begins the test design process in earnest, where we discuss how to create test specifications – the basic design documents that help us to build a test. This is where we learn to become 'test architects', shaping the materials and putting them together in plans that can be used to produce usable test forms. In Chapter 6 we look at how to evaluate the test specifications and test items, from initial critical discussions in specification workshops to trying out items and tests with learners. Chapter 7 contains a discussion of scoring, covering both traditional item types like multiple choice, as well as performance tests that require human judgement. Frequently, we have to use tests to make decisions that require a 'cut score' – a level on the test above which a test taker is judged to be a 'master', and below which they are still 'novices'. Establishing cut scores and linking these to absolute standards is the subject of Chapter 8. Chapter 9 discusses the practicalities of test administration, and why the 'rituals' of testing have grown as they have.

Finally, in Chapter 10, we return to the classroom and to the effect that tests have upon learning and teaching, and how we go about preparing learners to take tests.

Throughout the book I have included examples from real tests and assessments. Some of these are good examples that we can emulate. Others are provided for you to critique and improve. Some of them are also drawn from historical sources, as 'distance' is useful for nurturing critical awareness. However, I do not present sets of typical test items and tasks that you could simply select to include in your own tests. There are plenty of books on the market that do this. This book asks you to think about what item or task types would be most useful for your own tests. We discuss options, but only you can provide the answers and the rationales for the choices you make.

There are activities at the end of every chapter that you can attempt on your own, although many would benefit from team work. Sharing experiences and debating difficult issues is best done in a group. And it's also more fun. The activities have been designed to help you think through issues raised in the chapter, and practise the skills that you have learned. The activities are not exhaustive, and you are encouraged to add to these if you are using the text in a language testing course. Beginning in Chapter 4 there is also a Project that you may wish to do as you move from chapter to chapter.

This structure has been shaped not only by my own understanding of what an introductory book to foster 'assessment literacy' might look like, but also by what language teachers and students of applied linguistics have told me that they need to know, and be able to do. Prior to writing the book I undertook a large-scale internet-based survey, funded by the Leverhulme Trust. Almost 300 respondents completed the survey, and I was struck by the sophistication of their awareness of assessment issues.

Here is a selection of typical responses to a question about what teachers and students of applied linguistics most need in a 'practical' language text:

Evaluating reliability for our in-house tests, and checking questions at each stage in test development.

I don't understand statistics, but I know they can be useful. I need it explaining conceptually.

We need to know the jargon, but introduce it step by step.

Hands-on activities; examples of test specs; a glossary would be useful.

A book of this type must focus on the basics of item writing and test construction, the basic concepts of validity and reliability, particularly in regards to the assessment of speaking and writing. It must also cover the ethics of test use and test score interpretation.

Developing classroom tests, performance tests, setting score standards, deciding what to test, preparing learners for test situations.

Differentiation between classroom assessments, formative assessment, and large-scale assessment when discussing key issues.

Most of the assessment/testing practices are done by teachers; I think that a book should be aimed at 'normal' language teachers more than specialists in testing, they already have other sources of information and training.

Issues to do with ensuring validity and reliability in language testing. The test writing process from the creation of test specifications through to the trialling, administration and marking of tests.

Vignettes; glossary; application activities for individuals and groups, including some practice with basic test statistics and approaches to calculating grades.

Some information on testing as an industry, a multi-billion dollar concern and why we have to fight crap when we see it.

Luckily, many respondents said they realised that it is impossible to include everything in a practical language testing book. This is evidently true, as you will see. I am sure to have left out a topic that you think should have been included. One respondent understood this all too well: 'The book should be well-structured, clearly focused, and however tempted you might be to put everything into one book, you should be selective in order to be comprehensible and user-friendly.' I am not entirely sure that I have achieved this. But if I have got even halfway there, my time will have been well spent.

As another respondent said, 'The learning never ends.' In order to sustain you during your journey through the book, you may wish to pay regular visits to my website:

http://languagetesting.info

Here you will find a set of online videos that define and explain some of the key concepts and topics in language testing. To help you with additional reading, I have links to online articles, and other language testing websites. There are links to useful journals, and regular updates on testing stories that get into the news.

Constructive criticism is always welcome, via the website.

1

Testing and assessment in context

▶ 1. Test purpose

Language testing, like all educational assessment, is a complex social phenomenon. It has evolved to fulfil a number of functions in the classroom, and society at large. Today the use of language testing is endemic in contexts as diverse as education, employment, international mobility, language planning and economic policy making. Such widespread use makes language testing controversial. For some, language tests are *gate-keeping* tools that further the agendas of the powerful. For others, they are the vehicle by which society can implement equality of opportunity or learner empowerment. How we perceive language tests depends partly upon our own experiences. Perhaps they were troubling events that we had to endure; or maybe they opened doors to a new and better life. But our considered judgements should also be based upon an understanding of the historical evolution of testing and assessment, and an analysis of the legitimate roles for testing in egalitarian societies. This first chapter therefore situates language testing in its historical and social context by discussing a variety of perspectives from which to evaluate its practical applications, beginning with the most fundamental concern of all: the purpose of testing.

The act of giving a test always has a purpose. In one of the founding documents of modern language testing, Carroll (1961: 314) states: 'The purpose of language testing is always to render information to aid in making intelligent decisions about possible courses of action.' But these decisions are diverse, and need to be made very specific for each intended use of a test. Davidson and Lynch (2002: 76–78) use the term 'mandate' to describe where test purpose comes from, and suggest that mandates can be seen as either internal or external to the institution in which we work. An internal mandate for test use is frequently established by teachers themselves, or by the school administration. The purpose of such testing is primarily related to the needs of the teachers and learners working within a particular context. Tests that are under local control are mostly used to place learners into classes, to discover how much they have achieved, or to diagnose difficulties that individual learners may have. Although it is very rarely discussed, teachers also use tests to motivate learners to study. If students know they are going to face a quiz at the end of the week, or an end of semester achievement test, the effect is often an increase in study time near the time of the test. In a sense, no 'decision' is going to be taken once the test is scored. Indeed, when classroom tests were first introduced into schools, an increase in motivation was thought to be one of their major benefits. For example, writing in the nineteenth century, Latham (1877:

146) reported: 'The efficacy of examinations as a means of calling out the interest of a pupil and directing it into the desired channels was soon recognized by teachers.' Ruch (1924: 3) was a little more forthright: 'Educators seem to be agreed that pupils tend to accomplish more when confronted with the realization that a day of reckoning is surely at hand.' However, the evidence to support the motivational role of tests has always been largely anecdotal, making it a folk belief, no matter how prevalent it has always been.

The key feature of testing within a local mandate is that the testing should be 'ecologically sensitive', serving the local needs of teachers and learners. What this means in practice is that the outcomes of testing – whether these are traditional 'scores' or more complex profiles of performance – are interpreted in relation to a specific learning environment. Similarly, if any organisational or instructional decisions are taken on the basis of testing, their effect is only local.

Cronbach (1984: 122) put this most succinctly:

> A test is selected for a particular situation and purpose. What tests are pertinent for a psychological examination of a child entering first grade? That depends on what alternative instructional plans the school is prepared to follow. What test of skill in English usage is suitable for surveying a high school class? Those teachers for whom clarity of expression is important will be discontented with a test requiring only that the student choose between grammatically correct and incorrect expressions.

If testing with a local mandate is ecologically sensitive, it is highly likely that it will have a number of other distinguishing characteristics. Firstly, we would expect much of the testing to be *formative*. That is, the act of testing is designed to play a role in the teaching and learning process, rather than to certify ultimate achievement. Secondly, the test is likely to be *low-stakes*. This means that any decisions made after the testing is complete will not have serious consequences for the person who has taken the test, for the teacher or for the school. Rather, the information from the testing or assessment procedure will be used by the teacher and the learner to make decisions about what the most immediate learning goals might be, what targets to set for the next semester, or which classes it is most useful for a learner to attend. If mistakes are made, they are easily corrected through dialogue and negotiation. Thirdly, the testing or assessment procedures used are likely to be created or selected by the teachers themselves, and the learners may also be given a say in how they prefer to be assessed. This ecological sensitivity therefore impacts upon how testing is used, the seriousness (and retractability) of decisions, and the involvement of the local *stakeholders* in designing and implementing tests and assessments.

An external mandate, on the other hand, is a reason for testing that comes from outside the local context. The decision to test is taken by a person or a group of people who often do not know a great deal about the local learning ecology, and probably don't even know the teachers and learners who will have to cope with the required testing regime. As soon as we begin to talk about external mandates loaded words begin to enter the discussion, such as 'regime', because teachers are naturally suspicious of anything that is 'imposed' from outside. The motivations for external mandates may also appear extremely vague and complex; indeed, policy makers often do not clearly articulate the purpose of the required testing, but it usually serves a very different function from internally mandated tests. External tests are primarily designed to measure the proficiency of learners without reference to the context in which they are learning. Also, the tests are *summative*: they measure proficiency at the end of a period of study, by which time learners may be expected to have reached a particular *standard*. The information therefore doesn't always feed back into the learning process, but fulfils an accountability role.

In summative testing we also expect test scores to carry *generalisable* meaning; that is, the score can be interpreted to mean something beyond the context in which the learner is tested. In order to understand this, we can turn to Messick (1989: 14–15), who said that generalisability is about 'the fundamental question of whether the meaning of a measure is context-specific or whether it generalizes across contexts'. Teachers wish the meaning of testing and assessment to be locally meaningful in terms of what comes next in teaching. If the outcomes are not particularly generalisable across people, settings and tasks – or different 'ecological conditions' – it doesn't matter too much. In externally mandated tests, however, there is an assumption that the meaning of test scores generalise to what learners are capable of doing across a wide range of contexts not necessarily contained in the test. Score users want to be able to make decisions about whether learners can communicate with people outside their immediate environment, in unfamiliar places, engaging in tasks that have not been directly modelled in the test itself. The greater the claim for generalisability, the more 'global' the intention to interpret score meaning. For example, an academic writing task may contain only one or two questions, but the scores are treated as being indicative of ability to write in a wide range of genres, across a number of disciplines. Or we could think of scores on a short reading test being used to compare literacy rates across a number of countries. The testers might wish to draw conclusions about the likely contribution of the educational sector to the economy. Indeed, the latter is the explicit aim of the Programme for International Student Assessment (PISA), carried out by the Organisation for Economic Co-operation and Development (www.pisa.oecd.org).

Generalisability is therefore an important consideration in tests with an external mandate, when they are used to certify an ability to perform at a specified level, or to compare and contrast the performance of schools, educational districts, or even countries. We refer to such tests as being *high-stakes*. Failure for individual learners may result in the termination of their studies. Or they may not be able to access certain occupations. For schools, a 'failure' may result in a Ministry of Education introducing 'special measures', including removal of staff, or direct management from the central authority. At the national level, perceived failure in comparison with other countries could result in the wholesale reform of educational systems as politicians try to avoid the implied impending economic catastrophe.

2. Tests in educational systems

One of the largest testing systems in the world is the National College Entrance Test in China (the Gaokao). Taken over a two-day period, students sit tests in Chinese, English, mathematics, sciences and humanities. The outcome is a score that can range between 100 and 900 points, and determines which college or university each student will attend. Each college and university sets its entrance score and allocates a number of places to each province. Millions of students apply for a place, and so the test is extremely high-stakes and very competitive.

Why do such tests exist? Testing is primarily about establishing *ways of making decisions* that are (hopefully) not random, and seen as 'fair' by the population. Whenever we establish ways of making decisions, we reveal what we believe about society and political organisation. So the practice of testing and assessment can never be separated from social and political values.

This may sound like an overstatement. But consider the university application situation again. There are a limited number of places in institutions of higher education and there must be some method of judging which applicants to accept. We could make the acceptance decisions using many different criteria. If the criteria that we use reflect our views about how society is (or should) be organised, what would it say about us if we decided to offer the best places to the children of government officials? Or to those who can pay the highest fees? If you find these two suggestions rather distasteful, perhaps you should ask this question of yourself: what do you think the goals of education are?

Here is another strong statement: 'the act of testing is the mechanism by which our social and political values are realised and implemented.' If we believe that the purpose of a test like the Gaokao is to provide equality of opportunity, we see meritocratic practices embedded within the testing process. Messick (1989: 86–87) was one writer who believed that this was the primary social purpose of testing. He argued that testing, when done well, was capable of delivering 'distributive justice' (Rawls, 1973):

> If desirable educational programs or jobs are conceived as allocable resources or social goods, then selection and classification may be viewed as problems of distributive justice. The concept of distributive justice deals with the appropriateness of access to the conditions and goods that affect individual well-being, which is broadly conceived to include psychological, physiological, economic and social aspects. Any sense of injustice with respect to the allocation of resources or goods is usually directed at the rules of distribution, whereas the actual source of discontent may also (or instead) derive from the social values underlying the rules, from the ways in which the rules are implemented, or from the nature of the decision-making process itself.

In the Gaokao there is an assumption that access to university places should be based on a principle of meritocracy that places a high value on ability, as defined by the tests. There is also a clear commitment to equality of opportunity. This means that there should be no discrimination or *bias* against any test taker or group of test takers. We could question these values, of course. Access to higher education has in the past been a matter of ability to pay, which in many countries was related to class; but social immobility is not something that we would wish to defend today. Other options might be to value effort above ability. Perhaps it is those individuals who strive hard to improve who should be given the better education? We might assess for progress from a baseline, therefore valuing commitment, dedication and staying power. In a world of global business where the principles of capitalism do not seem to be frequently challenged, perhaps the process should merely be opened up to market forces?

What we choose to endow with high value tells us a great deal about what we expect the effects of testing to be. It has even been argued that *effect-driven testing* begins by picturing the impact a test is intended to have upon all the stakeholders in a society, and work backwards to the actual design of the test (Fulcher and Davidson, 2007). This means that we cannot separate the actual practice of writing tests and assessments – the nuts and bolts of test design and creation – from our values. For teachers and other practitioners, this is liberating. It means that our philosophy and understanding of what is valuable and meaningful in society and education are highly relevant to the tests that we use. We can also see why things happen the way they do. And once we can see this, we can also imagine how they might change for the better.

▶ 3. Testing rituals

High-stakes externally mandated tests like the Gaokao are easily distinguishable from classroom assessments by another critical feature: the 'rituality' associated with the activity of testing (further discussed in Chapter 9). As the test marks the culmination of secondary education, it is a 'rite of passage', an event that marks a significant stage in life. It also determines the immediate future, and longer-term prospects, of each test taker. Such events are ritualised, following established practices that endow the activity with special meaning. But the rituals themselves are drawn from the values embedded in the educational and social system, in this case, meritocracy and equality of opportunity. Arriving at a pre-specified place at the same time as others, sitting in a designated seat a regulation distance from other seats, and answering the same questions as other learners in the same time period, are all part of this ritual. This testing practice is designed to enable meritocracy by imposing the same conditions upon all test takers. A *standardised test* is defined by Cohen and Wollack (2006: 358) in the following way:

> Tests are standardized when the directions, conditions of administration, and scoring are clearly defined and fixed for all examinees, administrations, and forms.

The principle at stake is that any difference between the score of two individuals should directly reflect their ability upon what is being tested. To put it another way, if two individuals have an equal ability on what is being tested, they should get the same score. If one person gets a higher score because she received more time to take the test, or sat so close to a more able student that she could copy, the principles of meritocracy and equality of opportunity would be compromised.

In the Gaokao, maintaining the principles is taken extremely seriously. Apart from the normal examination regulations, during the two days of testing building sites are closed, aircraft flight paths are changed to avoid low-flying aircraft disturbing students, and test centres are provided with their own police guard to reduce traffic noise and maintain security over test papers. The cost of these measures is extremely high. However, it is known from research that increased noise during a test can in some circumstances result in reduced scores (Haines *et al.*, 2002; Powers *et al.*, 2002) because it affects concentration. If some test centres are subject to noise levels that other tests centres do not experience, any difference in scores could be a result of noise. In testing jargon the impact of any variable like noise upon test scores is called *construct irrelevant variance*, or the variance in scores that is due to a factor in which we are not at all interested. Another such factor is cheating, and so students are often checked with metal detectors as they enter the examination room to ensure they are not carrying mobile devices or any other information storage equipment. *Invigilation*, or *proctoring*, is carried out with great care, and any case of examination fraud is dealt with harshly.

These rituals are repeated around the world. And the rituals are far from a new invention. China's Imperial Examination System was started in the Sui dynasty of 589–618 AD and only came to an end in 1905. Designed to select the most able to fill posts in the civil service, the examinations were free to enter, and open to anyone who wished to participate. Rules were formulated about leaving one's seat, the impropriety of exchanging or dropping test papers, talking to others during the test, gazing at others, changing seats, disobeying instructions from the invigilator, humming, or submitting incomplete test papers (Miyazaki, 1981: 28). These examinations also instituted the principle that the examiners should not know the identity of the test taker when marking work in order to avoid bias or discrimination (Miyazaki, 1981: 117). All of these ancient practices are features of the ritual of testing that teachers around the world are familiar with today.

▶ 4. Unintended consequences

If the consequences of testing are those that we intend, and our intentions are good, all is well. However, it is rarely the case that we can have things all our own way. Whenever tests are used in society, even for well-meaning purposes, there are *unintended consequences*. With high-stakes tests, unintended consequences are likely to be much more severe. Let us consider three unintended consequences of tests like the Gaokao.

Perhaps the most obvious unintended consequence is the fact that many students and teachers cease to study the language, and start to study the test. This is done in the belief that there are test-taking strategies that will raise a score even if ability, knowledge or communication skills have not been improved. The effect of a test on teaching is termed *washback* (discussed at length in Chapter 10). While this can be positive or negative, it is often assumed that teaching to the test is negative. Examples of the negative washback from high-stakes language tests are provided by Mansell (2007: 83–90) in the context of the United Kingdom's foreign language General Certificate of Secondary Education examinations. These include:

- Memorising unanalysed fragments of text that can be assembled to create a variety of 100-word essays on simple topics.
- Memorising scripted fragments of speech in relation to common oral interview-type questions, and extended chunks for presentation-type tasks.
- Teaching written responses to questions, followed by oral memorisation drills, for all common topics such as 'family and friends', 'holidays' or 'shopping'.

Associated with this kind of teaching is the publication of test preparation materials on an industrial scale, and the growth of private schools that specialise in test preparation. These 'cram schools' claim that they can raise test scores through specialised tuition in short time periods, primarily by practising test-type questions over and over again, and learning test-taking strategies. Parental and peer pressure may make students spend considerable periods of out-of-school time in test preparation classes, the value of which are questionable (see Chapter 10).

Another unintended consequence of high-stakes testing is the possibility of deteriorating health. Longer hours of study without periods of rest and relaxation, or even time to pursue hobbies or extra-curricular activities, can lead to tiredness. Given the pressure to succeed, stress levels can be high, and becoming run-down can add significantly to fears of failure. It is not surprising that this can lead to health problems among a growing percentage of the test-taking population. At its worst, some students become clinically depressed and suicide rates increase.

This is not an isolated problem. Mental health and stress-related illnesses have been reported in many countries with high-stakes standards-based tests for high school students. Suggested solutions have included the introduction of more schools-based assessment, the reduction in length of time spent on formal summative assessment, and a move toward test formats that reduce the overuse of memorisation activities in class. Teachers do not wish to see learners put under the kind of pressure that happens in many modern educational systems; it is therefore incumbent upon teachers to engage with testing systems and those who create them to develop less stressful approaches.

The final example concerns 'test migration'. Universities in China allocate numbers of places in advance to the various provinces of the country, for which the students in those provinces are competing. In rural provinces students have to get higher scores than their urban counterparts to get into top universities. This has led to the phenomenon of 'examinee migration', where families move to provinces where they perceive their children have a better chance of success. Some have used this example of 'unfairness' to call for the abolition of the examination system, but nevertheless it is still seen as 'the least bad method we have' of ensuring fairness (People's Daily Online, 2007). This phenomenon, in a variety of guises, is universal.

'Fairness' is difficult to define, but it is a concept that is conjured up to defend (or criticise) many uses of tests. Consider, for example, the *standards-based testing* systems that are now operated in many countries around the world. One of the uses of test scores in these systems is to create school *league tables*. The rhetoric associated with the justification of such tables emphasises 'openness' and 'transparency' in the accountability of schools and teachers, and the 'freedom of choice' that parents have to send their children to a successful school. However, in league tables there are some schools that will appear towards the bottom of the table, as well as schools that appear towards the top. It is often the case that those at the bottom are situated in areas where families are from lower socioeconomic groups. The 'catchment area' of the school is such that the children are likely to be those with fewer life opportunities and experiences on purely financial grounds. There is a resulting pressure upon families to move into the catchment areas of the better schools so that their children are more likely to receive what they perceive to be a better education. The additional demand for houses in these areas pushes up the price of housing, thus reinforcing the lack of mobility of poorer families, and the association between income and education (Leech and Campos, 2003).

In these examples I have attempted to show that testing is not just about creating tests to find out what learners know and can do. When testing is practised outside the classroom and leaves the control of the teacher, it is part of the technology of how a society makes decisions about access to scarce resources. The decisions to test, how to test and what to test are all dependent upon our philosophy of society and our view of how individuals should be treated (Fulcher, 2009). Teachers need to become strong advocates for change and for social justice, rather than bystanders to whom testing 'happens'.

▶ 5. Testing and society

The defence of high-stakes externally mandated tests is that they provide fairer access to opportunities and resources than any other method that society has yet conceived. The testing system in China was established in order to reduce the power of the aristocracy in civil administration and open it up to talented individuals from whatever background they came. Spolsky (1995: 16–24) has called the testing practices associated with meritocracy the 'Chinese principle'. He shows how the principle affected the whole of European education in the nineteenth century, with a particular focus on language assessment. He shows that tests, or what Edgeworth (1888: 626) called 'a species of sortition', was a better way of sorting people than on the basis of who their parents were. And we are asked to believe that tests remain the best way of making decisions, even if they are imperfect.

But this is not the only position that we can take. Shohamy (2001a) argues that one reason why test takers and teachers dislike tests so much is that they are a means of control. She argues that many governments and ministries of education use tests to implement language policies and force teachers and students to comply. In her analysis, this takes place mostly within systems that have a strongly enforced national curriculum with summative high-stakes national tests that are used to ensure that the curriculum is delivered as intended. Shohamy is not reticent about passing judgement upon this use of tests:

> *Implementing policy in such ways is based on threats, fear, myths and power, by convincing people that without tests learning will not occur. It is an unethical way of making policy; it is inappropriate to force individuals in a democratic society. Thus, tests are used to manipulate and control education and become the devices through which educational priorities are communicated to principals, teachers and students.*
> (Shohamy, 2001a: 115)

This view is firmly based in social criticism drawn from Foucault's (1975) book on discipline and punishment, in which he analysed the history of the penal system as a means of state control. The fact that a discussion of testing appears in this context tells us a great deal about Foucault's views. He argued that authority can control individuals and make them do what it wishes through observation and classification. We can illustrate this with reference to Jeremy Bentham's (1787) views on the ideal prison. In this prison there is a guard tower situated in the centre of the prison with the cells arranged in a circle some distance from the tower (see Figure 1.1). No prisoner can see into the

Fig. 1.1. Jeremy Bentham's Panopticon in action. Credit: © Bettmann/Corbis

cell of another prisoner, nor can he see if there is a guard in the tower – but he assumes that he is being watched nevertheless. The guards in the tower, on the other hand, can observe what is happening in every single cell. Foucault takes Bentham's two principles as the basis for his analysis of control in society: that the exercise of power should be visible (always present), but unverifiable (you do not know if you are being watched at any particular moment). The current trend in some countries to cover the streets with closed-circuit television cameras that cannot always be either switched on or monitored is another realisation of the same theory. And in literature the famous novel *Nineteen Eighty-Four* by George Orwell describes a totalitarian state that uses surveillance of this kind to achieve complete control over the activities and beliefs of its citizens. Orwell coined the phrase 'Big Brother is watching you' that has now entered into everyday language.

In what ways might the examination be similar? It is worth listening to Foucault (1975: 184–185) at some length in his own words:

> *The examination combines the techniques of an observing hierarchy and those of a normalizing judgement. It is a normalizing gaze, a surveillance that makes it possible to qualify, to classify and to punish. It establishes over individuals a visibility through which one differentiates them and judges them. That is why, in all the mechanisms of discipline, the examination is highly ritualized. In it are combined the ceremony of power and the form of the experiment, the deployment of force and the establishment of truth. At the heart of the procedures of discipline, it manifests the subjection of those who are perceived as objects and the objectification of those who are subjected. The superimposition of the power relations and knowledge relations assumes in the examination all its visible brilliance ... who will write the ... history of the 'examination' – its rituals, its methods, its characters and their roles, its play of questions and answers, its systems of marking and classification? For in this slender technique are to be found a whole domain of knowledge, a whole type of power.*

For Foucault, the ritual is not a rite of passage, but a means of subjecting the test takers to the power of those who control the educational system. It is an act of observation, of surveillance, in which the test taker is subjected to the 'normalizing judgement' of those who expect compliance with the knowledge that is valued by the elite. After all, the answers that the test taker provides will be judged, and in order to do well they have to internalise what is considered 'right' by those in power.

How is this achieved? Firstly, of course, what counts as valuable knowledge and as a 'right' answer is externally controlled. The test takers are treated as 'cases' in a large-scale system that collects and analyses data. Each 'case' is documented according to any personal and demographic information that is collected. As the test data involves numbers, it is given the appearance of 'scientific truth' that is rarely questioned, and the objectification of the individual as a case within a system is complete. But do authorities really behave in this way? The evidence suggests that tests have been used as a means of state control over educational systems and individuals for as long as there has been an educational system. And this has not ceased today. Indeed, with the data storage capacity of modern computers, the tendency is for governments to try and keep much more integrated personal data on each individual unless this is curbed by data protection legislation.

If you have been convinced by this argument so far, it would appear that Foucault has turned upside down the argument that tests are the 'least worst' method of being fair.

The natural reaction of most teachers to what Foucault describes, and what some governments try to achieve through the use of tests, ranges from distaste to outrage. In what follows I will attempt to investigate the origin of the distaste and illustrate it through historical example. The reason for this is very simple. When we read about language tests and educational testing more generally today, it tends to wash over us. The context is so well known, the arguments of the education ministers well rehearsed: Foucault would argue that we are desensitised to what is happening to the point that we become an unquestioning part of the system. It is much easier to see issues in examples that are now alien to us because time has lapsed. Once we are aware of these issues, we can problematise them for our own context, and through the process become more vividly aware of what may be happening. Awareness makes it possible for us to consciously avoid the negative uses of tests, and engage practices from design to implementation that encourage positive test use.

6. Historical interlude I

So let us step back into history for a while, and concentrate on the negative uses of tests, before we return to the positive. The first extensive treatment of the role of education in society is found in Plato's *Republic* (1987), written around 360 BC. In this famous text, Plato sets out his vision of the ideal state. It is constructed of three classes: the Guardians or rulers; the auxiliaries or warriors, who protect the state; and the workers, who generate the wealth. For Plato, the survival of the state depends upon its unity, and so the social structure with its three social castes must be maintained. Of course, this means avoiding any change whatsoever. Plato therefore requires that all people 'devote their full energy to the one particular job for which they are naturally suited' so that 'the integrity and unity of both the individual and the state ... be preserved' (1987: 190). The role of education is to perpetuate the class structure of society without change. It was therefore seen as essential that individuals should have no personality, no aspirations, no views, other than those invested in them by the state and their position in it. As Popper (2002: 55–56) puts it:

> *The breeding and the education of the auxiliaries and thereby of the ruling class of Plato's best state [are], like their carrying of arms, a class symbol and therefore a class prerogative. And breeding and education are not empty symbols but, like arms, instruments of class rule, and necessary for ensuring the stability of this rule. They are treated by Plato solely from this point of view, i.e. as powerful political weapons as means which are useful for herding the human cattle, and for unifying the ruling class.*

For Plato, testing was an essential part of the educational system that was designed for the preservation of the elite. It allows the rulers to decide what it was necessary to know, or be able to do, to be a ruler. And a centrally controlled curriculum maximises the stability of the system. Only those who are the most successful in the elite will be allowed to rise to the very top. Plato says of potential Guardians: 'we must see how they stand up to hard work and pain and competitive trials … And any Guardian who survives these continuous trials in childhood, youth, and manhood unscathed, shall be given authority in the state … Anyone who fails them we must reject' (Plato, 1987: 180).

This position is profoundly anti-egalitarian and has very little in common with the 'Chinese principle'. And in fact, it also had very little in common with actual education in democratic Athens of the time, as we know from other sources (Fulcher, 2009). However, Plato has had a very significant impact upon education and assessment practices down the ages. For example, one of Hitler's first acts upon coming to power in the 1930s was to take control of the educational system through the centralisation of curriculum, testing, teacher training and certification. The notion that education was about personal growth and development built into the German educational system by von Humboldt (1854) was replaced with the policy 'that people should not have a will of their own and should totally subordinate themselves' (Cecil, 1971: 428). Education and testing became technological tools to enforce compliance with a collectivist philosophy that required absolute acquiescence.

My experience has been that teachers are far from being anti-egalitarian. Being a professional teacher usually carries with it a desire to provide the very best education to all learners, to help each person achieve their full potential. Such a belief is egalitarian, and implies a commitment to individual growth and development. This is also the critical insight of Dewey (1916): that the goal of personal growth implies the freedom to experiment, make inferences and develop critical awareness. As the level of external control increases, it becomes difficult for teachers to see how this goal can be achieved. I believe that it is this fundamental tension between the tendency of external authorities to impose control through tests, and the ethical imperative of teachers to maximise freedom to achieve individual growth, that results in tensions and frustrations. The examples cited above, from Plato and Nazi Germany, are simply extremes. In both cases the role of the teacher is simply to act as an agent of the state. The teacher is disempowered as a stakeholder and an actor in the educational process. The teacher is de-professionalised.

7. The politics of language testing

It is to be hoped that the extreme educational philosophies and practices discussed in the previous section will never be resurrected. However, education and testing still play a significant role in imposing political policies today. This is particularly the case when testing is used as a tool for policy makers to impose systems that emphasise accountability. That is, the policy makers wish to make teachers and schools accountable to them for their practices. McNamara and Roever (2006: 213) have claimed that 'the politicization of assessment in these ways is perhaps the most striking feature of current developments in language assessment'. Why would policy makers wish to do this? There are two possible reasons, either or both of which may be operating at any given time.

Reason 1: The progress of individual learners is of central importance in education (an assertion with which teachers would agree). In order for each learner to get the very best education they can, information on institutional performance through tests should be publicly available. This freedom of information provides learners with informed choice (an assertion with which teachers may not agree). League tables also show which institutions are failing, and which are succeeding. This allows parents to choose where to send their children. It also enables central authorities to take remedial action; local information on class test performance allows local managers to deal with underperforming teachers (an assertion with which teachers almost always disagree).

The second two assertions in this reason only hold if we believe that the free-market economy extends to education, and that the role of 'managers' is the close monitoring of outcomes (in terms of test scores) against centrally established targets. In managerial systems success and failure must be measurable in ways that can be reported up and down the system. Test scores are the easiest measures of outcomes to aggregate and report, and for schools they represent the 'bottom line' of the balance sheet – investors in this institution need to know what profit they are getting (Mansell, 2007: 7).

Reason 2: Central authorities are concerned with the efficient operation of the economy, and it is essential to produce the human resources required by business. Many states and supranational organisations are concerned that they are in danger of losing ground in the global economy, and one way of measuring potential economic effectiveness is the readiness of the population to contribute to the economy.

This is how governments use the data generated by PISA literacy tests. International comparisons can feed into national economic strategies that include educational policy. This is where language teachers and educational policy makers are most likely to find themselves in disagreement, for it implies a managerial view of language education that measures success for both teachers and learners in financial terms. The following extract from a popular European magazine is an excellent example of the new managerial view of education.

Recently, education has been made the subject of public discussion from the point of view of economic usability. It is seen as some important human resource and must contribute to an optimization of location in a global competition as well as the smooth functioning of social partial systems. Whereas education in former times was associated with the development of individuality and reflection, the unfolding of the muse and creativity, the refinement of perception, expression, taste and judgment, the main things today are the acquisition of competence, standardisation and effective educational processes as well as accreditation and evaluation of educational outcomes. (Swiss Magazine; translation provided by the magazine from the original German)

The reasons for learning a language shift under this philosophy. In the past, as this text puts it, we may have learned a second language to travel and widen our horizons, appreciate other cultures, their ways of life and their literatures. These reasons were certainly uppermost in Lado's mind when he wrote the first book on language testing in 1961. In the new view, language learning primarily serves the need to do business in the global economy.

How do we judge if a learner can communicate at a required level for a particular role in the economy? In language testing, *rating scales* (also called *rubrics*) have been used since the Second World War to grade performance on writing and speaking tasks (Fulcher, 1998a) (discussed extensively in Chapter 7). Rating scales typically consist of a number of levels, along with a short verbal descriptor of what the learner 'can do' at each level. A specific level on a scale becomes associated with a standard when some authority declares that this is the level required for the award of a privilege or qualification. This is a huge step in reasoning, but one that is quite easy for a bureaucracy that wishes to set targets for the educational system, or to implement other policies for which language is particularly suitable. It is also a long way from the original intention of scale designers: to provide a means of deciding whether an individual was capable of undertaking specific work-related tasks – originally military tasks – in safety:

> *The nature of the individual test items should be such as to provide specific, recognisable evidence of the examinee's readiness to perform in a life-situation, where lack of ability to understand and speak extemporaneously might be a serious handicap to safety and comfort, or to the effective execution of military responsibilities.*
> (Kaulfers, 1944: 137)

We face the same problem today that Kaulfers faced in his work during the Second World War: the need to describe minimum levels of performance for work in high-stakes areas, such as speaking in air traffic control or reading where machinery maintenance manuals are in a second language. It is accepted as one of the challenges inherent in language testing and teaching. We have a professional responsibility to ensure that our students are prepared to communicate efficiently in contexts where a failure to do so would put others in danger. We also have a responsibility to ensure that effective testing does not allow those who cannot perform at the required standard to gain a licence to practise.

But the real interest of many policy makers lies in using levels and descriptors to set minimum levels of achievement that help them to hold institutions and teachers accountable for delivering the outcomes specified as essential in their own policies. The standards-based systems provide the rationale for the infrastructure of controls that micromanage the behaviour of learners, teachers and institutions. As Mansell (2007: 9) notes: 'To many of those on the end of it, this system of surveillance carries Orwellian overtones.' However, it is equally true to say that there are many who believe that testing is a legitimate tool for the improvement of educational systems in service of the economy. It is a debate that is not going to abate, as the next section will illustrate.

8. Historical interlude II

The use of tests as a tool to improve the economy is not new. We have already seen the germ of the idea in Plato and totalitarian regimes: tests can be used to place individuals into the roles for which they are best suited. Even in benign states, the argument goes that if only we were able to ensure that the economy was provided with individuals to match the current needs – the correct size cogs for the machine – then efficiency would be achieved. The great economist and sociologist Max Weber argued that, in order to calculate the economic efficiency of a worker, it was essential to know '(a) the optimum aptitude for the function; (b) the optimum of skill acquired through practice; (c) the optimum of inclination for the work'. With regard to the first of these qualities, he argued, 'Aptitude, regardless of whether it is the product of hereditary or environmental and educational influences, can only be determined by testing' (Weber, 1947: 261). Economics had borrowed testing as a tool for optimising the selection of individuals from the military. It was during the First World War that the US Psychological Corps developed a test battery that was given to 1.7 million recruits in order to place them into appropriate roles. The theory was that the war would be won much more quickly if soldiers were put into those roles that were most suitable to their aptitudes. Terman (1919: 17) called the process 'determining vocational fitness'. Part of this battery of tests was the very first large-scale test of English for those whose first language was not English, to determine whether they were capable of understanding the language of other tests (Yerkes, 1921). We must also remember that the First World War was the first conflict that would be won or lost on the basis of the ability to organise efficient economies and factories to produce weaponry on an industrial scale; but the fears of economic and military 'inefficiency' had been around for a great deal longer. At the turn of the twentieth century, Britain was in decline; the empire was no longer stable. Britain's terrible performance in the Boer War of 1899–1902 was a serious shock to the nation, and there was a general fear that the growing economies of both the United States and Germany would push Britain into third place. This was the motivation for the introduction of great social reforms in education and health care by Sydney Webb to produce a population from which an army could be recruited (Semmel, 1960: 71–73). It was also the motivation for the development of test theory to weed out the inefficient. One of the earliest and most optimistic views of what could be achieved by testing comes from Spearman, in one of his co-authored papers, and deserves an extensive quotation:

> It seems even possible to anticipate the day when there will be yearly official registration of the 'intellective index', as we will call it, of every child throughout the kingdom ... In the course of time, there seems no reason why the intellective index (or system of indices) should not become so well understood, as to enable every child's education to be properly graded according to his or her capacity. Still wider – though doubtless dimmer – are the vistas opened up as to the possible consequences in adult life. It seems not altogether chimeric to look forward to the time when citizens, instead

of choosing their career at almost blind hazard, will undertake just the professions really suited to their capacities. One can even conceive the establishment of minimum index to qualify for the parliamentary vote, and, above all, for the right to have offspring.
(Hart and Spearman, 1912: 78–79)

The First World War provided the conditions upon which these theories could be tested. The rapid development of testing theory was the response of psychology to the emerging corporate world with which we are now so familiar (Evans and Waites, 1981: 74–75). By the 1930s the test makers and educational psychologists believed they had gone a long way to realising the dreams of Hart and Spearman, as this quotation from a respected educational psychologist makes starkly clear:

The future is going to see a far more effective use, both in peace and war, of the biological reserves of intelligence which we possess. (The Americans sorted their recruits by intelligence tests: we used some of the best brains from civilian life to stop bullets in the front-line trenches.)
(Cattell, 1937: 79)

One use of testing, and 'better tests', was to provide a good education only for those who were exceptionally talented:

The unhappiest children I ever see in a psychological clinic are those who, by a combination of excessive hard work and 'lucky' accidents, have got a scholarship to a secondary school when their real ability, as analytical tests shew, is quite insufficient for the demands of the secondary school curriculum.
(Cattell, 1937: 82)

These examples show that testing for efficiency was closely tied to views on social engineering and the eugenics movement (Black, 2003; Gould, 1997). While this link was largely brought to an end by the excesses with which we are all familiar, testing for educational access, vocational fitness and economic efficiency has survived to the present day. We do not argue that these purposes for testing are always wrong, or always harmful, within benign societies. But they must be critically assessed in terms of their effects, intended and otherwise.

The temporal distance between ourselves and these practices reveals for us what at the time were commonly held assumptions about hereditary ability, the importance of the survival of the collective (the empire or state) at the expense of the individual, and the need to achieve political goals through education and testing. It can also reveal other sources of our current frustrations with externally mandated testing. The first is that testing for economic efficiency has an air of elitism about it. What we seem to want to do is select 'the best' to receive the better educational opportunities, and to pursue the more (financially) rewarding careers. This implies that those who are not so able are not provided with similar opportunities after testing. Cattell (1937: 47), for example, said that a learner who cannot pass tests has to be kept in school even if there is no benefit only because 'if neglected he becomes defective also in general habits and character, leaving school as a permanent drug on the labour market and a persistent petty criminal'. Ironically, in many countries with national standards-based tests today, attention is directed away not only from the least able, but also the most able; the focus is on those perceived to be just below the borderline and may 'achieve the standard' with additional tuition. Small gains in the test scores of these learners have a much larger impact upon league tables. But whether policies target the most able, the least able, or those in the middle, there is a real sense in which teachers feel that they are being required to conspire in the creation of economic cogs for the system. Secondly, some externally mandated test systems are seen not only to challenge, but to remove, the professionalism of the teacher. They can do this by constraining the selection of content and teaching method through the imposition of a curriculum. The imposition carries the implication that the teaching profession is either not capable of deciding what is really in the best interests of learners and the economy, or is standing in the way of the progress which the politicians know is really needed. Mansell (2007: 212–213) explains this as a loss of trust in teachers by the bureaucracy. Their response is to introduce hyper-accountability mechanisms, defined as 'reforms designed to use market mechanisms to put pressure on these individuals to act in the public interest'. While Mansell traces this attitude to the 1980s, we can see in our analysis that it is in fact a much older issue.

It seems that politicians will always associate education with the creation or maintenance of the kind of society they wish to promote. What is taught, and what is tested, can become a battleground when teachers are not given much freedom to make independent professional decisions about content, method or assessment. Perhaps the largest challenge we face is engaging with these issues to find solutions that do not remove teacher professionalism in teaching and assessment, while satisfying society that the best interests of everyone are being served. Just because this has not been achieved in the past does not mean it is not possible in the future.

▶ 9. Professionalising language education and testing

Where does this leave us? This chapter has explained how tests can be used for social justice and the enhancement of meritocracy. This is part of what is termed *consequential validity*. But the very act of testing has unintended consequences, many of which are difficult to control and can be very harmful. On the other hand, tests have been used for as long as we can tell as tools to control teachers and educational systems to deliver the kind of society and economy envisioned by the powerful. The critics of testing and assessment analyse the social evils associated with them, but offer no way out.

One person who does offer us another view is John Stuart Mill. In his discussion of testing (Mill, 1859: 118–119) he argues that tests are essential to achieve meritocracy in democratic societies. He believed that the primary purpose of testing was to ensure that learners acquired the basic skills needed to participate fully in their society.

Literacy and language skills were seen as extremely important within this context. We must remember that in Mill's time suffrage was very limited. Mill saw the growth of national educational systems with assessment at key ages as preparing for universal suffrage through the production of critical, socially aware individuals, capable of making decisions about their own lives and how they wished to live (Mill, 1873: 257). Aware that tests could be used to control educational systems and indoctrinate individuals, Mill established three principles that place limits on what can be done with tests. The first relates to who makes tests, and thus to who is able to make judgements about which knowledge is valued. The second relates to test content and what may not be tested. The purpose is to avoid using tests for ideological purposes. The third relates to test use and the kinds of decisions made about people on the basis of test scores.

The first principle is that the tests and their content should not be controlled by the state or ministry of education, but by an independent authority. Mill does not discuss how this authority should be constituted, but it is clear that he sees the involvement of teachers as professionals contributing to such decisions. In this, Mill was hugely in advance of his time. The problem today, of course, is that governments and transnational institutions are often incapable of seeing that many of their policies on testing are not aligned to Mill's enlightened approach, but reflect a controlling agenda. They therefore ignore the warnings of democratic educationalists whose touchstone is 'whatever the exact character of the built-in safeguards, the best Ministry of Education is that which interferes least in the operation of the system' (Cecil, 1971: 4). For Mill, the role of a Ministry was merely to provide the infrastructure for the system to operate.

The second principle is that no test should ask questions that require the test taker to hold views or consent to believe anything which would require commitment to a 'disputed view'. A disputed view would be anything upon which the individual might reasonably come to hold some view that would result in getting the answer on the test incorrect unless he agreed with the principles or world view of the test creator. For Mill this was not just bad test design, but ethically reprehensible. As he says: 'The knowledge for passing an examination (beyond the merely instrumental parts of knowledge, such as languages and their use) should, even in the higher classes of examinations, be confined to facts and positive science exclusively' (Mill, 1859: 119).

The third principle is that the state should not take upon itself the task of saying which qualifications are recognised and which are not. This specifically puts a limitation upon the tendency to use tests and qualifications in gatekeeping, unless those concerned with specific professions and the public require the demonstration of specific skills or abilities for particular roles. It would certainly rule out the use of language tests as surreptitious restrictions on immigration, for example (McNamara, 2005). Mill puts it refreshingly in this way: 'public certificates of scientific or professional acquirements, should be given to all who present themselves for examination, and stand the test; but that such certificates should confer no advantage over competitors, other than the weight which may be attached to their testimony by public opinion' (Mill, 1859: 119).

These three principles provide a basis for an analysis of the current use of externally mandated tests in general, and language tests in particular. Although there is no direct reference to Mill, Shohamy's (2001b) notion of democratic assessment would utilise these principles, and particularly the inclusion of stakeholders in the discussion of test use. Shohamy also emphasises the responsibilities of test developers for their fair use, and the rights of test takers to be treated as valued individuals. Each of Mill's principles is concerned with justice and freedom for the individual in the testing process. Fulcher and Davidson (2007) deal with the same issue by claiming that test developers should explicitly state who a test is designed for and what its intended impact upon them is. If this intended impact is acceptable after democratic consultation, the test is designed with the effect in mind:

> The task for the ethical language tester is to look into the future, to picture the effect the test is intended to have, and to structure the test development to achieve that effect. This is what we refer to as effect-driven testing.
> (Fulcher and Davidson, 2007: 144)

Language testers have attempted to deal with their ethical responsibilities through open debate and the creation of an agreed Code of Ethics and Guidelines of Practice. These are published by the International Language Testing Association (ILTA), and are freely available from its website (www.iltaonline.com). Establishing shared understandings of what is and is not ethical within the context of a professional organisation is part of the process of the professionalisation of any body of practitioners (Davies, 1997). There are also Codes of Practice that cover testing and assessment generally, the most important of which is the *Standards for Educational and Psychological Testing* (AERA 1999). These Codes, Guidelines and Standards do not constrain the practice of language testing professionals in ways that are clear-cut and easily applied in every circumstance. However, they bring to bear principles for ethical test practices.

10. Validity

The codes and guidelines all place the concept of *validity* at the centre of the testing enterprise. It is the concept of validity that guides our work in testing and assessment. What is validity? Until 1989 the same definition had been echoed down the decades. This is taken from Ruch (1924: 13):

> By validity is meant the degree to which a test or examination measures what it purports to measure. Validity might also be expressed more simply as the 'worthwhile-ness' of an examination. For an examination to possess validity it is necessary that the materials actually included be of prime importance, that the questions sample widely among the essentials over which complete mastery can reasonably be expected on the part of the pupils, and that proof can be brought forward that the test elements (questions) can be defended by arguments based on more than mere personal opinion.

With this traditional definition, the key validity question has always been: does my test measure what I think it does?' If the evidence suggests that it does, the responsibility of the test developer is at an end.

However, since Messick's (1989) work, our understanding of validity has changed. It is now seen as a single concept, with a number of different facets, or aspects. The notion of consequential validity extends the possible responsibility of the test developer to all uses of the test. It raises the question of the extent to which the score is relevant and useful to any decisions that might be made on the basis of scores, and whether the use of the test to make those decisions has positive consequences for test takers.

The question of relevance and usefulness relates to whether it can be shown that the inferences we draw from a test score about the knowledge, skills and abilities of a test taker are justified. This is the substantive aspect of validity that replaces the traditional definition in the quotation above.

Next is the structural aspect, which is closely related to the substantive aspect. If we claim that a test provides information on a number of different skills or abilities, it should be structured and scored according to the skills and abilities of interest. Thirdly, the content of the test should be reasonably representative of the content of a course of study, or of a particular domain (such as 'aviation English' or 'travel Spanish') in which we are interested. We often wish the test score to be meaningful beyond the immediate questions or tasks on a particular test, as we cannot put all content, situations and tasks on any test; it would simply be too long. So the fourth aspect is generalisability of score meaning beyond the test itself, or whether it is predictive of ability in contexts beyond those modelled in the test. Finally there is the external aspect, or the relationship of the scores on the test to other measures of the same, or different, skills and abilities. We would hope that tests of a particular skill would provide similar results. Convergence gives us more confidence in the test outcomes.

Our interest in validity is all about trying to build tests for which there is a strong link between inferences and decisions, and ensuring that test use has a positive impact on people and institutions. Whether the test is for use in the classroom, or for large-scale administration, we need a convincing argument that it is useful for its purpose (Kane, 2006).

People engaged in language testing do believe that tests can be used to make fair decisions, and that classroom assessment can inform teaching and learning. Yet, we could easily fall into a counsel of despair when we see how tests of all kinds have been used in society. The practice of testing is itself a social construct. It is a practice invented by humankind to make difficult decisions, and to shape educational practices and institutions. Testing has been used to achieve goals of control and manipulation, and has been used to provide opportunities to those who would otherwise have none. Like all social constructs, it can be used for good or ill.

The rest of this book is about how to design and build tests, and how language teachers and testers can develop practices to use testing and assessment to good effect. With a clear definition of test purpose, and a vision of the effect that we wish our test to have, planned intention can inform the decisions we make along the way.

Activities

◯ 1.1 Why do you test?

It is traditional to talk about tests being used for one of five different purposes:

- achievement
- aptitude
- diagnosis
- placement
- proficiency.

However, we have already seen in our discussion that there are many other reasons for testing, including motivating learners to study. Reflect upon the reasons why:

(a) You give tests in to your own students. Make a list of the reasons.
(b) Your learners have to take tests that are externally mandated. List the test that they take and why you think they have to take these tests.

The reasons for testing will differ from one context to another, so now compare your answers to those of someone who works in a different country. What are the main similarities and differences in your reasons?

◯ 1.2 The grounds for selection

Throughout history people have been selected to receive an education or follow a particular career using a range of criteria. Look at the list below. Can you add to this list? Which of these criteria do you find acceptable or unacceptable, and why? If a society used a criterion that you find unacceptable, what values do you think it would hold?

Wealth	Socio-economic status	Social class	Effort	Motivation
Sporting prowess	Dedication	Ability	Physical strength	Ethnic background
Parental occupation	Physical disability	Health	Life expectancy	Aptitude
?	?	?	?	?

○ 1.3 Identifying unintended consequences

It is very rare for educational authorities or schools to explicitly consider the effects that testing might have on learners, teachers or institutions. But all of the effects of testing should be considered so that we can evaluate the overall impact that our actions have. Think about your own teaching and learning context. Make a list of all those things that you do because a test is going to be given. Or, if it makes the task easier, make a list of the things you wouldn't do, if the test was not there!

Once you have your list, go through and put a ✓ against each item that you think is a positive effect induced by the act of testing, and an ✗ against each item that you think is a negative effect.

○ 1.4 Mitigating unintended consequences

Read the following article, and decide what action(s) might be taken to alleviate the situation (short of abolishing the tests).

SHANGHAI, June 7 (AP) – A 16-year-old girl's suicide after she was barred from a key exam underscores mounting worries over academic pressures, as millions of Chinese students began annual college entrance tests on Wednesday.

The three-day exam, viewed as crucial to future career and financial success, has a record 9.5 million high school students across China competing for just 2.6 million university places. For kids and parents alike, it's a nail-biting ordeal that experts say causes undue emotional distress. 'Pressure from study and exams is a top reason for psychological problems among Chinese youth,' said Jin Wuguan, director of the Youth Psychological Counseling Center at Shanghai's Ruijin Hospital.

In China's increasingly success oriented, pressure-cooker cities, academic stress is seen as a rising cause of youth suicides and even murders of parents by children unhinged by overwhelming pressure to perform. According to her family and newspaper accounts, 16-year-old Wu Wenwen drowned herself after she was stopped at the exam room door because her hair wasn't tied back as her school required.

Returning in barrettes, she was then told the end-of-term exam had already started and she was too late to take it. In tears, Wu called her mother, and then disappeared. Her body was found the same night in a nearby lake.

China doesn't keep comprehensive statistics on student suicides, but Jin said health care professionals see the problem worsening, even among elementary students. Wang Yufeng, of Peking University's Institute of Mental, estimates the rate of emotional disorders such as depression and paranoia among Chinese students under age 17 at up to 32 per cent – a total of 30 million students. Others say that figure may be as high as 50 per cent. A survey last year by the government's China Youth and Children Research Center showed 57.6 per cent of students felt highly distressed by academic pressures.

○ 1.5 The Big Brother debate

Read the following article. Do you believe that that the creation of the database with individual dossiers for life is legitimate? Or does this just go to show that Foucault was right about the true intentions of governments? List the pros and cons on both sides of the argument. If you are working with a group of colleagues, you may wish to organise a formal debate, with the motion 'This house believes that a "testing record for life" is an infringement of personal liberties and damaging to the future of the individual.'

Every child in school numbered for life

All 14-year-old children in England will have their personal details and exam results placed on an electronic database for life under a plan to be announced tomorrow.

Colleges and prospective employers will be able to access students' records online to check on their qualifications. Under the terms of the scheme all children will keep their individual number throughout their adult lives, *The Times* has learnt. The database will include details of exclusions and expulsions.

Officials said last night that the introduction of the unique learner number (ULN) was not a step towards a national identity card. But it will be seen as the latest step in the Government's broader efforts to computerise personal records.

Last night teachers' leaders, parents' organisations, Opposition MPs and human rights campaigners questioned whether this Big Brother approach was necessary and said that it could compromise the personal security of millions of teenagers.

(Adapted from *The Times*)

○ 1.6 Finding the right level?

The following descriptor is from level B1 in the *Common European Framework of Reference for Languages: Learning, Teaching, Assessment* (Council of Europe, 2001). This has been selected by many European governments as the language standard required for immigration.

Do you and your colleagues believe that this is an adequate description of the minimum language requirements for a new immigrant to your country?

Do you believe that language requirements are relevant to immigration decisions?

Think of just one task that you might include on a test designed to measure whether an immigrant has reached this standard. Write your task down and ask a colleague to critique it using this question: would the expected response to this task provide (part of) the evidence I would need to make an admittance/non-admittance decision in an immigration application?

> Can understand the main points of clear standard input on familiar matters regularly encountered in work, school, leisure, etc. Can deal with most situations likely to arise whilst travelling in an area where the language is spoken. Can produce simple connected text on topics which are familiar or of personal interest. Can describe experiences and events, dreams, hopes and ambitions and briefly give reasons and explanations for opinions and plans.

◯ 1.7 The efficiency drive

Yoakum and Yerkes (1920: 185) describe the value of 'mental engineering' during the First World War in this way:

> *The work of the Committee on the Psychological Examination of Recruits was another of the notable mental engineering achievements of the war. Its original purpose was to help to eliminate from the Army at the earliest possible moment those recruits whose defective intelligence would make them a menace to the military organisation. But the military value of an early and reliable estimate of the general intelligence of each recruit proved enormously greater than had been anticipated ... in the enormous task of building up an efficient army organisation it proved important to discover at the earliest opportunity those recruits who could learn the new duties that were required of them as soldiers in the shortest time.*

The graph on p. 25 is reprinted from page 198 of their book. Each horizontal line on the graph represents the range of scores that men from various jobs scored on the Army tests. The vertical line through each horizontal line is the average score.

Yoakum and Yerkes argued that this data from the Army tests provided guidelines for how individuals might be allocated to jobs, in order to efficiently reconstruct countries after the end of the war.

Are you convinced by their argument and the data?

If you are not convinced, what do you think might be the flaws in their reasoning, research, or their interpretation of the data in the table?

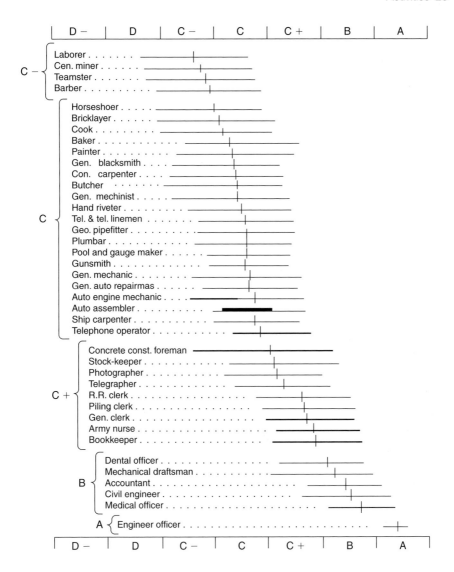

◯ 1.8 Whose values?

Look at this test item from the PISA literacy test (OECD, 2006) released into the public domain. Remember that this test item is given to students in many different countries around the world. Responses are scored and aggregated for the purpose of comparing literacy across countries. The OECD informs governments how it thinks its workforce compares with those of different economies around the globe. As you read the test item and the scoring guideline, ask yourself these questions:

1. What does the choice of topic say about the values of the test developer?
2. Would you need to share the values of the test developer in order to score well?
3. Are any of the values assumed in this test item specific to some countries or cultures?
4. Are any of the values assumed in this test item specific to learners from certain socioeconomic backgrounds?
5. Are there learners in some countries who could not do well on this item because they might not share the values of the test developer?
6. Does this reading item require background knowledge that would not be available to some subgroups of the test-taking population?
7. Is there anything else about this reading item that would lead to correct or incorrect answers due to factors other than reading ability?

Question 4A: What does the table on p. 27 indicate about the level of PLAN International's activity in Ethiopia in 1996, compared with other countries in the region?

A   The level of activity was comparatively high in Ethiopia.
B   The level of activity was comparatively low in Ethiopia.
C   It was about the same as in other countries in the region.
D   It was comparatively high in the Habitat category, and low in the other categories.

Question 4B: In 1996 Ethiopia was one of the poorest countries in the world.

Taking this fact and the information in the table into account, what do you think might explain the level of PLAN International's activities in Ethiopia compared with its activities in other countries?

Question intent: Reflecting on the Content of a Text: drawing on knowledge and experience to form a hypothesis which is consistent with given information.

Scoring guide

Full credit
Code 3: Student has answered Question 4A correctly (Key B). Explains the level of PLAN's activity by drawing on ALL the information supplied, with explicit or implicit reference to the type of activity conducted in Ethiopia by PLAN.

Answer must also be consistent with (though does not need to refer to) BOTH of the following:

(1) PLAN's low level of activity in Ethiopia (information supplied in the table); AND
(2) Ethiopia's poverty (information given in the stem).

- Aid organisations often start their work in a country by training local people, so I would say PLAN had just started working in Ethiopia in 1996.
- Training community workers might be the only kind of aid they can give there.

R099: Plan International

PLAN International Program Results Financial Year 1996

Region of Eastern and Southern Africa

RESA

	EGYPT	ETHIOPIA	KENYA	MALAWI	SUDAN	TANZANIA	UGANDA	ZAMBIA	ZIMBABWE	TOTALS
Growing up Healthy										
Health posts built with 4 rooms or less	1	0	6	0	7	1	2	0	9	26
Health workers trained for 1 day	1 053	0	719	0	425	1 003	20	60	1 085	4 385
Children given nutrition supplements > 1 week	10 195	0	2 040	2 400	0	0	0	0	261 432	266 237
Children given financial help with health/dental treatment	984	0	396	0	305	0	581	0	17	2 283
Learning										
Teachers trained for 1 week	0	0	387	0	970	118	565	0	303	2 320
School exercise books bought/donated	687	0	0	41 200	0	69 106	0	150	0	111 123
School textbooks bought/donated	0	0	45 650	9 600	1 182	8 769	7 285	150	58 387	131 023
Uniforms bought/made/donated	8 897	0	5 761	0	2 000	6 040	0	0	434	23 132
Children helped with school fees/a scholarship	12 321	0	1 598	0	154	0	0	0	2 014	16 087
School desks built/bought donated	3 200	0	3 669	260	1 564	1 725	1 794	0	4 109	16 331
Permanent classrooms built	44	0	50	8	93	31	46	0	82	353
Classrooms repaired	0	0	34	0	0	14	0	0	33	81
Adults receiving training in literacy this financial year	1 160	0	3 000	588	3 617	0	0	0	350	8 695
Habitat										
Latrines or toilets dug/built	50	0	2 403	0	57	182	23	96	4 311	7 102
Houses connected to a new sewage system	143	0	0	0	0	0	0	0	0	143
Wells dug/improved (or springs capped)	0	0	15	0	7	13	0	0	159	194
New positive boreholes drilled	0	0	8	93	14	0	27	0	220	362
Gravity feed drinking water sytems built	0	0	25	0	1	0	0	0	0	29
Drinking water systems repaired/improved	0	0	392	0	2	0	0	0	31	425
Houses improved with PLAN project	285	0	520	0	0	0	1	0	2	788
New houses built for beneficiaries	225	0	596	0	0	2	8	0	313	1 142
Community halls built or improved	2	0	2	0	3	0	3	0	2	12
Community leaders trained for 1 day or more	2 214	95	3 522	232	200	3 575	814	20	2 693	13 365
Kilometres of roadway improved	112	0	26	0	0	0	0	0	534	80.6
Bridges built	0	0	4	2	11	0	0	0	1	18
Families benefited directly from erosion control	0	0	1 092	0	1 500	0	0	0	18 405	20 997
Houses newly served by electrification project	443	0	2	0	0	0	0	0	44	494

Source: Adapted from PLAN International Program Output Chart financial year 1996, appendix to Quarterly Report to the International Board first quarter 1997.

- There might not be the hospitals or schools in which they could base the other kinds of aid work.
- Other foreign aid groups might be helping with medicine, etc. and PLAN sees they need to know how to run the country. *[Implicitly refers to training community leaders.]*

Partial credit

Code 2: Student has answered Question 4A correctly (Key B). Explains the level of PLAN's work by drawing on MOST of the information supplied. Answer must be consistent with (though does not need to refer to) BOTH of the following:

(1) PLAN's low level of activity in Ethiopia (information supplied in the table); AND
(2) Ethiopia's poverty (information given in the stem).

- It might be hard to distribute aid there because things are in such a mess.
- There may be a war on so it would be hard to give aid.
- They don't know how to help there.
- If other organisations are helping in Ethiopia, there is less for PLAN to do.
- I could imagine that the other countries received help first and that Ethiopia will be helped in the near future.
- The people of Ethiopia may have a certain culture which makes it difficult to interact with foreigners.
- I think they are giving a bit too much help in other countries and Ethiopia is missing out. PLAN International might not have enough funding and money for all the countries in need.

Code 1: Student has answered Question 4A correctly (Key B). Explains the level of PLAN's work by drawing on PART of the information supplied. Answer must be consistent with (though does not need to refer to) PLAN's low level of activity in Ethiopia (information supplied in the table).

- Ethiopia does not need PLAN's help as much as the other countries. *[Draws on information in the table but does not take into account the information about Ethiopia's relative poverty supplied in the stem.]*
- Ethiopia is not as poor as the other countries so it doesn't need PLAN's help as much. *[Draws on information in the table but is inconsistent with information about Ethiopia's relative poverty supplied in the stem.]*
- Ethiopia might only need more help with their community leaders than other countries. *[Draws in detail on information in the table but does not take into account the information about Ethiopia's relative poverty supplied in the stem.]*

OR: Student has answered Question 4A incorrectly (not Key B). Explains the level of PLAN's work by drawing on PART of the information supplied.

Answer must be consistent with (though does not need to refer to) BOTH of the following:

(1) the level of activity in Ethiopia which the student has indicated in Question 4A (the explanation itself need not be true); AND

(2) Ethiopia's poverty (information given in the stem).

- [Answer to Question 4A: The level of activity is comparatively high in Ethiopia.] Ethiopia is poorer than other countries in the region and therefore needs more help.
- [Answer to Question 4A: It is about the same as in other countries in the region.] Aid is distributed equally so there is no rivalry between countries.

No credit
Code 0: Gives insufficient or vague answer.

- They don't do as much work in Ethiopia. *[Restates information in Key to 4A without attempting to explain it.]*
- PLAN hardly does anything in Ethiopia.

OR: Shows inaccurate comprehension of the material or gives an implausible or irrelevant answer.

- They should be giving more to Ethiopia. *[Expresses an opinion rather than suggesting an explanation.]*
- They are only training community workers. They don't seem to be doing anything for health or learning of the people there. *[Does not explain the level of activity.]*
- The level of PLAN International's activities in Ethiopia compared with its activities in other countries is higher. *[Restates information in distractor to 4A without attempting to explain it.]*
- PLAN gives the same amount to every country. *[Restates information in distractor to 4A without attempting to explain it.]*

Code 9: Missing.

○ 1.9 Professionalism

Think of a test that you know well, and hate. This might be a test you have had to take, or it might be a test that it used in an institution you have worked for. Why do you hate it? Why do you think it is unfair? Write just one paragraph to make your views explicit.

Now go to the website of the International Language Testing Association (www.iltaonline.com) and read the ILTA Code of Ethics and the ILTA Guidelines of Practice. Is there anything in these documents that would help you understand why you hate the test you have selected?

○ 1.10 A thought experiment

Imagine that you are in a universe in which you have the magical power to change history. You can decide if you wish to remove all testing from human history, and from our current society. After the spell has been cast, it isn't just that there won't be any more tests – there won't even be the concept of a test. And that means that you won't ever be able to bring tests back.

Before you decide whether to cast the spell, make a short list of tests that are commonly used in society. Include language tests for a variety of purposes, but don't limit yourself to them. For example, you might include the driving test in your list. When you have a list of ten tests, for each one state how you would make the same decision *without the use of the test*.

When you have done this, you arrive at the moment of truth. With a number of colleagues decide whether you wish to begin a new universe without tests and testing.

2 Standardised testing

 ## 1. Two paradigms

If you are reading this sentence I have to assume that you did not wave your magic wand in the thought experiment at the end of Chapter 1, and testing is still a fact of our social life. In this chapter we are briefly going to describe two paradigms in educational measurement and language testing, and then concentrate on describing the dominant first paradigm. This first paradigm of *norm-referenced testing* is the normative approach in educational testing generally. In this paradigm individuals are compared to each other. The meaning of the score on a test is derived from the position of an individual in relation to others. This was the historical basis for testing, and remains the paradigm for many externally mandated high-stakes tests. It is not difficult to see why. If the purpose of testing is to distribute scarce resources (like university places) fairly, we need a test that separates out the test takers very effectively. The primary requirement of the test is that it should discriminate between test takers – but in this use of the word, *discrimination* is a positive quality. The high-scoring test takers are offered places at the most prestigious institutions, while those on lower scores may not be so fortunate. The decision makers need the test takers to be 'spread out' over the range of test scores, and this spread is called the *distribution*.

The second paradigm is that of *criterion-referenced* testing (Glaser, 1963). The idea of a criterion-referenced test was first discussed in the 1960s, and informs testing and assessment that is related to instructional decisions much more than norm-referenced testing. This is because the purpose of a criterion-referenced test is to make a decision about whether an individual test taker has achieved a pre-specified criterion, or standard, that is required for a particular decision context. For example, the International Civil Aviation Authority requires that air traffic controllers achieve a criterion level of English before they may practise as air traffic controllers. The holistic description of the criterion is shown on p. 32.

The purpose of this test is not to select the best speakers of English to be air traffic controllers, but to establish a criterion by which an individual can be classified as 'operationally proficient'. Sometimes these are also called mastery tests.

We are going to look more closely at the assumptions underlying both of these paradigms in this chapter and in Chapter 3. We will introduce the basic tools that you will need to evaluate a test from each paradigm, and to make your own tests. However, all the test design tools that you will need to build a test are described in detail in Chapters 4 to 7. We are going to start with the norm-referenced paradigm because it has a much

A speaker is proficient to Operational Level 4 if they can:

a communicate effectively in voice-only (telephone/radiotelephone) and in face-to-face situations;

b communicate on common, concrete and work-related topics with accuracy and clarity;

c use appropriate communicative strategies to exchange messages and to recognise and resolve misunderstandings (e.g. to check, confirm, or clarify information) in a general or work-related context;

d handle successfully and with relative ease the linguistic challenges presented by a complication or unexpected turn of events that occurs within the context of a routine work situation or communicative task with which they are otherwise familiar; and

e use a dialect or accent which is intelligible to the aeronautical community.

longer history, and because its principles and assumptions still dominate the testing industry today.

2. Testing as science

In Chapter 1 we saw that the rise of testing was a social correlate of the development of our corporate world that really began during the First World War. For the first time in history it was essential that industry was organised on a large and efficient scale in order to produce the materials necessary for military success. Lloyd George's reorganisation of the British munitions industry to meet the demand for shells on the Western Front is widely considered to be the beginning of modern industrial and corporate efficiency (Adams, 1978). With it came the need to count, measure, and quantify on a completely new scale. In an early study of labour efficiency, Greenwood (1919: 186) takes as his rationale the dictum of the natural scientist, Kelvin:

> *When you can measure what you are speaking about and express it in numbers, you know something about it, but when you cannot measure it, when you cannot express it in numbers, your knowledge is of a meagre and unsatisfactory kind.*

The statistical analysis of production mushroomed from 1915 onwards. Greenwood (*ibid.*, 187) reminded his readers that 'the compilation of such industrial statistics had never been attempted in England before the war'. But the war created the conditions in which the new technologies of efficiency flourished. As we saw in Chapter 1, the First World War also saw the dramatic rise of large-scale testing. Psychologists wished to contribute to the war effort and show that testing was a scientific discipline (Kelves, 1968).

The idea was simple enough. Tests are about measuring knowledge, skills or abilities ('KSAs') and expressing their existence, or degree or presence, in numerical form. The assumption is that, once we are able to do this, we have 'genuine' knowledge. Shohamy (2001: 21) correctly identifies this as one of the key features of the 'power of tests':

The language of science in Western societies grants authority, status and power. Testing is perceived as a scientific discipline because it is experimental, statistical and uses numbers. It therefore enjoys the prestige granted to science and is viewed as objective, fair, true and trustworthy.

By the time the Great War broke out, it was taken for granted that measurement and scientific progress went hand in hand. Measurement had in fact been seen as the most important development in scientific research since the early nineteenth century. Babbage (1857: 289) had even proposed that scholarly institutions around the world should undertake research to write a volume entitled 'The Constants of Nature and of Art', which 'ought to contain all those facts which can be expressed by numbers in the various sciences and arts'. His paper outlines the extent of the measurements to be undertaken, from the natural sciences to buildings, mountains, and man. In a similar vein, arguing that testing was a measurement-based science, Cattell (1893) said:

The history of science is the history of measurement. Those departments of knowledge in which measurement could be used most readily were the first to become sciences, and those sciences are at the present time the furthest advanced in which measurement is the most extended and the most exact.

What did the early testers believe they could achieve that led to the explosion of testing theory and practice during the Great War? It is best explained with reference to a comment that Francis Galton was asked to write on one of Cattell's early papers (Cattell and Galton, 1890: 380):

One of the most important objects of measurement … is to obtain a general knowledge of the capacities of a man by sinking shafts, as it were, at a few critical points. In order to ascertain the best points for the purpose, the sets of measures should be compared with an independent estimate of the man's powers. We thus may learn which of the measures are the most instructive.

The metaphor of sinking a shaft comes from mining. Galton is suggesting that the use of tests is like drilling a hole into the test taker to discover what is inside. In language testing we would refer to this as a strong 'trait theory' of validity: what we think our test measures is a real, stable, part of the test taker. For early testers there was therefore no question that using tests was in principle no different from using scientific instruments to investigate natural phenomena. The second thing that we learn from this quotation is that, in order to make a decision about which tests are the best measures, we need to compare the results of the test with an independent estimate of whatever the test is designed to measure. That is, the value of our measurements can be judged by their relation with other measures of the same property. In the last chapter we called this the external aspect of validity, and we will return to this in Section 11 below.

A norm-referenced test, therefore, was seen as a scientific tool designed to discriminate among test takers in such a way that it placed those with 'more' of a property of interest higher on a scale, and those with 'less' of a property lower down on a scale. In a meritocratic use of such tests, those with 'more' are assumed to be more deserving, and are therefore awarded more of the available resources. In the Army tests the higher scorers were considered for officer positions. Today, test takers who get higher grades on modern international language tests have more chances of promotion, or can obtain places in the universities of their choice. The basic assumptions have not changed.

The early scientific use of tests therefore contributed to the efficiency of the war effort. The testers genuinely believed that through their efforts the war would be more successfully prosecuted, and victory would be achieved sooner. This faith in scientific testing can be seen very clearly in a contemporary song published in a camp newspaper, which poked fun at the testers (Brown, 1992: 113–114):

The March of the Psychos

The valiant, bespectacled psychos are we
Prepared to assign every man his degree
And the place he's best fitted for in the armee
By psychologee, psychologee.
Bill Kaiser will shake in this throne 'cross the sea
When he feels the earthquake of our efficiency
Pencils up! Forward march! to the great victory
Of psychologee in the Army.

It should be remembered that a view of testing as 'scientific' has always been controversial. Lipman (1922) was an early critic, arguing that:

Because the results are expressed in numbers, it is easy to make the mistake of thinking that the intelligence test is a measure like a foot rule or a pair of scales. It is, of course, a quite different sort of measure. For length and weight are qualities which men have learned how to isolate no matter whether they are found in an army of soldiers, a heap of bricks, or a collection of chlorine molecules. Provided the foot rule and the scales agree with the arbitrarily accepted standard foot and standard pound in the Bureau of Standards at Washington they can be used with confidence. But 'intelligence' is not an abstraction like length and weight; it is an exceedingly complicated notion which nobody has as yet succeeded in defining.

What Lipman is saying is that a strong trait theory is untenable. In fact, most of the traits or constructs that we work with (see Chapter 4) are extremely difficult to define, and if we are not able to define them, measurement is even more problematic. It also has to be remembered that the 'scientific testers' hit back at their critics with great force (Terman, 1922). Reading these newspaper and magazine articles today can help us to appreciate the controversy over the claim to be 'scientific'. Today it may seem to be part of a bygone age, but the issues are still alive.

▶ 3. What's in a curve?

First of all, let's consider the effect of a norm-referenced test. The intended effect is to discriminate between individuals so that decisions can be made about them. In the case of the Army test we would wish to select the better candidates as officers so that they are not 'wasted' doing tasks that are beneath them. Nor do we wish to place poorer candidates in officer roles where they may not be able to make quick and appropriate decisions. In both cases, according to this argument, military efficiency is compromised. Figure 2.1 represents the distribution of test scores on an Army test by different ranks of soldiers.

Although this diagram is hand drawn and not precisely to scale, the height of each curve roughly represents the number of individuals scoring at that level. Most of the officers score between A and B, for example, while most of the enlisted illiterate men score just below D, and most enlisted literate men score C, in the middle of the scale. If we give the same test to a new group of candidates and an individual scores C+, the argument goes that he is most likely to be corporal material. However, there are problems even with extreme groups. Consider the intersection of the curves for the enlisted illiterate men and the officers. In the diagram this is marked with the second vertical line (2) that I have added to Yerkes' original drawing. The right tail of the illiterate curve overlaps quite considerably with the left tail of the officer curve. What this tells us is that it is possible for an illiterate enlisted man to get a score that is similar to that obtained by a low-scoring – or even a middle-scoring – officer. But it is highly unlikely. Also, someone who is really officer material may get a score similar to that expected of a high scoring illiterate. Once again, this is highly unlikely, but possible. If we look at the intersection between the officer curve and the sergeants' curve, however, the possibility that an officer would get the same score as a sergeant and vice versa is much higher, and

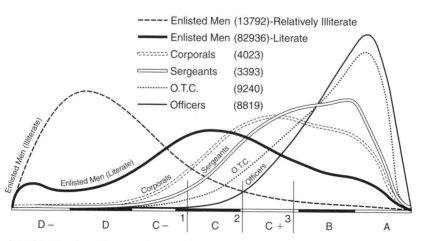

Fig. 2.1. Distribution of scores in typical army groups, showing value of tests in identification of officer material. From Yerkes (1941: 13)

placement into an appropriate category becomes more difficult. This is the problem of setting *cut scores* on tests in order to make decisions (see Chapter 8). At the end of the day, it is a matter of judgement. In attempting to make sure that no enlisted illiterates ever became officers, I might draw the cut score for entrance to the officer ranks at point 3, somewhere between C+ and B. I would of course need other criteria to distinguish between officers and sergeants! If, on the other hand, I wanted to allow all those who were genuinely officer material to become officers, I might set the cut score at point 1. But this would also let in most of the sergeants, corporals, and the literate enlisted men. And the test wasn't supposed to give the truly deserving a chance to be an officer – it was to place people in a rank where they would contribute most efficiently to the war effort. So selecting option 1 would not have been a likely outcome. Indeed, Yerkes (1941: 14) says:

> *Commissioned officers of the United States Army, with few exceptions, possess superior or very superior intelligence. A few of the good officers fall in the C+ class and a still smaller number, almost invariably unsatisfactory to the service, possess only average intelligence, designated by the letter C.*

However, we have made our point: decision making with norm-referenced tests involves value judgements about the meaning of scores in terms of the intended effect of the test.

▶ 4. The curve and score meaning

In norm-referenced testing the meaning of a score is directly related to its place in the curve of the distribution from which it is drawn, because it tells us how an individual with this score relates to the rest of the test-taking population. Each individual is compared with all other individuals in the distribution. We have known for a long time that when we measure most things, the observations form a curve of normal distribution, or a bell curve, which looks like Figure 2.2 below:

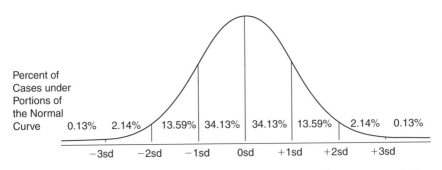

Fig. 2.2. The curve of normal distribution and the percentage of scores expected between each standard deviation

We know that most scores are fairly close to the mean, or average, which is represented by the line in the middle of the curve. This is the score that splits the distribution of scores into two. In fact, around 68 per cent of all scores cluster closely to the mean, with approximately 34 per cent just above the mean, and 34 per cent just below the mean. As we move away from the mean the scores in the distribution become more extreme, and so less common. It is very rare for test takers to get all items correct, just as it is very rare for them to get all items incorrect. But there are a few in every large group who do exceptionally well, or exceptionally poorly. The curve of normal distribution tells us what the probability is that a test taker could have got the score they have, given the place of the score in a particular distribution. And this is why we can say that a score is 'exceptional' or 'in the top 10 per cent', or 'just a little better than average'.

▶ 5. Putting it into practice

A test score is arrived at by giving the test takers a number of *items* or *tasks* to do. The responses to these items are scored, usually as correct (1) or incorrect (0). The number of correct responses for each individual is then added up to arrive at a total *raw score*.

Imagine that I have a test with 29 items (I really do – but I'm not going to show it to you yet!). Each item is scored as correct or incorrect, and I ask 25 language learners to take the test. Each person responds to each test item, and I then add up the number of correct answers for each test taker. The scores for my hypothetical language learners are presented as follows, from the lowest to the highest. Two learners only managed to answer one item correctly, and one learner answered 28 correctly. The rest are spread between these two extremes.

1	1	2	3	5	6	6	7	8	10	10	11	11	11	13	13	14	15	15	16	17	18	25	27	28

We can present these scores visually in histograms like the one in Figure 2.3. This tells us how many learners achieved a particular score. With this very small group of learners the most frequent score is 11. The most frequent score in a distribution is called the mode. We are also interested in the score that falls in the middle of the distribution, called the median score. If we had 24 students, the middle score would be 24 / 2 = the twelfth score. In this case that would also be 11. But we have 25 scores, so we take the twelfth and thirteenth score, add them together and divide by 2 to get the middle score. The twelfth score is 11 and the thirteenth score is 11, and so we have: 11 + 11 = 22; 22 / 2 = 11. Both of these figures tell us something about the mid-point of a distribution. We also know something very basic about our distribution, because we can see the range of scores from 1 to 28. This is a wide range, so we can infer that our group of learners are at very different levels of ability and that the test spreads them out reasonably well.

The most useful description of the mid-point for norm-referenced tests is the *mean*. This is calculated by adding all the scores together and dividing the total by the number of test takers. When we add the scores together we get the sum, which is represented

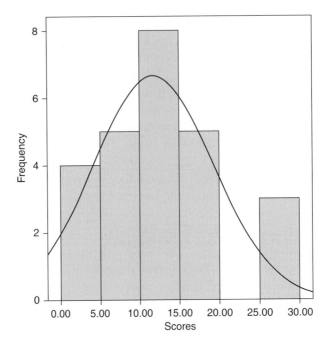

Fig. 2.3. A histogram of scores

by the Greek capital sigma (Σ). If I add together the 25 numbers above, $\Sigma = 293$. This is really the correct number of responses scored by all students on the test. When we divide it by the number of students we have 293 / 25 = 11.72. This is fairly easy, even if the formula for the mean looks difficult at first sight:

$$\bar{X} = \frac{\Sigma X}{N}$$

This is read as follows: X bar (the mean) equals the sum of X divided by N. Each individual score is an X (X_1, X_2, X_3, X_n) and N is the total number of test takers. The mean is the most important measure of the centre of the distribution of test scores because it allows us to calculate a much more useful description of the distribution of scores than the range, called the *standard deviation*. We will look at how this is calculated first. Then we will consider the formula, and finally consider the use of these descriptive statistics in language testing.

In our example, we know that the mean score on the test is 11.72. The mean has one very important property that the mode and median do not have. If we take away the mean from each of the individual scores we get a deviation score from the mean, and the mean of these scores is always zero. We illustrate this in Table 2.1. The first column contains the scores for each of 25 test takers (X_{1-25}). The second column contains the mean, which is of course the same in all rows. In the third column we subtract the mean from the score, giving the *deviation score*. This number shows how far an individual score is away from the mean, and may be a negative or positive number. If we add up the scores above zero, add up the scores below zero, and subtract one number from the other, the answer will always be zero. The final column is the square of the deviation score. That is, we multiply the deviation score by itself. On many calculators this function is achieved by pressing a button marked X^2 after inputting the deviation score. So with a score of 10 and a deviation score of -1.7, $1.7 \times 1.7 = 2.9$. We can then add up all of the squared deviation scores in the column.

Scores	$\overline{X}$	$X - \overline{X}$	$(X - \overline{X})^2$
1	11.72	−10.72	114.92
1	11.72	−10.72	114.92
2	11.72	−9.72	94.48
3	11.72	−8.72	76.04
5	11.72	−6.72	45.16
6	11.72	−5.72	32.72
6	11.72	−5.72	32.72
7	11.72	−4.72	22.28
8	11.72	−3.72	13.84
10	11.72	−1.72	2.96
10	11.72	−1.72	2.96
11	11.72	−0.72	0.52
11	11.72	−0.72	0.52
11	11.72	−0.72	0.52
13	11.72	+1.28	1.64
13	11.72	+1.28	1.64
14	11.72	+2.28	5.20
15	11.72	+3.28	10.76
15	11.72	+3.28	10.76
16	11.72	+4.28	18.32
17	11.72	+5.28	27.88
18	11.72	+6.28	39.44
25	11.72	+13.28	176.36
27	11.72	+15.28	233.48
28	11.72	+16.28	265.04
$\Sigma = 293$		$\Sigma = 0$	$\Sigma = 1345.08$
$\overline{X} = 11.72$			
$N = 25$			

Table 2.1 Deviation scores

From this table we can work out the standard deviation with the help of the following formula.

$$SD = \sqrt{\frac{\Sigma(X - \bar{X})^2}{N - 1}}$$

This formula states that the standard deviation is the square root of the sum of the squared deviation scores, divided by N − 1. From our table we know that the sum of the squared deviation scores is 1345.08 and N − 1 is 24; 1345.08 / 24 = 56, and the square root of 56 = 7.5. Our standard deviation is therefore 7.5.

What can we do with this information? We can place our figures back on to a curve of normal distribution as follows (Figure 2.4).

The mean (zero) is in the centre. We now know that each standard deviation = 7.5, and so for each standard deviation (marked on the diagram as −3sd to +3sd), we add or subtract 7.5. So, for example, the score we would expect at one standard deviation above the mean = 11.72 + 7.5 = 19.22 (for convenience we will call it 19.2 and round to just one decimal place). You will notice that the score at +3sd is not possible, as our test only has 29 items. Similarly, it is not possible to get a score at −2sd, as this would be a negative score. This is rare, and indicates quite a serious problem with this particular test. But we will return to this later. The most important observation at the moment is this: if a learner scores 19.2 (again impossible – but close to 19) we know that approximately 15.86 per cent of the test takers are expected to score higher, and 84.12 per cent of test takers are expected to score lower. We know this because of the probability of scores occurring under the normal curve. The meaning of the score is therefore its place on the scale measured in standard deviations.

However, we can be even more accurate than this. We do this by transforming the raw score – the number of right answers – into a new kind of score called a z-score. A z-score is simply the raw score expressed in standard deviations. So, if your score on the test was 11.72, you would in fact score zero. And if your score was 19.2, you would score 1. There is a very straightforward formula for transferring any raw score to a z-score:

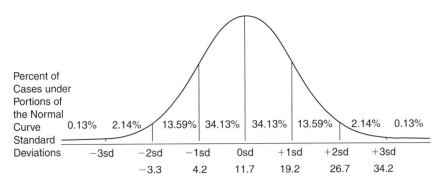

Fig. 2.4. The curve of normal distribution with raw scores for a particular test

$$Z = \frac{X - \bar{X}}{SD}$$

We read this as: Z equals X (the raw score) minus X bar (the mean score) divided by the standard deviation. If my score was 11.71 on the test, we can see what this means:

$$11.7 - 11.7 = 0; 0 / 7.5 = 0$$

Similarly, let's try it for 19.2:

$$19.2 - 11.7 = 7.5; 7.5 / 7.5 = 1$$

We can do this for all scores. The lowest score in the range for our test was 1. The z-score is:

$$1 - 11.7 = -10.7; -10.7 / 7.5 = -1.43 \text{ (standard deviations below the mean)}$$

The highest score, on the other hand, was 28. The z-score is:

$$28 - 11.7 = 16.3; 16.3 / 7.5 = 2.17 \text{ (standard deviations above the mean)}$$

To find where a test taker with any z-score stands in relation to all other test takers, all we need is a table that tells us the percentage of test takers we would expect to be higher, and the percentage would expect to be lower. You will find a copy of the table of z-scores in Appendix 1. Refer to it now, as you read the following explanation.

In the first column of the table you will find the z-score with the first decimal place. Along the first row of the table you will find the second decimal place of the z-score. We will consider our highest score first, which is 2.17. In the first column read down to 2.1, which is at the 22nd row. We then read across the top of the table to find the column headed 0.07. We then find the intersection of the row and column. The number in this cell is the percentage associated with a z-score of 2.17. The entry in this cell is .4850, or just 48.5 per cent (move the decimal place two places to the right). This number can be read as the percentage of test takers falling between the mean (zero, or 11.7) and the score of 28 (or 2.17). Also remember that 50 per cent of the scores are below the mean. Therefore, 50 per cent + 48.5 per cent = 98.5 per cent of test takers are expected to get a score of less than 28. Our test taker who scored 28 is therefore in the top 2 per cent of the population. We can see this visually on our curve of normal distribution (Figure 2.5).

What about our raw score of 1, giving a z-score of –1.43? If you read down the left-hand column to the row marked 1.4 and then find the cell along that row under the column 0.03, you will find the number .4236. Rounded to two decimal places, this means that 42 per cent of scores fall between the mean and this score. Of course, as the

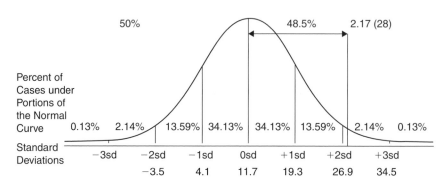

Fig. 2.5. The curve of normal distribution with the meaning of a particular raw score

score is negative, this means that all these scores are better than this score. As 50 per cent of scores fall above the mean, 42 per cent + 50 per cent = 92 per cent of scores are expected to be higher than the score of this test taker.

'But,' I can hear you saying, 'this means that 100 per cent – 92 per cent = 8 per cent of test takers are expected to get scores below –1.43, but in raw scores the only lower score is zero, and no one got all the questions wrong! And even if someone did, we wouldn't expect 8 per cent of test takers to get all the questions wrong.' And you would be right to point this out. We said above that there is (at least) one problem with the test from which these scores came, and now we know what it is. It is far too difficult for the population of test takers for whom it was designed. It just isn't sensitive enough at the lower end of the scale, and so we are told to expect test takers below a level at which they can actually score. The authors of the test admitted that this was the case. It represents a serious flaw in the test design.

6. Test scores in a consumer age

The normal curve has been the technological basis for testing for over a hundred years. It came into widespread use during the First World War, and it is alive and well today. Whenever you read about standardised tests, the tests are based upon the assumption that the distribution of scores (and test taker ability) are normal. However, when you see a score from a standardised test it won't be expressed as a number from –4 to +4. It would be fairly demotivating for a person to be told that his or her score on a test was –0.4 or +1.1. For this reason the z-scores are manipulated to create a standardised scale that is directly related to the z-scores but is much more palatable to the consumer.

In Chapter 1 we discussed the Gaokao examination at some length. This is a modern standardised test that works on precisely these principles. However, the reported score ranges from 100 to 900. The reported score bears little relationship to the actual number of items on the test. Indeed, the actual number of items may vary from year to year, but the score meaning on the scale remains the same. The descriptive statistics for the standardised Gaokao examination every year are as follows:

Mean = 500
Standard deviation = 100
Range = 100 – 900 (i.e. – and + 4 standard deviations from the mean)

In the example above, we know that the mean is 11.72 as a raw score, but we do not know what this raw score is for the Gaokao from year to year. It changes. What happens is that the z-scores, an abstraction of the raw scores in terms of the normal curve of distribution, are transformed using the following formula:

$$z * sd + \overline{X}$$

This reads: z multiplied by the new standard deviation plus the new mean. This is quite easy to understand. A z-score is simply the raw score expressed as a number on a scale with a mean of 0 and a standard deviation of 1. In order to transform this to a number on a scale with a mean of 50 and a standard deviation of 10 (often referred to as a t-score, giving a range of 10 to 90), I would simply fit the numbers into my formula. For a score of 11.7 (0 as a z-score, as it is the average raw score) this would be:

$$0 * 10 + 50 = 50$$

Similarly, if my score is 28 (+ 2.17 as a z-score), the new score would be:

$$2.17 * 10 + 50 = 71.7$$

The ratios between the new positive numbers are exactly the same as the z-scores. Thus, whatever the raw score a student gets on the Gaokao examination, it is standardised and the following formula applied:

$$z * 100 + 500$$

This creates the scale upon which scores are reported. In the case of the Gaokao, score meaning in terms of an individual's position in the population is made explicit. When learners log on to the test website to collect their score, they can see how well they did in relation to all other test takers and calculate their precise position in the population. This is done by means of a score conversion chart, which we reproduce in Appendix 2.

First, look at the column on the left-hand side of the chart. This provides scores on the Gaokao starting at 500 and rising by 10 for each row. The first row at the top of the chart provides the units from 0 to 9. In the cell for the first row and the first column, which is a score of 500, we have the entry 5000. Forget all the other zeros, as we usually round to two decimal places. This is read as a percentage – we expect 50.00 per cent of test takers to score below 500. This is intuitively obvious, as we have made 500 the mean score, which is the same as a z-score of zero. Now we will consider a score of 600. Once again we are looking at figures in the first column, but we read down to the eleventh row. The entry for this cell is 8413, or 84.13 per cent. We know that 600 is a score that is exactly 1 standard deviation above the mean, and if you refer back to Figures 2.3, 2.4 or 2.5 and add all the percentages below the line marking the first standard deviation, you will discover that they total 84.13 (actually 84.12, due to a small rounding error).

All Chinese students who take these examinations, with the all-important English test making up such a large proportion of the score, know that they are being compared with all other test takers. They know that their score meaning is their place on a curve of normal distribution as expressed through the standardised test score, and that this will determine the university or college they will attend. This is a critical moment in their lives. So let's take two test scores from two hypothetical students and imagine how they will feel in each case. Hui scores 717 on the standardised scale. Looking at the table we discover that the entry for this cell is 9850, or 98.5 per cent. (If you compare this with Appendix 1, you will see that 717 is a z-score of 2.17, with a value of 48.5 per cent between the mean and this score. (It is in fact the same as a score of 28 on the previous test we discussed.) This means that Hui is in the top $100 - 98.5 = 2$ per cent of the test taking population. This is wonderful news, and probably means that Hui can go to a top university. Zhi, on the other hand has a score of 450. As the table in Appendix 2 does not go below 500, we can select the entry for 550 instead, but treat the number in the cell as those who are above Zhi, rather than those below. This says that 69.15 per cent of test takers are expected to score higher than Zhi. This can be confirmed by looking at Appendix 1. We know that 1 standard deviation is 100, and so a score of 450 is .5 of a standard deviation below the mean. The entry for 0.5 in Appendix 1 is .1915 per cent. This means that 19.15 per cent of test takers fall between the mean and Zhi's z-score, and 50 per cent are above this mean. Adding these two together, we have 69.15 per cent of test takers score higher. This means that Zhi will probably have to be content with a second- or third-choice university.

▶ 7. Testing the test

The test we have been discussing in Section 5 above with a mean of 11.72 and a standard deviation of 7.5 was the first language test designed to be implemented on a large scale during the First World War. The linguality test, as it was called, was developed in two forms – one for individual administration and the other for group administration. The purpose of the test was clear: to establish whether a recruit needed to be sent to a 'development battalion' to learn English before he could undertake any other military duties:

> *The non-English-speaking and illiterate recruits constituted such a serious clog to military efficiency that development battalions were organized to train these men in speaking English and in reading and writing.*
> (Yerkes, 1921: 355)

These tests are reproduced in Appendix 3. In this section we are only concerned with the group test, for which you will recall we have already said that it proved far too difficult for the population of test takers for whom it was designed. The test designers developed two important validation techniques for the analysis of tests at this time, both of which are illustrated in Table 2.2 (Yerkes, 1921: 360).

Item	Group I (non-English)	Group II (English)	Item	Group I (non-English)	Group II (English)
			21	24	62
1	79	93	13	22	62
3	67	99	16	17	63
2	63	88	12	14	62
4	52	87	25	28	47
10	51	78	19	16	58
5	43	85	20	22	43
6	43	74	17	12	47
15	40	76	22	17	42
9	42	71	18	10	31
11	31	73	24	18	23
23	40	62	27	16	25
26	44	52	7	11	27
8	19	75	28	4	5
14	19	67	29	3	1

Table 2.2 Proportion of test takers from two groups answering individual items correctly

The first principle was to look at the proportion of correct responses to an item as a measure of the *item difficulty*. This is now referred to as the *facility index*. If we look at item 29, which we would probably all agree is the most difficult on the test, just 3 per cent of the test takers in the sample (around 660 test takers) answered this item correctly. The second principle was that it was important to compare the responses of non-native speakers to those of native speakers of the language. Again, if we look at item 29, only 1 per cent of the native English sample answered this item correctly, indicating that it is seriously flawed. Although we are very much aware of the fact that the definition of the 'native speaker' is problematic in applied linguistics (Davies, 2003), the comparison of native speaker responses with those of the target non-native test-taking population has become a basic source of information on whether the test is a language test, rather than a test of other cognitive or non-linguistic abilities. This principle is still applied today. For example, the first major study conducted to ensure that the Test of English as a Foreign Language (TOEFL) test was 'fair' to non-native speakers was a comparison of non-native and native speaker scores by Clark (1977), and when the test was computerised a similar study was immediately undertaken (Stricker, 2002).

8. Introducing reliability

Traditionally, the most prized quality of standardised language tests that are designed to implement meritocracy is *reliability*. The classic definition of reliability was provided by Lado (1961: 31) in the first book published on language testing:

Does a test yield the same scores one day and the next if there has been no instruction intervening? That is, does the test yield dependable scores in the sense that they will not fluctuate very much so that we may know that the score obtained by a student is pretty close to the score he would obtain if we gave the test again? If it does, the test is reliable.

Lado specifically separated the quality of reliability from *scorability*, which some current commentators confound. Scorability, which we discuss in more detail in Chapter 7, is the ease with which a test item or task can be scored. Thus, a set of multiple choice items is more scorable than a response to an open-ended writing prompt. But this does not necessarily make the set of multiple choice items more reliable. It is quite possible that they are easily scored, but produce unreliable scores, as defined by Lado.

If reliability is about the lack of fluctuation, or *consistency*, of scores, we can begin to identify and describe any factors that may threaten this consistency. Lado (1961: 330–331) focused upon variation in conditions of administration, the quality of the test itself and variability in scoring. As for the first, he noted that test scores may fluctuate over time, and may also fluctuate if the circumstances in which the test is taken change. Lado assumed that if no learning had taken place between two administrations of a test, we should not expect the scores to differ greatly. Similarly, if the test is held in two different places, or under slightly different conditions (such as a different room, or with a different invigilator) and the score changed as a direct result, this is a source of unreliability. The second source of unreliability is the test itself. No test, claimed Lado, is a perfect measure. He pointed to problems with sampling what language to test – as we can't test everything in a single test. He also noted that if a test consists of items that test very different things, reliability is also reduced. This is because in standardised tests any group of items from which responses are added together to create a single score are assumed to test the same ability, skill or knowledge. The technical term for this is *item homogeneity*. Finally, unreliability can be caused by the scoring. If humans are scoring multiple-choice items they may become fatigued and make mistakes, or transfer marks inaccurately from scripts to computer records. However, there is more room for variation when humans are asked to make judgements about the quality of a piece of writing or a sample of speech, and give it a rating.

Reliability is a slippery concept, despite its intuitively satisfactory definition. The reason is that the concept is drawn from the way in which instruments are developed in the natural sciences. It is assumed that nature behaves in consistent, predictable ways, and one of the goals of scientific observation is to develop instruments that can observe and plot these consistencies. This is why we spent time in Section 2 to understand why testing was viewed as a 'science': it is assumed that tests, like scientific instruments, provide the means by which we can observe and measure consistencies in human ability.

Any observed score on our tests is therefore assumed to be a composite, explained by the formula:

$$X = T + E$$

The observed score (X) is made up of the 'true' score of an individual's ability on what the test measures (T), plus the error (E) that can come from a variety of sources like those identified by Lado. This assumption has been questioned many times, and it is one that we shall return to in the next chapter. For the moment we will accept the assumptions underlying the concept of reliability so that we can ask ourselves the question: how do we understand and quantify error?

9. Calculating reliability

The method we use to calculate reliability depends upon what kind of error we wish to focus on. In the following discussion and explanation we will focus on the three areas identified by Lado. However, whichever method we use, a reliability coefficient is calculated that ranges from 0 (randomness) to 1. No test is 'perfectly' reliable. There is always error. Exceptionally high values should always be questioned and investigated, as there may be calculation errors or something wrong with the scoring key (Wainer, 1986).

Test administrations

We are always concerned about the consistency of scores across different times or test forms. In order to address this, we use the statistical technique of correlation, which is a measure of the strength of a relation between two interval level variables, such as test scores. The full name of this statistic is the Pearson Product Moment Correlation, after Karl Pearson who invented it. How this works can best be explained by considering Figure 2.6. This represents a scatterplot of the scores from the same test given at two different times. The score that each student got on the test at administration 1 and 2 is plotted. We can see visually that there is a strong positive relationship between the two sets of scores: it is highly likely that a student who scored highly on one administration will score highly on another administration, but there will be some fluctuation.

The strength of the relation between the two sets of scores can easily be quantified on a scale of –1 (there is an inverse relationship between the scores – as one goes up, the other comes down), through 0 (there is no relation between the two sets of scores) to 1 (the scores are exactly the same on both administrations of the test). The closer the result is to 1, the more test–retest reliability we have. The formula for the correlation between the two sets of raw scores is:

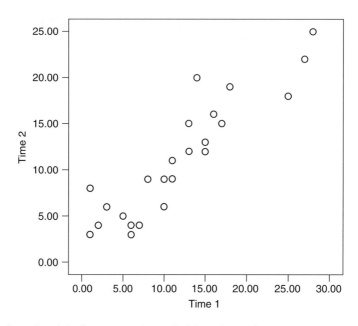

Fig. 2.6. A scatterplot of scores on two administrations of a test

$$Rxy = \frac{\Sigma xy}{N(Sd_x)(Sd_y)}$$

This may look rather impenetrable, but it is easy to calculate by hand when the range is low and we don't have too many scores. In this example we will take the 25 scores from the example above (Table 2.1), and assume that we asked the same group of students to take the same test again at a separate time. We set the distance between the two administrations so that the students will (hopefully) not remember the test content, but not too far in the future that their knowledge or abilities have greatly increased. The score on the first test is 'x' and the score on the second test is 'y' (Table 2.3).

Figure 2.6 is the scatterplot of these data. We can now take our formula and put the numbers in, remembering that the variance is calculated as the square of the standard deviation.

$$Rxy = \frac{1028.24}{25(7.5)(6.3)} = \frac{1028.24}{1181.25} = .87$$

As Bachman (2004: 86) warns, when calculating by hand it is usually necessary to use as many decimal places as possible. To get maximum accuracy it is necessary to do the calculation using a suitable program, such as the Statistical Package for the Social Sciences (SPSS, see http://www.spss.com/UK/). However, when using some packages

Scores x	Scores y	X – X̄	Y – Ȳ	XY
1	3	–10.72	–8.16	87.48
1	8	–10.72	–3.16	33.88
2	4	–9.72	–7.16	69.60
3	6	–8.72	–5.16	45.00
5	5	–6.72	–6.16	41.40
6	4	–5.72	–7.16	40.96
6	3	–5.72	–8.16	46.68
7	4	–4.72	–7.16	33.80
8	9	–3.72	–2.16	8.04
10	6	–1.72	–5.16	8.88
10	9	–1.72	–2.16	3.72
11	11	–0.72	–0.16	0.12
11	11	–0.72	–0.16	0.12
11	9	–0.72	–2.16	1.56
13	12	+1.28	+ 0.84	1.08
13	15	+1.28	+ 3.84	4.92
14	20	+2.28	+ 8.84	20.16
15	12	+3.28	+ 0.84	2.76
15	13	+3.28	+ 1.84	6.04
16	16	+4.28	+ 4.84	20.72
17	15	+5.28	+ 3.84	20.28
18	19	+6.28	+ 7.84	49.24
25	18	+13.28	+ 6.84	90.84
27	22	+15.28	+ 10.84	165.64
28	25	+16.28	+ 13.84	225.32
X̄ = 11.72	Ȳ = 11.16			Σxy = 1028.12
Sd = 7.5	Sd = 6.3			
N = 25	N = 25			

Table 2.3 Calculating a correlation coefficient between two sets of scores

you should be aware that they may not use the unbiased estimators of the population standard deviation as we do here (placing $N - 1$ in the denominator). In other words, the program assumes that you are not estimating from a sample, but know the true value for the entire population. This will inflate the correlation. With this reservation in mind, while the use of machine calculation is much more accurate than doing calculations by hand, it is important to understand what the machine is doing, and why, to be able to interpret the output.

In order to interpret the correlation coefficient we square the result, and $.87^2 = .76$. This number (or r^2) can be interpreted as the percentage variance shared by the two sets of scores, or the degree to which they vary together (as the score on one test increases, so it increases proportionally on the other test). In our case, 76 per cent of variance is shared. A visualisation of this is presented in Figure 2.7.

The shared variance is represented by the shaded area of overlap between the two boxes, whereas the white area of each box represents variance that is unique to each administration. This suggests that the test tends to produce similar results across administrations at different times.

The test itself

We noted above that Lado argued test items should be homogenous. What this means in practice is that when we give a test a name (or a *sub-test* in larger *test battery*) we are labelling the *construct* that we are claiming to measure. If, for example, we call our test 'reading comprehension', all the items should measure the construct of 'reading comprehension'. Similarly, if we call it a test of 'vocabulary', all the items should measure 'vocabulary'. One of the most difficult parts of test development is deciding upon these labels and defining precisely what we mean by them. We return to this problem in Chapter 4. However, for our current purpose we need to be clear about the assumption underlying standardised tests: that if we add the responses from items together to create a score, the aggregation is meaningful in terms of the label we give to it.

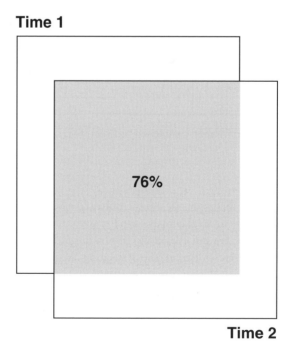

Time 1

76%

Time 2

Fig. 2.7. Shared variance between two tests at $r^2 = .76$

The items must be homogenous. In technical terms, they must all be highly cor-related. Once again, we find the notion of correlation at the very centre of the notion of reliability. We will consider two ways of addressing reliability in terms of item homogeneity.

The first is the split-half method. After a test has been administered the first task is to split it into two equal halves. This might be done by placing item 1 in test A, item 2 in test B, item 3 in test A, item 4 in test B, and so on. Once this has been done we notion-ally have two tests, each of which is half the length of the original test. We then calculate the correlation between the two halves in exactly the same way as discussed above. The correlation coefficient is the reliability coefficient for a test half the length of the one you have actually given. However, reliability is directly related to the length of a test: generally speaking, the longer a test, the more reliable it becomes. So we must correct the correlation for length in order to arrive at the reliability estimate for the whole test. For this we use the Spearman Brown correction formula, which is:

$$R = \frac{2r_{hh}}{1 + r_{hh}}$$

where r_{hh} is the correlation between the two halves of the test.

The most common method, however, is to investigate the internal consistency of the test using the items themselves. Imagine all the possible split halves you could have by dividing the items on a test into two parts, calculating the reliability for each, and then finding the mean of all the reliability estimates. Using internal consistency methods essentially simulates this process.

The most frequently used and reported reliability coefficients is Cronbach's alpha (or α). The formula for *dichotomously scored items* (scored 'right' or 'wrong') is:

$$R = \frac{k}{k-1} \left\{ 1 - \frac{\Sigma pq}{S^2} \right\}$$

In this formula k is the number of items on the test, S^2 is the test score variance, which is the square of the standard deviation, and Σpq is the sum of the variances of individual items. We know for the linguality test that $k = 29$ and $S^2 = 56.25$. In order to calculate Σpq I have adapted Table 2.2 above to create Table 2.4. In Table 2.4 the item columns are identical to Table 2.2, and the columns labelled 'p' are identical to the columns in Table 2.2 labelled Group I (non-English), but with a decimal point before the number. These are the proportions of non-English speakers who answered each item correctly. The next column is 'q', or the proportion of non-English speakers who answered the item incorrectly ($q = 1 - p$). The final column is 'pq' which is p * q, so for item 1, .79 * .21 = .17, and so on. In order to get Σpq, we simply add up all the values in the pq column, to discover that $\Sigma pq = 5$.

Item	p	q	pq	Item	p	q	pq
				21	.24	.76	.18
1	.79	.21	.17	13	.22	.78	.17
3	.67	.33	.22	16	.17	.83	.14
2	.63	.37	.23	12	.14	.86	.12
4	.52	.48	.25	25	.28	.72	.20
10	.51	.49	.25	19	.16	.84	.13
5	.43	.57	.25	20	.22	.78	.17
6	.43	.57	.25	17	.12	.88	.11
15	.40	.60	.24	22	.17	.83	.14
9	.42	.58	.24	18	.10	.90	.09
11	.31	.69	.21	24	.18	.82	.15
23	.40	.60	.24	27	.16	.84	.13
26	.44	.56	.25	7	.11	.89	.10
8	.19	.81	.15	28	.04	.96	.04
14	.19	.81	.15	29	.03	.97	.03
$\Sigma pq = 5$							

Table 2.4 Item variances for the linguality test

We can now put the numbers into the formula (α for dichotomously scored item is also called KR20):

$$R = \frac{29}{29-1}\left\{1 - \frac{5}{56.25}\right\}$$

$$R = 1.04 * (1 - .09)$$

$$R = 1.04 * .91$$

$$R = .95$$

This estimate shows that the test is highly reliable.

Marking or rating

Our next concern is with the reliability of marking, or rating. As we have already said, the scoring of closed response items like multiple choice is much easier than open response items because there is only one correct response. Rating is much more complex because there is an assumption that whichever rater is making the judgement should be a matter of indifference to the test taker. What this means in practice is that if I produce an extended written response to a writing prompt, I should get the same score irrespective of who rates the writing sample. That is, if there is variation by rater this is considered to be a source of unreliability, or error. If our concern is with variation between raters because some raters are more lenient than others, or some raters may rate some test takers higher than others (perhaps because they are familiar with the first language and are more sympathetic to errors), then it is common to quantify this error.

This can also be done using Cronbach's alpha. The formula is now a little different from its instantiation for dichotomous items, because raters usually make *partial credit* judgements, perhaps judging a piece of writing on (for example) a scale of 1 to 6 (see Chapter 7). If we have two raters and we need to discover their *inter-rater reliability*, the formula is:

$$\alpha = \frac{k}{k-1}\left\{1 - \frac{S^2_{r1} + S^2_{r2}}{S^2_{r1} + S^2_{r2}}\right\}$$

This should now be easy to read. k is the number of raters, and S^2 is the variance of their scores. R1 and R2 merely stand for rater 1 and rater 2. The procedure used is identical to the calculations for the standard deviation in Table 2.1, but we need the variances for each rater separately for the numerator, and together for the denominator. In Table 2.5 we calculate the descriptive statistics for rater 1 and rater 2 separately, and in Table 2.6 we add the scores from both raters in order to calculate the variance of the combined scores.

	R1 Scores	$\bar{X}$	$X-\bar{X}$	$X-\bar{X}^2$	R2 Scores	$\bar{X}$	$X-\bar{X}$	$X-\bar{X}^2$
Essay 1	5	3.9	1.1	1.21	4	3.4	0.6	0.36
Essay 2	5	3.9	1.1	1.21	2	3.4	−1.4	1.96
Essay 3	4	3.9	0.1	0.01	4	3.4	0.6	0.36
Essay 4	5	3.9	1.1	1.21	5	3.4	1.6	2.56
Essay 5	3	3.9	−0.9	0.81	2	3.4	−1.4	1.96
Essay 6	3	3.9	−0.9	0.81	4	3.4	0.6	0.36
Essay 7	2	3.9	−1.9	3.61	3	3.4	−0.4	0.16
Essay 8	4	3.9	0.1	0.01	3	3.4	−0.4	0.16
Essay 9	6	3.9	2.1	4.41	5	3.4	1.6	2.56
Essay 10	2	3.9	−1.9	3.61	2	3.4	−1.4	1.96
	$\Sigma = 39$		$\Sigma = 0$	$\Sigma = 16.90$	$\Sigma = 34$		$\Sigma = 0$	$\Sigma = 12.40$
$\bar{X} =$	3.9				3.4			
N = 10	k = 2			Sd = 1.37 $S^2 = 1.88$				Sd = 1.17 $S^2 = 1.37$

Table 2.5 Descriptive statistics for two raters, rating ten essays

	R1 + R2 Scores	$\bar{X}$	$X - \bar{X}$	$X - \bar{X}^2$
Essay 1	9	7.3	1.7	2.89
Essay 2	7	7.3	−0.3	0.09
Essay 3	8	7.3	−0.7	0.49
Essay 4	10	7.3	2.7	7.29
Essay 5	5	7.3	−2.3	5.29
Essay 6	7	7.3	−0.3	0.09
Essay 7	5	7.3	−2.3	5.29
Essay 8	7	7.3	−0.3	0.09
Essay 9	11	7.3	3.7	13.69
Essay 10	4	7.3	−3.3	10.89
	$\Sigma = 73$		$\Sigma = 0$	$\Sigma = 46.1$
$\bar{X} =$	7.3			
$N = 10$	$k = 2$			$Sd = 2.26$ $S^2 = 5.11$

Table 2.6 Descriptive statistics for combined scores

We can now plug the numbers from Tables 2.5 and 2.6 into our formula:

$$\alpha = \frac{2}{2-1} \left\{ 1 - \frac{1.88 + 1.37}{5.11} \right\}$$

$$\alpha = 2 * (1 - .64) = 2 * .37 = .74$$

This result shows a reasonable degree of agreement between the two raters, although with training the level of agreement may rise.

10. Living with uncertainty

One of the most important tools in the armoury of standardised testing is the *standard error of measurement*. If we assume that a test taker has a 'true score' on the test, which genuinely reflects their ability on the construct of interest, their observed score might be different because of error. While the reliability coefficient tells us how much error there might be in the measurement, it is the standard error of measurement that tells us what this might mean for a specific observed score. This statistic is therefore much more informative for interpreting the practical implication of reliability. The formula for the standard error is:

$$Se = sd \sqrt{1 - R}$$

In this formula Se is the standard error, sd the standard deviation, and R the reliability coefficient. We already have all of this information for two tests: the linguality test and our hypothetical writing test from the last section (we will use the combined scores of two raters with a possible range of 12 for ease of reference). Here are the numbers again, with their associated standard errors:

Linguality test
Sd = 7.5
R = .95
Se = 7.5 $\sqrt{.05}$ = 1.7

Writing test
Sd = 2.26
R = .74
Se = 2.26 $\sqrt{.26}$ = 1.15

We can now use the standard error to calculate a *confidence interval* around an observed test score, which tells us by how much the true score may be above or below the observed score that the test taker has actually got on our test. To do this we return to our curve of normal distribution and our table of probabilities in Appendix 1. In Figure 2.8 we show the 95 per cent and 99 per cent confidence intervals. In language testing we normally select a 95 per cent confidence interval, which tells us we can be 95 per cent confident that the true score will fall within a certain range above and below the observed score.

The 95 per cent confidence interval falls at 1.96 standard deviations, and the 99 per cent confidence interval at 2.58 standard deviations. If you turn to the table of z-scores in Appendix 1 and look up 1.96, you will find the value .475 in the cell. This is the proportion of scores between the mean (0) and a z-score of 1.96. If 47.5 per cent of scores are between the mean and this z-score, the same is true for the distance between the mean and –1.96. We therefore add the two proportions together: .475 + .475 = .95, or

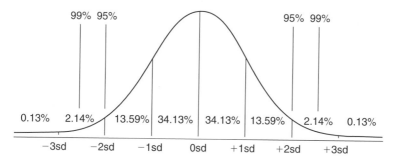

Fig. 2.8. Confidence intervals

95 per cent of all scores fall between the z scores of +1.96 and –1.96. Only 5 per cent of scores fall outside this range. Next, look at the cell for a z-score of 2.58. The value in the cell is .4951. Once again we do our calculation: .4951 + .4951 = .99, or 99 per cent of all scores fall between the z-scores of 2.58 and –2.58. Only 1 per cent of scores fall outside this range.

The standard error is multiplied by the level of certainty (95 per cent or 99 per cent) we wish to adopt in interpreting the value of the observed score. This is what we mean by our level of confidence in a score. To understand how this works we return to our two tests.

Linguality test
Se = 1.7
95% Confidence Interval = 1.7 * 1.96 = 3.33
99% Confidence Interval = 1.7 * 2.58 = 4.39

For any observed score on the linguality test we can be 95 per cent confident that it will fall within a range of + or – 3, and 99 per cent confident that it would fall within a range of + or – 4. For example, if I scored 14 on the test, I could be 95 per cent confident that my true score would lie within the range: 11 < 14 < 17. We can see that even with a very reliable test, a small amount of error feeds through into a level of uncertainty that means a score could really fall anywhere within a range of 7 raw marks. This information becomes critical if a particular score falls close to some cut/decision point, as we then do not know whether a learner is genuinely above or below the established cut score (see Chapter 8).

Writing test
Se = 1.15
95% Confidence Interval = 1.15 * 1.96 = 2.25
99% Confidence Interval = 1.15 * 2.58 = 2.97

For any observed score on the writing test we can be 95 per cent confident that it will fall within a range of + or – 2.25, and 99 per cent confident that it would fall within a range of + or – 2.97. For practical purposes we will call this 2 and 3. If, for example, I scored 6 on the test, I could be 95 per cent confident that my score would lie within the range: 4 < 6 < 8. Similarly, I could be 99 per cent confident that it would fall within the range 3 < 6 < 9. As the possible range of scores is 0 to 12 (the combined scores of two independent raters), an observed score may reflect a true score that could fall somewhere within half the range of possible scores.

Armed with this information we can decide whether it is possible to use these test scores for the kinds of decisions for which the test was originally designed. And, as test users, we should always ask the producers of standardised tests for information on the standard error of measurement.

11. Reliability and test length

The reliability of a test is determined mostly by the quality of the items, but it is also determined by the length of the test. As you will have noticed, the number of items in a test is included in the calculation of α. If you were to increase the value of k in the formula you would see that reliability would steadily increase. This is because in standardised tests with many items, each item provides a piece of information about the ability of the test taker. The more independent pieces of information we collect, the more reliable the measurement becomes. This is why the response to any specific item must be independent of the response to any other item; put another way, the test taker should not get one item correct because they have got some other item correct. The technical term for this is the *stochastic independence* of items.

Lado (1961: 339) provides us with the following formula for looking at the relationship between reliability and test length:

$$A = \frac{r_{AA}(1 - r_{11})}{r_{11}(1 - r_{AA})}$$

In this formula A is the proportion by which you would have to lengthen the test to get the desired reliability, r_{AA} is the desired reliability, and r_{11} is the reliability of the current test. Let us imagine a test with a reliability of .7, and you wish to raise this to .85. The illustrative calculation is as follows:

$$A = \frac{.85\,(1 - .70)}{.70\,(1 - .85)} = \frac{.85 * .30}{.70 * .15} = \frac{.26}{.11} = 2.36$$

In order to increase the reliability of the test to .85, the test would have to be lengthened by a proportion of just over twice its current length. In many cases this is simply not practical because of the time available to conduct the test, or the resources to produce the items. Assuming that the test is not very short, the best way to increase reliability is to produce better items.

12. Relationships with other measures

In Section 2 we observed that a key part of standardised testing was the comparison of two measures of the same construct. Since the time of Galton's work on correlation in the late nineteenth century, it has been assumed that if two different measures were highly correlated this provided evidence of validity (Pearson, 1920). This aspect of external validity is *criterion-related evidence*, or evidence that shows the scores on two measures are highly correlated, or that one test is highly correlated with a criterion that is already known to be a valid measure of its construct. It is also sometimes called evidence for *convergent validity*. In Appendix 3 we have reproduced both the individual and the group English language tests from the First World War. Yerkes (1921: 360) correlated these, and these are the results:

	Group I (non-English)	Group II (English)
Group with performance individual	.68	.72
Group with verbal individual	.76	.77
Group with total individual	.72	.80

Table 2.7 Correlations of group with individual linguality test scores

Yerkes observed that the group score is related at roughly the same level with both the performance and verbal individual scores, and that the correlations were similar for both the non-English and the English group. He therefore concluded that it was possible to combine the two parts of the individual test (performance and verbal), combine the non-English and English scores, and correlate the aggregated scores. The resulting correlation was .79, which 'was considered high enough to justify the selection of critical points on the group test as those corresponding to the critical points on the individual test, determined by way of the equation of correlation'. This produced the decision chart reproduced in Table 2.8.

Rating	Individual test	Group test
A	40 and up	23 and up
B	28 to 39	12 to 20
C	20 to 27	5 to 11
D	9 to 19	Up to 4
E	Up to 8	

Table 2.8 The relation between the two tests

The test developers realised that, as the group test was far too difficult, it was impossible to use it to place test takers into the lowest category. The individual test was presumed to be the criterion – a better measure of English language ability – and the relationship between the group test and its criterion at .79 ($r^2 = .62$) was strong enough in their view to make it 'usable' when it was not possible or practical to use the individual test. For decision purposes, we even see an attempt to provide verbal descriptors for each of the levels, A to E, which is a feature of more recent tests:

> In language the rating E means inability to obey the very simplest commands unless they are repeated and accompanied by gestures, or to answer the simplest questions about name, work, and home unless the questions are repeated and varied. Rating D means an ability to obey very simple commands, or to reply to very simple questions without the aid of gesture or the need of repetition. Rating C is the level required

for simple explanation of drill; rating B is the level of understanding of most of the phrases in the Infantry Drill Regulations; rating A is a very superior level. Men rating D or E in language ability should be classified as non-English.
(Yerkes, 1921: 357)

 # 13. Measurement

In this chapter you will have noticed that we have hardly talked about language at all. It has all been about measurement as understood in *Classical Test Theory*. All test theory assumes that scores are normally distributed and that all of the measurement assumptions we have discussed do in fact hold (Crocker and Algina, 1986). The measurement theory described in this chapter is therefore central to understanding how all standardised tests are built, and how they work. Content analysis also played a role. Yerkes (1921: 355), for example, comments on the content of the linguality test in this way:

> *A fairly accurate individual directions test was arranged, and a less accurate but usable group test, modelled after examination beta. The group test is too difficult at the start and is extended to an unnecessarily high level for purposes of calibration. The individual test is preferable, not only on the score of accuracy and level, but also because of its military nature.*

Deciding what to test is now seen as just as important as how to test it, and we return to this crucial matter in Chapter 4. However, we must acknowledge that the basic technology of language testing and assessment is drawn from measurement theory, which in turn models itself upon the measurement tools of the physical sciences. This leaves open the most important question of all: can human abilities, skills, or knowledge, be treated in the same way as natural phenomena?

In the next chapter we consider classroom assessment and the paradigm of criterion-referenced testing. The assumptions that we make in classroom assessment are shown to be very different indeed.

Activities

○ 2.1 The scientific debate

Read the statement from Baron Kelvin in Section 2 again. For Kelvin, measurement was important because it established the constants that described the world and forwarded science. His research into the measurement of temperature and the establishment of a definition of absolute zero remains the basis of scientific research today. When the astronomer Adolphe Quetelet turned his attention to the emerging 'social sciences', he wrote:

> We cannot … demand from those who employ themselves with social physics, more than we should have done from those who foresaw the possibility of forming an astronomical theory, at a period when defective astronomical observations and false theories, or their total absence, with insufficient means of calculation, only existed. It was especially necessary to be certain of the means of performing such a task; it was afterwards necessary to collect precise observations with zeal and perseverance, to create and render perfect the methods for using them, and thus to prepare all the necessary elements of the edifice to be erected. Now, this is the course which I think it proper to pursue in forming a system of social physics.
> (Quetelet, 1842: 9)

Is the measurement of man similar to the observation and measurement of natural phenomena? If you are working with a group of colleagues you may wish to organise a formal debate, with the motion 'This house believes that the only knowledge we have of man is what can be measured using the tools of science.'

○ 2.2 What is a Quincunx?

The Quincunx is a machine invented by Sir Francis Galton (1822–1911), the inventor of fingerprinting, and one of the first people to take a deep interest in tests. The Quincunx is a board made of equally spaced pins spaced like a '5' on a die. A ball is dropped from the top, and each time it hits a pin there is a 50/50 chance that it will fall to the right or the left. When it reaches the bottom of the Quincunx, it falls into a bin. This is repeated a large number of times. The experiment was designed to investigate the law of errors and the curve of normal distribution. There are a number of Quincunx simulators on the internet. Just type 'Quincunx' into a search engine, or try this excellent simulation:

http://www.jcu.edu/math/ISEP/Quincunx/Quincunx.html

Your time to play!

As you run the Quincunx, notice the distribution being built up, and at the end a normal curve will be superimposed upon the distribution. The larger the sample size, the closer the experiment will come to the normal curve. If you have an odd number of bins, a normal curve will be generated more quickly. Play with the different settings and watch what happens to the distribution. Note that if you change the probability away from .5 (randomness) you will get a skewed distribution. For example, if I make p = .8 (an 80 per cent chance that the ball will fall to the right) I will get a negatively skewed distribution, which is what I would expect from a criterion-referenced test where I expect students to pass! On the other hand, if I set p = .02, this means that the test is too difficult for the learners; perhaps the average facility value for items is too low for the intended test takers. Now what happens on the Quincunx? I get a positively skewed distribution, with most of the scores at the lower end of the distribution. This is almost always a sign of a poor test.

You can also use the Quincunx to investigate a question that many people ask: how many learners do I need to give my norm-referenced test to in order to find out if it is working well? Change the number of bins to an odd number (e.g. 5) and then run the program with these numbers of balls: first 10, then 20, and go on to run it with 30, 40, 50, and so on. What do you notice about the distribution as the number of balls (observations) rises? If you try this a few times (to avoid unusual chance distributions), what is the minimum number you would choose to ensure that your test (assuming that it is at an appropriate difficulty level for the intended population) would generate a normal curve?

The Quincunx is so popular that you can still buy one on the internet: http://www. does.org/masterli/ltcquincunx.htm. The reason for its popularity is that it shows how all measurement theory, in testing and all quantitative sciences, is related to probability. Any single score or measurement is nothing but a 'one-off' observation that could be close to what we might observe frequently. Or it might be an oddity (i.e. statistically unlikely according to probability theory). Our understanding of distributions helps us to calculate just what the range (or distribution) of possible scores might be. This is how we understand the fundamental uncertainty that exists in testing, and the universe. And it is a warning against treating any single number (in any discipline) as representing 'truth', rather than as a random sample from a distribution of possible numbers. Thinking about it in this way also explains why we should use multiple sources of evidence for decisions, rather than single test scores. Any test score is just a sample from a possible distribution, and it could be from anywhere in the range provided by the standard error of measurement.

⭕ 2.3 Non-native and native speaker performance

In Section 7 we presented the facility value of the items in the group linguality test for non-native and native speakers, and provided an analysis of what this meant for our evaluation of the test. Here is the same data for the individual linguality test, reproduced in Appendix 3. Analyse the statistical information and, referring to the appendix, decide which items are very good, average or poor. Decide why this might be the case for each item.

	Verbal scale			Performance scale	
Item	Group I (non-English)	Group II (English)	Item	Group I (non-English)	Group II (English)
1	1.0	1.0	1	1.0	1.0
2	.97	1.0	2	.99	1.0
3	.98	.99	3	.99	1.0
4	.98	1.0	4	.97	.98
5	.97	1.0	5	.95	.98
6	.97	.99	6	.94	.98
7	.92	.98	7	.93	.97
8	.90	.98	8	.91	.97
9	.85	.98	9	.82	.96
10	.85	.97	10	.73	.92
11	.63	.89	11	.71	.89
12	.48	.82	12	.64	.91
13	.23	.78	13	.55	.83
14	.26	.75	14	.54	.78
15	.21	.63	15	.39	.86
16	.08	.53	16	.21	.63
17	.09	.52	17	.14	.58
18	.12	.42	18	.11	.55
19	.08	.41	19	.09	.42
20	.03	.23	20	.09	.39
21	.03	.16			
22	.03	.12			
23	.02	.10			
24	.02	.09			
25	.01	.07			

○ 2.4 Practising your calculation skills I

| 11 | 12 | 17 | 18 | 21 | 22 | 24 | 24 | 24 | 26 | 27 | 27 | 27 | 28 | 29 | 30 | 30 | 31 | 32 | 33 | 33 | 35 | 36 | 44 | 45 |

a. Here are 25 scores on the individual linguality test, which has a possible range of 0 to 45. Calculate the mean and standard deviation. State which raw scores would be found at exactly −1 and +1 standard deviations (z-scores of −1.0 and +1.0).

b. Next, calculate Cronbach's alpha, and then use this to calculate the 95 per cent confidence interval.

c. What does this tell us about the reliability and usability of this test?

To do (a), fill in this table:

Scores	$\bar{X}$	$X - \bar{X}$	$(X - \bar{X})^2$
$\Sigma =$		$\Sigma =$	$\Sigma =$
$\bar{X} =$			
$N =$			

To do (b), you should fill in the following table. In order to calculate p, refer to the Group I (non-English) values for each item in the table above (Activity 2.3).

Item	p	q	pq	Item	p	q	pq
				23			
1				24			
2				25			
3				26			
4				27			
5				28			
6				29			
7				30			

Item	p	q	pq	Item	p	q	pq
8				31			
9				32			
10				33			
11				34			
12				35			
13				36			
14				37			
15				38			
16				39			
17				40			
18				41			
19				42			
20				43			
21				44			
22				45			
$\Sigma pq =$							

Suggested answers to this task can be found in Appendix 6.

○ 2.5 Practising your calculation skills II

Although we have shown you how to calculate correlation by hand, as soon as numbers get slightly larger, or the data set becomes larger, this becomes impractical. We then turn to the computer. But it is still essential that you understand what the computer is actually doing for you. In this activity we invite you to use machine calculation. If you have a statistical package like SPSS on your computer, the two columns of figures can be entered directly as variables. If you do not have access to statistical software, there are now many excellent online calculation tools.

One of my favourite webpages to search for statistical calculation tools is http://statpages.org/. In order to calculate a correlation coefficient using the data below I selected a calculator at the Institute of Phonetic Sciences in Amsterdam (http://www.fon.hum.uva.nl/Service/Statistics/Correlation_coefficient.html) which allows us to simply copy and paste data from a table into the webpage for ease of calculation.

Imagine that Yerkes and his team had created a second verbal linguality test. Instead of giving the 25 test takers just the form in Appendix 3, imagine that he got 13 participants to do form x first and form y second, and 12 to do form y first and form x second. This is a *counterbalanced design* to counter the potential effect of order on scores.

The scores from form x (Appendix 3) are taken from Activity 2.4, and invented scores from our hypothetical (y) form are listed in the second column of the following table. Calculate the correlation coefficient between the scores for the two forms. What do you conclude about the two forms of the test? Also see Appendix 6 for suggested answers.

Student	x	y
1	11	12
2	12	14
3	17	17
4	18	13
5	21	21
6	22	23
7	24	23
8	24	21
9	24	25
10	26	25
11	27	28
12	27	24
13	27	26
14	28	29
15	29	29
16	30	26
17	30	29
18	31	30
19	32	27
20	33	26
21	33	33
22	35	36
23	36	34
24	44	44
25	45	44

◯ 2.6 And what can you do with that score?

In Section 12 we saw that even in the early days of standardised test development there was an eagerness to state what a test taker can do with a score at a certain level. A rating of B was considered necessary to understand drill regulations, for example. However, there was no analysis of the drill regulations in comparison with test content, and no attempt to establish the validity of this claim through research. It was an intuitive assumption. Today, we still wish to make claims about what learners can do in the real world if they achieve a particular score on a standardised test.

The following example is taken from Educational Testing Service (2005: 67), and shows the likelihood that a test taker with a score in a certain range on the reading test is able to undertake certain real-world tasks.

How do you think the researchers began to establish the link between the score and the 'can do' statements in the left-hand column of the table? If you are working with colleagues, discuss possible methodologies in groups. When you have finished, compare your ideas and decide which method you would try first, and why.

TOEFL. TOEFL iBT – Reading Competency Descriptors

Competency Descriptors	TOEFL iBT Reading Score Levels (0–30)						
	1–5	6–10	11–15	16–19	20–23	24–27	28–30
I can understand major ideas when I read English.							
I can understand how the ideas in an English text relate to each other.							
When I read English, I understand charts and graphs in academic texts.							
I can understand English vocabulary and grammar when I read.							
When I read academic texts written in English, I understand the most important points.							
I can understand the relative importance of ideas when I read an English academic text.							
I can organize or outline the important ideas and concepts in English academic texts.							
When I read an academic text written in English, I can remember major ideas.							
When I read a text in English, I am able to figure out the meanings of words I do not know by using the context and my background knowledge.							
I can quickly find information that I am looking for in academic texts written in English.							
When I read academic texts in English, I can understand them well enough to answer questions about them later.							
I can read English academic texts with ease.							
I can read and understand texts in English as easily as I can in my native language.							

Likelihood of Being Able to Perform Each Language Task:

<50% Very unlikely	50–65% Unlikely	66–80% Borderline	81–95% Likely	>95% Very likely

3 Classroom assessment

▶ 1. Life at the chalk-face

Just how different is assessment in the classroom from the world of large-scale standard-ised assessment? Some believe that they are not only different paradigms, but exist in a state of conflict. Needless to say, it is standardised assessment that is seen as the villain. For example, Stiggins (2001: 12) argues that, while high-stakes tests may be motivating and challenging for the secure and able, for those who 'regard success as beyond their capacity' the outcome is usually demotivation and failure. Some would even go as far as to 'argue that teachers need help in fending off the distorting and de-motivating effects of external assessments' (Shepard, 2000: 7), even using 'the image of Darth Vader and the Death Star to convey the overshadowing effects of accountability testing' (Shepard, 2000: 8). The passion that testing arouses even calls up the rhetoric of the dark side of the force! What is evident in this battle between the practices of standardised test-ing and classroom assessment is that for the advocates of the latter, there is a sense of injustice, and a need to introduce 'bottom-up' practices that place the teacher in control (Shepard, 1995). The uneasy relationship between externally mandated test-ing and teacher assessment has been widely studied (Brindley, 1998, 2001), showing, in Rea-Dickins' (2008: 258) words, how 'the wider political context in which children are assessed may constrain desirable assessment practices'.

Even if we resist these external attempts to control what is done in the classroom, there will always be a place for the externally mandated standardised test. It is just that these tests do not do the kinds of jobs we want tests to do in the teaching and learning process. As we noted in Chapter 1, one area in which teachers have used standardised tests for learning is to improve motivation (although Stiggins would argue this is not always the case). Latham (1877: 40) saw why the teachers of his time liked tests: 'The value of examinations … is far greater as an engine in the hands of the teacher to keep the pupil to definite work than as a criterion.' The analogy of the test as an engine to drive other goals is a powerful one. The technology of standardised testing has been developed in order to produce an engine that is capable of driving a meritocratic social system. Tests encourage learning because they are gateways to goals. In the classroom, however, we wish to devise engines that encourage learning, not only by motivating learners, but also by providing feedback on learning and achievement to both learners and teachers. If learning can also take place through assessment, we may have achieved the effect to which classroom testing aspires.

In this chapter we will consider two major approaches to classroom assessment:

Assessment for Learning and Dynamic Assessment. While these have much in common, they have a different theoretical basis. One is a highly pragmatic approach to classroom assessment, while the other is driven by sociocultural theory. In both cases we will focus upon the practice associated with the movement, although we will explain and critique the theory upon which each is based. We also briefly consider self- and peer-assessment, and portfolio assessment, as useful techniques in assessment for learning. We then look at the link between assessment and second language acquisition in order to see if there is a 'learning sequence' that can be used to inform assessment for learning. We argue that all current approaches to classroom assessment have grown out of criterion-referenced testing, which we describe in some detail. The practice of designing test specifications is the most important practical application of criterion-referenced testing, and so we devote a whole chapter to this later in the book. In this chapter, however, we look at the concept of *dependability* in criterion-referenced testing for the classroom, which is the counterpart of reliability in standardised testing. This provides the tools you will need to investigate the dependability of your own classroom assessments. We close the chapter by assessing the state of the theory underlying classroom assessment.

▌2. Assessment for Learning

The traditional approach to classroom assessment is sequential (Cumming, 2009: 91). Firstly, teachers establish educational goals and objectives. Secondly, they construct the activities and tasks that will move the learners towards those goals and objectives. Thirdly, they evaluate how well they have succeeded. Since the 1980s, however, there has been a strong interest in the role that assessment can have during the learning process, rather than just at the end of it. The work of Black and Wiliam (1998) in particular, and the 'Assessment for Learning movement' more generally, has had a great deal of impact on many educational systems around the world (Leung and Scott, 2009). While most externally mandated testing is summative, Black and Wiliam focused on formative assessment. The latter are tests or assessments used in the process of learning in order to improve learning, rather than at the end of a period of learning. Unlike tests that are imposed upon the schools, their function is to aid in the diagnosis of individual learning needs. Further, it is not useful in formative assessment to compare learners with one another. The work of Black and Wiliam was not only theoretical. In a large-scale project the practical classroom practices associated with assessment for learning were trialled in schools (Black et al., 2003, 2004). Classes were selected to receive the assessment for learning 'treatment', so that outcomes could be compared with those of control classes at the end of the year. Unusually, the researchers reported the standardised effect size, rather than traditional significance statistics. This is the difference between the scores for the treatment group and the scores for the control group divided by the standard deviation. This takes into account differences in 'gains' as well as the distribution of the groups. An effect size of .3 was reported, which suggests that there are important effects associated with formative assessment.

The reason for this research was a desire to 'raise standards', by which Black and Wiliam meant improving the educational achievement of learners. They argued that the most important way in which standards can be raised is to gather information through assessment that can be used to modify or change teaching and learning activities to better meet the needs of learners. It was also claimed that the process of assessment, including self-assessment, could improve motivation and self-esteem, leading to additional learning gains. Achieving motivation within the classroom is, they argue, more associated with all learners gaining a sense of achievement, rather than encouraging the comparison that inevitably occurs when extrinsic awards are involved. Therefore, one of the most important practices they implemented in their trials was providing only feedback on work, rather than grades or scores. The findings showed that this was particularly beneficial to less able students who achieved much more than they otherwise would have done. It has to be acknowledged that this particular practice can raise larger problems for language teachers. In many institutions – particularly schools – there is an expectation from the learners, their parents and the school management that teachers will grade each piece of work. If a piece of work is not given a grade, the teacher is perceived to be failing in one of their most important tasks. However, research has shown that in a classroom context if a grade is given, a learner will probably pay very little attention to the feedback, however useful it might be. Teachers therefore face the uphill struggle to convince managers, learners and their families that giving grades is not always good practice.

Motivating learners is part of instilling a 'culture of success', where all participants feel that through active participation they can achieve more than they previously thought possible. Most important is giving feedback 'about the particular qualities of his or her work, with advice on what he or she can do to improve' with no comparison to the work of others. What the research discovered was that a number of simple practices led to significant levels of improvement. Firstly, in feedback to all tasks, teachers should try to make learners aware of what they have learned. It should be 'descriptive' rather than 'evaluative', so that it is not perceived negatively (Rea-Dickins, 2006: 168). Secondly, learners need to know what aspects of their performance can be improved and, critically, how they can make that improvement. It is the process of understanding what the goal is, where the learner is now and how they can move towards the goal. Thirdly, the researchers recommended that time for the learner to digest and respond to teacher feedback should be planned into the learning time so that the learners can start to develop metacognitive awareness of their own learning processes.

The practical steps that we have discussed so far have been designed to improve learning. There are also a number of practical teaching practices that support improved learning through assessment. The one that has received the most attention is questioning. Traditionally, teachers spend a lot of class time asking questions. Language teachers have known this for a long time from the discourse studies of classrooms that identified the Initiation–Response–Feedback (IRF) patterns (Sinclair and Brazil, 1982). What Black and Wiliam discovered was that teachers in the classrooms they observed did not leave sufficient time after a question for learners to think about what was being asked. Rather, if there was no immediate response, teachers would provide the answer themselves or move on to the next topic. The practical recommendation for this most basic form of classroom assessment is to frame questions that do not require the simple repetition of facts, but are more open-ended. Once a question has been asked, teachers should allow longer 'wait times' for the learners to think, and respond. This could very well involve learners discussing the question for a period of time before formulating an answer.

The other critical component of formative assessment is the choice and design of classroom tasks, and how the classroom is managed for learners to undertake these tasks. Designing tasks that engage the knowledge, skills or abilities that we are trying to teach is a complex process. It requires a sound knowledge of the subject area, discussion with colleagues, and a certain amount of technical know-how that we discuss in detail in Chapter 5. Classroom tasks frequently look very different from the kinds of items and tasks that appear in standardised tests. The main reason for this, as we have seen, is the requirement that standardised tests have many items in order to achieve reliability. The response to each item is a piece of information that is used to construct a picture of the test taker's ability. This is not a requirement for classroom assessment, where there is time for much more open-ended tasks that take considerable time to complete. The context of the assessment makes a great deal of difference. Tasks that involve group and pair work are particularly useful in the language classroom, providing the opportunity for production and learning from interaction. They create the opportunity for collaborative learning, in which language learning takes place through language use. As learners become aware of the communication problems that they face in achieving goals, they begin to focus on what they need to acquire next. Swain (2000: 100) put it this way:

> There are several levels of noticing, for example, noticing something in the target language because it is salient or frequent. Or, as proposed by Schmidt and Frota, in their 'notice the gap principle', learners may not only notice the target language form, but notice that it is different from their own interlanguage. Or, as I have suggested, learners may notice that they do not know how to express precisely the meaning they wish to convey at the very moment of attempting to produce it – they notice, so to speak, a 'hole' in their interlanguage.

Assessment of the gap between what is now possible and the goal in language learning has been a central theme of second language acquisition research in recent years, with a particular emphasis on the kinds of tasks that encourage 'noticing the gap' (Bygate, Skehan and Swain, 2001).

▶ 3. Self- and peer-assessment

Another important component of helping learners to develop a clear picture of the goals of their own learning compared to their current performance is self- and peer-assessment. Black and Wiliam were among the first to recommend that learners be given the criteria by which teachers (or examiners) judge the quality of work. In many cases, these may have to be simplified for learners. Alternatively, after being shown model samples of language performance, learners may be asked to produce their own rating criteria in groups, and use these to peer-assess each other's work. Following Frederiksen and Collins (1989), this is seen as introducing 'transparency' to the criteria for success, and which Shepard (2000: 12) sees as a basic principle of 'fairness'. The practice of self- and peer-assessment using transparent criteria is designed primarily to assist the development of the awareness of the 'gap' between what is being produced now, and the target performance, thus improving learning.

In order for self- and peer-assessment to work well, it is essential that classroom time be spent on training learners to rate their own work, and the work of their colleagues. This can take significant amounts of time, and the kinds of techniques are not dissimilar to those of rater training to use rating scales (see Chapter 7). Research has shown that, without substantial experience of applying the criteria to work samples, self-assessments can fluctuate substantially (Ross, 1998a; Patri, 2002), but that with training it can be dependable for short periods of time (Ross, 2006). Peer-assessments tend to be much more stable, although they may be more lenient than assessments made by teachers (Matsuno, 2009).

While consistency may be a virtue, dealing with self- and peer-assessment purely in these terms is rather to miss the point. Oscarson (1989: 2) famously argued that 'the question of subjectivity does not necessarily invalidate the practice of self-assessment techniques in language testing and evaluation and, furthermore … self-assessment may be motivated by reasons that go beyond mere evaluation'. He saw the primary value in the introduction of a shared responsibility between learners and teachers for deciding what constituted 'good' work. This, he contended, led to improved learning through raising awareness of the quality of writing or speech, and establishing a goal-orientation in study. Oscarson recommended the practical devices of getting learners to keep records of their work, and their own perceptions and ratings of how their work improves and develops. This may involve a diary, or a continuous assessment card like the one illustrated in Figure 3.1.

Today this could take other forms, such as a digital audio or video diary, or an online blog in which samples of work and a commentary are saved side by side. This naturally leads on to the use of portofolios, where students collect together samples of writing, or digital copies of speech, into a collection of their work. However, it may also contain reading and listening texts, with an assessment of how well they were understood, and reactions to them. A portfolio represents a wide sample of the work of a particular student to show what they can do with the language. It can be assessed by themselves, their colleagues, the teacher, and even parents. Genesee and Upshur (1996: 100) see the primary benefits of portfolio assessment in conjunction with self- and peer-assessment to be collaboration, inclusiveness, involvement and responsibility, in both learning and assessment. This, they believe, leads to increased motivation.

CONTINUOUS ASSESSMENT CARD		Name ... *Peter Anderson*	
Test No ⟶	1	2	3
Type of test and date	Interview 21 January	Role-playing tasks 19 February	...
Self assessment	'I thought I could answer about half of the 10 questions satisfactorily. Weak on pronunciation'	'Went very well. But there were a few words and phrases I didn't remember (Important?)	...
Test result	7/10	Good	...
Comments (by teacher or learner)	'Slight under estimation Pronunciation not too bad' (Teacher) 'Better than I thought' (Student)	'You sounded a bit blunt, perhaps (Teacher) 'Must practise polite phrases' (Student)	...

Fig. 3.1. Continuous assessment card (Oskarson, 1989: 6)

▶ 4. Dynamic Assessment

Assessment for Learning in the classroom is therefore premised upon the belief that activities should focus upon making the learner aware of the gap between current abilities and performance levels, and the target or goal that the learner wishes to achieve. Dynamic Assessment (DA) makes the same assumption, but is built upon the work of Vygotsky. Based in sociocultural theory, it provides what advocates claim is 'a new understanding that cognitive abilities are developed through socially supported interactions' (Shepard, 2000: 7). From Vygotsky, DA takes the notion of the Zone of Proximal Development (ZPD) to describe the gap between the learner's current stage of development and the next stage of development. This differs from learning for assessment, as the learner is not necessarily shown what the final target performance is, but shown the gap to the next level of development in a sequence of acquisition or learning. The second difference is in the conceptualisation of the role of the teacher. Rather than 'just' a provider of feedback, teachers are 'mediators'. Lantolf and Poehner (2008a: 273) say:

> *In DA, assessment and instruction are a single activity that seeks to simultaneously diagnose and promote learner development by offering learners mediation, a qualitatively different form of support from feedback. Mediation is provided during the assessment procedure and is intended to bring to light underlying problems and help learners overcome them.*

Mediation is about intervening in the learning process in a way that aids learners to modify their use of language or communication, so that they constantly improve. In terms of the kinds of tasks that learners are given, DA holds that teachers should use activities that learners cannot complete independently, so that mediation is required. The ZPD is then defined as the gap between what the learners can do unaided, and what they can do with assistance (Lantolf, 2009: 363). The nature of the mediation is also important. It can be of two types. If it is 'interventionist', the mediator standardises the mediation, so that it is common across learners. Indeed, this kind of intervention could be provided by a computer in what was traditionally known as programmed learning. DA practitioners, however, recommend 'interactionist' mediation, in which the mediator interacts with each learner depending upon the ongoing assessment of the current stage of the individual's development. It is this 'interaction' that provides DA with the rationale for the use of the word 'dynamic' in its title.

The three methods most closely associated with DA are the 'graduated prompt', 'testing the limits', and the 'mediated learning experience' (Lantolf and Poehner, 2007: 53). The first two are interventionist techniques, and the latter an interactionist technique. In the 'graduated prompt', the mediator creates a task with a graded series of questions to ask a learner who has problems completing a task. The questions start from the most implicit to see if a learner can overcome a difficulty through guided thinking, to very explicitly focusing on the nature of the problem. These prompts are prepared in advanced, and not varied. In 'testing the limits', learners are given feedback on their performance on a task, and then asked to verbalise the problems they feel they have faced, and what they will try to do to overcome them. This technique requires a teacher to work with a single student on a task, and to provide whatever scaffolding is necessary to enable the learner to complete it successfully. The preferred 'mediated learning experience' is a one-to-one interaction in which the mediator interactively helps the learner move toward the next stage of learning through scaffolding attempts to communicate.

Each technique can also be used in a 'cake' or 'sandwich' approach. In the 'cake' approach, mediation takes place after each item or task, and so can only really be used with individuals. On the other hand, the 'sandwich' approach involves mediation at the end of a test or series of activities, and so can also be used with groups.

Whichever combination is used, during the process the teacher notes the extent of mediation necessary in order to evaluate the current level of the learner. This information is used to select the next task. Lantolf and Poehner (2007: 68–69) provide an example of how an interventionist mediation might occur with reference to an item from a language aptitude test (see Figure 3.2).

If the examinee's first attempt to complete the pattern is incorrect, s/he is provided with the following implicit hint: 'That's not correct. Please, think about it once again.' If the second attempt is also unsuccessful, the examiner offers a more explicit hint: 'That's not correct. Think about which rows are most relevant to the one you are trying to complete.' In this case the first row is not relevant ... If the third attempt fails to produce the correct response, the examiner offers an even more explicit hint: 'That's

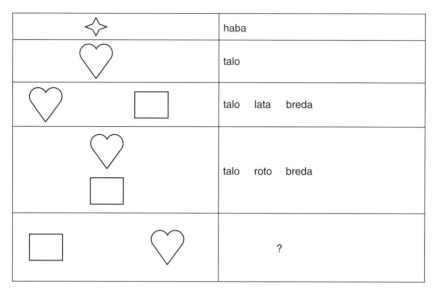

Fig. 3.2. An item from an aptitude test

not correct. Let's look at rows three and four.' At this point, the examinee's attention is drawn to several important pieces of information: heart is talo; that the language has words (lata and roto) that indicate relative horizontal and vertical position of objects; that the subject or topic of a sentence is given first; that sentence in the third row most likely means "the heart is above the square".

If the learner still doesn't get the answer correct, it is given by the mediator.

Examples of the much freer interactionist techniques are provided (Lantolf and Poehner, 2007: 72–73), in which an examiner helps a learner to select the correct verb ending.

> Example 1
> S: *Juegué al tenis* [I played tennis]
> [the correct form for the third person is *jugó*]
> E: *Jugué o jugó* [I played or she played?]
> S: *Jugó* [She played]
>
> Example 2
> E: Very good. And here you said, what did she do?
> S: *Comí* [I ate]
> E: *Comí o comió?* [I ate or she ate?]
> S: *Comió* [She ate]
> E: *Comió* [She ate]

One of the first reactions to examples like these is to wonder just what the difference is between 'mediation' and what teachers normally do in classrooms to get learners to notice their mistakes. Teachers assume that noticing and correcting leads to learning, even if acquisition may require several instances of noticing over a considerable period of time; research supports this assumption (Long and Robinson, 1998). We therefore have to ask why such an elaborate sociocultural theory is necessary to explain how teachers are constantly assessing in the language classroom. But perhaps this is to miss the point. Perhaps the contribution of DA is to show that teachers are in fact constantly assessing, and that this assessment is part of the learning process. The additional layers of theory are perhaps attempts to explain what already happens, although to what degree this is successful is a question that has not been thoroughly investigated. As Rea-Dickins (2006: 166) correctly asks: 'But what, exactly, constitutes an assessment or an assessment event? How are these differentiated from, say, a teaching event? Is it even possible to distinguish between them? Teachers, so it seems to me, may engage in a continual process of appraising their learners.'

For practical purposes, however, the fact that most of DA has to occur with individuals is problematic. Despite the references to group DA in the 'sandwich' approach, many teachers around the world are faced with large classes where this kind of mediation is not possible. These restrictions upon the use of such techniques should be acknowledged.

What is important to recognise, however, is that adopting DA as the paradigm of choice in classroom assessment makes assessment an entirely local practice. Growing as it does from sociocultural theory, DA practitioners argue that the meaning of the assessment is contextually dependent, where 'language teaching and learning need to be conceived as integrally interactive, jointly constructed, and negotiated processes between teachers and learners, which cannot be prescribed or predicted by general curriculum policies' (Cumming, 2009: 93). The reason it is important to understand the claim is that anything learned from DA is only meaningful in context; with these particular participants, these particular tasks, at this particular time. It cannot have, and does not claim to have, any generalisable meaning beyond the instance of occurrence. As a theory, it therefore embodies the essence of a postmodern social constructivism that restricts meaning to the moment.

▶ 5. Understanding change

What is not in dispute is that learning for assessment generally, and DA in particular, are more concerned with change than with stability. Indeed, the whole purpose of 'feedback' or 'mediation' is to cause change. If the intervention or interaction is successful, learning takes place and the learner is no longer the same person. In standardised testing, on the other hand, we assume that the learner's state will remain stable at least for a period of time. Some large-scale testing programmes issue certificates that are recognised for the purpose of university entrance for a period of two years – the period over which little language gain or loss is expected to occur. And the purpose of these tests is certainly not to cause change. This observation is not in dispute, and so it has been recognised for some time that it is not possible simply to 'map' the validity criteria of standardised testing onto formative assessment (Taylor and Nolan, 1996; Teasdale and Leung, 2000). The idea of calculating a correlation coefficient between the scores of an assessment given at two different times, as we did in Chapter 2, would seem bizarre to DA practitioners. As we have seen, the claims made for DA are that significant changes can be seen over relatively short periods of time. Lantolf and Poehner (2008a: 280) see the difference this way:

> *Both psychometric concepts [reliability and validity] are built on a foundation that privileges the autonomous individual as the site from which performance and development emerge. DA, on the other hand, is built on a foundation which privileges the social individual, or as Wertsche (1998) puts it 'person-acting-with-mediational-means.' It also must be remembered that DA is not an assessment instrument but is instead a procedure for carrying out assessment.*

All the contextual features of DA that lead to change would be classed as threats to reliability in standardised testing. Lantolf appears to have fewer problems with traditional notions of validity. He focuses specifically on predictive validity, as the purpose of assessment in DA is to predict (and assist) learner development from their current stage to the next. This does not appear to be problematic, as long as the claims made by those who practise DA are never generalised, and the measure of the validity of the practice is the extent to which a learner moves from his current stage to the target stage. Or, as Poehner (2008: 3) puts it, 'validating the activity of teaching-assessment requires interpreting its impact on learner development'. When it comes to other aspects of validity, DA practitioners have more serious problems. Discussing the definition of learner competencies, for example, Poehner says: 'In some sense, this is akin to two artists arguing over who has more accurately rendered an autumn landscape, with neither noticing that the seasons have changed' (2008: 9). I think that this argument misses the point. We need to be able to define competencies, skills and abilities even if they change over short periods of time; but this lack of interest in definition shows that DA is not at all concerned with anything but change itself.

Nevertheless, even this weak notion of validity as successful change is not without its problems, as we cannot be sure that the intervention is the cause of the learning. This is because, by definition, there can be no comparison with what any other learner is doing, or even with what a given learner might have been doing if he had not been doing DA. The kinds of control groups used by Black *et al.* (2003) would be meaningless in DA. We therefore do not know whether the learner would make more, less or essentially the same progress under different conditions. But this is the price to be paid for the relativism that comes with social constructivism.

This is not, of course, to say that classroom assessment should adhere to the same validity criteria as standardised tests. We have seen that it is a very different paradigm, with different rules. To this extent I agree with Moss (2003; see a discussion in Fulcher and Davidson, 2007: 192–202) that evaluation has to be in terms of pedagogical decisions made, and their effectiveness. And this has to be done in a paradigm where 'the context is part of the construct' (2007: 25). Validity evidence, however, will not have the power of generalisability beyond the case study.

▶ 6. Assessment and second language acquisition

Perhaps one of the most intractable problems associated with DA is the notion that the mediator, who is always a person with more knowledge (the teacher) who can act as a guide, is able to identify and describe both the present state of the learner and the next level of development. It assumes that learning is a progression along a known pathway. This implies a strong link between assessment and second language acquisition (SLA) theory. The kind of theory that is required is a model of SLA that 'includes two dimensions: 1) development, which [is] regular and predictable, and 2) variation, which is largely the result of individual differences' (Bachman, 1998: 190). However, SLA does not provide us with a theoretical model that can be used to construct the kind of progression required to describe the current stage of an individual learner, or the most likely next step on the path. The closest that SLA research can offer is Krashen's (1981) natural order hypothesis and Pienemann's acquisition-based procedures for assessment (Pienemann and Johnston, 1986; Pienemann, Johnston and Brindley, 1988). The problem is that regular and predictable development has only been described for the very limited area of morpheme acquisition in English, and word order in German and English. Extensive research has shown that there is a reasonably stable implicational hierarchy, in which certain forms tend to be learned before others as if they were the building blocks of an interlanguage grammar. Pienemann *et al.* (1988) report these (in acquisitional sequence) as:

Structure	Example
1. Single words, formulae	How are you?
2. SVO, SVO?	*The tea is hot?
3. Adverb Preposing	*Yesterday I work
4. Do fronting	*Do he work?
5. Topicalisation	This I like
6. NEG + V (don't)	*He don't eat meat
7. Pseudo-inversion	Where is my purse?
8. Yes/No-inversion	*Have he seen it?
9. Particle shift	*He turn the radio on
10. V-'to'-V	We like to sing
11. 3rd-SG-s	She comes home
12. Do-2nd	They did not buy anything
13. Aux-2nd	Where has he seen you?
14. Adv-ly	They spoke gently

| 15. Q-tag | It's expensive, isn't it? |
| 16. Adv-VP | He has often heard this |

Explanatory notes

Adverb preposing: In English some, but not all adverbials, may be placed in sentence initial position.

Topicalisation: The placement of objects or subordinate clauses in sentence initial position, such as 'Because I feel ill, I can't work.'

Pseudo-inversion: In wh-questions with a copula, the subject and copula must be inverted.

Yes/No-inversion: In questions to which the answer is 'yes'/'no', the modal or auxiliary comes to sentence-initial slot.

Particle shift: The verb and preposition of a phrasal verb are split.

Do-2nd and Aux-2nd: In main clauses the auxiliary and the model are in second position in positive sentences and wh-questions.

In acquisition studies it was found that these features were acquired in five discrete stages that could be used in a speaking test to place a learner in an acquisitional level (Pienemann *et al.,* 1988: 228):

> Stage 1: Single words and formulae
> Stage 2: SVO, plural marking
> Stage 3: Do fronting, topicalisation, adverb preposing, Neg+V
> Stage 4: Pseudo-inversion, Yes/No-inversion
> Stage 5: 3rd-SG-s, Aux-2nd, Do-2nd

Pienemann *et al.* (1988: 221) argue: 'If the teachability of grammatical forms is constrained by the learner's current stage of language development, and furthermore if this development is the same for all learners, then teaching and by extension, testing, can be geared to what is currently learnable by profiling the learner's present state of development.' This became known as the 'teachability hypothesis' (Larsen-Freeman and Long, 1991: 282), which puts constraints on what can be learned next, and also predicts what will be learned next. The problem for language testing is that we normally do not wish to restrict ourselves to testing grammatical structures.

How does DA cope with this problem? Lantolf (2009: 357–358) explicitly rejects any view of second language acquisition that posits a universal process that is regular and predictable. He also rejects any general learning theory, like Piaget's, that posits a developmental sequence. Rather, Lantolf claims that DA prioritises action, so that 'effective instruction must precede and indeed lay down the path for development to follow' (2009: 358). This implies that it is the mediator who is able to influence the acquisitional path of the learner, so that the next stage is decided by the current intervention. This position is theoretically unsatisfying. If we are unable to make predictions about acquisition based on the theory, there is no way, even in principle, of observing any changes that might bring the theory into question. So, while SLA offers only limited findings that can help us establish an acquisitional sequence, DA appears to abandon any hope that it may exist in favour of a view that if we only use the recommended technique, anything is possible.

This raises a crucial question about the relationship between theory and data. We have observed that the kinds of interventions recommended by DA are not dissimilar to what most language teachers would see as regular teaching practice. Further, no one is questioning that these interventions are highly likely to lead, however slowly, to language acquisition. The problem is in explaining why. Whenever we observe phenomena like these exchanges leading to learning, we attempt to create explanations (theories). The value of these theories lies in whether they are capable of predicting what will happen under certain conditions in new contexts. In other words, it should be testable. DA appears to be based on a theory that is not testable, but is self-validating in each new context. While the practice may be useful, the theory may be just so much unnecessary baggage.

7. Criterion-referenced testing

The insights that have led to Assessment for Learning and DA come from criterion-referenced testing and assessment (CRT). Whether we decide to use these integrated approaches to classroom assessment or traditional linear classroom testing, one of the key features of classroom testing is that test takers are not compared with each other. As Stiggins (2001: 10) puts it, the change is 'from merely sorting students to ensuring attainment of specific competencies'. If there is a 'score' at all, its meaning is not derived from the distribution of scores. Furthermore, we do not expect a set of scores to be normally distributed. If the purpose of assessment for learning is to improve performance on tasks or any kind of test that is a measure of what has been learned, we expect (and hope) that most of the learners will do well. The kind of distribution that we wish to see is *negatively skewed*, as shown in Figure 3.3.

When this happens, the technology of standardised testing fails. The engine no longer runs in the way predicted, and the statistics that we discussed in Chapter 2 can no longer be used. Those statistics depend on the assumptions of normal distribution, and good discrimination. We have neither of these when assessment for learning is working well.

This recognition led to the evolution of the second paradigm in assessment, which was named 'criterion-referenced testing' by Glaser (1963: 519), and he described it as follows:

> *Achievement measurement can be defined as the assessment of terminal or criterion behaviour; this involves the determination of the characteristics of student performance with respect to specified standards.*

The first thing to note in this quotation is the use of 'standards'. We have already noted that this has multiple meanings in the language testing literature, and here it is interpreted interchangeably with 'criteria' in real-world performance. The principle is that

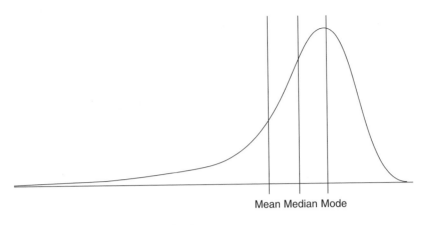

Mean Median Mode

Fig. 3.3. A negatively skewed distribution

if we can describe the target performance, and stages along the route to that perform-ance, we can assess where a learner is on the trajectory. This is the same principle that we see in Assessment for Learning and DA, but there is an assumption that we can spec-ify a 'continuum of knowledge acquisition' (Glaser, 1963: 519). The fact that Glaser's work was done in relation to the use of new technologies in programmed learning indicates the fact that this progression was seen as a linear 'building-block process', in a behaviourist learning model (Shepard, 1991; Glaser, 1994b: 27). However, what was completely new was the focus upon the description of what was to be learned, and what came to be called 'authentic assessment' (Glaser, 1994a: 10). This was essentially a new interest in the content of tests that had not been taken so seriously in earlier large-scale, standardised tests. While recognising the role played by closed response items in stand-ardised tests, the criterion-referenced testing movement also saw that they were not the most efficient way of representing real-world performances in tests (Frederiksen, 1984). Glaser (1994b: 29) overtly argued:

> as assessment departs from the confinement of multiple-choice testing, freer formats will enable many of the processes and products of learning to be more apparent and openly displayed. The criteria of performance will be more transparent so that they can motivate and direct learning. The details of performance will not only be more open for teacher judgement but will also be more apparent to students so that they can observe and reflect on their own performances and so that they can judge their own level of achievement and develop self-direction. If this occurs, in an appropriate social setting in the classroom, then students along with teachers can observe one another and provide feedback and guidance as they learn to help and receive help from others. In this scenario, one can ask: In such classroom assessment, where do the performance criteria reside?

The challenge is in producing such criteria, a topic to which we turn in Chapters 4 and 7. However, we should note here that criterion-referenced testing is no longer linked to behaviourist theories of language learning. Secondly, as Shepard (1991: 5) points out, within this model, testing is not used to 'drive instruction'. Rather, the test is used to aid and monitor instruction. It is in the service of teaching, rather than being its master. Or as Latham (1877: 8) would put it: 'It makes all the difference whether the teaching is subordinate to the examination or the examination to the teaching.'

In criterion-referenced testing the teaching comes first, and the results of the tests are used to make decisions about learners and instruction. As Popham and Husek (1969: 3) pointed out, criterion-referenced testing was therefore not the tool of choice for selection purposes. As we have already seen, there is no expectation of discrimination, or large standard deviations. If, as they argued, the meaning of any score 'flows directly from the connection between the items and the criterion', the critical feature of criterion-referenced testing is the *test specification*, which describes the nature of the items and the rationale for their use in the test. It is in the test specifications (see Chapter 5) that the link between test and the real world is established (Popham, 1994) which has been called 'item–objective congruence' (Hambleton, 1994: 23).

8. Dependability

In classroom testing we wish to know whether the results of the assessment are dependable. This concerns whether an estimate of a learner's current stage would change if a different teacher conducted the assessment, or if a different (but comparable) task was used. Dependability is the criterion-referenced correlate of reliability in standardised testing.

The traditional methods of investigating reliability that we considered in Chapter 2 cannot be used, as the lack of variance 'would lead to a zero internal consistency estimate' (Popham and Husek, 1969: 5). Cronbach's alpha would always be very low. Rather, we need to turn to estimates of the consistency or dependability of decisions. These are the kinds of decisions that teachers make when they decide that a learner has or has not achieved a certain level. This decision is sometimes called a 'mastery/non-mastery' decision, or even 'pass/fail' (Brown and Hudson, 2002: 151). Alternatively, we may have three or more levels, each indicating a stage in the learning process. Each level would normally be carefully described, and in some cases a *cut score* on the test would be established to place learners into levels (see Chapter 8 for a discussion of cut scores and how to decide where a cut score should be placed on a test). These are referred to as 'absolute decisions', defined as 'one in which we select or reward test takers on the basis of their level of knowledge or ability, according to some pre-determined criteria' (Bachman, 2004: 11).

The most common ways of calculating dependability are known as the 'threshold loss agreement approaches'. These require the same test to be given twice, just as in calculating test–retest reliability. The purpose is to calculate whether learners are consistently classified as 'masters' or 'non-masters'.

The first approach that we discuss is called the agreement coefficient, or P_0 (Bachman,

2004: 200), and is very easy to calculate. The teacher gives a test or assessment twice, and on each occasion the decision to class a learner as a 'master' or 'non-master' is recorded. Table 3.1 sets out the results using a fictional group of 60 learners.

Classification		2nd administration		Total
Classification		Master	Non-master	
1st administration	Master	41 (A)	6 (B)	47 (A + B)
	Non-master	5 (C)	8 (D)	13 (C + D)
Total		46 (A + C)	14 (B + D)	60 (N)

Table 3.1 A classification table

With this information, the calculation of the agreement coefficient is now very simple:

$$P_o = \frac{A + D}{N}$$

With our sample data, this translates into:

$$P_o = \frac{41 + 8}{60} = .82$$

In other words, there is an 82 per cent agreement in the classification of students across two administrations.

As this calculation only requires information about classification of learners on two administrations, it can be used independently of the type of assessment used. It could be a normal classroom test, a collaborative communication task, or a piece of writing. The problem normally comes with conceptualising giving the task twice, because this is not something that teachers would normally do. But this is an illusory problem for the teacher. In most syllabuses we return to skills and subjects in a cyclical manner. We know that learners do not acquire language ability without repetition and practice. Teachers therefore design multiple tasks to practise the same skills, or use similar linguistic forms. For example, when we teach the skill of skim reading to get the gist of a text, we are likely to use multiple texts, each with its own prompts. If we have two such tasks that have been 'generated' by the same target skill (from a task specification – see Chapter 5), and the texts are equally difficult in terms of structure, vocabulary, length and cognitive load, we can treat them as equivalent.

It has been argued that there is a problem with the agreement coefficient. Whereas Cronbach's alpha can range from 0 to 1, P_o can never be 0 because just by chance, cells A and D in Table 3.2 would have a positive entry (Brown and Hudson, 2002: 169–170). This chance factor in the assessment can be calculated easily from the data in Table 3.1.

The formula for the chance factor is:

$$\text{Pchance} = \frac{(A + B) * (A + C) + (C + D) * (B + D)}{N^2}$$

For our example, this would be:

$$\text{Pchance} = \frac{(47) * (46) + (13) * (14)}{3600}$$

$$\text{Pchance} = \frac{2162 + 182}{3600}$$

$$\text{Pchance} = \frac{2344}{3600} = .65$$

This tells us that 65 per cent of the 82 per cent classification agreement between the two teachers could have occurred by chance alone. In order to correct the agreement coefficient for this chance element, we normally use the kappa coefficient, which is easily calculated as follows:

$$k = \frac{P_o - \text{Pchance}}{1 - \text{Pchance}}$$

We can fill this in from the calculations that we have already made:

$$k = \frac{.82 - .65}{1 - .65}$$

$$k = \frac{.17}{.35} = .49$$

The rule of thumb to interpret Kappa is:

.01–.20	slight agreement
.21–.40	some agreement
.41–.60	moderate agreement
.61–.80	substantial agreement
.81–.99	very high agreement

The figure in our example shows moderate agreement, and can be used as an indication that the working definition of 'mastery', or the tasks, may not be as stable as they might be to achieve higher levels of dependability.

Threshold loss agreement approaches estimate consistency in classification, and it does not matter what kinds of tasks or activities are used in making the classification. There is no requirement that there is a 'score', only a decision; but it is assumed that the tasks used measure the same constructs and are of roughly equal difficulty. Another approach to estimating consistency is squared-error loss agreement. Instead of looking at just the consistency of classification, this approach takes into account the degree of mastery or non-mastery, rather than just the classification (Brown and Hudson, 2002: 193–197). However, it also means that it must be possible to get a range of scores on the test; as such, it can only be used with more traditional tests that contain many items, and the items must be scored right or wrong. *Partial credit* is not possible. The most useful statistic, which is very easy to calculate by hand, is Phi Lambda (written Φλ). The formula for this statistic is:

$$\Phi\lambda = 1 - \frac{1}{K-1} \left(\frac{\bar{X}_p (1 - \bar{X}_p) - S_p^2}{(\bar{X}_p - \lambda)^2 + S_p^2} \right)$$

The symbols in this formula mean:

K	number of items on the test
$\bar{X}_p$	mean of the proportion scores
S_p	standard deviation of the proportion scores
λ	cut-point expressed as a proportion

All of these elements are familiar from Chapter 2, with the exception of λ. This is the 'cut score', or the score on the test over which a teacher will judge learners to be masters. In order to illustrate the use of this statistic, I will assume that a teacher creates a ten-item test of skimming for the gist of a passage, which she gives to fifteen learners. This is for illustrative purposes only. We would normally prefer to use more items than this. We will also assume that the cut score has been established at 6, using one of the procedures described in Chapter 8. The purpose of the test is to assess whether this skill has been acquired in the reading classes. The results are presented in Table 3.2. An entry of 1 in a cell indicates that the item has been answered correctly, while an entry of 0 indicates that the response is incorrect. These are added up in the column headed 'total' for each learner, giving each person's score. The final column is the proportion correct for each learner, which is the total correct, divided by the number of items (ten). The mean and standard deviation of the proportions are then calculated, in the same way that we learned to calculate the mean and standard deviation in Chapter 2.

Learner	\multicolumn{10}{c}{Item number}	Total	Proportion correct

Learner	1	2	3	4	5	6	7	8	9	10	Total	Proportion correct
1	1	1	1	1	1	1	1	1	1	1	10	1.0
2	1	1	1	1	1	1	1	1	1	0	9	0.9
3	1	1	1	1	1	1	1	1	0	0	8	0.8
4	1	1	1	0	1	1	1	1	1	0	8	0.8
5	1	1	1	0	1	1	1	0	1	0	7	0.7
6	1	1	1	1	0	1	1	1	0	1	7	0.7
7	1	1	1	1	0	1	1	0	1	0	7	0.7
8	1	1	1	1	0	0	1	1	0	0	6	0.6
9	1	1	1	1	0	1	1	0	0	0	6	0.6
10	1	1	0	1	0	1	1	1	0	0	6	0.6
11	1	1	0	1	0	1	1	0	0	0	5	0.5
12	1	0	1	1	0	1	0	0	0	0	4	0.4
13	1	1	0	1	0	1	0	0	0	0	4	0.4
14	1	1	1	1	0	0	0	0	0	0	4	0.4
15	1	0	0	0	0	0	0	0	0	0	1	0.1
											$\overline{X}_p$	.61
											S_p	.23

Table 3.2 Results of a reading test

These figures can now be plugged into the formula:

$$\Phi\lambda = 1 - \frac{1}{10-1}\left(\frac{.61\,(1-.61)-.23^2}{(.61-.60)^2+.23^2}\right)$$

$$\Phi\lambda = 1 - \frac{1}{9}\left(\frac{.24-.23^2}{.00+.23^2}\right)$$

$$\Phi\lambda = 1 - .11\left(\frac{.19}{.05}\right)$$

$$\Phi\lambda = 1 - (.11 * 3.8)$$

$$\Phi\lambda = .58$$

With the cut score at 6, we have a moderate value of dependability. This could be increased by using a different cut score, but if the cut score has been established on substantive grounds, it is much more appropriate to go back to investigating whether the test really assesses the construct in a satisfactory way. This may involve reviewing test specifications, changing or increasing the number of items, and reviewing decisions relating to the cut score.

Just as we looked at the standard error as one of the most important statistics in estimating the reliability of a standardised test, we can also calculate its equivalent for a criterion-referenced test. This is called the *confidence interval* (CI) around a score (Brennan, 1984), which allows us to see whether learners near the cut score may be below or above just by chance. The formula for the confidence interval is:

$$CI = \sqrt{\frac{\bar{X}_p (1 - \bar{X}_p) - S_p^2}{K - 1}}$$

The meaning of these symbols is the same as in the calculation of $\Phi\lambda$ above, with one exception. The standard deviation is calculated with N (rather than N − 1) in the denominator. The formula is therefore slightly different from that given in Chapter 2:

$$SD = \sqrt{\frac{\Sigma(X - \bar{X})^2}{N}}$$

For our data, this actually makes no difference at all to S_p^2, but with a larger number of items or learners, there may be differences.

We can therefore calculate CI as follows:

$$CI = \sqrt{\frac{.61 (1 - .61) - .23^2}{10 - 1}}$$

$$CI = \sqrt{\frac{.24 - .05}{9}}$$

$$CI = \sqrt{.02} = .14$$

This figure tells us that if an individual took the reading test a number of times, their score may go up or down by .14 proportion score points (or 14 per cent of raw score), around 68 per cent of the time (Brown and Hudson, 2002: 186–187). This is very important information when making decisions about learners whose score falls near to the cut score. For our reading test with a cut score of 6 this would be any score between 4 and 8; we could only be fairly certain that learners with scores of 1–3 had not mastered the skill, and learners with scores of 9–10 had. In fact, additional information is needed to make decisions about anyone who has a score within the CI of the cut score. Once again we have discovered that in assessment we need to develop strategies to deal with uncertainty.

9. Some thoughts on theory

Shepard (2000: 10) argues: 'I believe we should explicitly address with our teacher education students how they might cope with the contesting forces of good and evil assessment as they compete in classrooms to control curriculum, time, and student attitudes about learning.' It is probably not useful to see testing as quite so black and white. All forms of testing and assessment are socially constructed activities to achieve certain goals. There is a very important role for classroom assessment, and the integration of assessment with learning. Unlike Shepard (2000: 6), I would argue that there is also a place for tests that do not require teachers to make judgements about their own students. We know that sometimes teachers are influenced by factors other than the knowledge, skills and abilities of some students. This is inevitable when people work together in a learning environment over an extended period of time. This extended contact is essential for learning; it creates the social learning context. It also means that the learning context differs from teacher to teacher, and school to school. When testing or assessment is being used for high-stakes purposes, or where learners are being compared with each other across contexts, there is a case for using external tests. This does not mean that teachers should be excluded. They are stakeholders in the process. It is important that they are consulted and included in decision-making processes.

Sometimes the use of externally mandated tests can protect teachers. If they are personally responsible for high-stakes decisions, they are open to the accusation of personal bias. And, whether teachers or test designers like it or not, politicians are going to use test scores for more than informing learning and teaching. For example, Obama (2006: 161) has an insight into the good that testing and assessment can do in the classroom when he calls for 'meaningful, performance-based assessments that can provide a fuller picture of how a student is doing'. But he is also concerned with the statistics of failure, which come from national and standardised test scores.

> *Throughout our history, education has been at the heart of a bargain this nation makes with its citizens: If you work hard and take responsibility, you'll have a better life. And in a world where knowledge determines value in the job market, where a child in Los Angeles has co compete not just with a child in Boston but also with millions of children in Bangalore and Beijing, too many of America's schools are not holding up their end of the Bargain.*
> (2006: 159)

The fact is that there never was a time when testing was not high stakes, when it was not used to select individuals for 'a better life'. The scores have always had an economic value, even though, as Latham (1877: 6) says, 'people are hardly aware of how thoroughly the educational world is governed by the ordinary economical rules'. This is the reason for treating formative classroom assessment as a different paradigm. Its role is to aid learning, not to make high-stakes decisions. To create awareness of learning goals and stages of development, not to make awards or withhold prizes. To inform instruction and materials use, not report scores to external authorities.

Assessment for Learning and DA have much to offer the teacher. Both provide practical advice that has been found to lead to improved learning. Nevertheless, they differ in their theoretical underpinnings. Assessment for Learning attempts to combine the lessons learned from research in large-scale testing with a sensitivity to context. It does not adopt a strong constructivist stance, and so practitioners can conduct research to show that its methods are more successful (under some circumstances, with certain types of learner) than other methods. It is prepared to live with probabilistic statements of success. It is a position that is essentially experiential. The various practices have been seen to work in many (but not all) contexts, and to have benefited less able learners in particular. There is no strong theoretical claim to support the recommended practices, making it a pragmatic approach to what works in the classroom.

DA is different, because it is based upon sociocultural theory. Indeed, the jargon of DA is frequently impenetrable on first encounter with the literature. When it comes to looking at the examples of DA practice, they seem to differ little from what most language teachers would do anyway; and in many respects the techniques look less innovative than those of Assessment for Learning. This raises the question of why the associated theory is necessary to explain the evidence.

Perhaps the most serious problem for DA is that it does not appear to have any apparatus for rejecting alternative hypotheses for what is observed in case studies. Each case study is presented as a unique, non-generalisable event. What happens in each instance of DA involves the contextual interpretation of the participants who co-construct temporally bound meaning. Poehner (2008: 12) follows Luria (1979) in calling this 'Romantic Science'. Unlike regular science, this means that they 'want neither to split living reality into its elementary components nor to represent the wealth of life's concrete in abstract models that lose the property of the phenomena themselves'.

Indeed, this is not science. It is poetry, and art. It is an attempt to appreciate the whole as a piece, rather than create variables that can be investigated. There is a place for poetry and art. However, this is a fundamental flaw in DA. The purpose of any theory is to explain generalities in observable phenomena. But DA says that there are no generalities. In substantive theories systematic effects of interventions should be predicted and tested. This is one way to investigate the validity of theory. The effects may change according to the presence or absence, or degree of presence, of contextual or individual variables. These can be listed in the theory as moderating the predicted effects of the intervention or interaction on the outcomes. Only in this way can we know whether the theory has explanatory adequacy. DA denies this to us. Instead, it appeals to us to appreciate the holistic meaning of the event; to savour the landscape. The fundamental contradiction in DA is that it attempts to claim substantive theoretical justification, but abandons the need for it.

Formative classroom assessment is undertheorised. The rationales can be drawn from general learning theory, or from SLA, but where it has been attempted it has been found wanting. However, for all practical purposes what teachers and learners need are techniques that can be seen to lead to language acquisition, and improved communication skills. At this very practical level it is clear that the research described in this chapter has provided much needed guidance. Further, since the 1960s, a technology for the evaluation of classroom assessment has grown up in the form of criterion-referenced testing and assessment. The teachers' formative assessment toolbox is far from empty.

Activities

○ 3.1 The ten principles of Assessment for Learning

The United Kingdom's Qualifications and Curriculum Development Agency, through the Assessment Reform Group (1999), has produced an Assessment for Learning poster that may be freely copied for educational purposes. Download a copy from the QCDA website (http://www.qcda.gov.uk/4335.aspx) or from this source (http://language-testing.info/features/afl/4031aflprinciples.pdf). This contains ten principles of good practice that are supported by research that is discussed in this chapter.

With a group of colleagues, discuss each of the principles in turn. Which are operated in your own teaching context? What specific practices do you think would promote each principle?

○ 3.2 It's all about motivation

This isn't a book about motivation; but in any chapter on using Assessment for Learning it is bound to be a major theme. Traditional research into motivation has been based on the distinction between 'integrative' and 'instrumental' motivation (Gardner and Lambert, 1972). More recently, motivation is seen as coming about when learning is related to a learner's concept of his or her future L2 self (Dörnyei and Ushioda, 2009; Lamb, 2004). It is conceived as having more to do with self-perception and identity.

Watch the video of Martin Lamb talking about motivation theory on this website: http://languagetesting.info/features/motivation/mil.html. Take notes on this view of motivation theory. With your colleagues, describe *two* classroom learning/assessment activities that might encourage a strong sense of motivation. Provide reasons for your choice, and share ideas with other groups.

○ 3.3 Mind the gap!

Look at the following piece of classroom discourse, from Swain (2000: 107–108). Underline sections of the dialogue where language acquisition is taking place because learners are noticing the gap between their current stage of learning and the next. What strategies are these learners developing in order to assess their speaking and make improvements?

Two learners have been given a list of people, with descriptions, who have applied for a scholarship to attend college. They are discussing which of them should be awarded the scholarship.

G: Let's speak about this exercise. Did you read it?

S: Yes.

G: Okay. What are we supposed to do?

S: We have to speak about these people and ummm justify our position … you know our decision … our decisions about actions in ummm the past.

G: No. I think not just the past. We have to imagine our situation now. We have to give our opinions now.

S: So, for example, I choose Smit because he need it. No … it's a condition. I would give Smit … I would choose s/mit because he need the money. Right. I WOULD give …

G: Needs it.

S: Yes, because he need it.

G: Yes, but no. He needs. 's', you forgot 's'. He needs.

S: Did I? Let me listen the tape. (Listens to the tape.) Yes … yes. He needs. I have problem with 's'. Can you control … your talking?

G: It's a big problem. I still must remember 'had had'. But we try.

S: Yes, we try. But I don't know.

G: We don't try … you know we don't get better. We don't improve. We must practise to change old ways.

S: Okay. Maybe good idea to listen to tape after we each talk.

Once you have discussed this exchange, undertake a small piece of classroom-based research. Use one of the two tasks you designed in Activity 3.2 with a small group of learners (between two and four). Before they do the task, talk to them about the importance of monitoring and correcting their speech (focusing on form). Record the interaction, and make a transcription of a short section at random. Is there any evidence of 'minding the gap'?

◯ 3.4 Designing portfolio work for self- and peer-assessment

Portfolio assessment is extremely popular in language teaching, and in many other disciplines. It brings together many of the motivational elements that we have considered, from personal involvement and creativity, to group work and co-operation.

First of all, read more about the uses of portfolios at http://www.nclrc.org/portfolio/modules.html. Notice the importance of integrating assessment with portfolio work, including generating assessment criteria with learners so that they can see what they are aiming towards.

Secondly, visit http://electronicportfolios.org/portfolios/bookmarks.html, which has many links to electronic portfolios created by learners, and tools to create, manage and assess electronic portfolios. Alternatively, put 'electronic portfolios' into your favourite search engine and look at the links you get. Select *three* different web resources that you find useful. Write a short review of each site, with an account of how you might use the ideas or resources in your own classroom.

⭕ 3.5 Practising your calculation skills III

You and your team create two new forms of an end-of-year writing test to see whether your students have achieved the curriculum goals. You need two forms for reasons of test security. You pilot the tests on 40 learners selected at random from the institution. 20 students take Form 1 first, and the other 20 take Form 2 first, to counterbalance for an order effect. A cut score is established using an appropriate technique selected from those listed in Chapter 8. Once the writing tests are marked, you produce the following decision table.

Classification	Classification	Form 1		Total
Classification Form 2		Master	Non-master	
	Master	26 (A)	3 (B)	29 (A + B)
	Non-master	5 (C)	6 (D)	11 (C + D)
Total		31 (A + C)	9 (B + D)	40 (N)

- Calculate the agreement coefficient P_o.
- Calculate P_{chance}.
- Calculate Kappa.

What do these statistics tell you about your writing assessment?
What (if any) action might you take before using these two new forms?

⭕ 3.6 Practising your calculation skills IV

A placement test is used at upper intermediate level in your institution to decide if learners should proceed to academic language preparation, or continue to study general language skills. The test consists of 100 dichotomously scored items. The cut score has been established at 70. The mean proportion score on the test is .80, and the proportion standard deviation is .19.

- Calculate $\Phi\lambda$.
- Calculate the confidence interval (CI).

Is your current test dependable enough for its purpose?

⭕ 3.7 It's good to talk!

Good and evil? Two different paradigms? Or is classroom assessment just small-scale testing? In a group, try to list any 'real' differences that you can perceive between externally designed tests and those used in your own institutions.

4 Deciding what to test

1. The test design cycle

In the previous chapters we have considered why testing exists, its origins, what benefits it brings, and what its costs are. We have seen that testing is a socially constructed enterprise that has been part of human civilisation for as long as we can tell. Its function within society can be to maintain the status quo, or it can be the means by which equality of opportunity is afforded to all. Testing is therefore never value free, and is inherently a political activity (Fulcher, 2009). We have shown that there are two main testing paradigms, although we admit that the boundaries between them are fluid. Large-scale standardised testing is the most prevalent form, is usually externally mandated and plays the most important role in selection. Classroom testing, on the other hand, is of most use in the learning process. Each paradigm has its associated technologies, methodologies and challenges.

We now turn to issues of test design. In this and the following chapters we concentrate on the process of test development, and how to evaluate the outcomes. However, we will not be able to leave aside the social, political and ethical issues entirely. They still have an impact upon the key decisions that are made when building a new test or assessment.

We begin with the test design cycle. When asked to produce a test, many teachers start with writing test items. Managers frequently encourage this because they expect a teacher to produce the test in an afternoon, or over the weekend at best. It is something that is perceived to be the easiest part of the role of a teacher. In all fairness to the major testing agencies, they understand that standardised test development takes a long time and is very expensive. It is realised how important tests are for the lives of the test takers, and a great deal of effort is expended to investigate the reliability, validity and impact of the tests concerned (see, for example, Wall and Horák, 2007, 2008; Green, 2007). Writing test content is not normally the starting point of test design, for either standardised tests, or classroom tests.

The test design cycle is illustrated in Figure 4.1. In this chapter we will consider just the first three stages of the cycle, although 'Inferences' and 'Decisions' cannot be separated from our definition of test purpose; other stages will be considered in subsequent chapters.

The starting point in the cycle is normally test purpose. In Chapter 1 we quoted Carroll and Cronbach, warning us that without a clear statement of test purpose there could be no convincing rationale for selecting test content or format. This is equally true in classroom testing. For example, Harris and Bell (1994: 42–43) suggest that teachers ask the following questions when considering how to design their assessment for a learning programme:

- What do we hope to achieve?
- How can the important issues be identified?
- Who should be involved?
- What may be the effects of evaluating?
- How can information be collected and analysed?
- Who can best collect and analyse the information?
- What are the most applicable sources of information?
- What are the constraints (e.g. time, manpower, political)?

These are excellent questions that should be addressed. Before deciding to test, there has to be a reason for testing. Defining test purpose also incorporates another critical question: what do we test? Or, what is the information we need, and why do we need it? We define purpose and ask these questions first because it provides the basis of all further decisions. To explain this further, we will consider the arguments put forward by

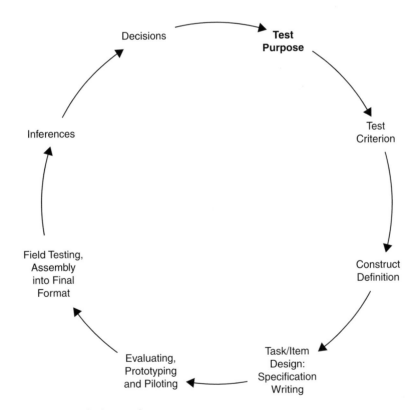

Fig. 4.1. The test design cycle

Fulcher (2006) and Fulcher and Davidson (2009), who use architecture as a metaphor for test development.

When architects begin to design a building, they must have a very clear idea of its purpose. If a client wishes to open a supermarket there is little point in designing a neoclassical residential town house. If the requirement is for a space to repair cars, the architect would not design a restaurant. And if I wished a to build a country retreat where I could get away from the city, light a fire on a cold winter evening and watch TV, I would be rather upset if the architect produced plans for a block of flats. Similarly, the materials needed for the construction of these buildings would be different, and the cost of the building would vary accordingly.

The same is true of language testing. As Ingram (1968: 70) once refreshingly put it, 'All tests are for a purpose. A test that is made up without a clear idea of what it is for, is no good.' If the purpose of my test is to assess the achievement of the learners in my class on the material covered in the last two months – which is a very common 'linear' requirement of teachers – I would need to design a test that was related to the course. There are a number of ways that teachers can do this. The first would be to sample content directly from the syllabus, and to design assessment tasks that reflect the kinds of processes and skills that were the target of learning. Another might be to look at the learning objectives or outcomes, and to base the assessments on these, rather than directly sampling from the syllabus. Or some combination of these might be used. Short cuts are often provided by course book publishers in the form of a 'test book' to accompany the course. However, teachers should use these with care, as it is not always clear that they provide the kind of learning information that we might need (see Chapter 3).

When tests are used for certification, the need to state the precise purpose of the test is even more acute. If we consider a situation in which it is necessary to certify the reading and writing skills for aircraft engineers the stakes could not be higher. Here there is a clear need to undertake a specified task in the real world that requires the use of language. In this case, the person has to be able to read a technical manual, follow the instructions carefully to inspect an aircraft and repair any faults that are found. At the end of the process they must write a report on what has been done so that it can be signed off by a supervisor to say that the aircraft is fit to fly. If the engineers are not capable of fulfilling these tasks in English, there is a clear and obvious safety hazard.

The purpose of the test is therefore very specific. It is to assess the ability of the test taker to understand the technical manual, to follow instructions provided in the manual, and to write a report in a specified genre that is acceptable to the supervisory engineers. This illustrates the next step on our test development cycle, which is defining the *test criterion*; in this case the criterion is successful use of the manual and effective communication through technical reports in the target domain. In order to study and describe the criterion, the test developer is fortunate in that it is possible to collect a representative sample of manuals that can be analysed. It is possible to design questions based on the sample manuals that can be given to proficient and non-proficient engineers in order to see which task types discriminate well between them (a 'group difference' study). Supervisors can be interviewed in order to discover what kinds of target behaviours are expected, and they can be asked to judge the adequacy of a range of sample reports collected from engineers in order to create a corpus of 'adequate' and 'substandard' reports. The key features of these could be described in order to create definitions of 'masters' and 'non-masters' for the purposes of scoring. In other words, it is test purpose that drives all the other activities associated with the development of a test.

As Fulcher and Davidson (2009: 123–124) put it,

> *a statement of test purpose is likely to include information on the target population and its ability range. Test developers normally state target domains of language use, and the range of knowledge, skills or abilities that underpin the test. This statement justifies the selection of constructs and content by articulating a direct link between intended score meaning and the use to which the scores will be put in decision making.*

Without this level of explicitness, we would have *design chaos*. This is a situation in which we are asked to design a structure without a purpose. Just as it is difficult to evaluate the success of a building without a purpose, it is impossible to evaluate a test. If we have design chaos at the beginning of the process, we have *validity chaos* at the end.

2. Construct definition

We come to the third label in the test design cycle. This is potentially the most difficult to understand and to apply, because the analogy with architecture does not help as much as it does with other aspects of seeing test design as 'building'. Constructs are the abilities of the learner that we believe underlie their test performance, but which we cannot directly observe. These begin as 'concepts', and we can identify them because they are usually abstract nouns. The oldest construct in education is probably 'intelligence', the meaning of which has been argued over for centuries; and it appears that we are no closer to having an agreed definition now than we were 100 years ago (Evans and Waites, 1981). Another construct that teachers often use is 'attitude'; we frequently say that a learner has a 'positive' or 'negative' attitude toward language learning. When judging how well a student communicates, we may talk about their 'fluency'. We can't point to a specific example of 'positive attitude' or of 'fluency'. Our judgement that these things exist, to some degree, is extracted from many examples of things we observe in the behaviour of the individuals concerned.

When we abstract from what we observe and create labels we are essentially building a basic theory to explain observable phenomena. Kerlinger and Lee (2000: 40) define constructs as 'concepts' that are adapted for scientific investigation in two ways. The first is that they are defined in such a way that we can measure them. This is usually termed an 'operational definition', which tells an observer what kinds of 'things' count towards positive attitude. Sometimes these 'things' have to be artificially manipulated in order to get a measurement. Measuring attitude normally has to be undertaken through a survey instrument of some kind, in which a learner is presented with statements regarding language learning and is asked to respond to indicate the degree to which they have a favourable or unfavourable reaction. These responses can be quantified, so that the variable 'attitude' can be plotted on a scale.

The point is that the definition of the construct is something that has to be undertaken carefully if it is to be assessed, as we need to know what it is we have to ask a learner to do, so that we can observe it , and decide whether (and to what extent) this abstract ability is present. Why does this matter? Isn't it good enough just to watch learners and get a general idea of what they can and can't do? Yes, in some circumstances. But we will use a non-language example in order to explain the power of 'construct' language.

Imagine that you are a local government official in a coastal district. In your district there are a number of wonderful beaches where people frequently swim during the warm weather, and for the coming season it is necessary to hire an additional lifeguard to meet health and safety regulations. An advertisement is placed in the local paper, and a fairly large number of people apply. The applicants are shortlisted, and the five finalists are asked to come to your district for an afternoon, at the end of which you will have to make a final choice. The task facing you is to decide what qualities you want your lifeguard to have, and how you will assess the shortlisted candidates against the qualities. What you need is a test (or tests) that can be held in one afternoon. Extending the selection period beyond that is not possible for economic reasons (a major constraint). The purpose of the test is clear: to select a person to work as a lifeguard. The criterion is a little more complex, however. We know what lifeguards are supposed to do: save lives in the sea. But the range of things they actually do is quite diverse. What follows is a summary job description, which is essentially our attempt to describe the criterion – what we expect the person appointed to be able to do when required. What it does not contain is as important as what it does contain, for it creates the frame around the picture that we can work with in designing a test.

The person appointed will be expected to:

- patrol an assigned area of beach, providing surveillance of swimmers, and assistance, including first aid; educate and advise beach-goers of dangerous marine conditions and beach hazards
- respond to emergency incidents, take actions to prevent injury, and perform rescues of injured or incapacitated victims in a dangerous marine environment; administer first aid, CPR and automatic external defibrillation, as necessary
- monitor beach and water population levels; recognise conditions warranting closing or reopening the beach areas
- provide high-level customer service, education and information to residents and beach visitors; identify lost individuals and coordinate reunification
- operate electronic communications, including mobile and portable radios, public address systems and computers.

The person appointed will have the ability to:

- perform physically demanding rescues on the surface and under water in large surf, and strong currents; make preventive actions under difficult, dangerous and stressful conditions; direct others in emergency situations
- resolve complaints from the public in a sensitive and tactful manner
- communicate clearly and concisely in speech and writing, under stressful conditions
- work for long periods of time in inclement weather conditions.

What are the constructs involved? Potentially there are many, but I will list just four:

Alertness
Affability
Strength
Stamina

If I could give each of the five shortlisted candidates a score on each of these constructs, I would be going some way towards making an informed selection. Of these, we will only discuss stamina. Although we have a general idea of what we mean by stamina, for the particular purposes of this test we define it as 'the ability to maintain arduous physical activity for an extended period of time without fatigue'. The definition of 'extended period of time' can be established by looking at the typical length of time it takes for lifeguards to retrieve swimmers in trouble from the sea. We will assume that this is up to, but rarely exceeding, twenty minutes. The reason this construct and its definition are so important is because we cannot possibly test each candidate under all the possible conditions that they may encounter in real life. If we consider just some of the variables involved, we might have to account for wave height, strength of current, water and air temperature, wind, distance to swimmer, condition of swimmer (unconscious, panicking, underwater, and so on), weight and size of swimmer. The list could go on. However, in a test we simply cannot replicate real life. Bachman (1990: 301–323) discusses what he calls the 'real-life' approach and the 'interactive language use' approach to defining test authenticity. In the real-life approach, we judge the 'authenticity' of the test on the basis of how well it replicates real life in the tasks. But we have seen that there are so many *performance conditions* for our stamina test that they cannot all be replicated. Further, in a test we frequently cannot replicate real life, anyway. In the stamina test we could not ask the candidates to take the test in the sea; health and safety legislation would prevent this. In addition, in the sea we couldn't replicate any particular performance condition that would be the same for all test takers, thus making the test fair. The test conditions would vary from administration to administration, because we cannot control the sea or the weather.

The definition of 'authenticity' that Bachman prefers is that of Widdowson (1978: 80), as 'a characteristic of the relationship between the passage and the reader and it has to do with appropriate response', or 'a function of the *interaction* between the test taker and the test task' (Bachman, 1990: 117, italics in the original). This is where the construct comes into play. The task is designed in such way that it is an index of the level of presence or absence of the construct, and we assume (and argue) that the construct is an ability that is used in all the performance conditions that we could list as part of what might happen in real life. The ability is therefore separate from the instances in which it might be displayed in real life.

Consider the following stamina test (Northwest Lifeguards Certification Test, 2008):

---

100 Yard Medley – 12 points possible

**Note: A person may not advance their position by using the bottom of the pool or the side walls. The end walls may be used for advancement.

A. Passive Drowning Victim Rear Rescue, 0, 1, 2, 3, or 4 points

1. Approach the victim from behind with the tube.
2. Reach under the victim's armpits and grasp his/her shoulders.
3. Squeeze the rescue tube between your chest and the victim's back.
4. Keep your head to one side of the victim's head to avoid being hit.
5. Roll the victim over so that they are on top of the rescue tube.
6. Move the victim to the other end of the pool.

B. Cross Chest Carry for 25 yards, 0, 1, 2, or 3 points

1. If the rescuer chooses to use the scissors kick, the hip must be in the victim's back; doing the whip kick, the rescuer must be on their back.
2. Hands must grasp behind the armpit.
3. Victim must be secure and controlled.
4. Victim must be level with face clear of the water.

C. Single Armpit Assist on Back for 25 yards, 0, 1, or 2 points

1. Thumb must be up on the inside of the armpit.
2. Eye contact must be maintained (except for quick glances forward for direction).
3. Rescuer must be PUSHING the victim with a smooth motion, no jerking.

D. Underwater Swim for 25 yards, 0, 1, 2, or 3 points

1. The rescuer has 3 seconds after placing the victim on the wall to begin the underwater swim. After the first 3 seconds, each 3 seconds after that will count as 1 breath (see D-3).
2. Rescuer may use the wall to push off underwater, but not over the top of the water. The rescuer must submerge vertically down and push off underwater from the wall.
3. Rescuer may come up once for air without losing points. More than once, a point is deducted for each time.
4. When the rescuer comes up for air, 3 seconds are allowed to get a breath and go back down.
5. Any part of the body breaking the surface is counted as coming up for air.
6. A person may not advance their position in the water (stroke at surface), when coming up for air.

A SCORE OF 0 POINTS ON SECTION D WILL AUTOMATICALLY FAIL A CANDIDATE.

The first thing to note about this task is that it is very controlled. The victim to be rescued is a real person, but the guidelines (not reproduced here) state the size and weight restrictions. Further, they do not struggle, but remain as limp as possible during the test. The test takes place in a pool, and practices that are not allowed (because they would not be available in 'real life') are clearly stated. Most importantly, the criteria for successful completion of each stage of the test are explicit.

The validity question that we face is: how good is the argument that performance on these tasks, as reflected in the scores, is an index of the construct 'stamina'? And, further, to what extent is our measurement of 'stamina' a predictor of successful performance in the real world?

To return to language testing, we can apply the same thinking to the reading test that we might construct for our aircraft engineers. Although this is a fairly limited language use domain, we recognise that we cannot describe everything that they might be expected to do. Nor, as Clark (1975: 23) pointed out, is it possible to place test takers into the actual role of an aircraft engineer and 'follow that individual surreptitiously over an extended period of time' to see if they carry out the tasks successfully in English. Not only would it be too costly, it would be unethical, and potentially extremely dangerous. The test must therefore be *indirect*, a number of steps removed from reality. In this sense, it is impossible to have a *direct test*, if this term is interpreted as actually doing what people do in real life as it was in the communicative language testing movement (Morrow, 1979). Designing a test for the engineers is not therefore simply a matter of conducting a job analysis and sampling for the test (Fulcher, 1999), although the analysis will be a crucial element of the research that will inform the selection of relevant constructs that will subsequently drive test design and inform the selection of texts for inclusion on the test.

What constructs are likely to be important for the engineers to undertake their tasks successfully and safely? Grabe and Stoller (2002: 21–30) describe reading constructs in terms of lower and higher processes. Among the lower processes, it is recognised that one of the most important constructs in reading any text is lexical access, defined as the speed with which readers can call up the meaning of a word when it is encountered on the page. This must be automatic if the reader is not to slow down to an extent that the general meaning of a text is lost because of short-term memory overload. Of equal importance is the syntactic parsing, or the ability to recognise groups of words in order to understand word ordering, subordination and other relationships between clauses. If lexical access and parsing are automatic, readers are able to access 'semantic proposition information', which allows clause-level meaning. Among the higher level constructs are the formation of a 'mental text model', which represents in the mind the main propositions of a text together with its supporting ideas and examples. The whole process may be supported or hindered by the activation of relevant background knowledge, as well as familiarity with the discourse organisation of the kinds of texts involved. A general description of reading constructs can be listed in more detail if necessary (Grabe, 1999), but for our purposes this will do. If the most important task for the engineers is to understand a process as it is described and follow that process exactly when checking and repairing an aircraft component, which, if any, of these constructs are relevant?

The first construct that is relevant to the engineers is lexical access to the technical vocabulary that they require in English. The second important construct is the ability to recognise and understand clausal relationships that indicate sequence and action. In order to make sense of information across clauses in texts that describe processes, it is essential to be able to maintain track of cohesive devices, which is a procedural skill to maintain a frame of reference (Fulcher, 1998b). The clausal relations that are most likely to be important in this context are situation–problem–response–evaluation (Hoey, 1983, 62–80), which can be illustrated in the following example:

> *(1) The release of oxygen masks should be checked at the required intervals only when the aircraft is outside the hangar. Personal cleanliness is imperative. Wash dirt, oil and grease from hands before working with equipment. Do not service during fuelling operations as oxygen under pressure and petroleum products may ignite when brought into contact. Release oxygen masks by activating the central release panel and ensuring that each mask in the aircraft has been released and a flow of oxygen is present. (2) The most frequent cause of non-release is the tube becoming twisted or catching on the housing. (3) Examine tangled tubes, gently releasing the mask and replacing as shown in diagram 3b. Any damaged tubes should be replaced with component 284XOM (4) to ensure smooth and easy release of the mask.*

(1) Situation
   Containing directions/instructions ('Wash … Do not service … Release … ')
(2) Problem
(3) Response
(4) Evaluation

Examples of clausal relations can be analysed from manuals so that suitable task types can be constructed. Along with a test of cohesion, the development of a test of technical vocabulary might be helped by the creation of a corpus of maintenance manuals to produce essential vocabulary lists. The ability to recognise steps in processes might be assessed using visuals, as might the ability to select the correct action for a given situation.

To define constructs of interest, language tests need to be developed for clearly specified purposes. A general language test would not target the precise constructs that underlie performance in any particular domain. This is one of the major problems with using 'off-the-peg' solutions for readiness to use language in specific domains. The scores on 'general' language tests are not necessarily built on constructs relevant to the decisions that need to be made in a specific context. If test scores vary because of constructs or other test features that are irrelevant to the decision we wish to make, it is construct irrelevant variance.

Constructs therefore need to be selected for their applicability to the context of test use. When we do this, we place the description of how we made these decisions in a document that narrates the design process. This document links the constructs to the purpose and context of the test, and is part of the *test framework* (Chalhoub-Deville, 1997). It forms part of the evidence to show that any inferences we make about the meaning of test scores are valid, and can be presented as part of the validation evidence.

▶ 3. Where do constructs come from?

Fulcher and Davidson (2009: 126–127) describe constructs as the 'design patterns' in architecture, which can be selected for use in a particular building project. They are abstractions with operational descriptions that can be relevant to many contexts in different ways, but are not useful in all contexts. The ability to comprehend processes and carry out procedures is highly relevant to aircraft engineers. It is also relevant to students who may be carrying out experiments in a laboratory. The context and materials are different, but the constructs may be largely the same. But these constructs will not be relevant to a test for a language test for tour guides, for instance. They may be partially relevant to a test for a travel assistant who may have to follow certain procedures in booking vacations for clients, but this would be a very small element in the broader communicative requirements of the context. If such a test only contained procedural questions, it would be *construct under-representative*. This means that the constructs tested are not enough to ensure that the score represents the abilities that a person may need to succeed in this role.

Constructs are usually described in *models*. These operate at a higher level than the test frameworks. They are general and abstract by nature, whereas the test framework is a selection of constructs that are relevant to a particular purpose. The relationship between models and frameworks is illustrated in Figure 4.2 (from Fulcher and Davidson, 2009: 127). You will notice that underneath a framework is a test specification. We will discuss test specifications in Chapter 5. Together, these three levels constitute the levels of test architecture, from the most abstract (models) to the most specific (specifications).

This conceptualisation recognises that there are a very large number of language constructs and infinite language use situations, but that only some constructs or abilities will be realised in each situation. Further, even the most proficient language users will not be equally 'proficient' in all contexts. As Lado (1961: 26) put it, 'The situations in which language is the medium of communication are potentially almost infinite. No one, not even the most learned, can speak and understand his native language in any and all the situations in which it can be used.' Lado was ahead of his time. He realised that language was not only a tool for humans to get things done, but the means by which personal and cultural meaning was encoded.

Language is more than the apparently simple stream of sound that flows from the tongue of the native speaker; it is more than the native speaker thinks it is. It is a complex system of communication with various levels of complexity involving intricate selection and ordering of meanings, sounds, and larger units and arrangements. (1961: 2)

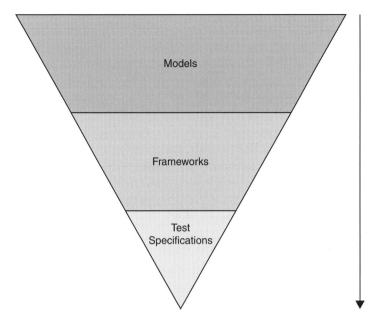

Fig. 4.2. The levels of architectural documentation

Lado (1961: 6) was the first to create a model of language use that contained constructs, as shown in Figure 4.3. For communication to be successful, he argued that language use had to be automatic – or 'habit' – as he put it in the behaviouristic terminology of the time. Lado's understanding is the same as that held in current SLA research: 'automaticity refers to the absence of attentional control in the execution of a cognitive activity' (Segalowitz and Hulstijn, 2005: 371). This automatic processing is important for the language user to select the form (sounds, words, grammatical units) to create meaning. The distribution is the 'permitted environments in which each form appears' (Lado, 1961: 5). This would include concepts such as collocation and colligation.

The linguistic meanings can only be understood if there is also an understanding of the cultural meanings behind the encodings. Lado said that it was difficult to describe these culturally bound meanings, but he saw them as the ways in which people from certain backgrounds used language to communicate the 'organization of behaviour', of ways of doing and of believing, through form, meanings and distributions. In order to penetrate meaning, cross-cultural communication issues were seen as critical, and could even be tested. Yet, Lado approaches this topic of differences between cultures with 'a basic assumption of and belief in the unity of all mankind. All races have the same origin and are capable of the same emotions and the same needs encompassing the whole range of human experience from hunger and the craving for food to theological inquiry and the seeking of God' (1961: 276). In this inspiring writing, Lado goes on to say that, apart from the culturally embedded meaning, individuals bring their own personal meaning which comes from life experiences. This stands outside culture, and

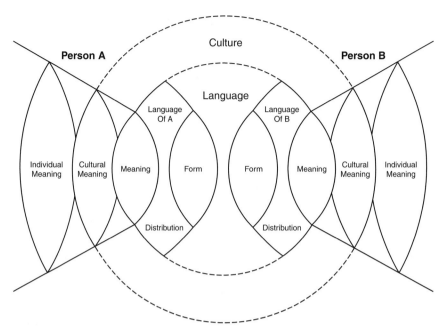

Fig. 4.3. Language, culture and the individual

represents the individuality that is expressed through language as an act of being. This model exists within each of the four skills of reading, writing, speaking and listening, and their interactive use (listening and speaking), in an infinite number of situations.

It is difficult to image now just how revolutionary Lado's argument was in 1961. At the time there was an assumption that language tests should limit themselves to language alone, usually considered to be grammar, lexis and the sound system. Carroll (1958: 8) is a typical example of this position, when he argues that 'it is assumed that we are concerned solely with the acquisition of a foreign language, not with the acquisition of the culture of a foreign people, nor the appreciation of its literature'.

Lado's work represents the beginning of model development for language and communication. This model, like others, can serve as an heuristic that can help us to select the constructs that are relevant to a test or assessment we need to design for a particular context. What it cannot do is tell us which forms we may wish to test, or what types of intercultural communication we should focus on, for any given context. That is the role of the test designer when creating a *test framework*. For example, if I wished to construct a test for shopkeepers in a tourist district, one element of intercultural communication that I may wish to test is the ability to establish rapport. In order to do this, it is critical to have the linguistic resources to follow a sales script, while also appearing friendly. It has been discovered that failure to comply with the cultural expectations of what happens in sales encounters can lead to hostility and loss of business (Ryoo, H.-K., 2005). We discuss this particular example in greater detail in Chapter 7.

Moving backwards and forwards between the architectural levels of model and framework is a challenging and fruitful way to look simultaneously at what happens in communicative situations and the constructs required for successful communication. It is also possible to use multiple models to inform choices. Other work on intercultural communication (Byram, 2000: 9–10) suggests that the following five additional abilities underlie the successful understanding of unfamiliar cultural meaning:

- attitudes: curiosity and openness, readiness to suspend disbelief about other cultures and belief about one's own
- knowledge: of social groups and their products and practices in one's own and in one's interlocutor's country, and of the general processes of societal and individual interaction
- skills of interpreting and relating: ability to interpret a document or event from another culture, to explain it and relate it to documents from one's own
- skills of discovery and interaction: ability to acquire new knowledge of a culture and cultural practices and the ability to operate knowledge, attitudes and skills under the constraints of real-time communication and interaction
- critical cultural awareness/political education: an ability to evaluate critically and on the basis of explicit criteria perspectives, practices and products in one's own and other cultures and countries.

Some, but not all, of these, may inform the development of a test or a related language course.

▶ 4. Models of communicative competence

Since Lado, models have evolved as we have learned more about what it means to know and use a language. They have also taken a variety of forms. Perhaps the most common models are those that attempt to present an abstract overview. The grain size of these models is very large. There are other models that attempt to reduce the grain size and give a great deal of detail about what kinds of competences or abilities are relevant to particular kinds of interaction. There are problems with both types. The more general and abstract models are much more difficult to apply to a particular context when we write our test framework. The more detailed models, on the other hand, often attempt to describe contexts of language use in ways that we do not recognise as being descriptions of what actually happens in communication. They lack both a theoretical and empirical basis for the detail they purport to offer.

Whatever their grain size, all models have been deeply influenced by the work of Hymes (1972). Breaking away from traditional linguistics, he argued that humans have an ability for language use that fulfils a social function. This ability, he argued, can be defined in terms of four kinds of knowledge. First of all, we know whether it is possible to say something (using the grammatical and lexical resources of the language).

Secondly, we recognise whether it is feasible to say it, even if it is grammatically possible. Thirdly, we know whether it is appropriate to the context. This kind of knowledge can be acquired through social interaction. And fourthly, we know whether or not something actually occurs (or is said), even if it is possible, feasible and appropriate.

In what is probably the most quoted section of any paper in applied linguistics, Hymes (1972: 15) says:

> Attention to the social dimension is thus not restricted to occasions on which social factors seem to interfere with or restrict the grammatical. The engagement of language in social life has a positive, productive aspect. There are rules of use without which the rules of grammar would be useless. Just as rules of syntax can control aspects of phonology, and just as semantic rules perhaps control aspects of syntax, so rules of speech acts enter as a controlling factor for linguistic form as a whole.

Hymes therefore talked about 'competence for grammar', and 'competence for use', as two aspects of knowledge. This is contrasted with performance – the actual use of language – which is judged by its 'acceptability' in the context of use (1975: 18). As Shohamy (1996: 139) notes, this early model brings into the picture non-linguistic elements to models of competence that have influenced all further developments. This is not to say that Lado's model did not have non-linguistic elements; it certainly did, but it did not have the notion of an underlying 'ability for performance' that later models contain.

In the rest of this discussion we will attempt to critically describe various models, beginning with mainstream models that attempt to define constructs underlying performance. We will then turn to performance models that try to describe language in behavioural or functional terms, rather than in terms of theoretical constructs.

Construct models

Perhaps the most influential post-Hymes model is that of Canale and Swain (1980). They draw directly on Hymes to create a model that could be used as the basis for syllabus or test design for communicative purposes. It is interesting to note that Canale and Swain's work began with a consideration of teaching and syllabus design rather than testing. It was not assumed that testing would drive teaching. Rather, they thought that a consideration of what it means to 'know a language' for use in context would inform both. Placing this understanding before the design of a teaching syllabus or a test had in fact long been part of sound planning (Spolsky, 1968). Communicative competence, they claimed, consisted of three components. The first was grammatical competence, which included knowledge of grammar, lexis, morphology, syntax, semantics and phonology. The second component was sociolinguistic knowledge, or the rules or use and discourse. Finally, they included strategic competence, which they defined as the ability to overcome communicative difficulties. Communicative competence was separated from 'actual performance' in real-life contexts. They argued that a theory of performance as advocated by Hymes was impossible, as it would include all the non-linguistic variables that could affect communication, such as individual or affective factors. Subsequent models have reintroduced non-linguistic variables. Lado (1961: 290–298) recognised that many non-linguistic variables would indeed impact on language learning, and performance on language tests. He included factors such as educational background, insight into language and culture (both one's own and those of others), attitudes towards minority groups, and interest in other peoples. But Lado knew that these things were too complex to take into account completely, or test with any reliability.

Nevertheless, the Canale and Swain model was soon expanded. In two subsequent papers, Canale (1983a, 1983b) began to include performance in the model, under the term 'actual communication', to mean: 'the realization of such knowledge and skill under limiting psychological and environmental conditions such as memory and perceptual constraints, fatigue, nervousness, distractions and interfering background noises' (Canale, 1983a: 5). The expanded model suddenly became much more complex; it included for the first time not only linguistic knowledge, but psychological and con-textual variables that would need to be modelled in the design of tests. Sociolinguistic competence was expanded to include pragmatics, including non-verbal behaviour and awareness of physical distance in communication, and discourse competence became a separate category, incorporating knowledge of textual organisation, genres, cohesion and coherence. This expanded model is portrayed in Figure 4.4.

The next adaptation of this model was undertaken by Bachman (1990), who altered it in two important ways. Firstly, he more clearly differentiated between what is classi-fied as 'knowledge' and what is a 'skill'. Secondly, he attempted to show how the various elements of the model interacted in language use situations. To this end, Bachman sepa-rated out strategic competence, which is said to include all communication strategies, rather than just compensatory strategies, from two separate knowledge components. The first knowledge component is language competence, and the second is knowledge

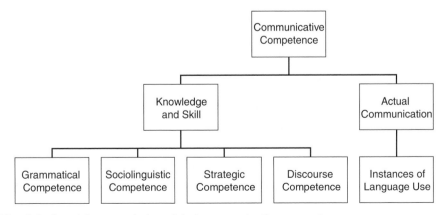

Fig. 4.4. Canale's expanded model of communicative competence

of the world. Both of these are said to affect strategic competence, and how we use it to communicate. In other words, it is strategic competence that draws on knowledge from both linguistic and non-linguistic competences to make communication possible. Strategic competence itself is said to consist of three separate components:

The assessment component:

- identifies the information we need to achieve a communicative goal in a specific context
- decides which language competences are needed to achieve the goal
- decides what knowledge and abilities we share with our interlocutor
- evaluates the extent to which the communication is successful.

The planning component:

- gets information from language competence
- selects modality and/or channel
- assembles the utterance or output.

The execution component:

- makes use of psychophysical mechanisms to realise the utterance.

While world knowledge encompasses what Lado would have called cultural and personal knowledge, language competence is more carefully described in Bachman, as shown in Figure 4.5.

The left-hand side of the Bachman tree contains the traditional linguistic components, while the right-hand side of the tree, under the new title 'pragmatic competence' lists the knowledge necessary to produce appropriate language. Illocutionary competence requires some further explanation. It draws on speech act theory (Austin, 1962), but speech acts are presented in terms of Halliday's (1973) language functions. Ideational functions are concerned with expressing propositions, information and feelings. Manipulative functions are concerned with affecting the world around us, or getting things done, including managing relationships with others. Heuristic functions are related to extending our knowledge of the world through questioning and learning, while imaginative functions concern using language for humour or aesthetic purposes.

Another element of communicative competence that has not appeared in the models we have considered so far is interactional competence. This was first proposed by Kramsch (1986), and it is a competence that relates to any use of language that involves real-time communication with others. The primary observation to support this construct is that, when individuals take part in spoken interaction, the 'text' – what is said – is co-constructed by the participants in the talk. No individual is completely responsible for any part of the talk, not even their own contribution, for it depends upon what else has been said, by whom and for what purpose. In speaking tests, for example, we have long known that proficient interlocutors are prepared to support, or 'scaffold', the speech of the test taker (Ross and Berwick, 1992). More recently, evidence has shown that the discourse style of the interlocutor can affect the performance of the same indi-

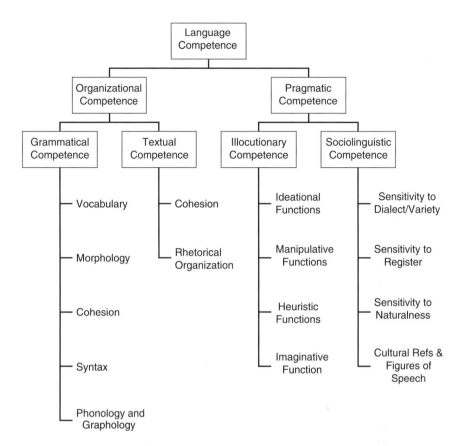

Fig. 4.5. Bachman's components of language competence (Bachman, 1990: 87)

vidual to such an extent that they may get a different score with a different interlocutor (Brown, 2003).

The nature of this competence is highly problematic, however. He and Young (1998) have argued that, because discourse is co-constructed between individuals, it does not make sense to say that interactional competence is something that an individual 'has', in the same way that we could say a learner has a certain degree of grammatical competence, for example. Nor, it is claimed, is this competence 'independent of the interactive practice in which it is (or is not) constituted' (He and Young, 1998: 7). The problem here is that there is no 'home', so to speak, for interactional competence. Young (2008: 101) makes this claim even more strongly:

Interactional competence is a relationship between the participants' employment of linguistic and interactional resources and the contexts in which they are employed … Interactional competence … is not the ability of an individual to employ those resources in any and every social interaction; rather, interactional competence is how those resources are employed mutually and reciprocally by all participants in a particular discursive practice. This means that interactional competence is not the knowledge or the possession of an individual person, but it is co-constructed by all participants in a discursive practice, and interactional competence varies with the practice and with the participants.

This understanding leads to difficulty in using interactional competence as a construct in practical language testing. As Weir (2005: 153) puts it, 'The real problem is that an individual's performance is clearly affected by the way the discourse is co-constructed with the person they are interacting with. How to factor this into or out of assessment criteria is yet to be established in a satisfactory manner.'

However, I believe that accepting the basic premise of interactional competence being disembodied from the individuals taking part in an interaction is flawed. Sociocultural explanations of constructs confuse the ability of an individual to recognise the contextual constraints and freedoms in communicating using available resources, with the actual communication itself. No one would wish to deny that each instance of communication, each instance of new discourse, arises within a context and is dependent upon the variables at play. But this does not mean that the competence to engage successfully in these new interactions is also newly generated in each instance of communication.

We can, however, understand why some applied linguists wish to avoid the distinction between individual interactional competence and its realisation in performance, which leads them to view interactional competence as a disembodied context-dependent phenomenon. It is the rejection of the neo-platonic distinction between competence and performance in the work of theoretical linguists like Chomsky (1965: 4). Recent trends in applied linguistics have favoured social rather than cognitive or psycholinguistic theory and research (Lantolf, 2000, 2002; Lantolf and Poehner, 2008b; Lantolf and Thorne, 2006), and this has also impacted upon language testing (McNamara, 2001; McNamara and Roever, 2006). With this approach, as we saw in Chapter 3 in our consideration of Dynamic Assessment, meaning resides in context and interaction, rather than individuals. It is therefore inevitable that sociocultural interpretations of competence understand all meaning as entirely local and non-generalisable. With every small change in every contextual variable, interactional competence changes. Each interaction is interpreted as an entirely unique realisation of the construct. When second language acquisition researchers have adopted this position, they have normally abandoned the use of the term 'competence' in favour of the word 'capacity' (Fulcher, 1995) to indicate that there is nothing inherently stable about an individual's ability for language use. This is a fundamentally postmodern understanding of language use. It reduces meaning to fleeting social interaction; it takes away from individuals their personal coherence as language-using human beings expressing their own being and existence. Indeed, sociocultural theory even contends that being and identity are only co-constructed through social interaction in which language is used, and that identity 'refers to what we do in a particular context, and of course we do different things in different contexts' (Young, 2008: 108). Nevertheless, Young is aware of the first (although less important) sense of identity as 'self-hood attached to a physical body' that remains the same over time, even though it changes and develops. But this is the least important meaning for sociocultural theory; it is merely an uncomfortable reminder that to have interaction it is necessary to have individuals.

My own view is that the stable individual takes priority. Without this emphasis on the willing participation of individuals in interaction there is no sense in which we hold any power over our own lives and our own sense of identity, which we express through language. The context does not control my contributions to an interaction, other than in the sense that I am sensitive to appropriacy (in Hymes' terms). But this is because I have acquired the necessary pragmatic competence through experience. Nor does the context define who I am. Nevertheless, the insight of sociocultural theory is not to be denied. Precisely how I interact with others in any context is dependent upon how they choose to interact with me.

> *The distinction between what is inside (knowledge, competence, capacity etc.) and what is external (interaction, communication, co-construction etc.) is fluid. The two interact. My 'competence' in Chinese is non-existent; I cannot co-construct discourse and meaning in Chinese. My competence in Greek is fair. I have a 'knowledge' of the vocabulary and structure of the language. Through interaction with other speakers I have gained other competencies which are useful in new situations, but not all. The strategies that I use to interact are simultaneously internal and external to myself. I am recognisable as myself when I speak in a variety of contexts, and yet in context my speech is always contextually bound.*
> (Fulcher, 2003a: 20)

Young (2008: 101–102) provides a simple example of co-constructed discourse between two teachers passing each other on a school corridor:

Ms Allen:	How are you?
Mr Bunch:	Fine.
Ms Allen:	That's good.

Young's analysis of this exchange is that the participants understand the process of turn-taking, that they can recognise when one turns ends and another one may start (transitional relevance places), and that questions and answers (with a response) are three-part conversational structures. In recognising the exchange as a formulaic greeting, each understands that this is part of a particular 'discursive practice'. Young (2008: 102) argues: 'The practice is co-constructed by both participants and in their skilful co-construction they are displaying interactional competence. Interactional competence arises from the interaction and is based on knowledge of procedure and practice that is shared by the participants.' He admits that this interaction is 'based on knowledge of procedure and practice' within the individual, but does not wish to call it 'interactional competence'. This may be illusory. Young himself asks what would have happened if Mr Bunch had responded something along the lines of: 'Well, I'm not too good actually. I had a meeting with my doctor yesterday and he said that I've got a stomach problem that may be stress related. In fact, I have had quite a bit of trouble with my wife recently, she's been …' Young says that this would be changing the discursive practice in a context that does not lend itself to such interaction. I would certainly agree with this. But the reason why the two participants can engage in formulaic greetings is because the participants possess interactional competence: they know what the rules of interaction are in this particular context, using this kind of formulaic language. Using Hymes' fourth kind of knowledge, they know that extended personal exchanges do not occur in such settings. Mr Bunch's interactional competence is the reason that he does not talk about his health.

It can therefore be argued that interactional competence is something much more substantial than a fleeting social co-construction. It is the knowledge of what is possible and what can happen in certain contexts, applied successfully to managing an interaction, with associated adaptivity to the speaker and other contextual variables.

We can see that there are two approaches to describing interactional competence. One approach sees it as a temporal, non-generalisable, social phenomenon. The other sees it as a set of abilities that an individual brings to the temporally bounded interaction set within a specific social context and discursive practice. If it is conceptualised in the former way, there is little that language testers can do with the construct, because testing is primarily about assigning a score to an individual that adequately reflects the ability of that individual. A group score may be useful in a classroom setting where decisions are made regarding the next task to be set to the group. In high-stakes testing, however, a group score is neither practical nor useful. This is why the construct of interactional competence has impacted on test method, rather than test content, or the way in which test performance is scored. The introduction of pair- or group-speaking methods in some large-scale tests is seen as a way of tapping into a richer interactional construct. The main claim is that when learners interact with each other it reduces the kind of 'interview language' that characterises interactions with a more powerful examiner-interlocutor (van Lier, 1989; Johnson, 2001).

Studies that have investigated the use of this format, with a focus on interaction between participants, have produced varied results. Many show that the percentage of speaking time for learners increases, as do the number and variety of language functions used. However, reservations have also been expressed. It has been suggested that test takers who are paired with partners of different ability levels, different nationalities, with whom they are unfamiliar rather than familiar, or even extroverts (if one is an introvert), may be at a disadvantage (see Fulcher, 2003a: 186–190, for a summary of the research). Studies conducted within a sociocultural paradigm have shown that, all other things being equal, learners in pair or group formats tend to produce more varied language and score slightly higher than they would otherwise on the same task (Brooks, 2009). However, these studies have nothing at all to say about how interactional competence might be scored. Indeed, it is noticeable that the rating scales used in these studies rely on the more established constructs of accuracy, fluency, ability to communicate, coherence and complexity of language. A study by May (2009) recognises that the problem lies both defining and operationalising the construct, but approaches this through rater perceptions rather than identifying the abilities that successful interactants bring to the interaction. She discovered that it is difficult for raters to identify the interactional abilities of individuals without a rating scale that guides the process, and also draws attention to the problems raters have in assigning any score at all to candidates who are less dominant in asymmetric discourse.

The story of research into pair- and group-speaking tests shows that construct definition within models is not entirely theoretical. It is an essentially practical activity. As teachers, we are constantly trying to describe abstractions from observation, and then relate them back to precisely what kind of observations gave them their genesis. In this to and fro between the intensely practical matter of whether we test speaking in groups, pairs and with individuals, we raise questions that pertain to teaching and learning, as well as to assessment: just what counts as evidence for 'interactional competence'? Unless we can produce an operational definition, it cannot be assessed, or taught.

Performance models

Rather than engaging with theoretical notions of competence, many language testers have relied on purely operational definitions of what it means to know and use a language. This began with the communicative language testing movement of the late 1970s and 1980s. There was a reaction against theory, against the use of multiple-choice items, and against what some called the 'statistical sausage machine' that treated human beings as 'subjects' (Underhill, 1987: 105). This was seen as a revolution in which 'there is more blood to be spilt yet' (Morrow, 1979: 156). Communicative language testing was more concerned with tasks and with test content. The closer these resembled what happened in teaching, the better they were. This has become known as an appeal to face validity: what looks good to an experienced teacher probably is; and there isn't much else to be said about testing. The evaluation of performance in a communicative language test was done purely on the basis of behavioural outcomes, defined as the degree to which the test taker achieved the intended communicative effect (see Fulcher, 2000a, 2010, for an extended discussion).

As Shohamy (1996: 145) correctly observes, 'The result was "theory-free" language tests, mostly performance-based, task driven, and considered to be communicative, functional, authentic, and direct.' The immediate appeal of this approach was that it was fairly easy to understand; it appealed to both teachers and the public who did not want to deal with the complexities of language competence and its realisations. But as we have seen in our discussion of the lifeguard test, the appeal to 'directness' and 'authenticity' is illusory. We are rarely concerned with single performances, bound as they are with all the contextual variables that we have outlined. Shohamy (1996: 147) is therefore correct when she says rather bluntly that 'the current performance-communicative task-oriented approach is wrong, simplistic and narrow'.

Nevertheless, performance models have flourished. The most widely used of these is the Common European Framework of Reference (CEFR) (Council of Europe, 2001). We will use this as our primary example to illustrate the nature of performance models.

The CEFR originated in the communicative language teaching movement of the 1970s, when the Council of Europe first raised the possibility of a European credit scheme for language learning, related to fixed points in a framework (van Ek, 1975). The first attempt to create such a fixed point was the Threshold Level (van Ek and Trim, 1990), first published in 1985, which described language learning in terms of the social tasks that learners would be expected to carry out at this level.

Over the years the documentation associated with the CEFR project has acquired the language of competence and constructs, but these do not really impact upon the approach adopted, which remains firmly behavioural (Little, 2006). For example, the CEFR claims to be an 'action-oriented approach' that

> *views users and learners of a language primarily as 'social agents', i.e. members of society who have tasks (not exclusively language-related) to accomplish in a given set of circumstances, in a specific environment and within a particular field of action. While acts of speech occur within language activities, these activities form part of a wider social context, which alone is able to give them their full meaning. We speak of 'tasks' in so far as the actions are performed by one or more individuals strategically using their own specific competences to achieve a given result. The action-based approach therefore also takes into account the cognitive, emotional and volitional resources and the full range of abilities specific to and applied by the individual as a social agent.*

(Council of Europe, 2001: 9)

The scales contained in the document contain no references to competences, only to what learners 'can do' in a variety of communicative situations, using functional language. The scales themselves have no basis in analysis of actual performance, or second language acquisition theory (Fulcher, 2004; 2008b; Hulstijn, 2007); and the primary authors of the scales admit that they are atheoretical (North and Schneider, 1998: 242–243). Rather, the verbal descriptors or 'can do' statements are drawn from a compilation of other rating scales (North, 1993), which were given to teachers to decide which were relevant to their own teaching context in Europe. From their experience, teachers were then asked to place the descriptors in an order from most to least difficult for learners to achieve. Those that could be scaled (that the teachers agreed on most) were used to create the scales in the CEFR. Therefore, as North (2000: 573) says, 'what is being scaled is not necessarily learner proficiency, but teacher/raters' perception of that proficiency – their common framework'. The 'common' in the title therefore refers to the shared perceptions of the teachers who participated in the study to scale the descriptors.

The lack of construct content, the focus on successful behavioural outcomes, and the relative incoherence of the situations across levels of the CEFR, can be seen in most of the scales. In order to illustrate this we reproduce the global scale in Figure 4.6.

Scales of this kind have a superficial attraction. On the surface, the ascending levels appear to increase in difficulty. Indeed, this is how they were created, through perceptions. However, there is little beyond gross observational categories, either in terms of abilities or specific tasks – or 'discursive practices'.

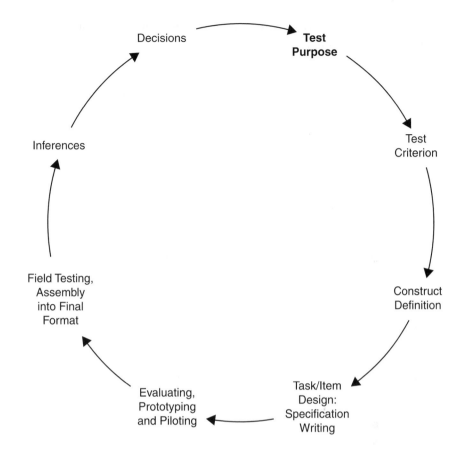

Fig. 4.6. The common reference levels: global scale

This discussion throws up an interesting question. Why is the Common European Framework called a 'framework', if it is a performance model? We have argued in this chapter that a test framework selects constructs from models and argues for their relevance to a particular purpose for testing. In fact, some people treat the CEFR as if it were really a framework – they take the scales and attempt to use them directly to score actual tests. This is a misuse of the CEFR, which we discuss in Chapter 8. It is indeed an abstract behavioural model, but it acquired its name for bureaucratic reasons. Trim (in Saville, 2005: 282–283) reports that the original intention was to call the CEFR the Common European Model. This name was vetoed by the French representatives in the Council of Europe because for them the word 'modèle' implied an ideal or perfect representation (of language use), and so the term 'framework' was adopted as a compromise. However, in English the term 'model' does not carry these implications; on the contrary, the implication is that it is a poor copy of reality, but may be good enough for its intended purpose. Perhaps in the same way we know that a map of the London underground bears no relationship to the geographical locations of the stations and the tunnels, but that does not stop it from being useful. However, the adoption of the term 'framework' has misled many users into thinking that it is directly applicable to teaching and testing.

This raises the question of just how a performance model like the CEFR can be useful. The answer is that, like all models, it is an attempt, however atheoretical, to describe language use. The descriptors are inadequate, and the levels are flawed because they are not based on primary data. But the text contains ideas that we might take away and use to build a framework for a particular context that is useful. It is a mine, out of which we may chip useful nuggets that, with crafting, can become useful instruments for testing and assessment. One example of how this might work is provided by Davidson and Fulcher (2007). They take the CEFR scale for 'transactions to obtain goods and services', which is reproduced in Appendix 4, and ask what ideas can be used to create a test for successful service encounters. It starts with the two key phrases in the CEFR that seem central to these types of encounters:

- 'Can ask people for things and give people things.'
- 'Can handle numbers, quantities, cost and time.'

As the CEFR does not provide any context or level of complexity, the study draws on discourse analysis of service encounters to create a basic template for a service encounter exchange so that a service encounter 'script' might be assessed at lower ability levels. The assumption for this decision is that one of the first things that learners of a second language need to do is get basic services, like buying a beer or a bus ticket.

Here are two sample items:

Item 1.
[The test taker hears]

Voice 1: Can I buy some apples?
Voice 2: Yes, They're two for 75p.

[The test taker sees]
What comes next?

(a) How much are they?
(b) How much are two?
(c) Thank you. I'll buy two.
(d) Thank you. How much?

Item 2.
[The test taker hears]

Voice 1: By when will my shoes be repaired?
Voice 2: Next Tuesday afternoon, I should think.

[The test taker sees]
What comes next?

(a) Thank you; I'll return Wednesday.
(b) Thank you; I'll return before then.
(c) Will they be ready by Tuesday?
(d) Can I get them on Wednesday?

While using the CEFR in this way can generate test purpose, a context and items, we note that it is still atheoretical. Its use can lead us to treat language use as a purely behavioural phenomenon. This is why further research is needed to supplement ideas mined from the CEFR. For example, in the Davidson and Fulcher study, it was noticed that a key construct in the literature, not mentioned in the CEFR, is the 'ability to establish rapport'. The construct 'rapport' is extremely difficult to define, and the most concise definition comes from the marketing literature:

> *Rapport is a customer's perception of having an enjoyable interaction with a service provider employee, characterized by a personal connection between the two interactants.*
> (Gremler and Gwinner, 2000: 92)

This raises a completely new set of questions relating to the kinds of constructs that might underlie successful service encounters, which may impact not only on testing, but providing both language courses and professional training for staff in a range of service industries. Such testing and training may offset the kinds of problems that have been studied by Ryoo (2005). It seems that one construct of primary relevance is the pragmatics of politeness. This could be operationalised in the talk of either the service provider or the customer, as in this next item, which is a modified version of Item 1 above. In this item, distractor (d) is possible and feasible, in Hymes' terms. It is therefore an alternative to the correct (c), but it is not pragmatically appropriate in this context if rapport is to be maintained.

Item 3.
[The test taker hears]

Voice 1: Can I buy some apples?
Voice 2: Yes. They're two for 75p.

[The test taker sees]
What comes next?

(a) How much are they?
(b) How much are two?
(c) Thank you. I'll buy two.
(d) Gimme two.

Behavioural models must be treated with care. It is not possible simply to use the content for practical language testing purposes. The content and scales need a great deal of applied linguistic work if they are to be applied successfully, and we can see that this work quickly leads us back to a consideration of theoretical constructs.

5. From definition to design

In this chapter we have looked at the test design cycle, and moved along the first three steps from defining test purpose, to construct definition. The amount of time that we spend on the tasks of defining purpose, identifying the criterion and teasing out the constructs that underlie performance will always depend upon the kinds of decisions we wish to make, and how serious those decisions are for the lives of the test takers. In large-scale, high-stakes tests, the process could take months, if not years. For classroom assessments it may be a single meeting of the staff involved. However, I would argue that even for the least important assessments, thinking through the issues in a structured process is professionally rewarding. It brings additional meaning to our understanding of just what it is we are testing, and so to what it is that we think we are teaching. The process of discussion and agreement is one that binds teachers together in a collaborative endeavour to improve teaching and assessment in an environment that encourages professional engagement and development.

While looking at the first three steps in the test development cycle we have also called upon the metaphor of architecture. We have tried to show that there are three levels of architectural design for any test or assessment. In this chapter we have been primarily concerned with the top, or most abstract, level. This is the level of models. We have described these as either construct-based models, or as behavioural-performance models. While we believe that the former are the most productive in test design, we have also tried to show that the latter can be useful if treated as heuristic devices to get us to the point where we have more to go on than the models themselves contain. They can act as starting points for our own ideas and research. But, ultimately, this is what all models are about. We attempt to select from them the constructs or other information that we think may be useful to our own situation.

It is describing our own testing purpose and context, and providing a rationale for the relevance of the constructs that we have selected to use, that constitutes the test framework. However, we have also seen that, in the process of constructing the test framework – of moving between the models and the framework – we may very well generate our own constructs that are particularly relevant to the context. These may be linguistic or, in the case of 'rapport', both linguistic and non-linguistic. We only considered the realisation of politeness in linguistic terms, but in a simulation task for more advanced learners we may wish to consider the role of body language and eye contact. These considerations open up both testing and language teaching to the wider world of communication in the criterion context.

Only at the very end of the chapter did we look at three test items. The test items or tasks, and the format of the test, are the lowest, or most specific level, in the test architecture. In Figure 4.2 these are called the test specifications. We turn to describing the test specifications and how they are constructed in the next chapter.

Activities

◯ 4.1 Just how specific is 'specific'?

This is not a new question. Language testing has been concerned for a long time with the extent to which general language tests are good enough for specific purposes, and whether specific purpose tests are so specific that they become tests of background knowledge (Alderson, 1988). Look at the two jobs below. To practise as a tour guide in Korea or a taxi driver in Wales, you are now required to pass a language test. For each job, make a list of the purposes for which you would use language. You may also wish to list the kinds of language functions, grammar or vocabulary that might be particularly relevant to the context. Also list required skills. Try to be as specific as possible.

Tour guides in Korea will have to go through a qualifying examination from September.

'Tour guides introduce Korea in foreign languages to tourists. If they don't meet certain qualifications, adverse side effects might arise,' said Kang Young-man of the Korea Tourist Guide Association. 'Speaking a foreign language fluently is not everything for a guide. They should also know Korean culture and history.'

The qualification test consists of a written examination, language test and a personal interview. Those who majored in the tourism industry will be exempted from part of the written exam, and the language test can be substituted for by other official foreign language tests.

The biggest difference in the new test will be the interview. The old interview assessed foreign language proficiency and tourism information separately, whereas now the information must be conveyed in the selected language.

[Shortened and adapted from the *Korea Times*, August 2009]

Your list

The tests, which include calculating how much change a customer is owed and identifying addresses read aloud to a driver, will be reviewed by the authority's licensing committee to see if taxi drivers' basic language skills need to be improved.

Anyone wishing to apply for a private hire driver licence must sit the exam which is split into four parts; listening and understanding the English language, choosing the best reply to sentences read out by an examiner, maths puzzles and matching road names to map grid references.

'The tests have been good for drivers,' said Mr Morris. 'If we really want to improve the relationships with our customers, we need to be able to converse and understand each other clearly.'

[Shortened and adapted from the *South Wales Argus*, September 2009)

Your list

○ 4.2 Identifying constructs

What other constructs do you think you may need to include in a test for lifeguards?

Look again at the two language use contexts provided in Activity 4.1. What key constructs would be critical for each test? Work with colleagues to make a list.

○ 4.3 Defining and operationalising constructs

In this chapter we discussed the constructs that would be relevant to a test for a lifeguard, but we only investigated stamina. Write a definition for each of the other three that we listed (or for those you produced in Activity 4.2). Then think of a task that might be used to measure that construct.

Alertness

Affability

Strength

What are the constraints that you face when designing your tasks?

How 'authentic' do you think your tasks are?

○ 4.4 Analysing domain-specific language

In order to decide what to test, we frequently have to analyse the language used in the criterion domain. This may involve collecting a corpus of spoken language, or a corpus of texts typically read (or created by) people who already work in that domain. The following text is a short extract from Taylor's (1996) *Introduction to Marine Engineering*. Imagine that you have been asked to create a reading test for potential students of marine engineering who will be expected to read texts like this in their first semester. How might the analysis of this (and similar texts) inform your decision regarding constructs and test content?

> *Ships are large, complex vehicles which must be self-sustaining in their environment for long periods with a high degree of reliability. A ship is the product of two main areas of skill, those of the naval architect and the marine engineer. The naval architect is concerned with the hull, its construction, form, habitability and ability to endure its environment. The marine engineer is responsible for the various systems which propel and operate the ship. More specifically, the means the machinery required for propulsion, steering, anchoring and ship securing, cargo handling, air conditioning, power generation and its distribution. Some overlap in responsibilities occurs between naval architects and marine engineers in areas such as propeller design, the reduction of noise and vibration in the ship's structure, and engineering services provided to considerable areas of the ship.*
>
> *A ship might reasonably be divided into three distinct areas: the cargo-carrying holds or tanks, the accommodation and the machinery space. Depending upon the type each ship will assume varying proportions and functions. An oil tanker, for instance, will have the cargo-carrying region divided into tanks by two longitudinal bulkheads and several transverse bulkheads. There will be considerable quantities of cargo piping both above and below decks. The general cargo ship will have various cargo holds which are usually the full width of the vessel and formed by transverse bulkheads along the ship's length. Cargo handling equipment will be arranged on deck and there will be large hatch openings closed with steel hatch covers. The accommodation areas in each of these ship types will be sufficient to meet the requirements for the ship's crew, provide a navigating bridge area and a communications centre. The machinery space size will be decided by the particular machinery installed and the auxiliary equipment necessary. A passenger ship, however, would have a large accommodation area, since this might be considered the 'cargo space'.*

You may wish to do this activity with a text selected from a field in which you have a particular interest, such as law, or medicine.

◯ 4.5 Searching for interactional competence

Read the following extract, from May (2009: 405–406). Two test takers, Hu (H) and Ling (L), read a passage about therapeutic cloning and are asked to discuss their opinions. The researcher (Res) is also present.

H: Hao le ma? (OK? In Mandarin)

L: (shakes her head, so Hu continues reading)

Res: that's five minutes

    Pause of several seconds

H: today we are talk about this very … have you opinions about the cloning?

L: yeah

H: ah first one is um banning all the research ah research … what do you think this … this this opinion?

L: mm they have both advantages and disadvantages [first]

H: mm

L: I think the advantage is that … er it's related to the … ethical opinions because cloned animals meet early meet early death and erm so we with find very cruel to kill living things

H: so we should ban [the]

L: [yeah]

H: the human cloning

L: ah there are also the disadvantages because cloning ah cloning can supply a new way to cure the disease um … especially the cancer cancer is a very terrible disease

H: yes

L: [that] destroys many many peoples for twenty years

H: ah yeah this is … ther … therapeutic cloning

L: yes so I don't agree about this opinion

H: yeah

What evidence is there of interactional competence in this dialogue?

Why might it be difficult to rate the contributions of (a) Hu and (b) Ling?

You may also wish to record two or three learners undertaking a communication task. Transcribe the interaction and identify key features of interactional competence. Present your findings to your colleagues.

◯ 4.6 Reverse engineering I

Reverse engineering involves looking at a test item or task and trying to work out what construct(s) it is trying to test. It is also useful when selecting tests to use for a group of learners, to discover whether the purpose of the test or item types matches their needs.

Look at the following writing prompt. Who do you think this item was written for? What does it test? What kinds of decisions might you take on the basis of scores derived from items of this kind?

Writing

Using the information below and the diagram, write a report of approximately 300 words evaluating the different methods of controlling traffic. Indicate which **two** methods you would choose to control traffic outside a school on a busy road.

Some traffic problems

- Traffic speed
- Overtaking
- Volume of traffic
- Lorries in residential streets
- Parking near junctions
- Pedestrians cross the road

Some possible disadvantages

- Awkward for buses
- Dangerous for cyclists
- Poor access for emergency vehicles
- Increased noise
- Loss of parking places

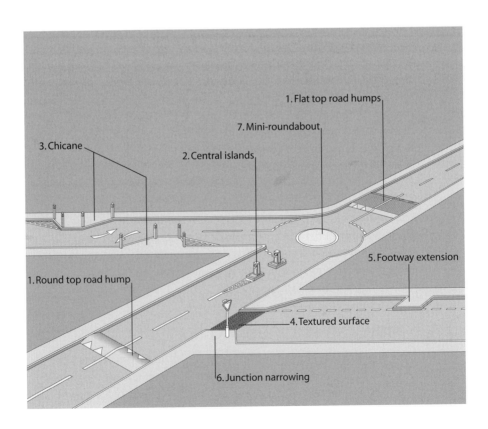

⭕ 4.7 Reverse engineering II

Look at this test item from McEldowney (1982). If you are working in a group, get two people to answer the item and verbalise their reasoning as they actually do it. The others should take notes on what they say. Using this data and your own analysis of the item, what construct(s) is it trying to test, and do you think it is doing this effectively?

Read the following text and then use the words in the list to complete the diagram.

Globbes

The four trug jigs of the globe are the colls, the solls, the pals and the tals. They are in wongs, one inside the other. First, there are the colls in the centre with the solls around them. Outside the solls is the polnth. Where the polnth has two wongs, the jigs of the outer wong are the pals, which tote the calyth. The jigs inside this are the tals toting the colnth.

calyth, colls, colnth, pals, polnth, solls, tals

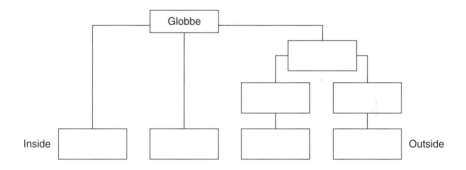

⭕ 4.8 Project work I

Select a particular group of people with language needs that you are familiar with. These may be your own students who are learning a language for a particular reason. However, it may also be learners who are studying to do a particular job that requires them to use and/or communicate in a second language.

Describe the target population and the contexts within which they are expected to use language.

Describe the purpose and means of communication, participants, the kinds of texts they may have to understand or create and the modalities of communication. This may involve a job analysis, or for students you may have to do a learning objectives/syllabus analysis.

If possible, collect some sample texts (spoken or written) that illustrate what the target population has to produce or comprehend.

List and define the constructs of interest.

Write up your report in a short test framework document. Justify your selection of constructs for test purpose.

5

Designing test specifications

 ## 1. What are test specifications?

In this chapter we look in detail at initial item design and writing test specifications in the test design cycle (Figure 4.1). Test specifications are the most detailed level of test architecture. They are also sometimes called test 'blueprints' (Alderson, Clapham and Wall, 1995: 9). The analogy is once again with architecture and engineering. Specifications are the design documents that show us how to construct a building, a machine or a test.

Test specifications can take many formats. It could be a single document that describes the test purpose, test constructs, the one or two item types that appear on the test, and a statement of the number of items that the test as a whole should contain. Alternatively, it may be necessary to have a separate document for each item type if there are going to be many types. The more complex the test, the more specification documents there are likely to be. It is possible to list all the possible specifications that we might need for a test, following the plan of Mislevy, Almond and Lukas (2003):

Item/task specifications:	Perhaps the most important part of a test specification, the item/task specifications describe the prompts that are designed to elicit the evidence upon which inferences are made about the targeted abilities of the learners. Minimally, these specifications should state what kind of input material the test takers will encounter, what the instructions look like, and any other features of the prompts that are important. They will also include variable features; these are ways in which the task may change, or which alterations are permissible. This is particularly important because it tells item writers just how much freedom they have to be creative when producing new items. It is normal to provide sample items with test specifications to illustrate what is intended by the description.
Evidence specification:	This is a description of what the test taker is expected to do – or what kind of response is expected – in each task. In some of the literature this is also called a 'response attribute'. An evidence specification also states how the response is to be scored (which is the

subject of Chapter 7). This is the measurement component. For a closed-response item such as a multiple choice, this may simply be that each response is scored as 0 for incorrect and 1 for correct; for performance tasks, it would be necessary to provide more complex rating scales or other devices to guide the judgements of human assessors.

Test assembly specification: This document provides the instructions for how the entire test is constructed. We might know that there are four item types, but we still need to know how many of each item type we need in the test. If the items are coded by context, topic, degree of pragmatic knowledge required to respond (as in our 'rapport item' at the end of the last chapter), or whatever other features we think characterise the criterion domain, we may need to specify how many items are required for each category. We also know from Chapter 2 that test reliability in norm-referenced tests is directly related to test length. We may therefore need to specify the target reliability and the minimum number of items needed to meet the target. The test assembly specification therefore plays a critical role in showing that the number and range of items in any form of the test adequately represent the key features of the criterion situation in the real world.

Presentation specification: Sometimes completely overlooked by many language test designers, the presentation specification tells the test production team precisely how the items and any support material is to be presented to the test takers. If it is a paper and pencil test, we need to specify the margin size, the font type and size, spacing, and where page numbers will appear. In computer-based tests the presentation specification is even more important, because we know that variation can cause fluctuations in scores that are construct irrelevant. Interface design and specification limit what it is possible to do, like the use of colour, scrolling, or the amount of text that can be presented on a single screen (Fulcher, 2003b).

Delivery specification: The delivery specification sets out the details of the test administration, test security, and timing. These specifications may include spacing between desks or computers, the number of invigilators/proctors required per number of test takers, what may or may not be used during the test (dictionaries, for example), how long each sub-test should take, and what the over-all time allocated to the test is.

Together, these specifications allow us to build and deliver a 'test form' for a particular administration. A 'test' is really an abstract term. In a very real sense, a 'test' is really the collection of specifications. Any realisation of the specifications is a test form. We can use the specifications to create three, four or a hundred test forms. And we don't use the term 'test version', for a very good reason. A test form means that it is generated from a test specification; one reason for having test specifications is to try to ensure that each form looks roughly the same because it is made up of the same item types, with the same number of items, representing the same set of constructs in each section. It is also designed to try to make sure that each form is of the same difficulty. Recall the discussion of fairness and equality in Chapter 2. One role for test specifications is to ensure that if we need two forms of a test on the same day for security reasons – say, one group of learners is taking the test in the morning and another in the afternoon – it should not matter to a test taker whether they are assigned to the morning or afternoon group. Similarly, if someone takes the test this year or next year, assuming that their ability on the construct has not changed, they should get a similar score (within the standard error of measurement), even if the forms are different. A critical feature of test forms, therefore, is that they are parallel; there is no change between them. However, when we talk about a version of a test, we imply that it has changed. Over time test designers learn new things about their tests. Some items are not as good as we thought they were at measuring the construct they were intended to measure. Perhaps some items are sensitive to variables like gender, or first language background, and so they have to be removed. Perhaps we see signs that the test-taking population is changing and so some items have to be made more difficult. Changes to the test require the test specifications to be changed so that we have a new version of the test. The new version, in its turn, generates new forms – but all the new forms are parallel and there is no change between them. This relationship between forms and versions is illustrated in Figure 5.1. Here we can see that a test was developed at a point in time and a number of forms were created. These are identical twins, as it were. The test has subsequently been changed and improved on two separate occasions. This is part of the natural evolution of a test specification. Each time, the previous forms have been discontinued and new forms produced. The test remains the same. It is still a test of the same constructs. The test specifications evolve into new versions of the test. The forms are realisations of a particular test version.

You will not be surprised to learn that test specifications are part of the technology that we discussed in Chapter 2. However, they are also a critical component of criterion-referenced testing.

Although the term 'specifications' is not used, the earliest discussion appears in Ruch (1924: 95–99). Indeed, the advice he gives to teachers covers pretty much the content of the five kinds of specifications listed above. While no early specifications appear to survive, we can see evidence of them in many early publications on testing. For example,

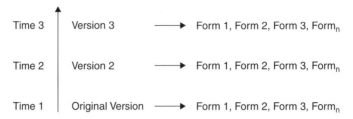

Time 3	Version 3	⟶	Form 1, Form 2, Form 3, Form$_n$
Time 2	Version 2	⟶	Form 1, Form 2, Form 3, Form$_n$
Time 1	Original Version	⟶	Form 1, Form 2, Form 3, Form$_n$

Fig. 5.1. Forms and versions

Yoakum and Yerkes (1920) contains multiple forms of ten army tests that are remarkably parallel, both in content and statistical performance. It seems highly unlikely that these forms could have been generated without a set of specifications, although sadly they skip over precisely how the test designers moved from initial ideas to multiple forms (1920: 2–3). We can also see evidence of specifications in some task descriptions, such as these from Burt (1922: 24–25):

Understanding Simple Commands
Procedure. 'Show me' ['put your finger on,' 'point to'] …

(i)   … 'your nose' …
(ii)   … 'your eyes' …
(iii) … 'your mouth' …

Each request (repeated several times, if necessary) should be given and answered separately.

Evaluation. All three injunctions should be correctly performed: but abundant repetition and free encouragement may first be used. (Opening the mouth, winking the eyes, etc., may be accepted.)

[Terman adds (iv) 'hair'; this requires three out of four to be correct; allows using a doll, and the question: 'Is this its (or your) nose? … Then where is its (or your) nose?]

In more open tasks that resemble modern-day speaking tests much more closely, we also have the following (slightly adapted) example (Burt, 1923: 26–27):

Describing Pictures
Three pictures chosen as containing people, and suggesting a story, and having a certain standardised difficulty.

Procedure. 'Look at this picture and tell me about it.'

'What is this?' If the child says 'a picture', 'Tell me what you see there.' It seems better to avoid leading phrases like 'What can you see in it?' which suggests enumeration, and 'What are they doing?' which suggests interpretation. Repeat instructions once for each picture, if there is no answer. Words of praise or encouragement may be

added: 'Isn't it a pretty picture? … Do you like it?' Or even, 'That's right' if the child is on the point of saying something, but is withheld by shyness.

Evaluation of Replies. Record the type of response given to the first picture. If doubtful, use the second and third, and record the type of response most frequently given.

Types of Response.

A.   *Enumeration. Replies giving a mere list of persons, objects or details.*
B.   *Description. Phrases indicating actions or characteristics.*
C.   *Interpretation. Replies going beyond what is actually visible in the picture, and mentioning the situation or emotion it suggests. For interpretation, the average order of ease appears to be: (i) man and woman, (ii) convict, (iii) man and boy.*

[Note on pictures: There can, I think, be little doubt that pictures better printed, larger, coloured … representing actions in progress … allowing children … would be much more appropriate than … engravings. Many investigators use pictures of their own. But the above alone have been standardised.]

The pictures associated with this are reproduced here from Burt (1923: 27, 49, 51).

In these two examples, we can identify a number of features from test specifications that we still use today. Firstly, it is stated what the item is intended to test. In the second example, we are informed what each picture should contain, which also implies what they should not contain. Each one should suggest a story. The three pictures should be

of slightly different difficulty, and be presented in order from the easiest to the most difficult. We note the reason for the selection of pictures: it is related to the expected response and scoring – or the evidence specification. The highest score is to be given to test takers who are able to infer context and meaning beyond what is in the picture.

Next in each example is the procedure. These are the instructions to the interlocutor/ examiner about precisely how the test should be conducted in a standardised manner. There is also guidance on just how far the examiner may vary the questions to be asked, and the degree of repetition and encouragement that can be given. Today, the levels of encouragement that are allowed in this picture description test would probably not be allowed in high-stakes testing, as it would be disclosing to the test taker what the outcome of the test is likely to be.

Next comes information on what kind of responses are expected, and the range of responses that can count as evidence of understanding. This is part of what we would now call an evidence model, and in the picture description task we also have a scoring model that tells the examiner what kind of evidence counts towards a grade at a particular level, with 'interpretation' being the highest.

Remarkably, in the picture description task we also have information on the presentation specification. Burt recommends that pictures should be large, in colour, contain children (the target population of this test) and be action scenes. It is clear from the note that users of this item specification put their own pictures in place of the ones provided. This is an element of freedom (variation) in the specification, although it is noted that there is no evidence to suggest that the other pictures are in fact parallel with the ones provided in the sample; the only evidence for how this item type works comes from the particular pictures presented here. Like all specifications, this one suggests a piece of research that is needed to support the test development process: trying out the item with a range of possible pictures to see what content and physical properties are likely to be permissible without significantly changing the difficulty of the items produced from the specification. This kind of research is very much in evidence today. For example, when the TOEFL test was computerised, it became possible to place visual images on the screen during the listening test. Ginther (2001, 2002) studied the relationship between the type of visual and the type of listening stimulus and discovered that when pictures carried information that supported the listening text, test scores improved. We may speculate that the pictures act as an independent means of 'knowledge activation', that calls up in the mind of the test taker a schema that is relevant to the easier processing of the text before they hear it for the first time (Rost, 2002: 62–64). As Buck (2001: 20) argues, 'schemata guide the interpretation of text, setting up expectations for people, places or events'. It should not be surprising that the extent to which a visual activates this knowledge accurately prior to listening would increase comprehension to some degree.

We can see that the concept of test specifications is not new. Specifications were originally conceived as design documents so that forms of a test would look as similar as possible, and work in the same way. The test is seen as a measuring device. As we saw in Chapter 2, reliable measuring instruments that produce the same results whenever and wherever they are used are essential to scientific progress. The test specification is part of the technology required to craft precision instruments that give the same measurement results. As the specifications evolve, the instruments themselves come into being. These are tested out, and sometimes we find that features of the instrument produce variability that we did not expect. The sources of variability are researched. If these prove to be part of what we wish to measure – the construct – the test specifications are changed to allow their continued presence in future versions. If they prove to be construct irrelevant they are a source of 'error', and the instrument needs to be redesigned to eliminate it. The test specifications are therefore changed to stop the further production of items with these features.

I have framed the last paragraph in terms of the classical view of test specifications. Test specifications are still used in the same way today. However, there are other ways of looking at test specifications. Not surprisingly, these come from the criterion-referenced testing movement.

▶ 2. Specifications for testing and teaching

In our discussion of criterion-referenced testing in Chapter 3, we saw that one of the key principles of the paradigm was the link between the assessment and the domain in the real world to which inferences were to be made. The movement that Glaser (1963) began was really concerned with linking assessment to teaching so that outcomes could be described and measured. Hambleton (1994: 23) puts this most accurately:

> One of the most important contributions of criterion-referenced measurement to testing practice was the central focus it placed on describing the intended outcomes of instruction – that is, the objectives. Requiring teachers and/or test developers to describe clearly the knowledge and skills to be tested provides the framework needed to write valid test items, to evaluate item–objective congruence, and to enhance the quality of test score interpretations.

The phrase 'item–objective congruence' refers to the relationship between the item or task and the learning objective that it is designed to test. As the objective is defined in the item specification, this is now more frequently referred to as 'item–spec congruence' or 'item/task fit-to-spec' (Davidson and Lynch, 2002: 44–45). The point being made is that specifications make us think, as teachers, very carefully about what it is we think the object of a learning activity is. When we ask our students to do this task, what knowledge, skill or ability do we think it is helping them to acquire, and why? The specification forces the language test designer to be explicit about the reason for the use of the item and what it is the item is intended to test. If we consider Figure 4.1 once more, we can see that after the test is assembled into its final form comes 'inferences' – the inferences we wish to make from the outcome of the test to what the learner knows or can do. A good specification is the explicit statement of the rationale for an inference to be made from successful performance on the item or task to the construct, and from the construct to the criterion. This is what Hambleton means in the rather terse ending: 'to enhance the quality of test score interpretations'.

Popham and Husek (1969: 3) were the first to see that this link, as expressed in the test specification, would be a major consideration in assessing the validity of a criterion-referenced test: 'The meaning of the score ... flows directly from the connection between the items and the criterion.' Later, Popham (1994: 16) claimed that 'the increased clarity attributed to criterion-referenced tests was derived from the test-item specifications that were generated in order to guide item writers'. We have already seen that test and item specifications were used well before the advent of the criterion-referenced testing movement. However, this is not to say that Popham was not largely responsible for making the value of specifications so evident to both teachers and testers. Popham's (1978) classic test specification format is reproduced in Figure 5.2, as it appears in Davidson and Lynch (2002: 14).

Specification Number. Provide a short index number
Title of Specification: A short title should be given that generally characterizes each spec. The title is a good way to outline skills across several specifications.
Related Specification (*s*), if any: List the numbers and/or titles of specs related to this one, if any. For example, in a reading test separate detailed specifications would be given for the passage and for each item.

(1) *General Description* (GD): A brief general statement of the behaviour to be tested. The GD is very similar to the core of a learning objective. The purpose of testing this skill may also be stated in the GD. The wording of this does not need to follow strict instructional objective guidelines.

(2) *Prompt Attributes* (PA): A complete and detailed description of what the student will encounter.

(3) *Response Attributes* (RA): A complete and detailed description of the way in which the student will provide the answer; that is, a complete and detailed description of what the student will do in response to the prompt and what will constitute a failure or success. There are two basic types of RAs:
   a. Selected Response (note that the choices must be randomly rearranged later in test development): Clear and detailed descriptions of each choice in a multiple-choice format.
   b. Constructed Response: A clear and detailed description of the type of response the student will perform, including the criteria for evaluating or rating the response.

(4) *Sample Item* (SI): An illustrative item or task that reflects this specification, that is, the sort of item or task this specification should generate.

(5) *Specification Supplement* (SS): A detailed explanation of any additional information needed to construct items for a given spec. In grammar tests, for example, it is often necessary to specify the precise grammar forms tested. In a vocabulary specification, a list of testable words might be given. A reading specification might list in its supplement the textbooks from which reading test passages may be drawn.

Fig. 5.2. Popham's (1978) five-component test specification format

The use of a specification template like Popham's is beneficial for teachers and test designers alike, in achieving clarity of purpose in testing. Even though this was developed in the 1970s, it is amazing just how well the sections of the picture description from Burt (1922, 1923) would fit into the template. The general description contains the construct or target behaviour that the task or item is intended to test. If used in classroom assessment, or to describe tasks that the language teacher is developing for learning purposes, the general description can be used to link the task type into the syllabus. This is particularly useful if a team of teachers is going to be generating a range of similar tasks to articulate a spiral syllabus.

The prompt attribute defines what instructions the test taker will be given, and what kind of input is required to generate the required response. It is important that all instructions can be understood by the test takers in the way intended by the test designers. Any source of potential misunderstanding needs to be ironed out well before any items that come from the specification are used operationally. The prompt attribute may also contain information relating to the source and difficulty of input materials, such as reading or listening texts. The text types, ranges and genres may be specified in order to link them directly to a criterion context. In performance tests we may specify who the interlocutors may be, and how they are to conduct the test. Next comes the response attribute, which describes precisely what the test taker is expected to do in their response to the prompt. This may be as simple as selecting the 'correct' answer from a selection of four options, or specifying the expected nature of an extended piece of writing, or production of extended speech.

All specifications contain sample items that illustrate what is intended by the specification. Sometimes 'anti-items' are also contained in the specifications to show what is not intended. In Chapter 4, Section 4, we presented a number of items from Davidson and Fulcher (2007). Here is the specification for these multiple-choice items designed to test understanding of service encounters. You will note that all the features from the Popham specification are included under the heading 'Guiding Language'.

Version 0.25 of the CEFR A1 Service Encounter Spec

Note: in the sample items, an asterisk ('*') indicates the intended correct choice, or 'key'.

Guiding language:

At the lowest level of the CEFR, simple transactions are mastered. These transactions share linguistic features, which are assessed by tasks generated by this spec. Transactions typically tested at this level include:

'Can ask people for things and give people things'
'Can handle numbers, quantities, cost, and time'

Tasks should focus on basic language constructions common to these transactions. Because this is a lower level on the CEFR, we envision (a) an objectively keyed test, and (b) one in which the response is a selection (on a paper or computer screen). The oral stimuli are presented in recorded formats, on a tape recorder or by digital playback. The examinee is instructed to pick the best response from among the four alternatives shown in each test item.

Each task should have a single target focus that reflects simple question construction about matters of quantity, time, cost, and so forth. Syntactic complexity of the prompts is permitted, provided that such complexity does not draw focus away from the target forms on which the multiple-choice task depends. The idea here is to focus the test taker on to the meaning-laden target components of the transaction. It is assumed that the particular format of the question is not as relevant as listening for the key details of time, quantity, etc.

Both acceptable and unacceptable tasks are illustrated in this spec. Transactions of multiple turns are not acceptable. Also not acceptable are turns that have many utterances or complex embedded syntax that prevents listening for the target constructions.

Distracters are permitted that test rapport. Consider the alternative version of Sample Task One. Note the change to (d) in which a somewhat more rude response is presented – while technically accurate in terms of focused listening, the more-rude choice (d) violates an expectation of politeness for the encounter, and it is therefore considered to be a wrong response.

(From Davidson and Fulcher, 2007: 239–240)

The sample anti-items are as follows:

[Unacceptable sample 1 – multiple turns]
[The examinee hears:]

Voice 1: Can I buy some apples?

Voice 2: Yes, happy to help.

Voice 1: These over here look good.

Voice 2: Yes, those are nice. They are two for 75p.

[The examinee sees:]
What comes next?

a) How much are they?
b) How much are two?
c) Thank you. I'll buy two. *
d) Thank you. How much?

[Unacceptable sample 2 – complex syntax]
[The examinee hears:]

Voice 1: I am not satisfied with the calculations you've produced for us. It seems to me that the total invoiced price should not exceed the average invoice in our audit from last year. What did we figure wrong?

Voice 2: I don't know. The numbers in this spreadsheet ring false to me, as well.

[The examinee sees:]
What comes next?

a) The figures seem satisfactory to me.
b) Everything seems OK, so far as my number-crunching takes me.
c) Perhaps we ought to crunch the numbers again. *
d) Can we put the numbers into a spreadsheet and figure out what's wrong?

We can see that anti-items give clear indications to item writers what they should avoid producing. When specifications go into operation, test developers can monitor the kinds of items that item writers produce. When items that they had not envisaged in the specifications are created, the specifications can be updated to exclude these items, and the samples included in the anti-item list.

Finally, a specification supplement may be added. This includes any additional information that would help the task/item writer to create parallel items. In a speaking test this may include an interlocutor frame. Milanovic *et al.* (1996: 17) describe a frame in this way:

> *The interlocutor is provided with a frame of topics and questions to be dealt with – the interlocutor frame. S/he is expected to follow this frame closely for all candidates, although, clearly the nature of the interaction is influenced by several factors such as background, personality and competence of the candidate. The range of topics covered in this phase include:*
>
> *greetings and introductions;*

giving information about self related to
  current job or status;
  work and travel;
 a built-in topic switch
 future career prospects
 interests;
 closing exchanges.

This spells out in much greater detail precisely how the speaking test is to be conducted, amplifying what may occur in the prompt attribute. In a writing test, the supplement may give additional information about the nature of the intended audience, the functions that might be covered, such as complaining or inviting. Again, these details may be related directly to the criterion domain of interest.

To conclude this section, we return to the most important argument. Only by using specifications can we generate large numbers of items or tasks that are parallel for use in multiple test forms. The specifications are also the focal point for elaborating an argument that shows how the test items are directly related to test constructs. However, in creating tasks for classroom assessment and for classroom activities, specification creation also serves an important role. The specification can be a focal point for teacher collaboration in defining what it is that is being taught and learned. Teachers can use the specifications to create multiple tasks in teams that can be used in delivering a spiral curriculum that offers multiple opportunities for learning.

▶ 3. A sample detailed specification for a reading test

In this section we present an example of an architecture for a reading test. This includes the test framework that presents the test purpose, the target test takers, the criterion domain and the rationale for the test content. The architecture is annotated with explanations in text boxes. This is a detailed test specification. The complexities of coding in test specifications of this kind are usually necessary in the design and assembly of high-stakes tests where it is essential to achieve parallel forms. There are problems with this type of specification for use in classroom assessment, which we deal with in Section 4 below.

Framework

Test purpose and target audience

In a globalised world there is increasing mobility of labour between countries. In economically difficult times there is evidence that workers with only a high school level of education are increasingly moving to other countries to seek manual and unskilled employment for a variety of economic reasons. Research evidence suggests that immigrants with a higher level of education, especially those who have already spent time in a second language environment, are capable of undertaking work and integrating socially much more easily. There is also a positive correlation between reading ability and earnings (Chiswick and Miller, 1999; Carnevale, Fry, and Lowell, 2001), and an inverse correlation between reading ability and ability to access critical services such as health care (Kefalides, 1999; Watters, 2003). It is therefore important to have a means of assessing the reading ability of migrant workers for two purposes: (a) to ensure that they have the linguistic and communicative skills that they need to seek work, and (b) to determine the level of ESOL support that they may require over an extended period of time when attempting to access necessary social services.

Given the target audience and the test purpose, it is unlikely to be appropriate for any immigrants who have already spent up to three years in the country prior to testing, as evidence suggests that the language skill differences between those able to work and integrate socially are by this time reduced (Chiswick, Lee and Miller, 2006). Nor is this test suitable for anyone below the age of 18.

> **Annotation 1**: The framework for this test is not terribly long, but presents a rationale for the purpose of the test and identifies the test takers. One important feature of this framework is that it states who the test is not designed for. A specification that limits the applicability of a test is a sign that the designers have clearly thought through the kinds of decisions that the test results may support.

General description

The primary purposes of reading for the target group have been identified as:

Reading to search for simple information (facts) relating to employment and social services.
Comprehending consequences and reasons.

Higher level reading such as synthesising information from various sources, reading for pleasure, or reading to critique texts, are not relevant to the test purpose. We are concerned with lower level text processing that supports survival reading in social and work-seeking contexts.

Background knowledge should not play a role in responding to test items.

Subject/topic knowledge is limited to everyday survival tasks.

Cultural knowledge should not play a role in responding to test items.

Linguistic knowledge is restricted to basic reading comprehension as follows:

Word recognition/identification
Priority is given to words in the most common 2000, although some less common work-specific vocabulary may be included as long as it is not too technical.

Cohesion
Pronominal reference (he, they)

Substitution (e.g. the same, one)

Skills: reading for factual information
Scan a text to identify a piece of information or a word quickly
Skim a text to extract main message

Understanding logical sequence clause relations (Winter, 1977)

Cause consequence: y is the consequence of x
e.g. 'more agricultural jobs are expected in Lincolnshire this year because of the excellent Spring' (explicit), 'more agricultural jobs are expected in Lincolnshire after good weather conditions this Spring' (inexplicit).

Instrument-achievement: By doing x, y occurs
e.g. 'Register with your dentist today. In this way you will get treatment in reasonable time if you experience toothache' (explicit) and 'Register with your dentist today and get treatment in reasonable time if you experience toothache' (inexplicit).

> **Annotation 2**: The general description sets out what should be tested. The knowledge and skills listed are those that are expected to be directly relevant to the target test takers and the purpose of the test. Notice that it also states what should not be tested – background knowledge, cultural knowledge or linguistic knowledge that a new arrival could not be expected to have mastered, and is not relevant to their early survival needs. This level of explicitness acts as a good guide for identifying anti-items.

Prompt attributes
All texts should be concrete, not abstract
All texts should be factual

Text types and genres

Descriptions	Advertisements, job announcements, notices, signs, directories
Procedures	Public information leaflets, forms
Recounts	News items

More complex text types such as exposition, argument and narrative are excluded. Topics that can be varied may include work, leisure, health, travel, accommodation and shopping. Texts should not be more difficult than Flesch-Kincaid 40, and should not exceed 150 words.

The following is a design template for text types with completed data for the sample text below.

Text title	Tractor Driver	
Text ID	#BR001	
Text type	A Description	1 Advertisement
		2 Job announcement
		3 Notice
		4 Sign
		5 Directory
	B Procedure	1 Public information leaflet
		2 Form
	C Recount	1 News item
Topic	D Employment	1 Work
	E Social Needs	2 Leisure
		3 Health
		4 Travel
		5 Accommodation
		6 Shopping
Difficulty	Flesch-Kincaid index	43 (Grade 9)
	Word Frequency	1000: 74.44%
		1001–2000: 5.56%
		(apple, camp, extra, excellent, skills)
		2001–3000: 8.89%
		(ASAP, tractor, strawberry, p.m., a.m., hr, mobile, caravan)
		Off list words: 11.11%
		(availability, role, tasks, accommodation, site, ethic)

Sample Text (Code: #BR001)

Work Availability:
ASAP until October (may be work after October).

Company Role:
Work is for a strawberry and apple farm as a tractor driver.

Job Description:
Experienced tractor driver needed for various work on the farm.
Must have experience driving modern tractors.
Work will include tasks such as bed forming.

Working Day:
7.00a.m.–3.00p.m.

Payment:
Depends on experience, between £6 and £7 per hr.

Accommodation:
Accommodation on the campsite (mobile home/caravan) this is shared with others.

What to bring:
Good work ethic.

Extra:
Excellent English skills.

Annotation 3: It is important that the text types and their features are carefully specified in a reading test for a group of test takers who are so clearly defined in terms of their language needs. Texts outside the fields and registers listed would not allow sound inferences to the constructs. The length and difficulty are also specified, and a sample text provided. Notice how the text is coded as A2–D1. As more suitable texts are found they can be coded, for example, B1–E3 for a leaflet explaining how to register with a Health Clinic. The coding can then be used to ensure that the Assembly Specification has an adequate number of texts from each category so that the test developer can claim that the test has adequate domain representation.

Response attributes

Response attributes are restricted to the selection of a correct response from four options (multiple choice). Selecting the key is taken as an indication that the test taker has the ability to extract basic factual information from a text, understand causes, or the reasons for actions. Measurement component: each item is dichotomously scored and items are summed as a measure of 'basic reading for work and social purposes'.

Annotation 4: Only multiple-choice items are going to be used in this test. Constructed response items that ask the test taker to produce language are considered too difficult for the intended test-taking population.

Item specifications

Below are templates for four item types, each followed by sample items and specification supplements where required. The items are related to the sample text above.

Item type 1	Word recognition			
Item ID	#WR001			
Text ID	#BR001			
Frequency	(A) 1000	(B) 2000	(C) 3000	(D) Off list
Stem	(1) Words from text		(2) Synonyms or paraphrase	
Facility Value	.86			
Discrimination	.45			

Sample item:

How much you can earn depends on your:

(a) English
(b) experience
(c) tasks
(d) driving

Specification supplement:

The stem may or may not contain words taken from the passage, or use synonyms or paraphrase for words taken from the passage, in the immediate vicinity of the target word. It is expected that stems containing words from the text are likely to be easier, as word recognition will be achieved by matching words in the stem to those in the text, rather than identifying similar meanings.

Item type 2	Cohesion	
Item ID	#C001	
Text ID	#BR001	
Reference	(A) Pronominal	(B) Substitution
Distance	(1) Closest to reference	(2) Distant from reference
Facility value	.42	
Discrimination	.51	

Sample item:

What will you share with others?

(a) a caravan
(b) a mobile home
(c) accommodation
(d) the campsite

Specification supplement:

The target word should be located within two sentences of the pronominal reference or substitution. Distracters are drawn from noun phrases in the vicinity of the target word, and may be closer to the pronominal reference or substitution.

Item type 3	Reading for factual information	
Item ID	#FI001	
Text ID	#BR001	
Reference	(A) Scan	(B) Skim
Facility value	.77	
Discrimination	.37	

Sample item

What time will you finish work each day?

(a) October
(b) 3 o'clock
(c) 6 o'clock
(d) 7 o'clock

Specification supplement:

Items should focus upon dates, times, numbers, facts, events, or names.

Item type 4	Understanding logical sequence clauses	
Item ID	#LS001	
Text ID	#BR001	
Clause type	(A) Cause consequence	(B) Instrument achievement
Explicitness	(1) Marked	(2) Unmarked
Facility value	.33	
Discrimination	.62	

Sample item

If you take this job, you may:

(a) be offered further work
(d) bring a good work ethic
(c) improve your English skills
(d) drive modern tractors

> **Annotation 5**: Each of the item specifications sets out what is and is not allowed. Codes are provided for the key variables. The example for item Type 4 is coded as A2. This coding is very helpful at this level of delicacy as it allows the assembly specification to say that so many items should test pronominal and substitution reference, and how many of each should be close to the referent (and therefore easier), how many should be distant. When devising coding systems for items it is necessary to remember that the more complex the coding system, the more complex the assembly specification will be. Also, as the number of codes goes up to reflect the complexity of variability in the criterion domain, so does the number of items that you will have to put on the test to adequately reflect the criterion domain!

Assembly specification

Targets: This test is intended to be used to provide English language support to newly arrived workers. Resources for language programmes are limited, and it is therefore essential that only those who are in genuine need are allocated to classes. Each form should therefore reach reliabilities of .8 or higher.

Constraints:

Form constraints

Each form contains 50 items attached to 10 texts.

Text constraints

5 description texts, 3 procedure texts and 2 recount texts.

Topic constraints

5 Employment texts and 5 Social Needs texts, one to be drawn from each sub-topic.

Item constraints

Item type	Code	No.
Type 1	1A1	4
	1A2	3
	1B1	4
	1B2	3
	1C1	1
	1C2	1
	1D1	1
	1D2	1
Type 2	2A1	4
	2A2	2
	2B1	4
	2B2	2
Type 3	3A	5
	3B	5
Type 4	4A1	4
	4A2	1
	4B1	4
	4B2	1

Text/Item constraints

Approximately 5 items attached to each text.

Delivery specification

Paper based, with one text and approximately five questions appearing on each page. Each text and questions to appear in Times New Roman 12pt. Length of test: 75 minutes.

> **Annotation 6:** The assembly specification attempts to ensure that the relevant text types and topics are well represented, and that there is at least one item from each code in the system. Using this assembly specification each form of the test should be parallel in both content and difficulty. Finally, we have the delivery specification that provides layout and length, but does not tell us how the test is to be administered.

4. Granularity

Many teachers do not like detailed test specifications like the example above. In fact, many have much stronger reactions than just dislike. Popham (1994: 16) is getting closer to the mark when he says that many teachers respond: 'These specifications are too damned long to pay attention to!' We had to present an example of a fairly detailed specification so that you could see just what is involved in developing the architecture for a high-stakes test where it is important to be able to defend the use of every text and every item in terms of test purpose. This is part of the argument that the inferences from scores are valid. But for teachers this level of detail is not always possible, nor indeed desirable. Popham (1994: 16) goes on: 'If item writers to whom I was paying salaries resisted the use of detailed test-item specifications because the specifications were "too damned long," how likely was it that classroom teachers would be willing to wade through sets of lengthy specifications in order to attain the clarity needed to provide on target instruction?'

There is another problem with highly detailed test specifications. They limit creativity. In fact, that is precisely what they are intended to do. The coding system tells the item/task writer precisely what is and is not allowed. This is all well and good in high-stakes tests where each form has to be as similar as possible. Teachers, however, do not often wish to have these kinds of constraints in the classroom.

The third drawback to using highly detailed specifications for classroom tests is the tendency for teachers to teach nothing apart from what is defined in the specifications (Popham, 1992). This has the effect of limiting rather than enriching the curriculum. What started as an attempt to introduce clarity into teaching and assessment frequently achieves clarity only at the expense of breadth.

In reaction to the problems that we have outlined, Popham suggested that for pedagogical purposes specifications could be 'boiled down' to contain just a general description and a sample item (like the one for service encounters in Davidson and Fulcher, 2007). This would outline 'the intellectual essence required by the item' (Popham, 1994: 17), but would leave the door open to teacher creativity in designing the item or task. The example that he provided is from reading comprehension (1994: 18), which we reproduce here:

Comprehending Central Messages

General Description

Items can be phrased in a variety of ways, but they all must require the student to have recognized or inferred the central message of the selection or designated part of the selection. Items may call for students to create or choose the most accurate summary of the selection or part of the selection, to identify or state the topic of all or a part of the selection, or to identify or state the main idea or central point of a selection or part of that selection. Items may or may not require the student to make an inference in order to select or construct the appropriate answer.

Illustrative, Non-exhaustive Items.

What is this selection mainly about?

Write a brief paragraph describing the theme of this passage.

Describe, in one sentence, the passage's central message.

What is the main point of this essay?

Orally, indicate what the main idea is of the passage's fourth paragraph.

Select the best statement of the essay's central message about human development
(a) Nature is much more important than nurture.
(b) Nurture is much more important than nature.
(c) Nature and nurture are equally important.
(d) Neither nature nor nurture are all that significant.

The sample items in this example leave plenty of room for diversity and creativity. While this would not be desirable in a high-stakes test, it is an excellent strategy for classroom assessment. Popham (1992: 17) argues that this middle level of specificity is 'amenable to the delineation of multiple, not single, assessment tactics', and that the use of multiple examples is more useful in a classroom context than the complexities of detailed specifications. Davidson and Lynch (2002: 53) agree with adopting a middle level of generality like the one proposed by Popham, and suggest that the kind of language it generates to guide teachers in designing tasks for teaching and assessment be termed 'speclish'.

5. Performance conditions

When we discussed the lifeguard test in Chapter 4, we drew attention to all the contextual variables that could not be replicated in a test. This example showed how difficult it is to design an 'authentic' test, if 'authenticity' is taken literally to mean 'replicating real life'. There is no such thing as the replication of real life in a test, because the test can only be held under one set of conditions. When a test specification attempts to list the conditions, these are frequently referred to as performance conditions. One of the clearest examples of performance conditions is provided in the Canadian Language Benchmarks (Pawlikowska-Smith, 2000; Canadian Language Benchmarks, 2006). The benchmarks are a set of task-based proficiency levels. They therefore constitute a performance model like the CEFR. However, the Benchmarks are task based, whereas the CEFR does not place specific tasks in its levels. The underlying assumption of the Benchmarks, therefore, is that there is a sequential order of task difficulty.

The example that we provide is taken from the Stage II, Benchmark 5 (Pawlikowka-Smith, 2000: 53–59). At this level learners are expected to be able to 'participate with some effort in routine social conversations and can talk about needs and familiar topics of personal relevance'. More specifically, in social interaction, they can: respond to small talk comments; extend, accept or decline an invitation or offer; express and respond to compliments; express and respond to congratulations. This involves basic conversational management skills such as indicating non-comprehension, showing interest, and turn taking.

Within the range of tasks indicated, the Benchmarks provide the performance conditions that limit the task variables that are permissible as follows (Pawlikowka-Smith, 2000: 56):

- Interaction is face-to-face, or on the phone.
- Rate of speech is slow to normal.
- Context is mostly familiar, or clear and predictable, but also moderately demanding (e.g. real-world environment; limited support from interlocutors).
- Circumstances range from informal to more formal occasions.
- Instructions have five to six steps, and are given one at a time, with visual clues.
- Topics are of immediate everyday relevance.
- Setting is familiar.
- Topic is concrete and familiar.

At higher levels we discover that rate of speech may increase, contexts become less familiar, as do topics, and so on. These do not reach the level of detail that we would expect with a test for a specific purpose, because the Benchmarks remain at the level of a model. The Benchmarks are not a curriculum; nor are they a test. However, the examples can be used to spark debate on the kinds of performance conditions that we may wish to impose on tests with a defined purpose. Like the CEFR, these descriptors can act as heuristics for test development.

▶ 6. Target language use domain analysis

One approach to designing item/task specifications that incorporates performance conditions is Target Language Use (TLU) domain analysis (Bachman and Palmer, 1996: 309–311). This approach involves describing the item/task according to features that exist in the target language use situation across a number of categories: the facets of the testing environment (such as place, equipment, personnel, and so on), the facets of the test rubric (organisation, time instructions), facets of the input (format and language), facets of the expected response (format, language, restrictions on response) and the relationship between input and response (whether reciprocal, non-reciprocal or adaptive).

In order to illustrate how this kind of test specification might work, we will return to the idea of designing a task to assess service encounter participation; in this case, a service encounter in a travel agency. The following specification was designed as part of a research project (Mills, 2009). The table contains the TLU style specification for a task designed to be used in a course for Korean learners studying the language of tourism. Despite following the TLU style, we notice that the introductory material (purpose, constructs), and the format of the sample item and related description, show that Mills has created a hybrid specification that suits her own teaching and testing context. This kind of adaptation is an excellent example of how teachers can and should craft specifications so that they are of maximum use in their own working environments.

A service encounter (travel agency) specification (Mills, 2009: 95–101)

Test purpose
The purpose of this test is to test whether students have learned the content of the course and to provide diagnostic feedback to the teacher so that the course and the final test can be tailored to the level and the needs of the learners.

Definition of construct
For this achievement test a syllabus-based construct definition is used:
Situation: 'the ability to perform a simplified simulated authentic dialogue to book or take a booking for a flight at a travel agency'.
Skill: Comprehend and write down important facts. Negotiate for meaning when breakdowns in communication occur by asking for clarification and reformulating information.

	Characteristics of target language use (TLU) task	Characteristics of test task
	Booking a flight	Requesting price and availability of seats/giving flight information
SETTING		
Physical characteristics	Location: travel agency office Materials: telephone and computer	Location: teachers' office. It's sometimes noisy Materials: simplified flight schedule, paper and a pencil
Participants	Travel agent and customer.	Classmates and teacher (as assessor)
Time	Daytime	Afternoon

INPUT AND RESPONSE		
Format		
Channel	Aural and visual (flight schedule on computer)	Aural (from classmate) and visual (flight schedule)
Form	Language	Language
Language	Aural is target (English) Visual is Korean	Target (English)
Length	Quite short	Quite short (but customer's role is shorter than the agents)
Speed	Moderate: the speed cannot be too slow or the customer would be dissatisfied	Unspeeded, with classmate
Vehicle	Live	Live
Type	Limited production response	Limited production response. The customer has more constructed responses to listen for.
PROPOSITIONAL CONTENT		
Degree of contextualisation	Context-reduced language (often on the phone)	Context-embedded. The task is simplified by specifying the language to be used and be performed face-to-face
Distribution of new information	Negotiated	Negotiated
Type of information	Factual	Factual
Topic	Booking a flight	Booking a flight
Genre	Customer service	Customer service
LANGUAGE CHARACTERISTICS		
Grammatical	Vocabulary: general and specialised for flight reservations Syntax: standard English	Vocabulary: general and specialised for flight reservations Syntax: standard English
Textual	Conversation with features such as interrupting	Simplified conversation, suggested speaking pattern given in role-play

Pragmatic characteristics		
Functional	Ideational and manipulative, including: accepting; requesting; explaining; asking for clarification; and being polite	Ideational and manipulative, including: accepting; requesting; explaining, asking for clarification; and being polite
Sociolinguistic	Variety: Varied Register: Semi-formal	Variety: interlanguage
RELATIONSHIP BETWEEN INPUT AND RESPONSE		
Reactivity	Reciprocal	Reciprocal
Scope of relationship	Narrow	Narrow
Directness of relationship	Direct	Direct

Sample Item

One student is the travel agent and one is the customer. The customer wants to know the price and availability of seats. Both students need to write down 5 pieces of information.

Rubrics

The customer will receive a role card stating the destination, preferred travel day, and class of ticket. The travel agent will receive one of the following flight information tables.

Information gap

Travel agent

City	Travel date	Round trip/ one way	Class	Companions
e.g. Osaka	Wednesday	Round trip	business	No

Customer

Flight days	Direct or stopover	Departure time	Arrival time	Price
e.g. Monday Wednesday Friday	Direct Stopover Direct	11.20a.m.	6:40p.m.	$750

	Starlight airlines Fares and flight Schedules						
Destination		Schedule	Stop-over	Departs	Arrives	Price (Economy / Business / First Class)	
						One way	Return
South Korea	Incheon	Monday	no	9.20a.m.	4.30p.m.	$477 / $753 / $1240	$877 / $1453 / $2240
	Incheon	Wednesday	Beijing	9.20a.m.	6.30p.m.	$427 / $723 / $1140	$827 / $1383 / $2140
	Incheon	Friday	no	9.20a.m.	4.30p.m.	$477 / $753 / $1240	$877 / $1453 / $2240
Japan	Osaka	Tuesday	no	10.15a.m.	5.40p.m.	$476 / $752 / $1100	$776 / $1352 / $2100
	Osaka	Thursday	no	10.15a.m.	5.40p.m.	$476 / $752 / $1100	$776 / $1352 / $2100
	Osaka	Saturday	Tokyo	10:15a.m.	7:40p.m.	$426 / $722 / $1100	$726 / $1252 / $2000

	Candidian Airlines Fares and flight schedules						
Destination		Schedule	Stop-over	Departs	Arrives	Price (Economy / Business / First Class)	
						One way	Return
South Korea	Incheon	Tuesday	no	7.50a.m.	3.00p.m.	$480 / $800 / $1400	$880 / $1500 / $2700
	Incheon	Wednesday	Manila	7.50a.m.	4.10p.m.	$460 / $780 / $1300	$860 / $1450 / $2600
	Incheon	Friday	no	7.50a.m.	3.00p.m.	$480 / $800 / $1400	$880 / $1500 / $2700
Japan	Osaka	Monday	no	9.40a.m.	4.10p.m.	$515 / $780 / $1540	$915 / $1480 / $2540

Osaka	Thursday	Hong Kong	9.40a.m.	5.30p.m.	$505 / $780 / $1540	$905 / $1420 / $2500
Osaka	Friday	no	9.40a.m.	4.10p.m.	$515 / $780 / $1540	$915 / $1480 / $2540

Specification supplement

The students will be told two weeks before the test that they will receive a joint score (out of 10) for writing down the correct information. Students are encouraged to ask for clarification and provide repetition to help each other complete the task.

 # 7. Moving back and forth

The test design cycle (Figure 4.1) implies that test designers complete one activity and move on to the next in a linear fashion. In reality, this never happens. Test designers move back and forth all the time. When a criterion (or target language use) domain is identified, it is natural to start thinking about the kinds of tasks that people have to perform in the domain. The constructs that underlie successful performance are described, and initial ideas for test tasks take shape. The first draft of the specifications is started. As the task descriptions evolve, it is natural to return to the construct definitions and sharpen them up, which in turn raises questions about whether the tasks can elicit the information necessary for the inferences we wish to make. Rather than being linear, the process is iterative. At times, it can even seem quite messy. Some ideas for tasks may be discarded, and new task types are suggested.

In this way test specifications evolve. In Section 2, you may recall that the service encounter specification from Davidson and Fulcher (2007) was given a version number: version 0.25. Test specifications go through versions. Keeping track of these versions and the decisions that led to each change is part of a validity narrative. A specification that is ready for use might be version 1.0, and numbers on the way to 1.0 show the specification's current state of evolution.

We conclude this section by reflecting briefly on what Davidson and Lynch (2002: 57–59) call 'ownership'. As they correctly point out, the creation of specifications is a dynamic process that is almost always the work of a group, rather than an individual. Specifications therefore reflect the theoretical and practical beliefs and judgments of their creators. When used by teachers to craft teaching and assessment tasks, they can become the focus for collaboration, action and clarity of purpose. When the team feels that the ideas in the test specification can work in practice, it is time to write sets of prototype items and try them out. This stage in the test design cycle is the subject of the next chapter.

Activities

⭕ 5.1 Specifications on the internet

Go to your favourite internet search engine and type in 'test specifications'. You will probably be surprised at what you get. Look through a number of websites at the specifications available. How many of them follow a structure similar to the ones that we have looked at in this chapter? Are there any that follow a very different structure?

Select one test specification that you find on the internet and write a brief report. What kind of a test is it? Who is the specification written for? What is the purpose of the specification? Is it useful for its intended purpose?

⭕ 5.2 Writing an item to spec I

Read Burt's specification and sample item again. Can you use it to create a modern item to this specification? Select three appropriate pictures and write improved instructions for the interlocutor.

⭕ 5.3 Writing an item to spec II

Look again at the detailed specification in Section 3. The sample item is a job announcement relating to employment. Select another text type and topic. Search for a suitable text that meets the specifications. When you have found one, write three to five items for the text to meet the specifications. Code each item.

As you are doing this activity, make notes:

> What problems do you encounter searching for a suitable text? What does this tell you about writing specifications for the selection of material to place in the prompt?
>
> What problems do you have writing the item? Are the specifications too restrictive? Or would you prefer the specifications to give more guidance? You may wish to revise parts of the specification as a result of your experience.
>
> What problems do you have using the coding system? Do you find the coding system is at the right granularity, or is it too detailed? What changes would you like to make to the coding system as a result of your experience?

⭕ 5.4 Reverse engineering III

In Chapter 4 we looked at two items to try to work out what they were testing. In this chapter we are going to do the same task, but this time you should try to generate an item specification. Treat the following item as the 'sample item' from a specification, and write the specification to go with it. You may use the Popham template for convenience, or adapt it in any way you think is appropriate. You may also decide on the granularity of the item spec. (You or your colleagues may wish to select another item from a test with which you are familiar, but unsure about what the items are designed to test.)

You have just arrived in England and plan to spend some time travelling around. You have heard that York is an interesting city to visit and you read about it.

One of the finest cities in Europe, York has buildings and architectural remains which span almost 2000 years. A good introduction to the city is a walk along the top of the well-preserved city walls, parts of which date from Roman times. They provide a splendid vantage point from which to view the landmarks of the city enclosed within.

The major monument in York is the great Minister. It was built over a period of almost 500 years and is one of the largest churches in Europe, and especially noted for its early stained glass. An exhibition in the undercroft tells graphically the story of the buildings which occupied the site before the present church was constructed (open daily).

The Vikings, like the Romans, settled in York and the sights, sounds and smells of their daily life in the city are realistically recreated in the Yorvik Viking Centre (open daily). A stroll through the Shambles will conjure up life in the medieval city. This narrow street is lined with half-timbered shops with overhangs that almost touch the buildings on the opposite side.

A large part of York's heritage has been preserved in its exciting museums. For example, in the Castle Museum, an entire cobbled street with shops of various periods has been reconstructed (open daily). The history of railways in Britain is displayed in the National Railway Museum where you can see old locomotives, rolling stock and memorabilia.

You will certainly enjoy your stay in York. Not so much a city, more a living museum.
(0904) 21756
From King's Cross at 0935, 1000, 1025 and 1100.
Typical journey time 2 hours 10 minutes.
InterCity Saver Return £30 or £37.

1. According to the brochure, what is York's greatest attraction?
   a. the city walls
   b. the Minster Church
   c. the Viking Centre
   d. the Shambles

2. According to the brochure, York is interesting because
   a. it has a fascinating history
   b. it contains both new and old architecture
   c. it has good shops
   d. there are many museums
3. How far back do the earliest remains in York date?
   a. to prehistoric times
   b. to the first century
   c. to Viking times
   d. to medieval times

You are thinking of staying in a hotel in the city of York. You see some advertisements for places to stay.

4. Which hotel sounds closest to the Minster?
   a. Disraelis
   b. Hudson's
   c. Savages
   d. Novotel

5. Which hotel is next to the river?

   ┌─────────────────────────────┐
   │   │
   │   │
   └─────────────────────────────┘

6. You also want to check how much it would cost to rent accommodation in the city. Which telephone number should you ring?

   ┌─────────────────────────────┐
   │   │
   │   │
   └─────────────────────────────┘

7. You decide to take the train to York. You want to arrive before midday. Which train should you catch from King's Cross?

   ┌─────────────────────────────┐
   │   │
   │   │
   └─────────────────────────────┘

○ 5.5 Write an item specification

In Activities 4.1 and 4.2 you attempted to define the constructs relevant to a test for tour guides and taxi drivers. With your colleagues, design a specification for one item type that you would include in a test to measure one of these constructs for either tour guides or taxi drivers. (You may, if you wish, select some other language use context – but try to make it very specific.)

○ 5.6 Project work II

In Activity 4.8 you wrote a framework document for a test.

Using a suitable template, which you may adapt as you wish, write a test specification based upon your framework document. Consider carefully how many item types you will include in your test. Remember that the more item types you include, the more complex the test will become and the longer the activity. However, using only one item type can sometimes restrict the range of constructs you can test, and may also introduce a *method effect*.

Include at least one sample item for each item type you specify.

[Remember that test specifications are normally written by teams of people. If you can work within a group this would be preferable, but if you are reading this book on your own, the practice will still be useful.]

6

Evaluating, prototyping and piloting

1. Investigating usefulness and usability

In this chapter we move on to the next stage in the test design cycle. The test specifications and sample items are subjected to close scrutiny in the early stages of design. In fact, evaluation begins in the test specification design workshops; this shows that the 'stages' of test design, as portrayed in Figure 4.1, are much more fluid than a diagram can suggest. If an item or task survives this initial scrutiny, a small pool of items is created and taken forward to the next stage, which is called *prototyping*. It is at this point that the tasks are tried out with two or three small groups of learners to see how they react to them. If it appears that the responses of the learners are similar to those predicted by the test designers, more items are written to form a pool large enough to pilot. This usually involves giving a set of items to a much larger number of learners so that statistical information can be collected. If the items are embedded in a test form that is created using an assembly specification, the *piloting* is usually referred to as 'field testing'. If the tasks/items and the test assembly model appear to be working well after all these checks, it is possible to move towards making the test operational. This is the point at which everyone concerned with the test development has to make a critical 'go no-go' decision (Fulcher and Davidson, 2007: 89). If a 'go' decision is made, it is then possible to set up task/item shells so that large-scale production can begin. As items are produced they are subjected to another round of review before they are placed in the growing item pool. Once in the operational item pool, they can be used to create test forms.

This process may sound complex, but for high-stakes tests it is very important. The narrative of the process is part of the evidence that can be used to support claims of validity for score meaning. In classroom testing many of the steps may be missed out, although the first is probably the most valuable for teachers. We therefore turn first of all to the evaluation of sample items and test specifications as they begin to take shape in the specification workshop.

2. Evaluating items, tasks and specifications

Davidson and Lynch (2002: 98–120) discuss at some length the importance of reviewing test specifications and items in teams. They stress the importance of putting time aside for cohesive groups to really take items and specifications apart in critical discussions. The purpose is to ensure that only robust items emerge from the process, for which there is wide agreement that the item type will not only work, but that it will elicit a response that provides valuable information on the construct of interest. Initial evaluation is undertaken by the test developers themselves, usually with help from other applied linguists or teachers with a range of experience in teaching and assessing.

In order to illustrate this I am going to use an example from a real test specification workshop, conducted for Oxford University Press, similar to the one described in Fulcher and Davidson (2007: 316–317). The context is the development of a computer-delivered placement test. The project brought together more than twenty experienced teachers and item writers. The workshop was divided into a number of stages, as follows:

Stage 1   Groups of teachers are formed and engage in an ice-breaking activity.

Stage 2   Review test constructs and create task/item specifications with sample items.

Stage 3   Groups swap sample items but not specifications. Each group attempts to reverse engineer the sample item from the other group.

Stage 4   Groups are given the original task/item specification and asked to critique the sample item in preparation for giving feedback to the group that designed the item.

Stage 5   Plenary session in which each group receives feedback on specifications and items, then responds to the critique.

Two concepts are critical to this process. The first is *reverse engineering*, and the second is *item–spec congruence* (or item–spec fit). We have already encountered reverse engineering in previous chapters; as a group evaluation technique it is a very powerful tool. Although there are different types of reverse engineering (see Fulcher and Davidson, 2007: 57), the most common is critical reverse engineering, in which we take a sample item and analyse it to ask what it is testing, whether it is a useful item, and consider what problems we might face if we use the item. The outcome may be to revise an item, or to abandon it completely. Item–spec congruence is particularly relevant to Stage 4. Here, a group sees the original item specification and checks to see whether the item could reasonably have been generated from the specification, and whether they have been able to reverse engineer the general description. The group has to consider whether an item and its specification are both congruent and useful.

We will begin by considering Stage 2 briefly. The participants had been asked to consult a range of sources on listening and reading constructs. These sources included books and articles, models like those we have discussed in Chapter 5, including the CEFR and the Canadian Language Benchmarks. In Stage 2 the groups focused on which constructs would be most relevant for a placement test to be used in a language school that is following a particular syllabus with an associated set of materials. Many constructs were selected and agreed upon; one of these was 'ability to identify facts in short, clear, simple messages and announcements'. One of the groups was given the task of designing a listening item type to test this construct.

Here is the item that was produced by the design group. Remember that this item is to be presented on a computer, so answers require the manipulation of the mouse and keyboard.

Tapescript (from the teaching materials)

Woman:	Yes?
Man:	I'd like some information about the rock concert tonight.
Woman:	Certainly? How can I help?
Man:	Where is it on?
Woman:	At the Regent Theatre in Bank Street.
Man:	What time does it start?
Woman:	At seven-thirty.
Man:	And how much are the tickets?
Woman:	Well, the ten-euro tickets are all sold – the only ones we have left are fifteen euros.
Man:	That's fine – I'll have those.
Woman:	How many would you like?
Man:	Four, please.
Woman:	We have four in the front row or in the middle of the theatre.
Man:	I'll take the ones in the middle, please. The front row will be too close to the stage.

We would make this an answerphone message or recorded announcement covering the message.

Click on the word or number which is not correct on each line. Key in the correct information in 1 to 6 below. You will hear the recording twice. You can key in your answer at any time. Once you have heard the recording, you will have 60 seconds to fill in your answer.

City Ticket Agency

0	Event	Jazz concert
1	Place	Regent Cinema
2	Address	Bank Road
3	Time	8.30

Tickets bought

4	Price	10 euros
5	Number	5
6	Seat(s) row	front

0	rock
1	[_____]
2	[_____]

3 [   ]

4 [   ]

5 [   ]

6 [   ]

You have already been told what this item is supposed to test. Remember that the evaluation group only had access to the item and nothing else during Stage 3 of the workshop. Before we move on to discuss Stage 3, you may wish to spend some time writing your own critique of this sample item. You can then compare your own views with those of the group.

Rather than simply listing a set of questions or criticisms that came out of Stage 3, I am going to present the transcript of the discussion with annotations. The reason for this, following Davidson and Lynch (2002), is that item development and review must be seen as a collaborative group activity. Individuals do not always see problems with items or tests. The problems and solutions emerge in discussion and debate, and good specifications evolve in the process. The following transcript is not exact. I have not recorded all overlapping speech, or attempted to transcribe hesitations, false starts, and so on. At points the discussion drifted from topic, and I have removed those sections that were not directly relevant. Nevertheless, the transcript does accurately reflect what was said in the workshop. As you read through the transcript, consider what ideas are being generated, where agreement starts to form, and where disagreements remain. At various places there are observations within text boxes to bring out salient points.

For ease of reading, our four participants in the discussion are Angela, Bill, Carol and Dave, although these are not their real names. We join them in Stage 3, in which they have been asked to reverse engineer the specification for the task.

Angela: We would make this an answerphone recorded message covering the conversation the information

Bill: what's it say?

Carol: Oh they've taken that dialogue, that's interesting, isn't it?

Angela: we would make this an answerphone recorded message covering the information

Bill: okay, yeah

Angela: click on the word or number which is not correct

Bill: just one that's not correct

Angela: on each line

Bill: oh okay

Dave: hm hm and the lines are

Angela: Key in the correct information in one to six below

Dave: so we need an input box as well

Carol: alright then we need to see this really

Angela: click on the word or number which is not correct

Bill: okay so I think what you have to do is well that's quite compli-cated isn't it? I mean technically. But I imagine what you're doing is in each line you have to kind of like select a word that's not right so jazz is wrong it's rock and you have to select 'regent' and change it to 'odeon' or something. That's what it is isn't it?

Carol: key in the correct information in one to six so alright

Bill: so the next one is theatre not cinema

Carol: so you click on that and then put in what it should be here. You will hear the recording twice. You can key in your answer at any time. Once you have heard the recording you will have sixty seconds to fill in your answers. It's very complicated.

Bill: It's very complicated it's very complicated to achieve as well

Carol: why doesn't it it's more than yeah what it's doing is actually very simple isn't it? It's just correct the answers

Bill: yeah

Carol: what's the point of clicking on it and then typing the thing in why can't you just

Angela: well exactly it seems to be a very long-winded way of just selecting the answers

Carol: you've actually got to hear it without any prompt haven't you? So is it notes? Can I just have a look is it is it erm so presumably you get a few seconds to read it through the city ticket agency jazz concert I'd like some information about the rock concert tonight you select jazz

Bill: technically it's quite difficult isn't it because you've got to have selectable text and you've got to have

Carol: and something that you can key

Bill: key in boxes it's technically quite hard

Carol: hm it seems uneconomical

Bill: procedurally very tough yeah

Carol: for what you're getting out of it

Angela: so why don't you just give them two words and they click on the right one?

Carol: hmmm

Bill: yes exactly yes

Dave: so you've got rock jazz
            and you just click on one of these
Angela: just click on it yes

Looking at a dialogue of an item review is fascinating from many points of view. In the preceding section the lexical cohesion between turns and the ways in which members contribute to building consensus is particularly interesting. You may wish to mark the text to show how this happens; for example, by highlighting each use of the words 'complicated', 'complex', 'difficult', 'hard' and 'simple'. In the opening discussion the group has not attempted to identify the intended construct. Rather, they are clearly having difficulty understanding just what it is the test taker has to do in response to the item. In focusing on the response attribute they also become involved in the delivery specification. It seems to them that just producing this item in a computer environment is likely to be difficult. But the difficulty is not just in the technicalities, it is also in the 'procedure' that the test takers are being asked to follow, as Bill makes clear.

We rejoin the discussion, where it takes a very interesting turn.

Bill: because you wouldn't have to write it out you might
Angela: because you would have a difficulty here you've got the spelling
Dave: so do you
            think then they've made this a spelling test? If they're not giving you the
            answers written then it's also a spelling test
Angela: yes but it's also a hearing test
Dave: yes but it's also but they are giving you the answers
            I think they are giving you the answers down the bottom
Carol: are they
Dave: one two three
            four five six will have alternatives won't they
Bill: no they're writing boxes they're
            empty fields
Angela: you have sixty seconds to write in
Carol: where do so so you have to
            remember what they were I mean you can write this down or
Angela: it's very confusing
Carol: because you
            may know what's wrong but then you've got to remember what's right and
            then you put the answers in and you can put them in any time
Angela: shall we try it? I'll read it and
            you try doing it
Carol: yeah

Angela: first of all you have to identify I suppose you mark
                  on there
Carol: I suppose you identify it on the first
                  listening and answer on the second I think

> At this point Angela attempts to read out the prompt and the dialogue while the
> others attempt to answer the item. However, we note that in this short period of
> discussion Angela and Carol have raised two serious problems with the item as their
> understanding of it develops. The first is that by getting the students to type the
> correct response into a box the item may be testing spelling. This is a computer-
> based test, and the computer will score the answers. But the item is clearly a
> listening item – the group appears to agree on this even though it hasn't been
> explicitly stated. The second issue is more subtle. Carol has seen that typing in the
> correct answer can only occur after listening to the text all the way through. This
> means that the test takers must remember the correct answer for each incorrect
> word. The implication of this observation is that the item is likely to be sensitive to
> short-term memory capacity, and the test is not meant to be a memory test. The
> group has identified two potential threats to score meaning from construct irrelevant
> variance.
>
> We rejoin the conversation after the group has had the opportunity to do a 'try-out' of
> the item.

Carol: It's all very complicated
Angela: I think it's fine but I think it just needs simplifying
Bill: It's a
                  variation on a blank fill really isn't it
Angela: yes
Bill: where you've got to identify which
                  blanks which blanks to fill in
Dave: so general description this would be identifying
                  specific information or is there a special phrase or
Angela: listening for specific
                  information but it's correcting wrong information
Bill: yes correcting year or just correcting information
Carol: they're not even similar sounding words are they they're just totally differ-
                  ent things it's not like
Dave: but are we supposed to use this tapescript here?
Bill: yes but
Carol: I'd like some
                  information about the rock concert tonight
Angela: rock
Carol: jazz

Angela: so then you have to
          what do you do then?
Dave: well they say they're going to make it a monologue aren't they it's
          going to be an answerphone message okay so they take that information
          about the concert and say 'hi this is Bob. I wonder if you want to come to
          the jazz concert tonight it's at the Leicester Square cinema'
Carol: Hang on a minute it's an
          answerphone it's a recorded answerphone message isn't it
Angela: trouble is an illustrative item or task reflects the specification it's difficult to
          do a listening without the script isn't it
Bill: well we can imagine it's not hard to
          imagine from that 'yes hello this is the regent cinema tonight's concert is
          a rock concert which starts at eight fifteen and the tickets are eleven euros
          fifty the ten euro tickets are all sold'
Angela: So it's the ability to identify the wrong information and replace it with the
          correct information

In this section it is interesting to see that members of the group have made very
different assumptions about what the answerphone message is. Dave assumes that
it is an invitation left on the answerphone of the test taker, while Bill's explanation is
that it is a recorded message from the cinema. This appears to be ambiguous in the
sample item because the designers have presented a dialogue and not rendered it
in the genre required. Despite this serious problem, the group appear to agree about
what the item is designed to test. Bill's interpretation and the conclusion summarised
by Angela at the end of this section show that they have managed to discern the
intentions of the item designers.

The discussion drifts back to whether this item can really be called a 'gap fill' or a
'cloze', and they decide that it doesn't really fit into either category. We return to the
discussion as the group begins to look at the prompt attribute.

Angela: Where does that leave us then? Prompt attributes. So you need a recorded
          answering machine message of around you want a word limit
Dave: fifty words
          would be more than enough
Angela: in order to extract information thirty seconds
          is one hundred and ten words in listening
Dave: yes yes you're right
Angela: so one hundred and ten to one
          hundred and twenty or something it's difficult to get the exact number of
          words but you need a kind of parameter and that would be a short snippety
          listening
Bill: and then the
          students correct the notes

Angela:	no I think you need to say students read the text and then listen
Dave:	no they read the notes
Angela:	well notes yeah the information in the task they need a ten second period they read that and they
Carol:	listen
Angela:	to the recorded message presumably as many times as they like
Carol:	twice
Angela:	does it say twice?
Carol:	it says twice
Angela:	I mean is the first listening to do the task and the second listening to check what they've done or
Carol:	well surely the first one is to to identify the mistake and the second one to write the answer
Angela:	but don't you want to do that together
Carol:	they can do it any time can't they they can put it in any time
Angela:	you will hear the recording twice and key in the answer any time once you have heard the recording you will have sixty seconds
Carol:	that's very difficult because presumably you have time to identify and then write it in so you're going to have to remember what the answers are
Dave:	six lines six questions there's one question for each line so that makes it a bit easier so it's not just a completely random set of notes so you know that in each line there's one error that you have to correct
Carol:	these would be better off next to
Angela:	yeah they would I think it's a bit of a layout problem
Carol:	and you've only got two words to choose from haven't you?
Dave:	yeah you have
Carol:	which word is wrong what should it have been and that's it
Bill:	once you get to the second part the first part ceases to be of any relevance
Dave:	does clicking on the incorrect word have any purpose?
Carol:	that's what I'm wondering was it just for them to be able to remember what it was
Bill:	it would make more sense to provide a task with the word underlined so they could listen for what the correct word is

The first thing the group notices is the length of the listening text. We don't expect to see this information in a sample item, and for the moment they don't have the specification in front of them. However, this is flagged up as something they would expect to see. The second issue is much more problematic at this stage. Carol had raised the problem before, but here it is picked up. Precisely what do the test takers do during the first and the second hearing of the text? This is not at all clear from the sample item. Three potential options appear: the second listening can be for writing in the answer, for checking the answer after it has been written in, or checking understanding of the passage before the answer is written in during the allotted sixty seconds. Carol again raises the problem of memory if this third option is intended.

The other issue raised concerns the presentation specification. Why aren't the text boxes into which the answer is typed next to the identification questions? Why are they kept apart? This isn't followed through, because of Bill's devastating observation: 'once you get to the second part the first part ceases to be of any relevance'. For a test taker to have any chance of answering the second part correctly, they must have answered the first part correctly. This takes us back to Carol's question: is the purpose of the first part just to get the test takers to notice and remember, so that they can complete the second part? If so, the first part should not be scored. At this point it appears that the rationale for the item is beginning to unravel.

It was at this point that the group was given a short break. They were then given the specification for the sample item. The specification was written using a Popham-style template, which we reproduce here.

Title of Specification
Listening Correction Task

General Description
Integrated listening/reading/skimming item. Ability to listen for specific information. Listening to a recorded announcement and following a written text to identify and correct differences between the two.

Prompt Attributes
Tutorial/example given. Recorded messages or announcements giving information about times, places, number, events, prices, telephone numbers, etc. Students read/ follow a text and listen to an automated message giving information. On each line there is a mistake. Students click on the mistake and then key in the correct wording in the numbered space beneath the text, as in the example. There are 6 mistakes, as in the sample item. There are 6 mistakes, 3 of which must be numbers and 3 of which must not. Level can be variable, and could also depend on speed of delivery.

Response Attributes
The student listens and follows the text and clicks on each mistake and attempts to key in the correct word/number. Students hear the recording twice and have one minute to fill in their answers once the recording is over.

Specification Supplement
The sample item is set at an intermediate level.
Key is the main problem and multiple key is necessary. Scoring would have to allow
for a given number of misspellings. Numbers can be written as digits or in full.

We now move into Stage 4, in which the Group has to produce a final critique of the sample item and its specification in preparation for the feedback session. Before you read the Stage 4 discussion you may wish to go over the specification a number of times and write down your own critique. (In the following section note that the term 'rubric' is used with its UK meaning of 'instructions'.)

Carol: It says variable levels
Angela: I don't know whether this is worth testing at higher
          levels
Carol: there's only three though isn't there
Dave: they want half as numbers and that
          seems quite a lot
Carol: it does say this would be variable maybe the items would
          be variable
Dave: no the level would be variable
Angela: yes that's how I took it to mean. I would say
          at the higher levels no more than one number
Bill: I would say don't specify
Angela: Okay well
          that's the description
Dave: well that's more or less what we said but there's more

[At this point Carol reads out the entire specification to the group]

Dave: I can't see the benefit of hm the errors in the notes why don't they just have
          blanks
Angela: yes I agree with that
Bill: yes
Dave: well they obviously have to come up with a
          different task but I can't see that the inclusion of errors makes it any
Bill: I think any
          kind of task should be one stage once you have to start doing two stages
          with a task the rubric becomes too complicated that's the thing if you have
          two stages to do this and then do that the rubrics get really complicated
Angela: and we don't want to test their typing
          skills and we don't want to test the speed with which they can key in
          another answer while they're listening to something else

Carol: it also says here which
is interesting the key is the main problem and multiple key is necessary

Bill: well because of spelling
mistakes

Angela: and as scoring would have to have a given number of spellings one
must be written in digits or not. It's too complex unless we just give them
alternatives

Bill: yes
I think that would work as a multiple you know just rock classical folk and
they just have to click A you know

Angela: any item what they have to key in
themselves is problematic because it means you can only test very simple
items because of the constraints of spelling

Carol: yes how do you say one is close
enough in spelling and one isn't

Angela: but the trouble is once you've got the distractors into a sentence
often you can identify what is wrong without actually listening because
some of them aren't options. The distraction comes from somewhere else
I mean that's where true distraction is quite interesting the true distraction
will be well 'I'll see you at six o'clock oh gosh i can't see you at six'

Bill: we'll make it half an hour later

Angela: and it's feasible
distraction so that's not going to happen with an answering machine
message you're not going to get any distraction there because it's purely
factual

Dave: as an item writer I can't
work with this

Bill: it's all too complicated

Angela: and I don't know how this will work
with upper levels

Dave: well if it were a stock market crisis or something

Angela: but would
that work because it's a specialist field

Bill: it could be anything statistical

Angela: okay maybe
you're right

Dave: Our real problem is with clicking on the errors. It's a dual stage task

Bill: yes a dual
stage task

Dave: and clicking on errors hasn't got much of a point. And we've got
problems with spelling.

This final section acts as a summary of the problems the group has identified with the item. There is some disagreement over whether the item difficulty (level) can be varied without moving into domains where background knowledge is going to be needed to comprehend the listening text. However, they are agreed that having two steps in the response attribute is a major flaw in the item design. The problem with testing spelling is raised once more, but this time more attention is paid to the problem of producing a workable scoring key that would have to list all acceptable variants of every target word or number. Producing such a key would be a major undertaking, and there is no guarantee all acceptable alternatives would be included. Clicking on the errors is again raised as a problem because it is unnecessary.

The solution the group comes up with is to abandon the item type completely and turn it into a multiple-choice item because it would be much easier to construct, and less complex. However, there is one final blow: the type of listening text envisaged in the specification would not lend itself to the generation of distractors.

In this detailed look at the evaluation of a single item, we can see how groups can work collaboratively to tease out problems that the design group had not thought through, even though they were vaguely aware of some of them, such as creating the scoring key, which is part of the evidence specification. Indeed, the problem with scoring is not only the creation of the key, but whether scoring the first part of the two-stage task should be included given the fact that it is 'irrelevant' once a test taker has reached the second stage.

The group has identified layers of complexity, in processing information, following instructions, layout and selecting appropriate content. It is not surprising that in Stage 5 the feedback included a recommendation that this item type was abandoned because they did not see any way of fixing the problems identified. The design group accepted this critique with grace.

What we must recognise is that the design group had attempted to create a novel item type to gather evidence about the construct they had identified as being relevant to the testing context. This kind of creativity is very important in the early stages of developing a new test, but we should not underestimate the difficulties of getting a new idea from inspiration to operational item. The evaluation group, on the other hand, has moved from creativity to wondering whether it would be best to operationalise this construct as a multiple-choice item. Nothing could be less creative than this option. But we must also recognise that there is a reason for this. Fulcher and Davidson (2007: 56–57) suggest that as teachers and language testers we carry 'archetypes' of tasks and items in our heads. When we are asked to design a new test, what we normally do is reproduce an archetype, which is a kind of unwritten specification. This is precisely what the evaluation group has done. Nor is the choice of archetype surprising. The multiple-choice item has a long history, as we have already seen in this book; and we know that the reason for its long history is that we know how it works, we know how to construct them well, we can score them easily, and we know how to build *norm-referenced* tests by manipulating the properties of the items. The multiple-choice item is therefore the ultimate archetype, against which all newcomers are but upstart challengers.

Awareness of the forces working against creativity is therefore essential if we are to encourage it during the early development stages. Inevitably, creativity requires more time, more thought, and much more debate.

▶ 3. Guidelines for multiple-choice items

Multiple-choice items are popular because new item types are difficult to design and bring through initial evaluation. They have been used for so long that we can provide general guidelines for how to write 'good' items. These guidelines are reproduced in many books on testing (Haladyna, Downing and Rodriguez, 2002), and examples of the kinds of multiple-choice items we can write are provided in books on testing particular skills or knowledge, such as grammar (Purpura, 2004: 129).

Multiple-choice items are made up of a stem, which provides the prompt. This is followed by options (usually four). One of these options is the key, which is the correct answer. The other three options are distractors, or incorrect responses.

Most guidelines contain the following advice:

- The stem should contain all the information necessary to select the key, but should not contain unnecessary material.
- The stem should not contain vocabulary that is unknown to the test takers, unless it is a vocabulary item.
- Avoid giving clues to the key in the stem (e.g. by using words from the key, or writing distractors that are not grammatically consistent with the stem).
- Each multiple-choice item should test only one construct (e.g. if it is a vocabulary item, it should not also test grammar, and so on).
- The key to any item should not give a clue about the key to another item. This often happens in reading tests where multiple items are based on the same text.
- Ensure that the key cannot be selected without reading the stem, or any other textual material upon which the item is based.
- Avoid trick items. These usually include ambiguous content, too much information in the stem, and too little difference between some of the options with the possibility of more than one correct answer. While trick items may distract some students, others could get the item correct just by using a test-taking strategy.
- Avoid negatives such as 'not' and 'except' if at all possible, as such questions increase cognitive processing and make the item more difficult.
- Make sure that only one option can reasonably be keyed.
- Randomise the location of the key. If you don't, you will find that (on average) option (C) will tend to be the key more often than other options.
- Options should be similar in structure and (most importantly) length. If all else fails in a multiple-choice test, students will select the longest option.
- Avoid options that use 'all of the above' or 'none of the above'.

- Avoid using qualifiers such as 'always' or 'never', which are less likely to be in the key than qualifiers like 'sometimes' or 'probably'.

Finally, always proofread items very carefully. If a spelling mistake creeps into a multiple-choice item, it will almost always find its way into a distractor.

When multiple-choice items have been piloted (see the discussion below), it is essential to carry out *distractor analysis*. This involves counting how many test takers selected each distractor to discover which are not working as intended. Consider the following item:

In the last paragraph the author introduces the topic of how to analyse a(n)

(a) assessment
(b) distractor*
(c) test
(d) none of the above

After the pilot we can assemble the responses as shown in Table 6.1. We take the top one third of test takers, the middle one third, and the bottom one third, and record the number in each group who selected each option.

	(a)	(b)	(c)	(d)
Top group	0	10	0	0
Middle group	0	9	1	0
Bottom group	0	9	1	0
Totals	0	28	2	0

Table 6.1 Distractor analysis

We can see that options (a) and (d) are not distracting, and that (c) is only distracting a small number of test takers. The options would need a radical rewrite or, perhaps more likely, the item would be discarded. Of course, as this item is designed to be awful we hope it would never have been placed in a pilot test to begin with.

 # 4. Prototyping

If items survive the design and review process, they are taken on to the next stage, which is prototyping. The concept of prototyping is taken from engineering. A prototype is a mould, or pre-production model, which can be used to test out ideas for making new products without the necessity to tool machines on production lines. If new products were taken straight from the drawing board (the specifications) to mass production, there is every chance that some of the parts might not fit together, perform as well as expected during the design phase, or even work at all. Making mistakes like these is very expensive if the machines and production lines have to be redesigned every time a fault is found. Specialist prototyping engineering companies have grown up that make the prototypes of parts or entire machines that can be tested before production starts. These prototypes are 'mock-ups' or 'models' (in the sense of model car or model aircraft). In testing, the prototypes are the first half a dozen or so tasks that are produced to a specification in addition to the sample item.

When the prototypes are ready, they are usually subjected to two types of trials. In alpha prototyping, subject experts are asked to comment on the items and the specifications to see whether they believe the content and format are relevant and useful. This is not very different from the original review process during a specification design workshop, but uses people who were not involved in the initial item design and evaluation. Alpha prototyping often throws up a number of issues that can only been seen by people coming to the items completely fresh, with no background in the complex discussions that have gone before. In beta prototyping the items are used for the first time with small groups of learners.

Beta prototyping is particularly important. It allows the test designers to check out a number of assumptions that they have made in the specifications. Perhaps the most important is whether the response attributes are accurate: whether the test takers actually respond in the way anticipated. However, the first thing is to identify five or six people to do the tasks. This small sample should be drawn from the intended test-taking population at large. No more than this number is needed in the first instance.

As an example we will consider the task designed by Mills (2009) from Chapter 5, as the specification has already been presented and discussed. Mills prototyped the task designed to her specifications with students in the tourism classes at her institution. As students took the tasks their performances were recorded for later analysis. In this example we see the interaction between Students 7 and 8 (S7 and S8):

```
 1. S8:   I need a ticket to.. osaka japan>
 2. S7:                                    <7> er....we..we have
 3.        three flights to osaka weekly ....monday::/ thursday::/ and
 4.        friday::\....the flight on monday:/ and friday:/ are direct\
 5.        and..the one..on....thursday:/.... has a stopover in
 6.        hong kong/\..when were you thinking of flying to osaka:>/ =
 7. S8:   =....er <4> [p] sorry..can you/....can you repeat that please/ =
 8. S7:   = <3>thursday::/ }
 9. S8:              { [p] thursday:\ }
10. S7:                      { thursday:/ <4> on thursday:/..
11.        <has a stopover in hongkong>/\
12. S8:                      [p] ah yes <5> I would
13.        prefer/....[p] thursday:\ =
14. S7:                      = [p] thursday:\ <4> er <5> will this be
15.        round trip or one way/ =
16. S8:                      = round trip <3> round trip
17.        returning....following – ..monday\=
18. S7:                              = er..how would you like to
```

19.	fly/ economy:/ busine:ss/ or first class/ =
20. S8:	= business class
21.	please – =
22. S7:	= <3> and..will anyone be traveling with you/ =
23. S8:	= <5> no..I'm traveling alone\ =
24. S7:	= <3> er <3> OK then\ ….
25.	<please give me a minute while I check price and availability>
26.	<17> the flight/..the flight/..departs at/..nine/ [<forty am\>
27.	<and arrives in osaka:>/ <3> osaka:/..at.. < five thirty
28.	pm>\….local time\….the price/ ..i:s/ one thousand/\ ..four
29.	hundred/\..twenty:/ dollars\ <4> <shall I book it for you>/ =
30. S8:	= ….not yet\ ..I'll get back to you\ <thank you very much for
31.	your help\>

Mills argues that in this example the two candidates are capable of co-constructing a dialogue in which the customer acquires the information needed, and shows an ability to ask for clarification when this is necessary. The student playing the role of the travel agent is capable of giving the correct information and doing this with an acceptable degree of politeness. Learners who performed less well were either not able to read the flight schedules, or were unable to seek clarification and therefore proceeded with the task without getting the information needed to meet the task completion criteria. Six samples were collected during prototyping. It was discovered that the task encouraged active participation; all tasks elicited the functions of requesting and giving information; each task could be completed within three minutes; the function of requesting clarification was sometimes evident, and all participants attempted to negotiate meaning.

However, there were problems with the prototypes in relation to the primary construct of interactional competence. We saw in Chapter 4 that defining interactional competence has been problematic. We can now outline another reason why it is so problematic, and use Mills' data to understand it. There has been an assumption in language testing going back to the work of van Lier (1989) that oral proficiency interviews are inferior language tasks because of the power difference between the examiner/interlocutor and the test taker. This view takes casual conversation as the norm in human communication, where two (or more) individuals with equal status engage in a 'natural' conversation. It makes 'informal, natural conversation' the gold standard of spoken communication, which should be replicated in tests. But why should this be the case? Arguably, in most situations in life, communication is not so equally balanced. In schools, colleges and universities, it is rarely the case that any two participants in an interaction are of equal status. Similarly, in all service encounters it is the customer who has the right to interrupt, challenge or bring the conversation to an end. Impoliteness on the part of the service provider is never a communicative option. What happens when a test includes a task that has a power differential, but one of the scoring criteria is interactional competence?

Mills discovered that on average the learner playing the customer spoke around 37 words, and the function most often used is giving information. The learner playing the travel agent uses 106 words on average, and has the opportunity to both ask for and give information. The travel agent role also requires using language marked for politeness. In other words, the two roles require very different speaking styles. It would therefore seem important that each participant should have the opportunity to take on each of the two roles. In other words, what Mills has discovered is that it makes a great difference to the test taker which role they are allocated in the task. This does not mean that the task cannot be used; only that there are problems with the distribution of roles that would need to be addressed before it could be used operationally.

The discourse approach to prototyping is very productive and can also be used with testing writing. For example, Cumming *et al.* (2006) were interested in discovering whether the writing elicited by tasks that were preceded by listening or reading and required a reaction to those texts (*integrated tasks*) was different from stand-alone tasks (*independent tasks*). They collected a corpus of more than 200 essays and analysed discourse features that occurred in the independent tasks, and those in the prototype integrated items. These features included text length, lexical sophistication, syntactic complexity, and quality of argument. They also looked at the ways in which test takers used the input material in the integrated tasks. They discovered that in the integrated tasks test takers wrote less, but used a wider range of vocabulary and produced longer clauses. However, the essays did not contain a strong argument structure; rather, they contained more paraphrase and summary of the input material with a reaction. This evidence was used to take forward the prototype items that are now used in live tests. It was argued that the integrated items:

> require complex cognitive, literature, and language abilities for comprehension as well as for producing written compositions that display appropriate and meaningful uses of and orientations to source evidence, both conceptually (in terms of apprehending, synthesizing, and presenting source ideas) and textually (in terms of stylistic conventions for presenting, citing and acknowledging sources).
> (Cumming et al., 2006: 46)

For a language test that is designed to predict the ability to use language in an academic setting, it seems reasonable to test the ability to use source material (both listening and reading) in this way. University students never write assignments without first reading widely and being asked to use sources critically.

Another important tool in prototyping is the verbal (or 'think aloud') protocol. This is a special technique where a test taker is asked to talk while they are doing a particular task. In prototyping the test taker is normally asked to verbalise how they arrive at the answer. In speaking and listening tasks the verbal protocol is retrospective, or after the event, as the test taker can't actually talk while doing the task. With all other test tasks the verbal protocol can be collected simultaneously. The verbal protocol is recorded and transcribed for analysis. The underlying assumption of verbal protocol analysis is that it 'is based on the assertion that an individual's verbalisations may be seen to be an accurate record of information that is (or has been) attended to as a particular task is (or has been) carried out' (Green, 1998: 2–3). From the protocol, the item developer makes inferences about the cognitive processes or other strategies the test taker uses to respond to the task. In other words, it is another way of attempting to discover if the processes being used by the test taker are identical, or similar, to those the test designer intended to engage. For the most part, learners solve problems without verbalising the steps they go through (Gass and Mackey, 2000: 23), and so it is important that in verbal protocol studies learners are given opportunities to practise verbalising with simple tasks before they undertake more complex verbalisations. Green (1998: 46–47) provides an example in which students were asked to verbalise the steps in answering a simple maths problem – multiplying 16 by 25.

> *Protocol: Well, if I set it out as a sum, I can see that six twenty-fives are one hundred and fifty. That leaves one to multiply by twenty-five and add a zero, so that's two hundred and fifty. Two hundred and fifty plus one hundred and fifty gives me four hundred. That's the answer.*

In the following much more complex example from Norris (1998: 8–9), the test taker is given a short text, and asked which of three statements is true beyond reasonable doubt. The item is designed to test critical thinking skills in reading.

> *Text*
> *Pat had poor posture, had very few friends, was ill at ease in company, and in general was very unhappy. Then a close friend recommended that Pat visit Dr Baldwin, a reputed expert on helping people improve their personalities. Pat took his recommendation and, after three months of treatment by Dr Baldwin, developed more friendships, was more at ease, and in general felt happier.*
>
> 1. *Without Dr Baldwin's treatment, Pat would not have improved.*
> 2. *Improvements in Pat's life occurred after Dr Baldwin's treatment started.**
> 3. *Without a friend's advice, Pat would not have heard of Dr Baldwin.*

The keyed (correct) option for the item writer was option 2, the important clue being in the phrase 'after three months'. Options 1 and 3 were the distractors. It is assumed that Pat could have improved even if she had not been treated, and it is also conceivable that she would have heard of Dr Baldwin even if she had not talked to her friend.

When this item was used in a verbal protocol study some test takers selected option 1 as correct. Here is a sample protocol:

> *The statement is ambiguous between 'would not have improved ever' or 'would not have improved during the three month period'. It is obvious that there is insufficient information to say beyond reasonable doubt that Pat would never have improved without the help of Dr Baldwin, so the statement must mean 'would not have improved during the three month period'. But is it beyond reasonable doubt that she would not have improved during this three-month period had she not received Dr*

Baldwin's treatment? Well, from the description, I assume that Pat had been suffering in this way for a long time. Problems such as this typically do not occur overnight, nor go away quickly by themselves without professional help. I therefore assume that Pat's problem was not one that would have gone away quickly on its own. Given these assumptions, the most plausible explanation of Pat's improved condition is that it was brought about by the treatment and therefore, while I cannot be certain, it seems beyond reasonable doubt that without Dr Baldwin's treatment there would not have been such an improvement during the three months.

What has happened in this example is that the test taker has made a set of assumptions about the context and Pat's condition that are different from the assumptions made by the item writer. The different assumptions lead to a correct inference, but one that is incorrect on the basis of the item writer's assumptions. This shows very starkly that individuals bring their own interpretative baggage to each test item; this will inform their reasoning processes, and can lead to incorrect answers for reasonable reasons. This is particularly the case when we attempt to measure any construct that is related to 'comprehension'. Take this example from Buck (1991), in which he administered a prototype listening comprehension to a group of six female Japanese learners of English, and collected verbal protocols after they had completed the items. The items were all open-ended questions that required a constructed response. The listening text was a short narrative, the beginning of which is reproduced here:

Text
My friend Susan was living in West Africa and while she was living there she had a problem with burglars. For a period of about two months every Sunday night someone was breaking into her house through her bedroom window and was stealing something very small from her house and she tried many things to prevent this from happening like putting bars over the windows and hiring a guard to watch the window. And still, every Sunday night, somehow someone came through the window and stole something …

Question:
What did Susan do about the problem?

One of the learners answered this question as follows: 'she employed a guardman and jammed the window closed with a bar.' If this question had been allocated two marks, one for the guard and one for placing bars on the window, the test taker would receive only one mark. However, in the protocol analysis Buck (1991: 74–75) discovered that the learner was unable to imagine bars over windows; in Japan she thought of all windows as sliding, and could therefore only imagine the possibility that Susan had used a piece of wood to somehow stop the window from being slid open.

In this case, using protocol analysis in prototyping has brought to light a cultural problem with the kind of texts selected. Language teachers and testers are very aware of potential cultural problems in the use of reading and listening materials, and it may very well be that specification supplements in item specifications need to highlight particular problems that may arise with identifiable subgroups of test takers to avoid the inclusion of culturally unfamiliar material. Buck's study shows just how difficult this is in practice. We come back to this issue when we discuss operational item review below.

Other problems with tasks have been brought to light through this technique. Johnstone *et al.* (2008), for example, have successfully used it to identify tasks in which the content is too difficult for the test takers, where the instructions are ambiguous or confusing, or where test takers universally misunderstood what they had to do.

Prototyping can lead to item types being discarded before they are put into production for large-scale testing, or used for classroom assessment. Most often, however, prototyping leads to a careful reworking of the specifications. Perhaps we discover that the item is sensitive to a cognitive strategy that is highly relevant to our criterion domain, but which we had not considered. In this situation, prototyping has helped to make our construct definition and the score meaning much richer. We would adjust the specifications accordingly. Alternatively, we may learn that most learners respond in ways that are different from those intended, but the item can be redesigned and taken to a second round of prototyping. In this way items and specifications evolve until we believe they are capable of providing the type of information we need for the test. The items and tasks that survive and exit prototyping are taken to the next stage, which is piloting.

5. Piloting

Piloting refers to the process of trialling items with a larger group of people than would normally be used in prototyping. When small numbers of test takers are used, it is only possible to collect qualitative data. As valuable as this is for investigating the validity of the items, we also need to collect quantitative data. Statistical evidence is important to show that the items are being produced at the appropriate level of difficulty for the intended test-taking population. In standardised tests we need to know that they are discriminating well, and that batteries of items in sub-tests are reliable. If the items are closed response, particularly multiple choice, it is also necessary to ensure that the distractors are working as intended in the specifications.

When items are piloted it is not necessary that the test takers are presented with a complete test. In piloting it is only essential that sub-tests are used that generally resemble what we think will probably be used in the final test; this may be just the reading section, for example. These sub-tests are any groups of items for which a sub-score will be reported, and for which separate reliability statistics will be calculated because together, we hypothesise that they are measuring the same construct.

The sample size for a pilot test does not have to be very large. For classroom assessments relatively small numbers can be used, as the kinds of statistical analysis that teachers would wish to carry out are those for criterion-referenced assessments described in Chapter 3. However, wherever possible, a sample size of 30 or greater is recommended. The reason for this is simple. Statisticians have discovered that at this number a distribution is most likely to approximate a curve of normal distribution (Lawn and Arbamowitz, 2008: 262). Hopefully, you will have discovered the same thing for yourself when you did Activity 2.2.

In addition to calculating descriptive statistics and a *reliability* coefficient (see Chapter 2), the most important part of piloting is item analysis. This has changed little since Lado (1961) outlined the procedures in the first book on language testing. We will look at the procedures using multiple-choice items as an example, as classical item analysis was designed for multiple choice. However, these techniques can be used with other *dichotomous item* types quite easily.

In order to illustrate item analysis, I am going to use a multiple-choice cloze taken from the Chinese College Entrance Test (2005).

Directions: There are 20 blanks in the following passage. For each blank there are four choices marked on the right side of the paper. You should choose ONE that best fits into the passage. Then mark the corresponding letter on Answer Sheet 2 with a single line through the centre.

Wise buying is a positive way in which you can make your money go further. The [67] you go about purchasing an article or a service can actually [68] you money or can add [69] the cost.

Take the [70] example of a hairdryer. If you are buying a hairdryer, you might [71] that you are making the [72] buy if you choose one [73] look you like and which is also the cheapest [74] price. But when you get it home you may find that it [75] twice as long as a more expensive [76] to dry your hair. The cost of the electricity plus the cost of your time could well [77] your hairdryer the most expensive one of all.

So what principles should you [78] when you go out shopping? If you [79] your home, your car or any valuable [80] in excellent condition, you'll be saving money in the long [81]. Before you buy a new [82], talk to someone who owns one. If you can, use it or borrow it to check it suits your particular [83]. Before you buy an expensive [84], or a service, do check the price and [85] is on offer. If possible, choose [86] three items or three estimates.

67. A. form B. fashion C. way D. method
68. A. save B. preserve C. raise D. retain
69. A. up B. to C. in D. on
70. A. easy B. single C. simple D. similar
71. A. convince B. accept C. examine D. think
72. A. proper B. best C. reasonable D. most
73. A. its B. which B. whose D. what

74. A. for B. with C. in D. on
75. A. spends B. takes C. lasts D. consumes
76. A. mode B. copy C. sample D. model
77. A. cause B. make C. leave D. bring
78. A. adopt B. lay C. stick D. adapt
79. A. reserve B. decorate C. store D. keep
80. A. products B. possession C. material D. ownership
81. A. run B. interval C. period D. time
82. A. appliance B. machinery C. utility D. facility
83. A. function B. purpose C. target D. task
84. A. component B. element C. item D. particle
85. A. what B. which C. that D. this
86. A. of B. in C. by D. from

As this is for illustrative purposes, I gave the items to just fifteen learners. When the test had been scored, I produced the following table of results. You will notice that in the left-hand column I have placed the learners in order, from the highest scoring at the top, to the lowest scoring at the bottom. I have also grouped the learners into three groups: high, middle and low scorers, by shading three parts of the table. Along the top of the table I list the items. I have only included the first eight, so that the table is easily readable. You will have to imagine the columns for the remainder of the items, so that if the responses to those questions were added to items 67–74 we would have the total score for each student in the final column. In each cell of the table we find the option which the learner selected, followed by a code for correct (1) or incorrect (0).

Student	Item 67	Item 68	Item 69	Item 70	Item 71	Item 72	Item 73	Item 74	Total
1	C1	A1	B1	C1	D1	B1	B0	B1	19
2	C1	A1	B1	C1	D1	B1	B0	B1	17
3	C1	A1	A0	C1	D1	B1	B0	B1	16
4	C1	B0	B1	A0	D1	B1	B0	B1	15
5	C1	A1	B1	C1	D1	B1	B0	B1	15
6	C1	A1	B1	D0	D1	B1	B0	C0	14
7	C1	A1	A0	C1	D1	B1	B0	A0	14
8	C1	B0	D0	C1	D1	B1	A0	C0	12
9	C1	A1	A1	D0	D1	A0	B0	C0	12
10	C1	A1	A1	C1	D1	B1	D0	A0	12
11	C1	C0	C0	A0	D1	B1	C1	C0	10
12	C1	B0	A1	A0	D1	A0	C1	A0	9
13	B0	D0	B0	D0	D1	B1	C1	C0	9
14	D0	A1	D0	A0	D1	B1	A0	C0	8
15	C1	C0	D0	A0	D1	B1	C1	A0	7

Student	Item 67	Item 68	Item 69	Item 70	Item 71	Item 72	Item 73	Item 74	Total
FI	.87	.60	.53	.47	1.0	.87	.27	.33	
FI Top	1.0	.80	.80	.80	1.0	1.0	0.0	1.0	
FI Bottom	.60	.20	.20	.00	1.0	0.8	0.8	0.0	
DI	.40	.40	.60	.80	.00	0.2	−0.8	1.0	

Table 6.2 Responses of 30 students to items 67–74

The first statistic that we calculate is the facility index, or item difficulty. This is the proportion of the test takers who answered an item correctly, and is shown in the row marked 'FI'. To calculate this we simply add up the number of correct responses for an item and divide by the number of test takers. For item 67 we can see that thirteen test takers have answered the item correctly, and 13/15 = .87. Normally in a test we wish to see many item difficulties of around .5. Items 69 and 70 come closest to this ideal. Why .5? When an item is of average difficulty for the test-taking population, it provides more information about their abilities on the construct. The variance of an item (the item variability) is expressed as:

$$S^2 = pq$$

S^2 is the variance, p is the proportion correct (the facility index) and q is the proportion incorrect. If the facility index is .5, then p = .5 and q = .5. By multiplying these we get .5 × .5 = .25, and .25 is the maximum amount of variance that an item can have. Therefore, items with these properties contribute more variance and hence information to the test. If we take item 69, its variance is: .53 × .47 = .249 (or almost .25). Item 1, which is fairly easy, is .87 × .13 = .11. Item 71, which everyone got correct, is .1 × .0 = 0. That is, it contains no variance at all, and therefore provides no useful information.

Of course, we never have a test populated only from items with a facility index of .5. All tests have a range of items, and the general rule of thumb is that items within a range of .3 to .7 should be included. Even some easier items may be retained. If the items are not linked to a text, the easier items are usually placed at the beginning in order to encourage test takers at the start of the test. If we look at the FI row for our test we appear to have a good spread, with the exception of Item 71. On a *criterion-referenced test* this would not matter, but on a norm-referenced test the item would normally be deleted.

The next statistic in which we are interested is the *discrimination index*. This tells us how well an item discriminates between those who score higher on the test, and those who score lower. In Table 6.2 this figure is found in the final row marked 'DI'. First, we have to calculate the facility index for the top group of students – in this case the five students in the unshaded area of the table. Next, we calculate the facility index for the lower group of students – those in the more heavily shaded bottom section of the table. We record these as 'FI Top' and 'FI Bottom' respectively. The calculation for the DI is FI

Top – FI Bottom. For item 67, 1.0 – .60 = .4. Ideally, we wish to retain items that have a DI of .3 and higher.

We will consider four items from our test. Item 74 has a DI of 1. This means that all the high scorers get this item correct, while all the low scorers get it wrong. It therefore discriminates perfectly between the two groups. Item 71 was answered correctly by everyone. We have already seen that it carries no information, and so it is not surprising that it does not discriminate at all. The DI is 0. Item 72 has a DI of .2, which is very low. We can soon see the reason. Only one student in the lower group answered this item incorrectly. It is both too easy, and does not discriminate well. This item is a candidate for rewriting or deleting. Finally, we consider item 73. This has a DI of –.8, something that test designers never wish to see. A minus sign indicates that the item is discriminating, but it is discriminating in the wrong direction. We can see that four of the five students in the lower group have answered the item correctly, whereas all of the better students have answered the item incorrectly. They have all been distracted by B. When this happens it is always difficult to know precisely why it is happening, and perhaps the only way to find out is to conduct a verbal protocol study. However, items with negative discrimination are almost always discarded.

Another useful measure of discrimination is the *point biserial correlation*. Correlation was explained in Chapter 2, as the relationship between two continuous variables. The point biserial correlation is also a measure of the relationship between two variables, but in this case one is continuous (the test score – here potentially ranging from 0 to 20), and the other is dichotomous (each item is correct, or incorrect, 1 or 0). The point biserial correlation therefore tells us what the relationship is between the overall test score and the response to each individual item. The larger the correlation, the greater the association between the two, thus making the point biserial a measure of discrimination.

The formula for the point biserial correlation is as follows:

$$R_{pbi} = \frac{\bar{X}p - \bar{X}q}{SD} \sqrt{pq}$$

where

R_{pb} is the point biserial correlation
$\bar{X}p$ is the mean total score for the test takers who answer the item correctly
$\bar{X}q$ is the mean total score for the test takers who answer the item incorrectly
SD   is the standard deviation of the total test score
p   is the proportion of test takers who answer the item correctly (FI)
q   is the proportion of test takers who answer the item incorrectly

We can calculate the standard deviation from the total scores in Table 6.2 using the formula in Chapter 2. This is presented in Table 6.3.

Scores	$\bar{X}$	$X - \bar{X}$	$(X - \bar{X})^2$
19	12.6	6.4	40.96
17	12.6	4.4	19.36
16	12.6	3.4	11.56
15	12.6	2.4	5.76
15	12.6	2.4	5.76
14	12.6	1.4	1.96
14	12.6	1.4	1.96
12	12.6	–0.6	0.36
12	12.6	–0.6	0.36
12	12.6	–0.6	0.36
10	12.6	–2.6	6.76
9	12.6	–3.6	12.96
9	12.6	–3.6	12.96
8	12.6	–4.6	21.16
7	12.6	–5.6	31.36
$\Sigma = 189$		$\Sigma = 0$	$\Sigma = 173.6$
$\bar{X} = 12.6$			SD = 3.52
N = 15			

Table 6.3 Standard deviation

We will now calculate the point biserial correlation for item 70, which is statistically one of the best from our set of items. This is done in Table 6.4 and the following calculation.

$\bar{X}p$	$\bar{X}q$
19	15
17	14
16	12
15	10
14	9
12	9
12	8
	7
$\Sigma = 105$	$\Sigma = 84$
N = 7	N = 8
$\bar{X}p = 15.00$	$\bar{X}q = 10.5$

Table 6.4 Means for p and q for item 70

We know from Table 6.2 that the proportion correct is .47, and so the proportion incorrect is $1 - .47$, or .53. We now have all the numbers we need to calculate the point biserial correlation for item 70:

$$R_{pbi} = \frac{15.0 - 10.5}{3.52} \sqrt{.47 * .53}$$

$$R_{pbi} = \frac{4.50}{3.52} \sqrt{.25}$$

$$R_{pbi} = 1.28 * .5 = .64$$

The general guidelines for interpreting a point biserial correlation is that any value above .25 is acceptable. In this case, it is not surprising to discover that item is performing exceptionally well.

6. Field testing

In large-scale language testing it is useful to draw a distinction between piloting and field testing. Generally speaking, a field test is a large-scale trial of a complete test once decisions have been made about the assembly model, including the number of sub-tests and the number of items for each sub-test. The sample sizes are much larger for a field test, so that the sample reflects the test-taking population in general. A field test provides an opportunity to obtain more stable estimates of item statistics, but it also allows more complex statistical analysis. For example, we may wish to investigate whether scores differ by subgroup of the population, such as first language background, gender or disability. We would not wish to see variation by group, which would show that there was bias in the test. Another study may look at the internal structure of the test, using a technique such as factor analysis. This would allow the test developer to see whether sub-tests that were designed to measure different constructs showed divergence (see, for example, Sawaki, Stricker and Oranje, 2009). The principle behind such analyses is that we expect items which test the same construct to converge, or be more highly correlated, whereas we expect them to have a divergent relationship with items designed to measure another construct. This is known as establishing *convergent* and *divergent* *validity*. Factor analysis cannot be conducted by hand, and is always done using powerful statistical programs, such as SPSS.

It is also the ideal time at which to find out if test takers generally can use the delivery system, especially if it is computer based, and to discover if there are any problems for students with disabilities, such as poor eyesight.

Finally, the field test is an opportunity to see whether the timing allocated to the test as a whole, and its components, is long enough to ensure that the test is not speeded. If test takers are rushing to complete the test it becomes a test of speed, rather than of the intended constructs. On the other hand, the time allowed should not be so long that test takers complete the test with a great deal of time to spare. This is not cost effective for the test producer, and is demotivating for the test takers.

7. Item shells

In large-scale testing the final decision about what to include and exclude, the final shape of the delivery system, and the timing of the test, is made when field testing is complete. It is at this stage that large numbers of items and tasks have to be developed according to the specifications. While item writers can work directly with specifications, many testing agencies also provide them with *item shells*, to guide writing. These are electronic templates into which the item writers drop new content. The shell would minimally contain a standardised set of instructions and layout that could not be changed (Haladyna, 1999: 126–133). These can easily be set up in word processing software, such as Word. Consider the following item:

Feeling the strain of commuting by train

SOMETIMES people shout in the street. Quite often it is because they are deranged.

Sometimes I would like to shout in the street. I would like to think that I am not deranged, but these days I'm not sure.

I travel on the Gravesend to London Bridge rail service every morning. Against my better judgement I repeat the exercise in the opposite direction at night. After more than two years using the line, shouting in the street could now be an option.

The service is without question the least excellent in the southern region. I refuse to refer to it as Network SouthEast because on the day British Rail changed the name my train was half an hour late.

I have monitored the performance of the service over the past week or two — the situation leads one to this kind of behaviour. On one occasion the train from Gravesend was a minute early arriving at London Bridge. The rest of the time it was anything between three and thirty minutes late.

It wouldn't matter if the accommodation were civilised. Unfortunately by my estimates the carriages are not far off 30 years old.

One could of course bury oneself in one's *Independent* and forget all about it. There is a catch here however, because it is virtually impossible to read on the train. The samba-like gyrations affected by the carriages make the term "rattler" a puny epithet indeed.

At Slade Green near Dartford, women not used to the route are sometimes moved to scream because they think the train is coming off the track.

Just outside London Bridge the train rests at least once so that it can maintain its record of exemplary tardiness.

It is of little comfort to me than when British Rail has finished with me, I am passed on to the least excellent London Underground service — the dreaded Northern line. Commuters were so terminally bored with this service the other day that they hijacked a train to ensure that it ended up where it was supposed to.

How do you begin to complain about such services?

Barrie Clement

While reading a newspaper you come across an article called 'Feeling the strain of commuting by train'.

Below are a series of common complaints against British Rail services. Which of them does the writer mention?

(a) infrequency of the service
(b) lack of punctuality of the trains
(c) state of the carriages
(d) swaying of the carriages
(e) fact that the trains stop for no apparent reason
(f) absence of a buffet car
(g) fact that there is not a complete ban on smoking

Put a tick (✔) next to the appropriate letters in the answer column.

a	
b	
c	
d	
e	
f	
g	

Item writers would be instructed in the specifications to select or write an article that complains about a service or facility, along with other textual features that impact upon difficulty. The item shell would look like this, allowing the item writer to add text only between the brackets:

While reading a newspaper you come across an article called '[insert title]'.

[Insert text]

Below are a series of common complaints against [name of service or facility]. Which of them does the writer mention?

(a) [complaint]
(b) [complaint]
(c) [complaint]
(d) [complaint]
(e) [complaint]
(f) [complaint]
(g) [complaint]

Put a tick (✔) next to the appropriate letters in the answer column.

a	
b	
c	
d	
e	
f	
g	

An added advantage of the use of item shells is the reduction in editorial work required when item writers submit new items for review, which happens before they are placed into the item pool for the construction of test forms.

8. Operational item review and pre-testing

As items and tasks are produced to create the pool, the review process continues. Each item must be checked in four ways.

Content review

In this first stage the reviewers check that the item and any associated materials or texts match the specification. This is to ensure item–specification congruence.

Key check

The reviewers check to make sure that the suggested answer is in fact correct. In a multiple-choice item, care must be taken to ensure that none of the distractors are really plausible responses. In constructed response items the scoring or marking sheet should indicate the range of responses that can be considered correct, so that all potentially acceptable answers are included, and all unacceptable answers are excluded.

Bias/sensitivity review

In the bias review we check items to ensure that they do not contain references or material that is likely to lead to bias against a certain subgroup of the test-taking population. This involves cultural sensitivity, and so in high-stakes testing the review is often undertaken by a panel of reviewers who represent the cultures of the various target test takers, or who have had extensive experience working with those cultures. Hambleton and Rodgers (1995) suggest that reviewers identify 'designated subgroups of interest' (DSIs), and for each DSI ask if any member is likely to suffer because the content is beyond their educational or cultural experience, whether it is inflammatory, offensive or portrays some DSIs stereotypically.

Editorial review

The final check on an item is to make sure that there are no spelling or grammatical errors, and that formatting is appropriate.

If an item fails a review, it goes back to the item writer for correction. When it is resubmitted, the item goes through the review process again. This is iterative, and continues until an item passes all checks. It then makes its way into the item pool, and will eventually be included in an operational test form.

You may feel that all the procedures and checks that we have discussed in this chapter seem rather convoluted. If you feel like this because it is all too much to do when preparing assessments for learning, then I would be the first to agree. Some, but not all, of the steps described in this chapter may be relevant to a specific institutional context. However, when high-stakes decisions are being made on the outcome of tests, it is critical that the test designers can defend the interpretation of scores. The procedures that I have described in this chapter have been developed to increase the reliability and validity of tests, and reduce the possibility that any test taker is unfairly treated as a result of having taken a test.

There is one feature of the design process that we have so far only mentioned in passing, which is ensuring the items can be scored. This is the measurement component that must be included in the specifications, and is the topic of the next chapter.

Activities

○ 6.1 Project work III

In Activity 5.6 you wrote a test specification and at least one sample item for each item type in your test. Arrange a workshop like the one described in this chapter. Give your sample item(s) to colleagues to critique. You may sit and listen to the discussion, or get feedback once they have completed the task.

Make a list of problems the group has raised. Can you use the item(s) that you have designed? Do they need to be changed in any way? Will the test specification need alteration? Make all the design changes necessary, and document the reasons for the change.

○ 6.2 Spot the mess

Look at the following multiple-choice items. Can you identify the problem(s) with each? The first four are a 'set' (there were no visuals in the actual test):

1. This man has dark
   a. heads
   b. head
   c. hairs
   d. hair
2. and a _____
   a. beard
   b. barber
   c. moustaches
   d. facehair
3. He is _____ a jacket.
   a. wearing
   b. carrying
   c. having
   d. holding
4. and he is _____ a piece of paper.
   a. wearing
   b. holding
   c. having
   d. getting

And now these:

'Things can only get _____!,' Jim said.

A. better **B.** bester **C.** worser **D.** worst

If I _____rich I _____travel around the world.

A. were / would **B.** am / would **C.** will / will **D.** is / will

Finally, try this sample (all originally reading items, but the texts are not reproduced here):

Which railway station does the text suggest does not have interesting nineteenth-century ironwork.

      a. Paddington   b. Central   c. Newchurch   d. Stirling

Which country sends more students to study abroad per head of population than any other?

      a. Britain   b. Canada   c. China   d. Australia

When restringing a guitar it is important not to loosen all strings at the same time because

a.   some might snap
b.   the truss rod's tension is relaxed, which may cause the neck to warp
c.   it may go out of tune
d.   the tone may be affected

◯ 6.3 Distractor analysis

Look again at Table 6.2. Each cell contains the option selected (A, B, C or D) and a code (1, 0) for correct and incorrect. Which items contain distractors that are not selected, or only selected by a very small number of test takers? Look again at the items and see if you can think of a reason why these distractors may not be operating as intended.

    If you have multiple-choice items from a test that you have written, conduct a distractor analysis. What do you discover about your items?

◯ 6.4 Practice in prototyping

Take any item that you have written. This may be the one you wrote for Activities 5.2 or 5.5. Ask a learner (or a colleague – as this is only for practice) to do the task. Ask them to verbalise how they are answering (either during, or after, the task, depending on the modality). What do you learn about your item and your specification?

◯ 6.5 Practising your calculation skills V

You give a test with 30 items to fifteen students. We reproduce the responses for just the first five items on the test below. Complete the table. Which items would stay in your test, and why? Which would you investigate further, and why?

Student	Item 1	Item 2	Item 3	Item 4	Item 5	Total
1	C1	B1	A1	D1	D1	28
2	C1	B1	A1	D1	A0	27
3	C1	D0	A1	B0	A0	25
4	C1	B1	A1	D1	A0	25
5	A0	C0	A1	D1	A0	20
6	C1	D0	A1	D1	A0	19
7	C1	B1	A1	D1	B0	19
8	C1	B1	B0	C0	B0	17
9	C1	D0	C0	C0	D1	15
10	C1	D0	D0	D1	D1	15
11	C1	D0	D0	C0	A0	13
12	B0	B1	C0	C0	D1	12
13	C1	D0	D0	D1	B0	12
14	C1	D0	C0	C0	D1	11
15	C1	D0	C0	C0	D1	10
FI						
FI Top						
FI Bottom						
DI						

You can check your calculations by turning to Appendix 6.

◯ 6.6 Item review

The following four items were designed to test conversational implicature. Review each item and identify any flaws that you find. Each item may contain multiple problems.

Item 1

Tony: Finishing the packing for our holiday is going to take forever at this pace.
Linda: Yes, and we've had quite a few late nights recently.

Linda implies that they:

(a) will miss their flight
(b) will be up packing late into the night*

(c) are both very tired

(d) need to work faster

Item 2

Presenter: So, what do people on the streets feel about binge drinking on the streets of our towns and cities, and particularly the rising incidence of drunkenness among young girls? We went out and about with our microphone to find out. Here's what Tom, an office worker from Middlington, had to say.

Tom: Well, I mean, it's up to them isn't it? Okay, you know, perhaps they don't have the money, so they have to get it from somewhere, and it could damage their health. But it's what they want to do. So I don't see the problem.

Tom's view is that:

(a) drinking causes social problems

(b) young people need more money

(c) heavy drinkers get liver disease

(d) the young can do as they please*

Item 3

Listen to the exchange and answer the question.

Rebecca: There are only three tickets for the concert on Friday, and I've invite Sonya and Terry.
Angela: I guess I'll get over it in time.

Angela:

(a) is very upset

(b) feels loft out*

(c) doesn't have time

(d) has her own ticket

Item 4

Economist: It is highly likely that the credit crunch will become excessively tighter as the year progresses, forcing more and small to medium-sized businesses into liqui-dation, and even resulting in many larger companies and high-street brands being forced into the hands of the administrators. As governments become more involved with the banking sector, many analysts foresee increasing levels of regulation that will bring an end to many opaque practices such as the trade in derivatives.

The economist argues that in the coming year:

(a) we will all have a harder life
(b) governments will buy banks
(c) some businesses will close*
(d) shops will get better managers

When you have completed this activity you may wish to compare your views with some suggested answers, provided in Appendix 6.

○ 6.7 Ahoy there!

One of the problems that beset item writers is selecting material that avoids involving 'background knowledge' as a construct irrelevant variable. Unless background knowledge is part of the construct – as in a test of English for economists, for example – we try to exclude the possibility that some test takers will get higher scores just because they are familiar with the topic and can therefore activate schemata that are not available to others. This is why many tests deal with topics that are bland and frequently uninteresting. Try answering the following item. What are the item writers trying to achieve? Do you think that there is a problem with this approach to background knowledge?

The following terms are used to describe parts of a schooner. Read the definitions and choose the most suitable words from the list below to label each part. Write the number of the chosen word for each part in the appropriate circle on the diagram. Write 'X' if there is no suitable definition. This question carries 10 marks.

1. *Bowsprit*
   A large spar projecting forward from the bow of a schooner.
2. *Flying jib*
   A sail outside the jib on an extension of the bowsprit.
3. *Foresail*
   The lower sail set behind a schooner's front foremast.
4. *Forestaysail*
   The triangular headsail of a schooner.
5. *Gaff*
   The spar upon which the head of a fore and aft sail is extended.
6. *Jib*
   A triangular sail set on a stay extending from the head of the foremast to the bowsprit.
7. *Luff*
   The forward edge of a fore and aft sail.

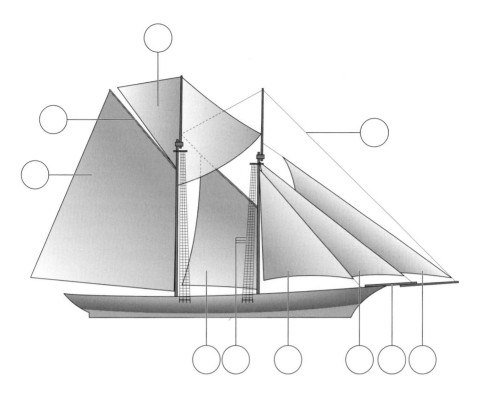

8. *Main gaff topsail*
   T-triangular topsail with its foot extended upon the gaff and its luff upon the
   main topmast.
9. *Mainmast*
   A sailing ship's principal mast, usually second from the bow.
10. *Main topmast*
    The mast next above the mainmast.
11. *Ratlines*
    One of the small transverse ropes attached to the shrouds.
12. *Shroud*
    One of the ropes leading usually in pairs from a ship's mastheads to give lateral
    support to the masts.
13. *Stay*
    A large strong rope usually of wire used to support a mast.
14. *Stay sail*
    A fore and aft sail hoisted on a stay.

What do you think this item is designed to test?

◯ 6.8 Project work IV

Following Activity 6.1, with any luck you should have produced a polished item (or a few items) for your test. It is now time to see how well they work.

First of all, select three or four suitable learners and prototype your item(s). Which prototyping methods will you use, and why? Based on the data from prototyping, make any changes you need to your item(s), and the specifications.

Next, write another ten items to the specification. If it is a performance test (speaking or writing), you may only need to produce one or two additional tasks at this stage.

Select as many learners as you can (ideally 30, but fewer if necessary) and conduct a pilot study. Calculate relevant statistics.

Write up the outcome of the prototyping and the pilot study, and add this to the growing test documentation. Make any revisions to the specifications that may be needed, remembering that test development is an iterative process.

7 Scoring language tests

▶ 1. Scoring items

There is little point in creating a novel item type if it is impossible to score. As an item type is being designed, the measurement component of the evidence specification also needs writing (see Chapter 4). We have already seen what can happen when this is not done. You will recall from the item evaluation dialogue in Chapter 6 that one of Bill's criticisms of the sample item was that 'once you get to the second part the first part ceases to be of any relevance'. Look at the item again. You will see that in the first part of the item clicking on the incorrect word is far too easy, and in the case of questions 3, 5 and 6, the response must be correct as there is only one thing to click on. However, Bill's point is really that if you can answer 'theatre' for the first blank in the second section, the only possible answer to item 1 in the first section is 'cinema'. This gives two marks for one piece of information, which is inadvertently weighting the item. The other problem with scoring, raised by Angela, was how it is possible to take into account all potential spellings in the second part, which requires typing a word. The scoring key may have to become exceptionally complex for the item to work correctly in a computer-scored test.

Problems with the measurement component are much more common than we might think, but they are not usually documented and published because they are part of the test development process. This is to be regretted, as research on scoring particular item types is part of the nitty gritty of practical test development. One exception is Alderson, Percsich and Szabo (2000). In testing reading, a *construct* of great interest has always been the ability to recognise logical relations between clauses, such as those indicating situation–problem–response–evaluation patterns (Hoey, 1983), which we discussed in Chapter 4. One way of testing this is to use a multiple-choice approach, as in the following example from Fulcher (1998b):

Most human beings are curious. Not, I mean, in the sense that they are odd, but in the sense that they want to find out about the world around them, and about their own part in the world		
1a. But they cannot do this easily.	1b. They therefore ask questions, they wonder, they speculate.	1c. Or, on the other hand, they may wish to ask many questions.

What they want to find out may be quite simple things: What lies beyond that range of hills? Or they may be rather more complicated inquiries: How does grass grow? Or they may be more puzzling inquiries still: What is the purpose of life? What is the ultimate nature of truth? To the first question the answer may be obtained by going and seeing. The answer to the next question will not be so easy to find, but the method will be essentially the same.		
2a. So, he is forced to observe life as he sees it.	2b. Although, often, it may not be the same.	2c. It is the method of the scientist.
A method that may reasonably be summed up by the phrase: 'Going and Seeing'. The last set of questions would normally be thought of as philosophical, and it would not be easy to find answers to them that would command general agreement. Some people would say that they are unanswerable.		
3a. But those who have tried to answer them in the past have used the method of speculation rather than of investigation, of sitting and thinking rather than going and seeing.	3b. Therefore, they have sat at home and not been too concerned about such questions.	3c. The reason for this is clear to see: they are indeed, even in principle, unanswerable.
'Leisure,' as Thomas Hobbes remarked, 'is the mother of philosophy'; the same relationship, it will be noted, as that which proverbially exists between necessity and invention. This should not be taken to imply that philosophers are not busy people, but their activity is likely to be mental rather than physical.		
4a. This is not to say that all of the scientists do nothing but think about problems of science and physics.	4b. Therefore, the philosopher must be free from all more practical duties and problems of everyday life.	4c. It would be a misleading over-simplification, however, to identify science with investigation and philosophy with thinking.
The scientist who is investigating the world around him will certainly do some sitting and thinking about the results of his inquiries; and mathematicians, often as a result of pursuing lines of thought which seemed at first to have no practical applications, have made enormous contributions to modern discoveries in physics. The philosopher who is speculating about the nature of truth, though he may not do much going, is likely to do a certain amount of seeing. He must have some data for his reflections, even if it is only that which is provided by the fact that he is reflecting. And modern philosophers especially often undertake detailed investigations into the ways in which language is used.		
5a. Nevertheless, it is on the whole true that for science the emphasis has been on investigation, and for philosophy on speculation.	5b. Reflecting is thinking, while it is obvious that investigating involves doing things.	5c. Thus, science is a matter of pure investigation, and philosophy is merely thinking, for which it has often been criticized.
It will be useful now for us to examine more closely what the word 'philosophy' has been and is used to describe.		

You may wish to spend some time looking at this particular task to identify problems. You may also wish to reverse engineer a specification and attempt to improve it. Many testers prefer to use a sequencing item type rather than multiple choice, in which the learners have to reconstruct the original sequence of sentences in a text, as in the following example (Alderson *et al.*, 2000: 425).

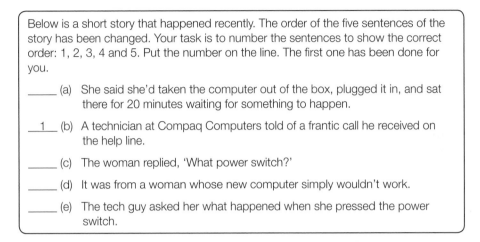

Assuming that a mark is given for each sentence placed in the correct slot, the most obvious scoring problem with an item like this is that, once one sentence is placed in the wrong slot, not only is that sentence incorrect, but the slot for another correct answer is filled. The correct sequence for this item is (d), (a), (e), (c). Suppose that a learner selects (a) for number 2. This immediately means that only two marks are available even though one error has been made. Further, it is possible that learners could place two or three sentences in the correct sequence, but not in the correct slots, and would therefore get no score even though they have understood the links between the sentences. This would occur, for example in the sequence (b), (c), (d), (a), (e). Most seriously, because it does not take into account the ability to sequence correctly 'it fails to take into account correct sequences of elements, the ability to organize which is thought to be central to the construct' (Alderson *et al.*, 2000: 437). This is critical, as the scoring method can seriously interfere with what it is we wish to test, even if the item looks like a reasonable test of the construct.

Alderson *et al.* suggested four different ways of scoring this item type:

Exact match: Allowing one mark for each sentence in the correct place in the sequence. This is the most obvious way to score the item, but one that suffers from the problems we have already outlined above.

Classic: One mark for an exact match, one mark if the previous sentence is the correct one in the sequence, one mark if the following sentence is the next in the sequence, and one mark if the sentence is the last in the sequence and no sentence follows it (an 'edge' score).

Added value: Same as the classic, but with no score for an exact match.

Full pair: The sum of previous and next scores, excluding an 'edge' score.

The only advantage of the exact match method is that it is simple and easy to score and calculate. The classic procedure keeps the exact match element, but gives scores for correct pairs and triplets in the right order, even if they are not in the same position. The added value method simply removes credit for the correct position, and gives credit for correct sequencing in pairs or triplets. The full pair method also credits pairs and triplets, but has no exact match score and no 'edge' score.

It is hypothesised that the classic approach would provide the best measure of the intended construct, followed by added value, then full pair, with exact match being the worst measure of the construct. In their study, each of these scoring methods was tried across four different sequencing tasks:

Task 1 Short story (as above).
Task 2 Short story (as above) but with no example, so that all five sentences had to be placed in the correct sequence.
Task 3 A text with seven sentences rather than five.
Task 4 A task with an intact text to read, after which the test takers were asked to sequence sentences that summarised the text.

The findings of the study were as follows:

- If the first sentence in the sequence is not given, the item is harder, irrespective of scoring method.
- The exact match method always produces the lowest score, and the classic always the highest, showing that test takers always benefited from sequences being taken into account.
- The correlation between individuals' scores on specific tasks and test total score are higher for tasks without the example at the beginning *when the text is short, or the task easier.* This means that this combination discriminates better, and is therefore assumed to be a better measure of the construct.
- Over all variations of the item type, the exact method has a marginally higher correlation with test total score than any other method.
- The correlations between all four scoring methods were higher for the task in which an intact text was presented first, and test takers were asked to sequence summary sentences.
- The results of all scoring methods are highly correlated, suggesting that they are sensitive to the same construct.

It seems reasonable to surmise that taking sequence into account in the scoring is a much better representation of the construct than exact matching. The disadvantage is that it is extremely difficult for humans to score all the possible acceptable sequences. Error rates would probably be very high. In classic scoring, this would also require checking exact match, and would take a great deal of time. The only way this scoring method could reasonably be adopted would be in a computer-scored test.

The lesson that we have learned through this and other experiences with developing new test items is that the scoring method should be developed at the same time as the item is developed, and the item specifications are written. As Bill pointed out in his critique of the item discussed in Chapter 6, if it is unclear how an item is to be scored, or if credit is being denied or given for construct-irrelevant reasons, the item is not going to provide useful information that contributes towards the meaning of the test score. Finally, the most suitable scoring method needs to be considered in relation to its practical *scorability* depending on the delivery method.

 # 2. Scorability

Lado (1961: 31) included 'scorability' in his list of desirable test qualities, as we mentioned briefly in Chapter 2. Scorability is highly desirable, whether tests are delivered by paper and pencil, or on computer. We first consider traditional paper and pencil tests, which are still widely used in educational systems and classrooms around the world.

Even with closed response items, Lado saw that if the answers are 'scattered in the pages', the time taken to score a test is extended, and the chances of making errors when marking and transferring results to a mark book would increase. He therefore recommended the use of separate answer sheets upon which test takers could record their responses. Scoring speeds up significantly, and errors are reduced. Separating the answers in this way also makes a number of other options possible. The first of these is the use of keys that reduce error rates. The most commonly used keys are stencils that enable the scorer to see whether a response is correct or incorrect without having to read the question. One of the earliest references to the use of marking stencils is found in Yoakum and Yerkes (1920: 159), describing the scoring of tests during the First World War (Figure 7.1):

> *Scoring is done by means of stencils, one for each of the eight tests. A test is scored by placing the stencil upon the appropriate page of the record booklet and comparing the responses given with the marks on the stencil. The stencils may be made of cardboard suitably marked to indicate the correct answer. For tests 4, 5, 7 and 8, stencils made of thin, transparent strips of celluloid are preferable. If celluloid cannot be obtained, stencils for these tests may be made of cardboard. In this case, the scoring of tests 7 and 8 will be facilitated by perforating the cardboard stencils so as to show where the correct responses are located.*

Even today, many teachers construct 'templates' to score tests much more quickly. The technology has changed little. An acetate sheet commonly used with overhead projectors is marked up so that when it is placed over an answer sheet the correct answers below can be counted off quickly.

SCORING GROUP EXAMINATION *a*, CAMP LEE, OCTOBER, 1917.
The transparent celluloid stencils used in scoring are shown at the near end of the table.

Fig. 7.1. Marking scripts in 1917. Notice the transparent celluloid templates on the table. From Yerkes (1921: 91). Courtesy Archives of the History of American Psychology – The University of Akron

From the very earliest days, a further perceived advantage of scoring closed response items was cost. Of course, increasing the speed of marking through the use of stencils reduced cost, but using clerical or other untrained staff also reduced personnel costs. Ruch (1924: 36) comments:

The increased ease of scoring calls for no additional comment except to point out that scoring can be done by clerical workers without previous experience or training. In some cases, pupils can be used successfully for this task. Even where the teacher must do the grading of the papers, the task is economically and mechanically carried out. This is a conserving of nervous energy and largely obviates the tendency to slight the job under the press of circumstances.

With the emphasis on speed, cost and accuracy, there were many ingenious attempts to make scoring easier. Lado (1961: 365–366) mentions two of these. The first was the Clapp-Young Self-Marking test sheets. This consisted of two pieces of paper sealed together with a sheet of carbon paper between them. When the test taker marks an answer on the sheet it is printed on the second sheet, which already has the correct answers circled. The marker separates the sheets and counts off the correct answers from the second sheet of paper. A second method was the punch-pad self-scoring device, by which a test taker removed a perforated dot from the answer sheet; if the response was correct, a red dot was revealed below.

The real solution to scorability was the computer. In 1938 IBM revealed the IBM 805 multiple-choice scoring machine (Figure 7.2). Test takers marked their answers on a sheet, which was fed into the machine. If a pencil mark was detected against the keyed

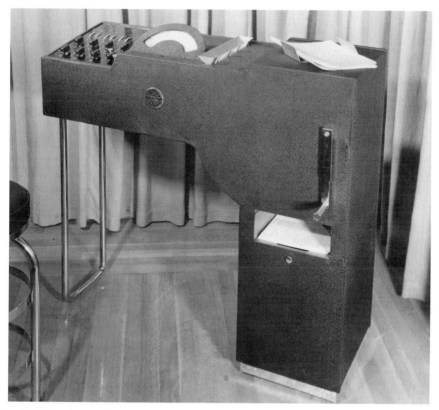

Fig. 7.2. The IBM 805 multiple-choice scoring machine. Courtesy of IBM Corporate Archives

answer a single electronic pulse was set off, which added one mark to the total. It could handle up to 150 multiple-choice items per sheet, and could score between 800 and 1000 test papers per hour, depending upon the skill of the operator.

Lado (1961: 365) noted that the machine was very expensive. Although rental was possible, he did not think that the cost justified the time savings for any but the largest testing programmes.

Many companies still build and sell test scoring machines. It is even possible to purchase portable devices that are relatively cheap. Most of them still use the 'bubble sheets' that were first developed during the 1930s. These are still extremely popular solutions with many institutions around the world, especially when there are larger numbers of test takers.

Not surprisingly, computer-based testing has become exceptionally popular (Fulcher, 2000b). Computers are capable of delivering tests efficiently, and can produce immediate scores for both the test takers and the score users. In the early days of computer-based testing a critical issue was whether the computer-based forms produced equivalent results to paper and pencil forms of the test (Fulcher, 1997). This was because language testers simply 'moved' their paper-and-pencil tests into computer delivery. The concerns with equivalence were particularly acute for assessing writing, where asking test takers to type answers rather than use a pen or pencil might disadvantage some learners (Russel and Haney, 1997). Similarly, before the Test of English as a Foreign Language was rolled out in its first computer-based form in 1998, a great deal of research was conducted into whether mouse and keyboard manipulation would prove difficult for subgroups of the test-taking population (Kirsch *et al.*, 1998). Studies have also been conducted to investigate whether reading from a screen and having to scroll text is such a different process from reading from paper that test scores are affected (Sawaki, 2001). In all of these studies the assumption was that computer delivery may have negatively affected some test takers. Most of them found that any effect, if present, was so small that it was of no practical significance. The designers of TOEFL introduced a practice section to the first computer-based version in order to get test takers used to using a mouse and scrolling; it is significant that this was removed after a relatively short period of time. We may now take it for granted that most test takers will be more familiar with using a computer and typing than they are with writing by hand.

The debate has therefore moved on, and such concerns are now only relevant if a test is being offered in both paper-and-pencil and computer-based delivery modes. But most tests are now specifically designed for one mode or the other. Of more concern today is the general design of the test. This primarily concerns avoiding construct-irrelevant variance that might be due to issues of *interface design*, which can be addressed through *usability testing* as set out in Fulcher (2003). Usability testing is actually the prototyping of a computer interface as well as test items during the design phase. Chapelle and Douglas (2006: 83–86) extract useful tables from Fulcher (2003) to create an evaluation framework for computer-based tests, which can be used as the basis for validation studies of computer-based testing systems (Labardo, 2007).

What matters most in terms of how computer-based tests are scored is the relationship between the response of the test taker to the items, and the reaction of the computer to the response (Chapelle and Douglas, 2006: 31–34). There are three basic options.

Option 1: Linear tests

In a linear test the test takers are presented with items in a set sequence, just as if they were encountering them in pencil-and-paper format. In a computer environment, of course, there is the opportunity for multimedia input; but all the test takers get the same questions, in the same sequence. The items are keyed, so that as the test taker responds to an item a '1' or a '0' is placed in a database and keeps a running raw score total for each person. From an item design and assembly perspective, there is little difference from the design and construction of a paper-and-pencil test.

Option 2: Branching tests

In a branching test, on the other hand, there is level of adaptivity to the test taker. All test takers may be presented with the same block of items at the beginning of the test, but then test takers with a score over a certain cut point may be directed to a more difficult set of items, whereas others may receive easier items. This level of adaptivity is still essentially linear, but not all students will receive the same blocks of items. One advantage is that test takers are almost never presented with items that are far too difficult, and thus demotivation is avoided. The main problem with branching is that the scores for students following different paths through the test are not comparable unless they are scaled according to the difficulty of the items presented. A popular alternative is to allocate the test taker to a level depending on which 'block' they end up completing successfully. For example, if a test taker answers most of the Block 1 Items correctly and is sent to Block 3, answers most of these items correctly and is sent to Block 7, struggles with these items and is sent to Block 6, where the performance is adequate, the student would be assigned to level 7. This is illustrated in Figure 7.1.

Option 3: Adaptive tests

The third option is to have adaptive tests at the item level (Dunkel, 1999; Chalhoub-Deville, 1999). In these tests the computer estimates the ability of the test taker after they respond to each individual item. If a test taker answers an item correctly, the computer selects a more difficult item. If the test taker answers an item incorrectly, it selects an easier item. This means that no two test takers are likely to face the same set of items, assuming that the item pool is large enough. For most teachers and institutions this is the critical problem. For adaptive tests to work successfully, there must be very large item pools with particularly large numbers of items within one standard deviation of

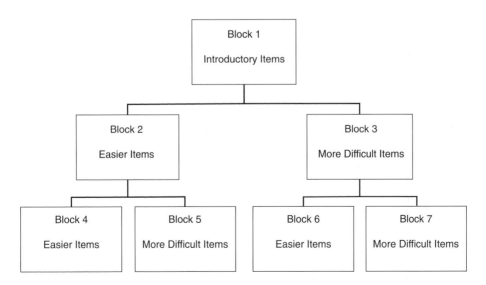

Fig. 7.3. Example of a branching routine

the mean ability level of the test takers. If there are not enough items, the pool is very soon exhausted and levels cannot be accurately estimated. However, there must also be many items along the entire ability scale so that the level of particularly low or high ability students can be estimated. This places a heavy burden on item-writing resources to produce enough, and to keep replenishing the pool of items.

In order to illustrate this, consider Figure 7.4. This is a map of the distribution of a set of items in a pool used to pilot an adaptive test. In computer adaptive testing the measurement model most frequently used is called the Rasch model (Bond and Fox, 2007). Using this approach, all test takers are placed on an ability scale, with 0 as the mean. Items are also placed on the same scale. However, while the level of the test taker is interpreted as ability, the level of the item is interpreted as its difficulty. The lower the number, the easier the item is. Similarly for the test taker, the lower the number, the lower the ability estimate is. The meaning of any particular point on the scale is probabilistic. For example, if an item has a difficulty of 0.2, and a test taker has an estimated ability of 0.2, this means that the test taker has a 50/50 chance of correctly answering an item of this difficulty. As the items become easier, the test taker has an increased chance of answering them correctly. Inversely, as the items become harder, the test taker has less chance of answering them correctly.

In Figure 7.4 we can see that the items are generally too difficult for the test-taking population, and there are not enough items at the lower end of the scale to estimate the ability levels of many test takers. The item writers would be required to significantly increase the item pool, producing very large numbers of easier items, before operational adaptive testing could be launched.

Adaptive testing is not frequently used by teachers for classroom assessment or by smaller institutions, mainly because of the resource implications. It is only a viable option with very large educational programmes where testing is used for high-stakes decisions, such as graduation or certification. Normally the institution will need to employ a number of staff simply to maintain and manage the testing system.

Computer adaptive testing was once seen as a panacea to language testing problems. Adaptive tests were thought to enhance test security, individualise the testing experience, and provide the maximum amount of information about individuals in the shortest possible time span (Burstein *et al.*, 1996; de Jong and Stevenson, 1990). When the computer-based TOEFL appeared in the late 1990s it was adaptive, and yet by 2005 when the internet-delivered version (TOEFL iBT) appeared, the design had reverted to a linear form delivered at set periods during the year. The main reason is because

> We have learned that computer adaptive testing is hideously expensive in large-scale tests. Item pools became vats, then lakes, then oceans, just to maintain test security in environments like China. The era of adaptivity in mass international language testing is dead.
> (Fulcher, 2005)

There is still a place for adaptive testing, but this is more likely to be in large institutions or at national level, where on-demand testing is not available. What we have learned is

Items	Persons	Items/People
	+−4.0+	0/ 0
	|−3.8 |	0/ 0
	|−3.6 |	0/ 0
	|−3.4 |	0/ 0
	|−3.2 |	0/ 0
	+−3.0+	0/ 0
	|−2.8 |	0/ 0
#|	−2.6 |	1/ 0
	|−2.4 |	0/ 0
#|	−2.2 |	1/ 0
#+	−2.0+	1/ 0
###|	−1.8 |	2/ 2
###|	−1.6 |	2/ 2
#####|	−1.4 |	5/ 2
####|	−1.2 |#	4/ 6
#######|	−1.0 |#	6/ 9
####|	−0.8 |##	3/ 19
####|	−0.6 |###	3/ 29
####|	−0.4 |####	3/ 37
#####|	−0.2 |#####	5/ 54
########+	<0.0+######	7/ 56
########|	0.2 |######	7/ 60
#######|	0.4 |#######	6/ 69
#####|	0.6 |######	4/ 62
####|	0.8 |########	3/ 77
####+	1.0>+#######	3/ 83
#|	1.2 |######	1/ 61
#####|	1.4 |#########	4/ 92
###|	1.6 |#####	2/ 47
|	1.8 |#####	0/ 54
+	2.0+####	0/ 38
###|	2.2 |#	2/ 13
####|	2.4 |####	3/ 43
###|	2.6 |##	2/ 16
|	2.8 |#	0/ 9
+	3.0+#	0/ 11
|	3.2 |#	0/ 10
|	3.4 |#	0/ 6
|	3.6 |	0/ 2
|	3.8 |	0/ 0
+	4.0+#	0/ 13

```
+—+—+—+—+—— −+−−+−−+−−+−−+
20  15  10   5        5   10   15   20
```

Percent of	Percent of
Items	Examinees

Fig. 7.4. An Item–person distribution map

that there is nothing at all wrong with the linear form, and from a practical point of view it has a great deal to recommend it. Once again, the older tried-and-tested technology appears to have prevailed.

3. Scoring constructed response tasks

If scoring closed-response items seems to be problematic, the situation becomes more complex when we turn to constructed responses, such as extended writing tasks, or speaking. Assessing writing or speech is normally done by a *rater*, using a rating scale. As Weigle (2002: 108) says, the two things with which we are most concerned are defining the rating scale, and training the raters how to use it. The purpose is to define the quality of the language and its communicative effectiveness within the boundaries set out in the specifications (Fulcher, 2008a).

Rating scales are traditionally constructed from a set of fairly arbitrary levels, each level being defined by a *descriptor* or *rubric*. Hamp-Lyons (1991) classifies all rating scales into one of three possible types, as follows.

Holistic scales

A single score is awarded, which reflects the overall quality of the performance. The descriptors are general and draw on theories of communicative language ability as discussed in Chapter 4. Holistic scales are generally fairly easy to use and with extensive training high levels of inter-rater reliability can be achieved. However, the link between the descriptor and the language performance is usually weak.

Primary trait scales

A single score is awarded, but the descriptors are developed for each individual prompt (or question) that is used in the test. Each prompt is developed to elicit a specific response, perhaps an argumentative essay in an academic context, for example. The primary trait rating scale reflects the specific qualities expected in writing samples at a number of levels on the scale. Samples of writing at each level are provided to exemplify what is intended by the descriptor. This is an improvement over holistic scales, but a different scale has to be developed for each prompt or task type, which increases the investment of time and resources in scale development. Also, scores are likely to be less generalisable to task types beyond those defined in the specification.

Multiple trait scoring

Unlike the two scale types already mentioned, multiple trait scoring requires raters to award two or more scores for different features or traits of the speech or writing sample. The traits are normally prompt or prompt-type specific, as in primary trait scoring. The argument in favour of this type of scoring is that richer information is provided about each performance. In the case of an essay this may include traits like organisation, coherence, cohesion, content, and so on. For testing speaking, they may include task completion, turn taking, fluency, appropriate vocabulary, etc., depending on the constructs of interest. If multiple trait rating scales are carefully designed to match the prompts and instructional goals, the scores can provide useful diagnostic information for learners and teachers in classroom testing. The main problem with multiple trait rating scales is that raters are highly likely to suffer from the *halo effect*. Originally identified as a problem by Thorndike (1920), this is a phenomenon where the act of making one judgement colours all subsequent judgements. In language testing we commonly find that if a rating is made on one scale it is carried over to others. The effect is the creation of a flat profile, even if a learner is in fact more proficient in some areas than others. Nevertheless, for classroom assessment multiple trait scoring remains highly desirable because of its diagnostic potential.

As most rating scales are in the public domain, it is possible for teachers or language testers to select a rating scale 'off the peg' for their own particular purposes. In most cases, however, the new testing purpose requires a new rating scale. There are five identifiable methodologies that can be used to design a rating scale. In what follows, I will describe each methodology and indicate the steps necessary to create the scale. Examples of each type of scale are provided.

Methodology 1: Intuitive and experiential

Rating scales created using Intuitive and experiential methods are the oldest and most frequently used. I have called the approach to design '*a priori*' or 'armchair' methods of scale development (Fulcher, 1993: 33). Language teachers and testers with a great deal of experience, who are considered to be experts in their field, are asked to decide on how many levels they feel are appropriate for the testing purpose, and to write the descriptors for each level. These descriptors may be revised over time in the light of experience. The FSI scale (see Activity 7.4), and the scales that evolved from it, such as the Interagency Language Roundtable (ILR) and the American Council on the Teaching of Foreign Language Guidelines (ACTFL), are all examples of this type of scale (see Fulcher, 2003a).

These scales have been extensively criticised on the grounds that they have no theoretical or empirical basis (Fulcher, 1996b), and it is very difficult to see why any particular sample of language should be placed at a particular level (Bachman and Savignon, 1986; Kramsch, 1986). The descriptions are also dependent upon each other, using the language of 'more' or 'less' proficient than a lower of higher level (Lantolf and Frawley, 1985). Lowe (1986: 392) nevertheless defends the ACTFL/Educational Testing Service/ ILR scales (shortened to AEI) precisely on the grounds of experience:

> The essence of the AEI proficiency lies not in verbal descriptions of it, but in its thirty-year-long tradition of practice – making training in AEI proficiency testing a desideratum.

Lowe argued that users of the scale are 'adepts' who are socialised into the use of the scale and constantly use it in conjunction with other assessors (Wilds, 1975). This is perhaps the most important point. A scale may acquire meaning through use; users develop, share and reinforce the meaning of each level of the scale. The meaning remains entirely implicit, but gives rise to high levels of rater agreement. In a sense, the descriptors become almost irrelevant, other than as a hook upon which to hang the implicit 'socialised' meaning of each score. The problem, as has often been observed, is that there can be little evidence for the validity of score meaning, and interpretations are difficult to justify outside the context of the institution that uses the scores (Chalhoub-Deville and Fulcher, 2003).

Methodology 2: Performance data-based

Dissatisfaction with scales constructed through intuition and experience emerged in the late 1980s. In particular, we saw the claim that rating scale 'descriptors' did not actually describe the speech of L1 or L2 speakers in actual communication (Fulcher, 1987). Discourse analysis was becoming much more widely used in applied linguistics, and language testers soon saw the possibility of using these techniques to improve the quality of descriptors (Fulcher, 1993). In what I called 'data-based approaches', the data was the discourse produced by language learners undertaking test tasks. The intention was to write descriptors with an empirical basis in descriptions of what is actually said, so that the meaning of the descriptor (and hence score) can be justified.

This approach resulted in an unexpected advantage over intuitive/experiential scales. For the most part, they had relied on the notion of the 'educated native speaker' to define the top level in the scale, with 'no functional proficiency' at the bottom of the scale. However, it was being widely argued that the idealised notion of an educated native speaker was untenable (Lantolf and Frawley, 1985: 343), and the 'nothing-to-perfect' rating scale had had its day. In a data-based rating scale it is only possible to have levels for performances that can be described and separated. The bottom level is therefore not 'nothing', and the top level is not 'perfect'; they are merely the least and most proficient performances observed in the test-taking population.

This method can be illustrated with reference to a scale designed to assess spoken fluency (Fulcher, 1993, 1996a). A sample of students was asked to undertake a task in which they first read a text, and then discussed the text with an interlocutor/examiner. The interactions were recorded and transcribed for later analysis. Each recording/transcription was analysed for fluency markers, including fillers (such as 'er'), repetition of syllables or words, re-selection of cohesion markers, re-selection of lexical items, pausing, and changing syntax within an utterance ('anacoluthon'). It was discovered that many of the features observed were related to language processing. For example, pausing might not be a sign of lack of fluency in itself, but could be related to a range of other phenomena, such as planning content, planning grammar, or indicating a turn-transitional relevant place for the interlocutor. Surface features were therefore coded by processing/communicative intention, and used as independent variables to predict effective communication.

Variables that could be used to successfully predict communicative ability were then used to create verbal descriptors for the scale. The rating scale was then used to assess a second sample of students taking the same tasks to discover if its use was better able to discriminate between the test takers. In this cross-validation study prediction was highly reliable. The descriptors that resulted from this study were also used in the studies to develop the CEFR, which in turn showed that 'Empirically, the fluency descriptors proved to have a rock-solid interpretation of difficulty across sectors, regions, and languages' (North, 2007: 657). This is not surprising, as the development methodology was firmly anchored in performance data.

A copy of the fluency scale can be found in Appendix 5. You will notice first of all that the descriptors are quite lengthy, as they attempt to describe typical language use at each level that could be distinguished in the study. We can also see from the rating scale that there is an attempt to move away from the typical assumption that language learning is linear. There is no assumption here that, for example, pausing simply decreases as proficiency increases. Rather, it was discovered that as language use becomes more sophisticated the use of pausing increased to allow for additional planning time, and then decreased again as language use becomes more automatic.

Despite the advantages of the methodology there is a practicality problem. The question we face is whether and to what extent a scale like this can be used in operational language tests, rather than in a research study. We have already discussed Popham's view that many criterion-referenced tests have a granularity in the test specifications which makes them difficult to work with, and this may also be the case with scoring criteria. If complex scoring criteria are to be considered for operational use, they need to be carefully piloted with potential raters.

Methodology 3: Empirically derived, binary-choice, boundary definition (EBBs)

The third methodology we discuss is also empirical. However, the source of data is different. In EBB development it is essential to have samples of language (writing or speaking) generated from specific language tasks, and a set of expert judges who will make decisions about the comparative merit of sets of samples. The procedure for developing an EBB scale is as follows. First, give the task to a group of students drawn from the target population. Take the resulting language samples and ask the group of experts to divide them into two groups – the 'better' and the 'weaker' performances. This first division establishes a 'boundary', which has to be defined. The experts are asked to decide what the most important criterion is that defines this boundary; they are asked to write a single question, the answer to which would result in a correct placement of a sample into the upper or lower group. In the example provided by Upshur and Turner (1995) the students were asked to do a task in which they watched a short story on a video, and were then asked to retell the story in one minute. The question that experts decided split the group into two was: 'Is the story retell coherent?'

Attention is then focused on each of the two groups separately. The experts are asked to split both the upper and the lower group language samples into three piles, giving six levels in total, three in the upper group and three in the lower group. Once this has been done, the experts are asked to state which key feature of the performances marks the boundary between each level. Once again, a single question is written that would help a rater to arrive at a decision about which level a language sample should be allocated to. This resulted in the rating scale presented in Figure 7.5.

This methodology has a number of clear advantages over rating scales. The first is that the decision points are the boundaries between levels, whereas rating scales attempt to describe typical performances in the middle of a level. This makes it difficult for raters to decide whether some samples are really 'in' the level or not. Secondly, this is very easy to use, compared with a complex rating scale. Raters can easily keep the questions in their heads while listening to (or reading) a new response.

An EBB has to be developed for each task type in a speaking or writing test. This can be an advantage or disadvantage depending upon how many different task types there are. However, the development methodology is particularly satisfying for teachers who can use it to focus attention on precisely what it is they wish learners to achieve from undertaking particular classroom tasks. For classroom assessment it is relatively easy to use, and increases the kind of group collaboration and understanding that developing task specifications can achieve.

If the approach has a weakness, it may lie in the fact that the boundaries and their definition are arrived at through the 'perception' of differences between levels (Upshur and Turner, 1995: 10). However, as the experts are looking at real performance samples when arriving at their decisions, EBBs have a major advantage over intuitive (non-empirical) methodologies. The simplicity, while an advantage, also means that the EBBs do not clearly reflect theoretical models of language use; but there is no reason in principle why these could not be brought into play in the decision-making process. In short, the EBB approach has much to recommend it, particularly for classroom assessment.

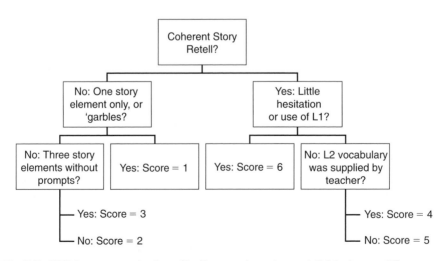

Fig. 7.5. EBB for communicative effectiveness in a story retell (Upshur and Turner, 1995: 6)

Methodology 4: Scaling descriptors

This is a methodology that language teachers (and most language testers) may never use. However, it is important to understand it, because it was developed to construct the Common European Framework (Council of Europe, 2001) that we briefly touched upon in Chapter 4. The first step in the process was to identify and collect as many existing rating scales as possible (North, 1993). The rating scales were then 'pulled apart' to create a pool of some 2000 descriptors. These were classified into types of communicative activities using expert judgement (North, 2000), and, where there were perceived gaps in a particular category, new descriptors were written. The descriptors were written on strips of paper and given to groups of teachers, who were asked to select those they felt were useful in their own teaching context. They were then asked to split the descriptors into three piles, describing low, middle and higher performance. The descriptors in each level were then divided into two in order to create the required six levels. Finally, sets of the descriptors were placed into questionnaires that were given to another group of teachers, who were asked to rate each descriptor according to its perceived difficulty, and the perceived difficulty estimates were scaled using Rasch analysis. The descriptors that could be statistically scaled were divided into equidistant groups and placed on to the six levels that we now see in the CEFR.

This methodology is empirical in the sense that there is data that guides the construction of the scales. The data is the perception of the difficulty of a descriptor for a typical group of students that is a personal abstraction from the experience of a teacher. These perceptions are scaled, and only those that can be scaled across teachers and language contexts find their way into the final rating scales. The scales are not grounded in theory, as we have already observed in Chapter 4. Rather, like Frankenstein's monster, they are constructed from previously used scale parts that are put together into a different configuration using a statistically driven model (North, 1995). This has left the CEFR scales open to the challenge that they do not describe the ways in which language is actually used, or acquired. The numbers, in terms of Shohamy's (2001a) critique, offer a sense of the certainty of scientific description where there really is none. The CEFR is likely to remain an influential document for the foreseeable future, and so a clear understanding of its construction is important for language teachers who are working in places where they may be asked to take account of its scales in their own assessment practices (also see Chapters 8 and 10).

Methodology 5: Performance decision trees (PDTs)

Finally, we describe performance decision trees. These are a combination of methodology 2 and methodology 3, to produce a binary-decision, data-based scale (Fulcher, Davidson and Kemp, 2011). In order to illustrate this method, we return to the example of service encounters in travel agencies that we have already discussed in Chapters 5 and 6. If we wished to score performances on the kind of task designed by Mills (2009), we would first have to collect data of actual service encounters and conduct a discourse analysis of the performances. We already know that there is a service encounter 'script' that participants must stick to (Hasan, 1985), as buying and selling services is an institutionalised social activity in which some kinds of communicative acts are acceptable, and others are not (Ylänne-McEwen, 2004). The normal pattern is: greeting, sale intention, sale request, sale, purchase closure and a closing routine. This may be punctuated at various points by sale enquiries. Interactions are also marked by side-sequences that help to establish temporary relationships, as in this example (SI = sale intention; SR = sale request; G = greeting; SS = side sequence) (Ylänne-McEwen, 2004: 523):

SI	=	Agent:	can I help you?
SR	=	Customer 1:	Kusadasi in er Turkey
SS	=	Agent:	ah! I'm going there in the summer
		Customer 1:	Eh?
		Agent:	I'm going there in the summer
		Customer 1:	are you?
G		Customer 2:	hiya
G		Agent:	hiya
		Customer 1:	er
SS		Customer 2:	it's nice in Turkey been in Turkey?
		Agent:	I haven't been before no
		Customer 2:	it's lovely
		Agent:	is it?
		Customer 2:	yeah

This is frequently termed 'relational management', and is designed to establish rapport (Gremler and Gwinner, 2000). Such insertions are the norm, rather than the exception, in service encounters. They turn a purely 'getting things done' interaction into a much more pleasant experience. Indeed, trainers encourage sales staff to use such interaction to improve the buying experience of the customer, as marketing researchers have discovered a relationship between relational management talk and brand loyalty (Zeithaml, 2000). Part of the success of the communication is also non-verbal, involving smiling, and maintaining regular eye contact (Gabbott and Hogg, 2000). In terms of communicative models (see Chapter 4), these elements relate to discourse and pragmatic competence. A scale resulting from such an analysis is presented in Figure 7.6.

The first question we ask is whether the obligatory elements are present; that is, whether the participants have produced a sale intention, sale request, and so on, so that the interaction is a complete and recognisable sales encounter, however short it may be. If the discourse is recognisable as a service encounter genre, the next question is whether non-obligatory elements (relational management) are present. If they are not, pragmatic competence is not assessed, but if they are, a score of 1 is added to the base score of 2 for each of the six identifiable markers of rapport building. Additional scores are added for the quality of discourse management in five identifiable categories. This creates a scale of 0 to 20 upon which the quality of the discourse can be graded.

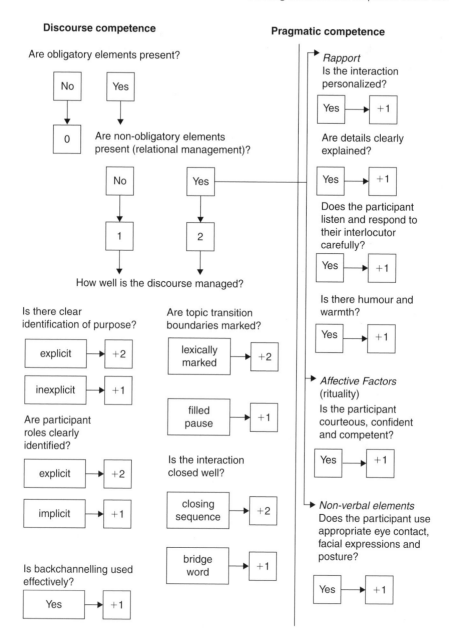

Fig. 7.6. A performance decision tree for a travel agency service encounter (Fulcher, Davidson and Kemp, 2011)

The addition of each additional point is a binary decision. In this way, the performance data-based methodology is combined with the EBB methodology to produce the kind of rich, thick description of the former, with the latter's ease of use.

▶ 4. Automated scoring

Lado (1961: 30) was particularly concerned with scoring that involved human decision. 'The examiner who is conscientious hesitates, wonders if this response is as good as another he considered good, if he is being too easy or too harsh in his scoring.' In fact, concerns about human reliability, including the impartiality of the teacher in classroom assessment, have been around for a long time (Ruch, 1924: 2–3). As part of the relentless drive to use technology to improve scorability, recent decades have seen a growing interest in scoring speaking and writing automatically (Wresch, 1993). Not surprisingly, the most successful automated scoring procedures are used in assessing writing. One system, e-rater, is widely used in the United States to score large-scale writing tests, and even to act as a second rater for the TOEFL iBT (Burstein, 2003). The software is capable of analysing syntactic features of the essay, word and text length, and vocabulary. Although these are often thought to be low-level textual features (Quinlan, Higgins and Wolf, 2009), by analysing patterns between discourse markers (e.g. 'however', 'therefore', 'first', 'second', and so on) and lexical sets, and comparing these with its database of actual essays upon which it has been trained, it is capable of providing a score for discourse organisation and topical relevance that is highly correlated to human scores (Lee, Gentile and Kantor, 2008). While the development of such systems is beyond the bounds of what is possible in most teaching contexts, if teachers are faced with exceptionally large numbers of essays to mark (or double mark), it is possible to purchase essay marking services online.

The automated scoring of speaking is a much more difficult task. The first such system was called PhonePass (Bernstein, 1999a). The kinds of tasks utilised by computer scored speaking tests include reading sentences aloud, repeating sentences, providing antonyms for words, and uttering short responses to questions. The validity claim is that the score is sensitive to basic listening ability and facility in the spoken language. By measuring pause length, pronunciation (graded against a training database of acceptable word pronunciations), timing and rhythm, the scores correlate moderately to highly with human raters.

The validation of automated scoring systems has primarily been approached through correlating the machine scores with human scores. This is known as a current criterion-oriented approach to validity. It treats human scores on a construct as the 'gold standard', and assumes that if the machine and human scores are highly related, the test is measuring a similar construct (Bernstein et al., 2000; Xi, Higgins, Zechner and Williamson, 2008). For example, Bernstein (1999b) presents the following table relating PhonePass scores to those of human raters on the constructs that the test is claimed to measure:

Score	Correlation
Repeat Accuracy	.89
Listening Vocabulary	.89
Pronunciation	.79
Reading Fluency	.86
Repeat Fluency	.87
Overall	**.94**

Table 7.1 Correlations between human and machine scores on PhonePass SET-10 (Bernstein, 1999b: 3)

We concede that all the evidence suggests that machines can indeed predict human ratings, and when used as a second marker the machine score is as highly related to the score of the first marker as the scores of human second markers (Atali, 2007). It is also the case that the machine scores are highly reliable. However, this does not necessarily mean that the machine and the humans are paying attention to the same qualities of speech or writing. When considering the claim that paper-and-pencil tests were capable of predicting speaking ability, Kaulfers (1944: 138) argued:

> The tests must not be guilty of the 'correlation fallacy', the common delusion that a certain level of ability on a pencil-and-paper test of vocabulary, grammar, or reading comprehension can automatically be interpreted to mean a corresponding level of ability to understand the spoken language, or to speak the language fluently.

The correlation fallacy has been studied in many disciplines where there is a tendency to assume that because two measures tend to co-vary, they measure the same construct. If they do indeed measure the same construct, we would expect them to correlate. But additional evidence is needed to show that the cause of the correlation is sensitivity to the same construct, which causes the variation in both measures. It is questionable whether a machine can bring to the rating process the same understanding of text and nuanced meaning that a human is able to. Many teachers therefore remain sceptical about the value and meaning of machine-generated scores for performance tests (Haswell, 2006). This scepticism is unlikely to dissipate in the near future either, for as Philips (2007) observes, most of the published research comes from employees who work for companies that produce the software or are eager to use automated scoring to reduce the costs of assessing speaking and writing in large-scale testing operations. This is compounded by the seeming inability of the computer to generate feedback for learners that even begins to approximate what a teacher can do, even if learners enjoy using automated scorers and appear to benefit from their use because of the novelty factor (Scharber, Dexter and Riedel, 2008).

The advantages of automated scoring for large-scale testing is clear, even though there is a question mark over whether the score is arrived at in the same way, and for the same reasons, as those assigned by humans. For teachers, perhaps the main advantage is freeing up time for other activities that marking seems to demand. Ruch (1924: 7) said of marking essays that 'The task at best is uninteresting and monotonous after the first dozen papers have been completed.' Perhaps there are times when the quality of feedback is not as good as we would wish to make it, in which case the computer can do a much more efficient task. Ruch continues:

> *Final examinations in particular are likely to be corrected on the day that all the multitudinous tasks incident to the closing of a semester of year or school rush in on the tired teacher, who must finish the papers, make out the report cards, balance the register, pack her trunk, and catch the earliest train home. Where, then, does the opportunity for training in the correct use of English come in under the situation as it really is?*

Such is the appeal of automated marking, even if teachers today are unlikely to be packing their trunks at the end of the semester.

5. Corrections for guessing

There is a widespread assumption that students may guess the answers to closed response items, such as multiple choice (e.g. Burton, 2001). Nothing could be further from the truth. In reality, guessing only occurs if the test is so speeded that test takers do not have time to complete the test within the time set. If this happens, it is a failure of the test designers to conduct proper timing studies during field testing. All test takers have reasons for selecting the options they do. Admittedly, these may be reasons other than ones expected by the designers, as we have seen. But they do not select randomly.

Despite this, researchers have devised means to adjust scores for a guessing effect. Lado (1961: 366–367) recommended the following formula:

$$S = R - \frac{W}{n-1}$$

where

S = the score
R = the number of right answers
W = the number of wrong answers
n = the number of alternatives per item

Thus, if I took a twenty-item, four-option multiple-choice test, and scored 12, the correction would be:

$$S = 12 - \frac{8}{4-1}$$

$$S = 12 - 2.67 = 9.33$$

This is exceptionally harsh when no one knows if I have been guessing or not, and, in all probability, I haven't. Lado realised that this was the case, and did not recommend its use. More complex methods of calculating guessing have been developed, such as estimating a guessing parameter using Item Response Theory (described in Crocker and Algina, 1986: 352–354). However, as correction for guessing is not recommended, whether applied to individuals or groups, these methods will not be discussed further. There is no theoretical or empirical basis in test-taker behaviour for their application.

▶ 6. Avoiding own goals

In this chapter we have concerned ourselves with the measurement component of the evidence model for a language test. This spells out the rules for how we derive a number or letter from a performance on a task or set of items. Deciding how this is to be done must take place concurrently with the design of the test specifications and the prototyping. Ideally, scoring methods should be tried out during prototyping and piloting. The more complex the scoring procedure, the more effort should go into the design. This is especially the case when raters will be asked to make judgements about the quality of written or spoken performances. Leaving the design of scoring systems until after items have been written and a test is virtually operational is likely to lead to serious problems.

We have also recognised that there is a tension between ease of scoring and trying to create rich performance descriptors. Complex rating systems require a granularity that is difficult to implement, whereas simpler systems are quick and efficient. We have seen numerous times in our discussions so far that even very creative teachers fall back on multiple-choice items as being the easiest way to test what they wish to test, and also to score. This is why the multiple-choice item has had such a long and robust history. Nevertheless, we should not shy away from attempting to create novel, complex item types, when we believe that the responses better reflect the constructs of interest. The effort needed to develop a scoring system may be time-consuming, and sometimes expensive. The benefits we have to gain then have to be weighed against the costs that we incur.

Very frequently scores on tests are given special meaning. If a student gets a 6.5, or over 80, they are deemed 'ready for university'. If an employee scores 48, they may be eligible for an international posting. Endowing scores with special meaning is the practice of setting 'cut scores' and establishing standards, which is the subject of Chapter 8.

Activities

⭕ 7.1 More options than answers

Look once more at the item in Activity 6.7. What problems can you see in scoring this item? How would you score it?

Now look at the following item from the Vocabulary Levels Test (Schmitt, Schmitt and Clapham, 2000: 58). Does this item present a scoring problem?

You must choose the right word to go with each meaning. Write the number of that word next to its meaning.

1. *concrete*
2. *era*
3. *fiber*
4. *hip*
5. *loop*
6. *summit*

	circular shape
_____	
_____	top of a mountain
_____	a long period of time

⭕ 7.2 Editing tasks

Variously called 'editing', 'error correction' or 'proofreading', these items come in and go out of fashion at regular intervals. Try the following editing task. When you have completed it, compare your answers with those of a colleague. What might make this item type difficult to score?

In the following passage, one necessary word has been omitted from each numbered line. Mark where you think the word has been left out ⋀, and in the spaces on the right write the omitted word. The first line has been done for you.

Picture in Depth

1 A hologram of an object is made on a piece ⋀ photographic film   1   ....of............

2 by using a laser. The object lit by the laser, and this light   2   ....

3 is reflected by the object onto the film. Light the laser   3   ....

4 also strikes the film directly. The light from the object from   4   ....

5 the laser combine to produce a pattern shows when the film is   5   ....
   developed.

6 The pattern does resemble the object until the film is   6   ....

7 illuminated. When this happens a hologram the object appears.   7   ....

8 The image is three-dimensional, having depth like real object.	8	....
9 By moving your head can see round any corners in the image.	9	....
10 Each part of the film actually contains slightly different	10	....
11 image of the object; when you look a hologram, each eye there-fore receives a separate image and these images	11	....
12 combine give it its realistic three dimensional effect.	12	....
13 Holograms can also made in which very different images can	13	....
14 be seen when you move your head. The image may to move, or it may change completely.	14	....

○ 7.3 Adaptive tests

In order to see how a computer adaptive test works in practice, see Rudner's (1998) interactive tutorial: http://echo.edres.org:8080/scripts/cat/catdemo.htm. In this demonstration you can take a short test and see how your ability estimate changes as you respond to items.

What do you think are the advantages and disadvantages of adaptive language testing?

○ 7.4 Comparing rating scales

This is the 1958 Foreign Service Institute Rating Scale. It was the earliest rating scale designed to score samples of speech from a speaking test. What are the strengths and weaknesses of this scale? Compare it with the fluency rating scale in Appendix 5. What level of detail do you prefer in a scale? Finally, compare both of these scales to the performance decision tree described in this chapter. Which of the three styles do you think is the most practical for operational use?

> _Level 1_: Elementary Proficiency. Able to satisfy routine travel needs and minimum courtesy requirements.
>
> Can ask and answer questions on topics very familiar to him; within the scope of his very limited language experience can understand simple questions and statements, allowing for slowed speech, repetition or paraphrase; speaking vocabulary inadequate to express anything but the most elementary needs; errors in pronunciation and grammar are frequent, but can be understood by a native speaker used to dealing with foreigners attempting to speak his language; while topics which are 'very familiar' and elementary needs vary considerably from individual to individual, any person at Level 1 should be able to order a simple meal, ask for shelter or lodging, ask and give simple directions, make purchases, and tell time.
>
> _Level 2_: Limited Working Proficiency. Able to satisfy routine social demands and limited work requirements.

Can handle with confidence but not with facility most social situations including introductions and casual conversations about current events, as well as work, family and autobiographical information; can handle limited work requirements, needing help in handling any complications or difficulties; can get the gist of most conversations on non-technical subjects (i.e. topics which require no specialised knowledge) and has a speaking vocabulary sufficient to express himself simply with some circumlocutions; accent, though often quite faulty, is intelligible; can usually handle elementary constructions quite accurately but does not have thorough or confident control of the grammar.

Level 3: *Minimum Professional Proficiency. Able to speak the language with sufficient structural accuracy and vocabulary to participate effectively in most formal and informal conversations on practical, social and professional topics.*

Can discuss particular interests and special fields of competence with reasonable ease; comprehension is quite complete for a normal rate of speech; vocabulary is broad enough that he rarely has to grope for a word; accent may be obviously foreign; control of grammar good; errors never interfere with understanding and rarely disturb the native speaker.

Level 4: *Full Professional Proficiency. Able to use the language fluently and accurately on all levels normally pertinent to professional needs.*

Can understand and participate in any conversation within the range of his experience with a high degree of fluency and precision of vocabulary; would rarely be taken for a native speaker, but can respond appropriately even in unfamiliar situations; errors of pronunciation and grammar quite rare; can handle informal interpreting from and into the language.

Level 5: *Native or Bilingual Proficiency. Speaking proficiency equivalent to that of an educated native speaker.*

Has complete fluency in the language such that his speech on all levels is fully accepted by educated native speakers in all its features, including breadth of vocabulary and idiom, colloquialisms and pertinent cultural references.

○ 7.5 The halo effect

The halo effect is a constant problem for diagnostic language testing. In assessment for learning it would be ideal to have learner profiles that could guide further learning and teaching, but the assessment on one criterion often contaminates the assessment on others. Read more about the halo effect, including an extract from the work of Thorndike (1920), at this website:

http://languagetesting.info/features/halorating/rating.html.

When you have done this, can you think of any methods that you might use to (a) reduce the halo effect, and (b) investigate whether it is present in a context where multiple-trait rating scales are being used?

⭕ 7.6 The big debate: automated scoring

Readers who wish to know more about commercial services should consult Dikli (2006), which is available online.

Visit the websites of the following automated essay scoring services. What claims do the companies make about automated scoring? Are you convinced by these claims? Would you use any of these services?

Bayesian Essay Test Scoring sYstem (BETSY): http://echo.edres.org:8080/betsy/
Criterion: http://criterion2.ets.org/cwe/
Intelligent Essay Assessment: http://www.knowledge-technologies.com/prodIEA.shtml
Intellimetric: http://www.vantagelearning.com/school/products/intellimetric/

Research: type 'automated essay scoring' into your favourite internet search engine. You will discover more services and a great deal of published materials. Spend some time investigating how much is being done in this expanding area.

Debate the value and efficacy of the automated scoring of constructed responses. If you are studying in a group you may wish to debate a formal motion, such as 'This house believes that automated scoring can never reflect the rich constructs of human scoring', or 'This house believes that automated scoring is the only way to encourage the teaching and learning of writing'.

⭕ 7.7 Creating an EBB

Collect a number of scripts written by your students in response to the same writing prompt. Divide them into two piles – the 'better' and the 'poorer'. What single factor distinguishes the two? Write a question, the answer to which would determine into which pile a new essay would go. Follow the same procedure for the 'better' and the 'poorer'.

Give your EBB to a colleague, or another group, along with the sample scripts. Is the other group able to put the scripts into the same piles you did, using your EBB?

⭕ 7.8 Designing a rating scale

Look at the following speaking task, which was designed to assess the achievement of learners in an advanced conversation class.

From time to time, individual years are dedicated to a particular theme. We have had the International Year of the Child, and Information Technology Year. If you could choose one theme for a future year, which of the following suggestions would you select, and why?

- *wildlife*
- *climate change*
- *famine relief*
- *women*
- *sport*
- *health*

Which type of rating scale would be most suited to scoring the responses to this task? If you have the time and resources, develop the scale. If you do not, try to write just one descriptor that describes what you think an 'acceptable' performance might be for an advanced learner.

Make a note of the challenges and problems you face in the process.

○ 7.9 Project work V

Look carefully at the item(s) or tasks that you have designed so far, based upon your test specification. Can you see any scoring problems that you have not identified? If your test specification does not contain a section on how the item(s) should be scored, now is the time to write it up and add it to the documentation.

8 Aligning tests to standards

 ## 1. It's as old as the hills

Standard setting is 'the process of establishing one or more cut scores on examinations. The cut scores divide the distribution of examinees' test performances into two or more categories' (Cizek and Bunch, 2007: 5). 'Standards-based assessment' uses tests to assess learner performance and achievement in relation to an absolute standard; it is therefore often said to be a development of criterion-referenced testing, even though the tests used are most frequently of the large-scale standardised variety.

Although standards-based assessment and standard-setting seem to be a very modern concern, the problem of establishing 'standards' is as old as educational assessment, and certainly pre-dates the criterion-referenced testing move. Latham (1877: 367) drew a distinction between 'relative' and 'absolute' measurements well before the usually discussed timelines.

> Thus far we have spoken of a relative measure of proficiency, but in some cases we want an absolute measure as well. This absolute standard is supplied in University Examinations by dividing the candidates into classes.

He also prefigured the difficulty of deciding upon a *cut score*, which is the central topic of this chapter: 'The difficulty of drawing a line is proverbial, and frequently this separation into classes causes much discussion.' And we may add, not a little disagreement.

 ## 2. The definition of 'standards'

We have already seen that the term *'standards'* has many different meanings when talking about testing and assessment. Whenever it is used, the first thing we have to do is be absolutely certain how it is being used. The meaning that we are concerned with in this chapter is defined by Davies *et al.* (1999: 185) in the following way:

> Standard refers to a level of performance required or experienced ('the standard required for entry to the university is an A in English'; 'English standards are rising').

In our discussion of scoring performance tests in the last chapter, we looked at how rating scales are developed. We saw that hierarchical linear scales contain descriptors of what the scale developer thinks learners know, or can do, at each level. Now imagine that a policy maker decides that a particular level on a scale describes what someone 'ought to know or be able to do' for them to be admitted to a programme of study, be awarded a diploma or be allowed to work in a country. A level on a scale has now become a 'standard' that has to be met.

▌ 3. The uses of standards

Establishing standards and introducing a system of standards-based assessment can be exceptionally useful, even challenging and professionally rewarding for teachers; and in the field of language certification for the world of work, essential for the protection of the public. If the ability to use language for a particular purpose is critical to successfully performing a job, it is appropriate that individuals are tested to see if they have reached the 'standard' necessary. For example, aircraft mechanics are required to check aircraft in a very systematic manner, following step-by-step instructions from a manual that is written in English (see the example in Chapter 4). Any problems have to be reported to a supervisor, and after every check a report has to be produced to be signed off by a senior mechanic. As a member of the travelling public, I would be exceptionally worried if I thought that the aircraft in which I was going to fly had been checked by someone who could not read the manual, communicate with the supervisor or write the safety report clearly. Yet, we know that there are serious problems with establishing standards in the airline industry, and designing tests that are capable of measuring whether individuals meet those standards (Alderson, 2009).

While the certification of air traffic personnel is fairly uncontroversial, other uses of standards-based testing cause fierce debate and disagreement. For example, testing and assessment has long been used as a method of implementing all kinds of policies by the state and other bureaucracies. Perhaps the most widely discussed is that of accountability through high-stakes testing (Menken, 2008a). Under the No Child Left Behind (NCLB) legislation in the United States, for example, schools are required to demonstrate 'adequate yearly progress' (AYP) of English language learners. AYP is assessed by tests that 'have become the de facto language policy in schools: they shape what content is taught in school, how it is taught, by whom it is taught, and in what language(s) it is taught' (Menken, 2008a: 407–408). All states are required to implement high-stakes tests that are linked to standards of attainment (Menken, 2008b).

The external mandate for the tests comes from a state that fears its economic and scientific future is threatened by low achievement in schools; to raise achievement it sets in place standards that have to be met. The tests hold schools and teachers accountable, and severe financial penalties may be imposed for not making adequate yearly progress towards meeting the standards (Chalhoub-Deville and Deville, 2008; Menken, 2009).

Standards are therefore not simply statements of levels of achievement. They are powerful expressions of what political authorities wish an educational system to deliver in the interests of the nation's future. The tests are the technology by which the state checks whether the educational goals are being met. The rewards and penalties that accompany success or failure on the tests are the mechanisms for enforcement. This kind of testing is not always negative. Standards-based testing can sometimes drive forward educational improvements (Lee, 2008), but if poorly designed and implemented, it can also have terrible unintended consequences.

Even more controversial is the use of standards-based assessment in immigration policy. This issue raises ethical questions that lead to significant disagreement among teachers and test developers. Some find this use of tests distasteful, while others believe that it is reasonable to require a language standard for immigration on the grounds of social integration (Bishop, 2004). Whatever position we take, it is often the case that the standard required for immigration is changed depending upon economic conditions. For example, in order to work in Australia most immigrants first require a temporary work visa. In 2009, the 'standard' required to obtain such a visa was raised from 4.5 to 5.0 because the economic crisis reduced the need for imported labour. In this case the 'standard' is taken from the scale of the International English Language Testing System (IELTS). Bands 4.0, 5.0 and 6.0 are reproduced below from www.ielts.org:

Band 6: Competent user: has generally effective command of the language despite some inaccuracies, inappropriacies and misunderstandings. Can use and understand fairly complex language, particularly in familiar situations.

Band 5: Modest user: has partial command of the language, coping with overall meaning in most situations, though is likely to make many mistakes. Should be able to handle basic communication in own field.

Band 4: Limited user: basic competence is limited to familiar situations. Has frequent problems in understanding and expression. Is not able to use complex language.

Moving the standard to band 5 had the effect of reducing the rate of immigration. Some professional organisations, such as Engineers Australia (2008), have lobbied the government for even higher requirements, claiming that immigrants without a band 6 are not able to function effectively as engineers (effectively using the job certification argument to reduce immigration quotas in a particular profession). While it would appear likely that there is a link between language competence and the ability to successfully operate as an engineer, there is no evidence to suggest that a band 6 on IELTS is 'the standard' that is most appropriate.

This story illustrates the central problem with deciding upon what 'standard' is required when the purpose of testing is to implement a policy objective that is primarily political, rather than linguistic. The decision about what standard to impose is not taken on the basis of evidence about the relationship between a descriptor and the ability to function in the target domain. The process of decision making therefore violates the central principle of validity, that there should be a strong inferential link between the meaning of a score and the abilities of the test taker. In short, the purpose of the test is to reduce immigration, not assess the test takers.

▶ 4. Unintended consequences revisited

When standards are used as policy tools, there are usually unintended consequences. For example, under NCLB legislation in the United States, as we have already mentioned, failure of a school or school district to show adequate yearly progress towards meeting standards is financially penalised. However, when English language learners achieve the standard as indicated by the test score, they are no longer classified as English language learners (ELLs). The successful students are removed. This means that the average score of the ELL group is always lower than the standard, and it is very difficult to demonstrate AYP. In addition, the lowest mean scores occur in schools with the largest populations of English language learners, which invariably indicates a larger proportion of recent immigrants, and therefore the need for more resources. However, the policy reduces access to those resources because AYP does not show up in the statistics (Menken, 2009). The overall effect is that resources are not channelled to where they are most needed. This policy is not a matter of indifference to teachers who have to work with language learners in these schools (Harper, de Jong and Platt, 2007), as it encourages poor strategies to deal with the situation. For example, teachers often concentrate on raising the test scores of the weakest learners at the expense of those nearer to the score where they would be reclassified. In fact, it is not in the interests of the school to have higher scorers reclassified. In addition, as Shepard (2000: 9) puts it rather bluntly, 'accountability-testing mandates warn teachers to comply or get out (or move, if they can, to schools with higher scoring students)'. This cannot be in the best interests of the learners.

Another unintended consequence relates to the mandatory use of English in tests of content subjects. For example, in many Alaskan schools teaching and learning are conducted in the first language of the learners, Yup'ik. But they are expected to show progress on tests set in what is for them a foreign language. While the learners are quite capable, and achieve school leaving certificates when the tests are set in Yup'ik, on all federally mandated tests they show up as well below proficient in language, maths and science. The policy therefore has the effect of putting pressure on the indigenous people to abandon education in their own language. This example shows how the thoughtless use of tests to achieve policy objectives can inadvertently threaten the existence of minority languages and the ways of life of indigenous peoples.

The use of language tests for immigration can have even larger and more damaging unintended consequences. When tests act as the gatekeeper to a new life and economic prosperity, the opportunities to make a profit from fraudulent practices multiply quickly. This is endemic in India, where many will go to great lengths to obtain work visas for Australia. The problems are multiplied when the tests chosen to fulfil the gatekeeping role are also used for access to college and university. Economic migrants who cannot pass the test seek out potential spouses who can, and offer to fund their studies in return for a short-term marriage. Partners of bona fide students can obtain work visas much more easily. In turn, this creates business for lawyers who are prepared to ensure that the scam marriages are not detected, and agencies that specialise in the other services that will be needed.

This is an ethical minefield. Language testing agencies have typically said that the social consequences of test use are not their responsibility, and political authorities are equally swift to deny their culpability.

▶ 5. Using standards for harmonisation and identity

Using standards to achieve harmonisation is a very old phenomenon, especially in Europe. Powerful centralising institutions have frequently used tests and standards to eradicate diversity and impose norms. This is different from the practical uses of standards in education and certification, and even in gatekeeping, because the goal is much more overtly political. The purpose is to enforce conformity to a single model that helps to create and maintain political unity and identity.

The earliest example of using standards and tests for harmonisation comes from the Carolingian empire of Charlemagne (CE 800–814). Charlemagne expanded the Frankish Empire to cover most of Central and Western Europe. Within the new empire various groups followed different calendars, in which the main Christian festivals – particularly Easter – fell on different dates. Charlemagne used his new monastic schools to institute a new standard for 'computists' who worked out the time of festivals, which was based on Bede's book *On the Reckoning of Time*. A test was then put in place to assess whether trainee computists had met the standard before they were certified to practise. Jones estimates the date of the documentary evidence for the test as CE 809, and shows that 'the Carolingians pressed for uniformity, and as such an examination was one form of pressure' (1963: 23). This is a fascinating example of the use of a standard and a test for purely political purposes. There are no 'correct answers' for any of the questions in the Carolingian test. The answers that are scored as correct are 'correct' because they are defined as such by the standard, and the standard is arbitrarily chosen with the intention of harmonising practice. Whether the harmonisation is needed, or whether one method is preferable to another, are not really questions that arise. The goal and value of harmonisation are the establishment of a political identity, and this is reason enough.

We see today that little has changed since Carolingian times. A frequent defence of standards is to be found in the claim that they offer teachers, testers and materials writers, a 'common language' that they can use to talk about the levels of their learners (Fulcher, 2008a: 160). One of the goals of the CEFR, for example, was to introduce a common metalanguage for testing and teaching languages in Europe (North, 2007: 659). The six-level scales and their descriptors are said to be 'natural levels', which has nothing at all to do with the 'nature' of language, but more to do with the fact that they are designed to represent 'the conventional, recognized, convenient levels found in books and exams' (North, 1992: 12). The claim being made is that the CEFR is a set of standards (and guidelines) that provides a uniquely European model for language testing and learning, and establishes a common metalanguage that enhances European identity and harmonisation (Fulcher, 2004). Teachers are now frequently required to show that the results of their tests provide information about the standard that their learners have achieved in relation to the CEFR, and align their curriculum to CEFR standards. This process is also referred to as 'linking', and as Kaftandjieva (2007: 35) argues approvingly, 'the main goal of this linking exercise is to demonstrate compliance with a mandate'. Failure to comply means that many European institutions will not recognise any certificate that is awarded on the basis of test outcomes. Through this policy, the Council of Europe has succeeded to a very large degree in harmonising a system through bureaucratic recognition, making resistance genuinely futile for many teachers.

Numerous problems arise from this kind of harmonisation. The first, and most obvious for teachers, is that it stifles creativity (Davies, 2008b: 438). Once a set of standards is imposed, experimentation ceases. Yet, there is nothing 'natural' about the levels. As we have seen in Chapter 7, different levels and standards are appropriate for different contexts. The same set of descriptors is not appropriate for migrant plumbers, aircraft engineers and international students. Most of all, enforced harmonisation discourages teachers from developing their own standards for their own students, and monitoring their own achievement within a context of local professional responsibility.

Second is a question of validation. The harmonisation process in Europe is largely about the recognition of qualifications across borders. European countries have long been determined not to recognise the qualifications issued by their European partners. My certificates may be recognised in the United States, Japan, China and India. But not in Spain, Italy or Greece. Indeed, the origins of the CEFR lie in Switzerland, where each Swiss canton would not recognise the language qualifications of other cantons within the same country (Fulcher, 2008b: 21). The harmonisation argument says that if the outcomes of a test are reported in relation to the 'standard' CEFR, the meanings of the scores of the different tests are shown to 'mean' the same thing. The main activity of research is therefore to link a test to the CEFR so that it is 'recognised' by other institutions. When this linking has taken place, the testing agency proclaims the test 'valid'. This is not what validation is about, but the policy aim has successfully subverted the meaning of validation and reduced it to little more than 'bureaucratic acceptance'.

This leads directly to the third problem. The policy encourages the view that tests and assessments, however different they might be in purpose, structure or content, can be compared once their 'meaning' is made clear by linking them to the CEFR. If all tests can be mapped on to the CEFR to explain the outcomes in terms of level and what the test takers can do, the tests are stripped of their purpose. For language testing this is a tragic consequence. We have tried to show in this book that test purpose leads to design decisions, and the test architecture links score meaning very closely to the kinds of claims that we wish to make about test takers. Once the meaning of the test is its level on the CEFR, it is just another 'measure' of what the CEFR purports to describe.

While this use of the CEFR subverts validity theory, it is popular with some testing agencies because it serves a useful economic purpose. It is possible to produce a test without any particular purpose, claim a link to the CEFR, and seek recognition of its use for purposes as wide as licensing engineers, applying for immigration, or accessing higher education. Websites for some testing agencies proudly list the extensive uses to which their tests are put. Any idea that the test is not appropriate for any and all purposes can be swept under the carpet in the goal of maximising test volume, and hence income. In these cases, the interests of the political bureaucracy and testing businesses with little concern for validity go hand in hand.

Ultimately, as I have argued elsewhere (Fulcher, 2008b, 2009), the use of standards and tests for harmonisation ultimately leads to a desire for more and more control. Sometimes this can verge on megalomania, as in the case of Bonnet (2007: 672), who wishes to see the removal of all national educational policies and the imposition of 'a common educational policy in language learning, teaching and assessment, both at the EU level and beyond'. However, I suspect that world domination is not a realistic possibility.

The claim that harmonisation produces a common language, a common way of seeing the world, is not new. For example, Schulz (1986: 373) claimed that the ACTFL Guidelines provided testers and curriculum designers with a common terminology with which they could work for the first time. While it is true that the ACTFL Guidelines have had a significant impact on the development of what is commonly referred to as 'the proficiency movement', history has shown that no single set of standards can meet all needs, or satisfy all purposes. Proponents of the ACTFL Guidelines have had to admit their standards, like others, are but useful fictions (Bachman and Savignon, 1986). However, teachers can easily be frightened into thinking that they must comply with the demands of powerful institutions. It is important not to allow these institutions to try to make us think and talk in only one way about language and standards; it drains creativity and is a disservice to learners and our profession. It is important to be eclectic, selecting parts of what is on offer when it is useful, and devising our own standards when they are not.

This brings the first part of this chapter to a close. Once again we have been obliged to consider the social, political, philosophical and ethical concerns that surround language testing. We now turn to the practical matters of how to align tests to standards.

▶ 6. How many standards can we afford?

When discussing 'best practice' in establishing standard descriptors, Perie (2008: 17) writes: 'The first decision is the number of performance levels to use. Ideally, policy makers should choose the fewest performance levels needed to fulfil their purpose. The goals for and use of the test should be considered in determining the number of performance levels needed. In many certification or licensure tests, only two levels are needed: Pass and Fail.' This advice leads to the best conceptual clarity that we can achieve, as each classification is not 'watertight', but leaks into the one above and below. This is not a new observation. Latham (1877: 368) noted that 'the gradation from one of these groups to another is continuous, and sometimes there is no considerable break between the candidates near the place where the line, according to tradition, ought to be drawn.' Latham saw that cut scores and boundaries were always going to be problematic, and they still are.

There is also a measurement reason for choosing the fewest possible levels, which Latham also prefigured (1877: 368): 'the more numerous the classes, the greater will be the danger of a small difference in marks causing the difference of a class between two candidates'. And small differences are frequently unreliable. As we saw in Chapters 2 and 3, the reliability or dependability of a test affects the probability that a score has occurred by chance, and scores within a certain region around the cut score could easily have fallen into another category. Wright (1996) recommends the use of the Index of Separation to estimate the number of performance levels into which a test can reliably place test takers. The formula for the Index is:

$$G = \sqrt{\frac{R}{1-R}}$$

where G is the index of separation, and R is the estimated reliability of the test. In order to establish a single cut score that justifies two levels (pass/fail), the test would need to achieve a reliability of at least .5. While this may not be too hard, the confidence interval around the cut score is likely to be extremely high. To introduce a second cut score with three levels, the test needs to achieve a reliability of .8, and .9 to support a third cut score with four levels. These are very demanding levels of reliability to achieve.

Despite the general recommendation to have the minimum number of levels possible, there are times when language testers deliberately increase the number of levels even if it is difficult to empirically support the expansion. This is most frequently done in the assessment of school-aged or college language learners, because a small number of categories does not give them the sense of progression from year to year. This can lead to a sense of demotivation. For example, in a large-scale survey of language learning, Carroll (1967) reported that most modern language learners in US colleges did not achieve a level 2/2+ on the Interagency Language Roundtable scale after many years of study. This directly led to the expansion of categories at the lower levels, which resulted in the American Council on the Teaching of Foreign Language Guidelines, which we discussed in Chapter 7. Not surprisingly, Latham also foresaw this necessity, despite his own desire for few cut scores: 'young people, however, need close gradations of success; if the steps are too far apart they stagnate somewhere' (1877: 368). For the purposes of motivation in language learning we just have to accept that it is sometimes necessary to use categories that are too numerous to be theoretically or empirically defensible. However, we should not start to believe that they are, or that they represent, some kind of second language acquisition 'reality'. They are but a useful pedagogical fiction.

▶ 7. Performance level descriptors (PLDs) and test scores

The performance level descriptors (PLDs) are arranged in a hierarchical, linear sequence. As we have seen in Chapter 7, they can be arrived at in a number of different ways. Most often, they are developed using the intuitive and experiential method. The labels and descriptors are often simple reflections of the values of policy makers. Perie (2008: 18) suggests that there are frequently around four levels, labelled as 'advanced – proficient – basic – below basic', or 'Exceeds the standard – meets the standard – approaches the standard – below standard'. One example of the two top level descriptors from the assessment of literacy (2008: 24) is:

Proficient: *Reading Comprehension Skills*

- Usually identify the main idea in the passage.
- Usually identify salient details in a short reading passage.
- Usually identify the sequence of events in the passage.
- Usually identify cause and effect relationships.
- Usually determine character traits.

Proficient: *Writing Skills*

- Usually apply the rules of grammar correctly.
- Usually apply the rules of punctuation correctly.
- Demonstrate some understanding of the more advanced grammatical structures.

Advanced: *Reading Comprehension Skills*

- Consistently identify the main idea in a reading passage, even if it is not explicitly stated.
- Consistently identify details in a reading passage.
- Easily recall the sequence of events in a reading passage.
- Consistently identify cause and effect relationships.
- Consistently determine character traits.

Advanced: *Writing Skills*

- Accurately apply the rules of grammar on a consistent basis.
- Accurately apply the rules of punctuation on a consistent basis.
- Demonstrate understanding most advanced

Although it is often said that tests used in standards-based testing are criterion-referenced, as discussed in Chapter 3, for Glaser the criterion was the domain to which inferences would be made, and does not necessarily have anything to do with standard setting and classification (Hambleton, 1994: 24). Nevertheless, the standards-based testing movement has interpreted 'criterion' to mean 'standard'. This has frequently led to the confusion that rating scales for a particular performance (like those discussed in Chapter 7) are the same as PLDs. While it is true that any of the methodologies discussed in Chapter 7 can be used to develop PLDs, PLDs should differ from rating scales in that they provide a general description of the larger construct (if there is one) to be assessed, rather than the criteria for assessing a particular performance on a single item or task. As Cizek and Bunch (2007: 30–31) show, 'the focus within PLDs is on the global description of competence, proficiency, or performance; there is no attempt to predict how a student at a particular achievement might perform on a specific item. Scoring rubrics address only single items; PLDs address overall or general performance levels.' PLDs therefore differ from descriptors in rating scales in that they are not attached to any particular test or assessment instrument. The fundamental distinction between PLDs used as 'standards', and descriptors in scales that are used directly for rating, should be maintained for standard-setting to be carried out.

The PLDs therefore provide a conceptual hierarchy of performance. A test that is a measure of the construct(s) described in the PLDs provides the score that is an indication of the ability or knowledge of the test taker (Kane, 1994). Standard-setting is the process of deciding on a cut score for a test to mark the boundary between two PLDs.

Thus, if we have a system that requires a binary decision, we have two performance level descriptors: 'pass' and 'fail'. We therefore need a test with a single cut score. If a test taker gets a score above this they are classified as 'pass', and if they get a score below this, they are classified as 'fail'. On the other hand, if we have a system where learners are to be placed into four levels, a test of these abilities must have three cut scores – one to separate below basic from basic, one to separate basic from proficient and one to separate proficient from advanced.

 # 8. Some initial decisions

Deciding how many levels to have is necessarily judgemental, unless a performance data-based approach is used to construct the scale. In fact, most of what happens in standard-setting involves human judgement. The decisions that have to be taken first concern how the scoring is going to work, and what errors in classifying test takers you can afford to make.

Decision number 1: Compensatory or non-compensatory marking? Let us imagine that you have a school achievement test that consists of four sub-tests: listening, speaking, reading and writing. The test-total score is scaled out of 100, and the pass score is 70. Anyone who gains 70 or higher progresses to the next instructional level, whereas anyone who scores less than 70 is assigned to a remedial instruction class. The decision you have to make is whether any combination of 70 (or higher) is a pass. Assuming that each section contributes 25 points, a grade of 70 could be made up of 19 in listening, 9 in speaking, 22 in reading and 20 in writing. In a compensatory system, the 9 in speaking does not matter because the strength in other areas 'compensates' for this weakness.

However, you may decide that, in order to pass, a test taker must get 70 and achieve at least 15 in each sub-test. The decision depends on just how much you value each sub-test, and how important you think it is to the kind of decision that you are using the test to make (Bachman, 2004: 318–319). Everyone involved in making this decision should be aware of just how contentious debate in this area can be. It requires an explicit statement of what kind of knowledge and skill is valued for whatever decision is going to be made on the basis of test scores, and different groups of stakeholders frequently bring different views to the table.

Decision number 2: What classification errors can you tolerate? We know that no test is 'completely' reliable. There is always going to be error. This means that when setting cut scores some test takers will be misclassified. We usually think about this by using a philosopher's truth table, which we can set out in Table 8.1. This closely resembles Table 3.1 in Chapter 3, as this is essentially a decision about managing errors in a criterion-referenced or, more appropriately here, 'standards-referenced', assessment system.

	The 'true' classification (which we cannot know)	
The inference drawn from the test	Pass	Fail
Pass	A Successful classification	B False positive
Fail	C False negative	D Successful classification

Table 8.1 A truth table

As we saw in Chapter 3, ideally we wish to maximise the numbers in cells A and D, but we know that there will be entries in cells B and C. Using the same example as above, would you be prepared to tolerate more individuals passing who should not really pass (thereby going on to the next instructional level), or is it more important that everyone who has genuinely not passed should receive remedial instruction? In the latter case, some learners who are genuinely pass students will have to undertake the remedial instruction as well. If you decide you can tolerate more false positives, you would lower the cut score to ensure that all genuine pass cases pass. If you decide you cannot, you raise the cut score to reduce the number of false positives and increase the number of false negatives. The proportions of learners who will be affected can be calculated using the threshold loss agreement methods described in Chapter 3.

With achievement tests we frequently do not really have a preference. However, if the test was a listening comprehension for air traffic controllers, we would wish to reduce the probability of a false positive to zero, which would involve increasing the level of the cut score. In this example the number of false negatives may be much larger, but introducing what might be seen as this level of 'unfairness' is not as serious as allowing a single false positive. Raising the cut score then becomes a policy matter after conducting a standard setting study, with due attention being paid to issues of 'disparate impact' (Geisinger, 1991).

Decision number 3: Are you going to allow test takers who 'fail' a test to retake it? If so, what time lapse are you going to require before they can retake the test? These decisions are not as simple are you may think. Remember that no test is completely reliable, and so we do expect some fluctuation in scores. The more often a test taker can take the test, the more likely they may pass just by chance, thus increasing the possibility of a false positive (Plake, 2008: 4). Your decision may therefore need to take account of your response to your second decision.

▶ 9. Standard-setting methodologies

In the *Standards for Educational and Psychological Testing* (AERA, 1999: 59), standard 4.19 reads:

> *When proposed score interpretations involve one or more cut scores, the rationale and procedures used for establishing cut scores should be clearly documented.*

In the commentary, it is suggested that the only unproblematic case of setting a cut score is when a certain percentage of test takers are going to be selected for a particular purpose – perhaps the top 10 per cent, for example. This can be done using a reliable norm-referenced test. In all other non-quota cases the rationale for establishing the cut score must be documented. This involves explaining the process of establishing the cut score using an appropriate standard-setting methodology.

Cizek and Bunch (2007) argue that there is no foolproof method of classifying standard-setting methodologies. However, it is necessary for us to make some distinctions simply for the purpose of presentation. I have decided to adopt a fairly traditional distinction between methods that focus on the test, and methods that focus on the test takers (Jaeger, 1989). As we have said, all standard-setting procedures involve judgements being made by experts – teachers, testers, applied linguists. The more qualified and experienced judges there are, the sounder the process is likely to be. The distinction used here is whether the judgements concern the test in relation to the standards, or the test takers in relation to the standards. In test-centred methods judges are presented with individual items or tasks and required to make a decision about the expected performance on them by a test taker who is just below the border between two standards. We describe the Angoff method, the Ebel method, the Nedelsky method and the Bookmark method. In examinee-centred methods the judges make decisions about whether individual test takers are likely to be just below a particular standard; the test is then administered to the test takers to discover where the cut score should lie. The two most common methodologies that we describe are the borderline-group method and the contrasting group method.

In the following description of the process of standard-setting and the most commonly used methods employed, I draw primarily upon Berk (1986), Cizek and Bunch (2007), Hambleton and Pitoniak (2006) and Livingston and Zieky (1982).

Process

Irrespective of the standard-setting method selected, there is a common process to standard setting activities. These are summarised by Hambleton and Pitoniak (2006: 436–439) as follows:

1. Select an appropriate standard setting method depending upon the purpose of the standard setting, available data, and personnel.
2. Select a panel of judges based upon explicit criteria.
3. Prepare the PLDs and other materials as appropriate.
4. Train the judges to use the method select.
5. Rate items or persons, collect and store data.
6. Provide feedback on rating and initiate discussion for judges to explain their ratings, listen to others, and revise their views or decisions, before another round of judging.
7. Collect final ratings and establish cut scores.
8. Ask the judges to evaluate the process.
9. Document the process in order to justify the conclusions reached.

We now consider each of the common methods mentioned above to see how these can be used in practice, although anyone who intends to carry out a standard setting study in their own institution is encouraged to read the more detailed descriptions in Cizek and Bunch (2007), and consult the step-by-step instructions provided by Livingston and Zieky (1982).

Test-centred methods

Angoff method

The Angoff method is one of the most commonly used of all standard setting methodologies. The standard-setting judges are asked to imagine a hypothetical learner who is on the borderline between two standards. They are then presented with test items one by one, and asked to estimate the probability that the learner will answer the item correctly. The probability estimates of each of the judges is summed and averaged to arrive at a cut score. If the test contains *polytomous items* or tasks, the proportion of the maximum score is used instead of the probability that the learner will answer the item correctly. If step 6 (above) is added, the method is normally referred to as a modified Angoff.

The main problem with the Angoff method is that it is difficult for all judges to conceptualise the borderline learner in precisely the same way, even if they have experience of similar learners and attempt to establish what they mean by a borderline learner before making judgements. Even when this is possible, it is very difficult to estimate the probability of such a student getting a single item correct. For example, presented with a multiple-choice vocabulary item, a judge would have to state that a candidate at the pass/fail border would only be 40 per cent or 30 per cent likely to get the item right. Because of the cognitive difficulty of this task, some researchers have claimed that the Angoff method is fundamentally flawed (Hambleton and Pitoniak, 206: 441); but this has not stopped it from being the most widely used method today because of its practicality.

Ebel method

Like the Angoff method, judges are given test items one by one. However, they are asked to make a judgement about two facets of each item: its difficulty, and its relevance to the target performance. Difficulty is classed as easy, medium and hard; relevance as questionable, acceptable, important and essential. This gives a 3 × 4 matrix, and each item is put into one of the 12 cells. The second stage in the process is for each judge to estimate the percentage of items a borderline test taker would get correct for each cell. For example, a judge might decide that in the 'easy/essential' cell, a borderline test taker might answer 85 per cent of the items correctly.

Once each judge has done this, the percentage for each cell is multiplied by the number of items, so if the 'easy/essential' cell has 20 items, 20 × 85 = 1700. These numbers for each of the 12 cells are added up and then divided by the total number of items to give the cut score for a single judge. Finally, these are averaged across judges to give a final cut score.

Although relatively simple, this method has also been questioned for the complex cognitive requirements of classifying items according to two criteria in relation to an imagined borderline student. In addition, as it is assumed that some items may have questionable relevance to the construct of interest, it implicitly throws into doubt the rigour of the test development process.

Nedelsky method

Whereas the Angoff and the Ebel method can be used with dichotomously and poly-tomously scored items, the Nedelsky method can only be used with multiple-choice items. The judgement that the experts are asked to make is how many options in the multiple-choice item a borderline test taker would know are incorrect. In a four-option item with three distractors, the judge is therefore being asked to decide if a borderline candidate could rule out 1, 2 or 3 of the distractors. If they can rule out all three, the chances of getting the item right are 1 (100 per cent), whereas if they can only rule out 1 of the items, the chance of answering the item correctly is 1 in 3 (33 per cent). These probabilities are averaged across all items for each judge, and then across all judges to arrive at a cut score.

The method is easy to implement, but has two disadvantages. The first is purely conceptual. It assumes that test takers answer multiple choice items by eliminating the options that they think are distractors and then guessing randomly between the remaining options. However, it is highly unlikely that test takers answer items in this way. Most test takers have some reason for the selection they make, even if the reasoning is false (Livingston and Zieky, 1982: 21–22). In studies it has also been shown that the Nedelsky method tends to produce lower cut scores than other methods (Hambleton and Pitoniak, 2006: 442), and is therefore likely to increase the number of false positives.

Bookmark method

The bookmark method requires the test items or tasks to be presented to the judges in a book, ordered according to item difficulty from easy to most difficult. This is called an 'ordered item booklet'. It is therefore essential that items have robust difficulty estimates arrived at from operational or large-scale administrations of the test. Clearly, this method is much more appropriate for large-scale testing operations than it is for institutional tests. However, as this method is widely used in the United States to establish cut scores, we will briefly describe its use.

Judges are presented with the booklets containing the items. If the item requires a constructed response (written or spoken), the judge also receives a sample response for the item at the estimated difficulty level of the item. The judge also gets an 'item map' that shows each item's relationship to other items and its location on the scale. The item map is generated from the kind of data presented in Figure 7.2. Each judge is then asked to keep in mind a student who is a borderline candidate, and place a 'bookmark' in the book between two items, such that the candidate is more likely to be able to answer the items below correctly, and the items above incorrectly. For constructed response items the bookmark is placed at the point where candidates performing below the bookmark are not likely to be in the higher category. In some cases the judges are also provided with an *a priori* definition of a mastery level, such as '66 per cent correct' (Reckase, 2000) in order to guide judgements, but these are additional arbitrary decisions that complicate the interpretation of outcomes.

Examinee-centred methods

Borderline group method

This method is probably one of the easiest to use, but it does require a relatively large number of test takers and judges. Nevertheless, in a reasonably sized school it is possible to conduct a borderline group study with some ease, as long as it is not necessary to establish too many cut scores.

The judges are asked to define what borderline candidates are like, and then identify borderline candidates who fit the definition. If multiple cut scores are needed, the process is more complex, as more than one definition, and more than one group of students, are required. Once the students have been placed into groups the test can be administered. The median score (the score in the centre of the distribution) for a group defined as borderline is used as the cut score.

Although the method is easy to apply, the main problem with the method is that the cut score is dependent upon the group being used in the study. The cut score will be valid only in so far as the characteristics of the student population does not change over subsequent administrations. If there is a drift in student ability over time, cut scores will have to be recalculated.

Contrasting group method

In this method it is essential to be able to identify at least two groups of potential test takers, one of which is very clearly above a boundary between two PLDs, and one of which is below. The classification must be done using independent criteria, such as teacher judgements of their abilities in relation to the PLDs. The test is then given, and the score distributions calculated. This method can be used with more than two groups, but the more that are added, the larger the sample sizes become, and the more difficult it is to find a score that discriminates well between levels.

If we assume that there are three levels and therefore two cut scores, we would require three groups of test takers. The distributions may look something like Figure 8.1, which looks suspiciously like Figure 2.1. (In fact, the problem faced by Yerkes in 1917 was one of attempting to contrast groups who were not sufficiently separated by his tests.) There are likely to be overlaps in the distributions, and the decision then has to be made where to establish the cut score. If we consider the distributions of the basic and proficient groups (assuming that a classification of 'proficient' brings with it some entitlement or advantage), we have at least three options, marked on Figure 8.1 as (a), (b) and (c).

Selecting (a) as the cut score will increase the number of false positives, but it ensures that everyone who is really proficient is classified as proficient. If (b) is selected as the cut score, the false positives and false negatives will be roughly equally divided. The selection of (c) would ensure that no one who is genuinely basic is classified as proficient, but some proficient students who just happen to have lower scores will be classified as basic. Once again, there can be no guidelines for making these decisions, as they are policy matters that depend entirely on the potential consequences of misclassification at some point on the scale. It is also advisable to take into account any legal consequences that might follow if a test taker were to claim that they had been misclassified.

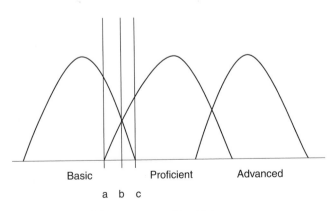

Fig. 8.1. The distributions of three groups of test takers

Of the methods that we have reviewed, which is the 'best'? This is a question that Livingston and Zieky (1982: 53) asked, and came to the conclusion that it all depended on what kinds of judgements you can get for your standard-setting study, and the quality of the judges that you have available. However, they recommended using the contrasting group approach if at all possible, on the grounds that it is the only method that allows the calculation of likely decision errors (false positives and false negatives) for cut scores. The difficulties lie in getting the judgements of a number of people on a large enough group of individuals.

10. Evaluating standard-setting

Kane (1994) suggested that three types of evidence are needed to evaluate a standard-setting study.

The first is procedural evidence, which shows that the standard-setting was carried out systematically, in such a way that the judges were properly trained in the methodology and allowed to express their views freely. Documenting what happens and how the standard-setting is conducted has gained a great deal of importance because of the arbitrary nature of the decisions being made, so that by analogy with legal proceedings, 'due process' is considered reasonable grounds for an outcome (also see Cizek, 1996).

The second is internal evidence, which focuses on the consistency of results arising from the procedure. For example, in the Angoff method we would hope that the probability judgements at each borderline decision would show low standard deviations, and that inter-judge agreement is high. Similarly, in a borderline group study we would also expect low standard deviations, and we would expect that the scores between lower and higher borderline groups are ordered and well apart (unlike those in the Yerkes data). It is also important to ask judges how confident they are in their own ratings. It is at least arguable that if they express self-doubt or reservations, any observed agreement is likely to be questionable. Agreement between judges is always reported in standard setting documentation. Although this can use Cronbach's alpha (see Chapter 2), the most commonly reported agreement statistic is Cohen's kappa, which is a measure of the percentage agreement between two judges, taking into account agreement by chance, when making qualitative (categorical) judgements. For example, a number of judges may be asked to classify 90 students into three levels for a contrastive group study. Judges A and B make their classifications, which are set out in Table 8.2.

Judge B	Judge A			
	Level 1	Level 2	Level 3	Total
Level 1	24	5	1	30
Level 2	6	21	5	32
Level 3	2	6	20	28
Total	32	32	26	90

Table 8.2 Classifications of students into three levels by two judges

Once the totals have been calculated, we add together the numbers in the shaded diagonals:

$$\Sigma d = 24 + 21 + 20 = 65$$

Where Σd is the sum of the diagonals.

In order to calculate the percentage agreement, we divide Σd by the total: 65/90 = 72 per cent. However, this does not take account of the fact that even if the judges had assigned individuals to levels randomly there would have been some agreement. In order to do this we calculate the expected frequency for each diagonal cell by multiplying the row total by the column total and dividing by the grand total. For each we get:

$$30 \times 32 / 90 = 10.67$$
$$32 \times 32 / 90 = 11.38$$
$$28 \times 26 / 90 = 8.09$$

These are the expected frequencies that we would get in the diagonals by chance alone, rather than the observed frequencies that we actually have. We now sum the expected frequencies:

$$\Sigma ef = 10.67 + 11.38 + 8.09 = 30.14$$

Kappa can now be calculated using the following formula:

$$k = \frac{\Sigma d - \Sigma ef}{N - \Sigma ef}$$

$$k = \frac{65 - 30.14}{90 - 30.14} = \frac{34.86}{59.86} = .58$$

The general rule of thumb is that levels of agreement of .8 and over show high rates of agreement, from .7 to .8 reasonable rates of agreement, and from .6 to .7 moderate rates of agreement. Results below .6 require attention. In our example we would go back to Table 8.2 and identify where judges disagree, and try to discover if this disagreement is because of inadequate PLDs, or whether one or both raters have not understood the PLDs at those levels.

The third is external evidence. This could be the correlation of scores of learners in a borderline group study with some other test of the same construct. Alternatively, it could be a comparison between the results of two standard setting procedures. If they agree, there is more assurance that the cut scores are being established at a defensible point (Livingstone and Zieky, 1982). However, it has to be acknowledged that conducting multiple standard-setting studies is both time-consuming and expensive, and can probably only be done for high-stakes decisions.

In addition to Kane's criteria, Hambleton (2001: 109) recommends that standard-setters should report the standard error of a cut score. As we have seen in Chapter 2, this is one of the most powerful ways of understanding the impact of unreliability on decisions that we might make. Hambleton recommends that judges are randomly split into two or more groups and the standard error calculated using the following formula:

$$SE_c = \frac{SD_c}{\sqrt{n}}$$

where SE_c is the standard error of the mean cut score for the groups of judges, SD_c is the standard deviation of this mean, and n is the number of groups of judges used. For example, if we have 4 groups of judges, whose mean cut score estimate on a test is 26, with a standard deviation of 3, the formula would give:

$$SE_c = \frac{3}{\sqrt{4}} = \frac{3}{2} = 1.5$$

It has been suggested that if SE_c is less than half the standard error of measurement for the test, the cut score adds little to measurement error (Cohen, Kane and Crooks, 1999).

Despite the range of evaluation tactics that can be used, we should always be aware that the link between standards and cut scores are never 'true', but arbitrary decisions made by human judges (Glass, 1978; Wiliam, 1996) (taking 'arbitrary' to mean 'involving variable human judgement' rather than 'capricious'; Hambleton and Pitoniak, 2006: 433). The outcomes of standard setting studies are also likely to vary depending upon which procedure is used, who takes part, and any variations in the conditions in which the study is conducted (Green, Trimble and Lewis, 2003). The standards and the cut scores also represent the values of those who devise the system (Kane, 1994: 434). It is therefore important to look at what would happen to the population of test takers if the system is implemented – how many would pass, how many would fail, and what the likely consequences are. If the consequences seem unpalatable or likely to lead to unfairness, Kane's criteria for evaluation should be put to one side, however convincing the outcomes of these analyses might be.

▶ 11. Training

The need to train judges is mentioned as a critical part of all standard setting procedures. We have even noted in the previous section on evaluation that if we don't get the kind of agreement that we expect, we can go back and train the judges even more until we eventually do get it. Disagreements can come about for many reasons. Judges may have different views on what constitutes 'mastery' or 'pass' or 'proficient'. They may interpret PLDs differently. Or they may simply bring different values to the process, perhaps beliefs about universal access to college in judging standards on a college access test. The training should not be designed to knock all this variation out of them. Rather, as Cizek and Bunch (2007: 51–53) make clear, the training activities should be constructed to allow free discussion among judges. If the judges do not converge, the outcome should be accepted by the researchers. Training activities include familiarisation with the PLDs and the test, looking at the scoring keys, making practice judgements and getting feedback. Judges can then openly discuss the process and make another attempt.

Only after this training process is the standard setting done for real. However, there should be nothing in the training process that forces agreement. Alderson, Clapham and Wall (1995: 108) have accurately described this kind of training as 'cloning'. The judges are subjected to a period of intense socialisation designed to remove their individuality and induce agreement. For many researchers this does not appear to be problematic, but it has been argued (Fulcher, 2003a: 145–147) that training judges to agree and then presenting the level of agreement as part of a validity argument is problematic. The classic example of this practice is the case of Dandonolli and Henning (1990) and Henning (1992), who took highly cloned judges and asked them to place samples of spoken data into levels. The samples had already been selected by a set of similar judges as typical of the levels. When they were able to do this, the evidence was presented as justifying the assessment procedure. This has been shown to be meaningless in a re-examination of the data presented in these papers (Fulcher, 1996b), and has since been recognised as a serious problem (Liskin-Gasparro, 2003).

With cloning, the only thing that is remarkable is the frequent failure to get higher levels of agreement than would be expected. Researchers who need agreement are often reluctant to realise that when it comes to language, communication and educational achievement, individuals see the world in myriad of different ways. There are those who wish to reduce this variation, and there are those who think that it is valuable. I confess to being among the latter. When using agreement between judges as validity evidence for a new rating scale, I deliberately avoided training them in advance (Fulcher, 1993). The issue at stake was whether I could produce sets of descriptors that would describe performance levels on particular tasks in such a way that untrained judges would be able to link the descriptors to the performances on their own. Simply training them to do it, to see no other possibility, is removing the richness of human judgement and reducing validity to a monotonic view of the world.

▶ 12. The special case of the CEFR

In the final version of *Relating Language Examinations to the Common European Framework of Reference for Languages: Learning, Teaching, Assessment (CEFR): A Manual* (Council of Europe, 2009: 7), it is explicitly claimed that the CEFR document (Council of Europe, 2001) contains performance level descriptors for standard setting. The terminology of the document is, however, confusing, partly because of the idiosyncratic nature of the approach adopted. The title refers to 'relating' tests to the CEFR, and this is glossed as 'linking' tests to the CEFR (Council of Europe, 2009: 7), which is said to 'presuppose' standard setting. In fact, standard-setting in the sense of establishing a cut score on a test to distinguish between two levels is only part of what this document is about.

The *Manual* recommends five processes to 'relate' a test to the CEFR. These are: familiarisation, specification, standardisation training/benchmarking, standard-setting and validation. Of these, familiarisation, standard-setting and validation are relatively uncontentious. The sections generally reflect common international assessment practice that is not unique to Europe. The other two sections are much more problematic. This is because the policy purpose of the PLDs in the CEFR is to introduce a common language and a single reporting system into Europe. In other standards-based systems the PLDs are evaluated in terms of their usefulness and meaningfulness in assessment terms; they can be discarded or changed if or when they cease to fulfil that specific purpose. In the CEFR their use is institutionalised, and their meaning generalised, across nations, languages and educational systems.

We consider content specifications in Chapter 10, where we discuss the effects of tests on what we teach. As this chapter is about standard-setting, we focus entirely upon standardisation, training and benchmarking. In all other standard-setting procedures that we have considered it is important for the judges to be familiar with the PLDs, and the 'training' or 'standardisation' that is required is to ensure that everyone understands the standard-setting method being used. However, judgements are freely made. There is no attempt to 'clone' judges. Rather, judges are usually given two or three opportunities to revise their judgements based upon feedback such as their judgements compared with others (normative), item statistics (reality-data, or how students actually performed) and impact data (what the effect of their cut scores would be on the population). It is hoped that the process of making judgements, looking at data and judging again, will lead to convergence in the light of information and discussion. As Cizek and Bunch (2007: 84) put it:

> The provision of such feedback often has the effect of 'convergence' by participants on a cut score, as they tend to make item probability estimates that are more accurate, the amount of between-participant variation in ratings is reduced, and/or the participants become aware of (and usually respond to) the consequences of their ratings vis-à-vis the projected passing rates for the examination.

In the *Manual*, however, standardisation is seen as facilitating 'the implementation of a common understanding of the Common Reference Levels' (Council of Europe, 2009: 10). This may look like 'familiarisation', but it is not. In a section on standardisation, it is made clear the intention is the 'standardization of judgments' (2009: 15) (this term was originally the title of the comparable chapter in the 2003 pilot version of the *Manual*, making the intention much clearer than it is in the 2009 edition). This involves acquiring 'a common understanding of the CEFR', which is 'maintained over time' (2009: 37), so that judges will come to the same conclusions after successful training. The Council of Europe approach here deviates from all other practices described so far in this chapter, in that judges are presented with items and samples of performances said to be 'benchmarked' at particular levels, and trained to reach the 'correct' answer for each. The *Manual* is quite specific in seeing the link between samples and levels as reflecting the 'truthful' outcome (2009: 37).

> *It should be remembered that, as in any assessor training session, asking trainees to estimate the level of an already standardised sample is an exercise with a right answer. The correct answer is released only at a later stage by the coordinator. Unlike in the benchmarking or standard setting activities that follow, at this stage the group is not being invited to form a consensus on the level of the sample irrespective of previous evidence – but rather to arrive at the pre-established correct answer by applying the criteria.*

When the judges come to rating specific 'benchmarked' samples against the CEFR scales the co-ordinators guide judges to the 'correct' answers, so that they will produce the 'correct' answers later, when asked to make similar judgements about samples from their own local context. For example, it is suggested that if judges cannot agree on levels for non-benchmarked samples it is because they 'start to apply other standards when now rating "their own" learners'. The recommended remedy to this is to 'Juxtapose CEFR sample and local sample directly to try and "force" people to apply the same CEFR standard' (2009: 53).

This training is 'cloning' rather than familiarisation, partly because it serves the policy purposes as well as standard-setting. By serving these two purposes another confounding factor is introduced. The term 'benchmarking' is not used in the standard-setting literature. It may be that typical performances are identified after standard-setting has taken place – these are examples of performances at particular score points from a test that illustrate how the test differentiates between standards. However, 'benchmarking' in the CEFR context refers to the process of rating individual performance samples using the CEFR performance level descriptors themselves. These are then described as 'typical', and used in a training process that also involves marking new performance samples using the CEFR scales. This is circular (Fulcher, 2008a: 170–171) and, as we have argued above, any subsequent agreement cannot be used to claim the validity of the judgments. However, it also violates the key standard-setting principle discussed in Section 7 above, that the scale used for rating an item or task performance on a test should not also be used as a performance level descriptor (Cizek and Bunch, 2007: 30–31). The effect is not only to introduce a circular (and self-fulfilling) argument, but to remove any need for standard-setting, for the score on any individual item or task is also the standard achieved. The role of a rating scale that describes task performance is confounded with PLDs that relate to more general performance, and throughout the *Manual* the CEFR descriptors are treated as if they can perform both functions simultaneously.

The various terminological and methodological confusions that the use of the CEFR has generated, together with the policy imperative that tests in Europe are 'linked' to the CEFR, cause additional complications. Frequently, what is called 'standard-setting' in

Europe is not establishing cut scores on tests, but an attempt to 'map' existing cut scores from tests onto CEFR levels. For example, Bechger, Kuijper and Maris (2009) conducted two studies. In the first they attempted to set the minimum CEFR level required for a beginning university student in Holland, and in the second attempted to ask whether students who passed the Dutch as a second language tests (on which the cut score is already set) met the standard established in the first study. I will discuss only the first study in order to show the lengths to which some researchers will go in order to produce a result that is politically acceptable.

In the first study a set of 114 CEFR can-do statements (CDSs: descriptors beginning 'can [do something] …') ranging from level A2 to C1 were randomly compiled into a questionnaire. After training, 57 judges were asked to label each descriptor as '1. certainly not required', '2. is not really necessary', '3. is often required' or '4. is definitely required' for university entry. The researchers report that there was not enough agreement between the judges to decide which of the CEFR levels (A2 to C1) is the standard required. As there is pressure upon test developers in Europe to show that tests have been 'related' to the CEFR, this is clearly not an acceptable outcome. The researchers therefore report:

> To deal with the present situation, we decided to collapse response categories 1 and 2, and 3 and 4. The idea behind this was that disagreement stems from the fact that adjacent response categories were confused … Now there is a majority verdict for each CDS, which we henceforth accept as the truth.
> (Bechger *et al.*, 2009: 132)

With a four-level scale from 'certainly not required' to 'is definitely required', there are very few adjacent response categories for judges to be confused by. The criterion for deciding which categories to collapse is the desired result, and so it is not surprising that the outcome was satisfactory.

Even after training the judges and manipulating the responses, no agreement was found. It was noticed that CDSs from a particular CEFR level (e.g. B2) still occurred in both the new 'not necessary' as well as 'necessary' categories. This implies that some of these abilities from the same level are not required, while some are. A single CEFR level could not therefore be chosen as 'the standard' on the basis of this data. How do they get around this problem?

> If the CEFR is correct, however, these CDSs do belong to the same language level. One possible explanation may be that CDSs that are not required may in fact be deemed irrelevant by the respondent. This suggests the following rule: A level is required if a majority of the CDSs pertaining to that level are required.
> (Bechger *et al.*, 2009: 132–133)

The researchers have decided that the CEFR is 'correct', and so clearly the judges must be in error when they make decisions about individual CDSs. In other words, the judges are not only confused, they are misinformed, perhaps even hold perverse views of what language abilities are needed for university, or just haven't responded properly to training. Of course, this invalidates the entire methodology and its rationale, but the researchers press on towards the desired goal. The descriptors that they have judged to be 'not required' are now accepted as 'required', as long as at least 50 per cent of the descriptors from that level in the questionnaire are judged to be required. This gives the 'correct' conclusion that a level B2 is required for university admission.

As Bechger *et al.* (2009: 139) lament: 'Bitter experience shows that experts often hold different opinions about the same person. This raises the question of how to deal with disagreement.' Indeed it does. We have suggested that the best standard-setting procedures do not clone, but bring together variety and difference through natural convergence. If this is not achieved, it cannot be 'forced' through manipulatory methods, and the use of circular arguments.

It is inevitable that some language professionals will be required to align their tests and teaching to the CEFR. If this is necessary it should be done with care, and sensitivity to the needs of local learners rather than the demands of centralised institutions. Above all, the CEFR and the *Manual* for relating tests to the CEFR should be treated with critical caution by teachers.

▶ 13. You can always count on uncertainty

Standards-based testing can be a positive experience. This happens when committed teachers are able to develop standards for their own context, or use standards that have been developed to reflect the breadth and depth of what is being taught well in language classes. It happens when people come together to reach a consensus, rather than being forced to see the world through a single lens. Developing PLDs and standard-setting in a local context for clearly defined purposes can be a focus of real professional development and curriculum renewal, just as creating test specifications can help to focus on what it is that we as language educators think really matters. Used in this way, standards are never fixed, monolithic edifices. They are open to change, and even rejection, in the service of language education.

When standards-based testing fails, it does so either because the PLDs are poor, unrepresentative of the construct, or narrow in focus; and when they are hijacked for high-stakes accountability purposes, as Shepard (2000: 9) has argued, 'the standards movement has been corrupted, in many instances, into a heavy-handed system of rewards and punishments without the capacity building and professional development originally proposed as part of the vision.' It fails when it is used as a policy tool to achieve control of educational systems with the intention of imposing a single acceptable teaching and assessment discourse upon professionals. It also fails when testing specialists bend to the policy pressures by manipulating data, procedures, or people, to get acceptable results. Standard-setting is far from being a science; the use of numbers in the pseudo-scientific manner encouraged by the requirement to conform is misleading. This would not matter too much if standard-setting studies did not have serious consequences for examination systems and learners. But they do. The lesson that we should learn, however, is aptly expressed by Blastland and Dilnot (2008: 132):

> *This is counting in the real world. It is not a science, it is not precise, in some ways it is almost, with respect to those who do it, absurd. Get down to the grit of the way data is gathered, and you often find something slightly disturbing: human mess and muddle, luck and judgment, and always a margin of error in gathering only a small slice of the true total, from which hopeful sample we simply extrapolate. No matter how conscientious the counters, the counted have a habit of being downright inconvenient, in almost every important area of life. The assumption that the things we have counted are correctly counted is rarely true, cannot, in fact, often be true, and as a result our grip on the world through numbers is far feebler than we like to think.*

Standards-based testing is controversial and will remain so. This is because it is the point at which the external political world collides with classroom practice, and number crunching can do little to tame the variability of human judgements. This doesn't mean that we have to throw up our hands and give up, because it has always been so. Latham (1877: 350) noted that once a test is given, there is frequently little argument about scoring it, but

> *It is only when the list has to be divided into classes that there is room for discussion; then the question 'Where are we to draw the line?' often gives form to debate, and the character of the work of the candidates on the debatable ground may then be canvassed in some degree.*

Judgemental standard-setting with reference to borderline candidates is clearly nothing new. And Latham was well aware of the uncertainty of decision making. Living with uncertainty and taking it into account in decision making is as important today as it was in the nineteenth century.

The controversy will also continue at the policy as well as the practical level. In some countries, like the United States, the debate about whether to impose national standards or maintain local state control will rage on (Barton, 2009). In Europe the fierce disagreement about the need for a common framework on the one hand, and freedom to have variety on the other, shows no sign of abating. These are ultimately political and philosophical questions; they are about educational values, and how people view a fair society. But they are also questions that impact upon our daily teaching and testing practices.

In this chapter we have attempted to outline the complexities of standards and standards-based testing, including the political, social and ethical issues surrounding their use. As teachers we need to evaluate what we are being asked to do, rather than simply aligning our assessments to the standards when required. But when there is such a requirement, or where we can see that there is something to be gained for the learners and ourselves, we need the skills to set standards as well as we can.

Activities

⭕ 8.1 Standards in context

Teachers are often asked to classify students in a variety of ways. Consider the institution in which you work, or one that you are familiar with. List the classification decisions that you are required to take. For each decision, list any test or assessment that you use to make these decisions. Finally, what 'standards' do you use to define the various categories within the classificatory system? You may wish to do this in the following table.

Classification decisions	Test or assessment	Standards

Compare your notes with a colleague. Where do the standards come from? Are they appropriate for the task?

⭕ 8.2 Standards for our safety

Throughout the book we have mentioned a number of jobs that require post-holders to have achieved certain 'standards' in language proficiency before they should be allowed to practise. These include pilots and aircraft engineers. What other jobs do you think should require language certification against a required standard? Make a list, and give a reason for each choice.

⭕ 8.3 Language tests in economic and immigration policy

The language 'standard' required for gaining an immigration visa to some countries is changed depending on prevailing economic circumstances.

Is the use of language tests to control immigration ethical?

Discuss with colleagues and prepare a response that you could share with others.

○ 8.4 The big debate: who's to blame?

Read the following article, which is shortened and adapted from *The Australian*.

THE personal advertisements dotted through Punjabi newspaper classifieds are as brazen as they are impossible to misinterpret. Headed 'Paper Marriage', they call for expressions of interest from girls who achieved good scores in the International English Language Test System exam and who are willing to study a course in Australia that leads to permanent residency for her and her sham husband.

All expenses will be paid and the marriage dissolved after permanent residency is secured. Through an interpreter, *The Australian* called one number to verify the demand. The advertiser was indeed looking for an IELTS-qualified marriage candidate, but the original vacancy had been filled. They were no longer looking for a girl who had passed her IELTS, but a boy.

The Australian rang another number and was told that a 32-year-old man from a backward caste, who had worked illegally in Britain for nine years, was looking for a girl who had passed the IELTS test to be his ticket to Australia. She would study; he would work. No dowry was required from her family and all expenses would be paid for study in a field of her choice.

While such arrangements can prove costly for the groom's family – $40,000 or more in agent fees, wedding and study costs, interests on loans and airfares – for many couples the deal is mutually beneficial.

In cities across Punjab, streets are littered with signs advertising IELTS trainers, as well as education, immigration and travel agents, all offering an easy path to a better future abroad. A journalist in Ludhiana told *The Australian*: 'People will do anything in Punjab to go abroad because they see it as an honour, even if it means selling their ancestral lands and putting their lives at risk.'

One Punjabi lawyer, who boasts of being able to help even students who have been knocked back for a visa, told *The Australian*: 'If you can find a girl (who has passed the IELTS test), you can go anywhere. That's very easy. Then both the husband and wife will go.'

(Adapted from *The Australian*, 14 July 2009)

- Is it reasonable to hold anyone responsible for the unintended consequences of tests?
- Who might be held responsible for the 'Paper Marriage' industry?
- What action would you take against those responsible?
- How is it possible to stop the practices described in the article?

○ 8.5 Writing PLDs

Imagine that you are required to classify learners into three levels according to their ability to listen to academic lectures. Those in the top group may undertake an academic course, those in the middle group will be required to spend one more semester in their listening class and be allowed to do a content preparation programme, while the lower group will continue with a language-only course of studies.

Write three PLDs with labels.

⟡ 8.6 Evaluating standards

Many standards documents and standards-based tests are available on the internet. Gottlieb, Cranley and Cammilleri (2008), for example, explain the widely used WIDA English language proficiency standards in this document: http://www.wida.us/standards/Resource_Guide_web.pdf. Some states also make available sample tests that are linked to standards at a range of grade levels. The California Department of Education, for example, runs the Standardized Testing and Reporting (STAR) website: http://www.starsamplequestions.org/. Here you can look at test items by grade level, subject and performance level. Basic item statistics are also reported for test items.

Open your favourite internet search engine and type in a query like 'standards-based assessment'. Select a set of standards, or a test that is standards based. Write a short critical review of its purpose, the design, and its likely impact (intended and unintended).

⟡ 8.7 Project work VI

If you have been doing the project work, you will by now have developed a short test, collected some data to investigate its properties and revised the specifications a number of times. Imagine that you are now required to establish a single cut score on your test to separate 'masters' from 'non-masters'. Which standard-setting technique would you choose, and why?

If you have access to the resources needed, you may wish to actually carry out the study and write it up.

9 Test administration

▶ 1. No, no. Not me!

Administration may not be much of an issue for informal, low-stakes, classroom assessment. But any teacher who has been asked to organise a more formal test or assessment for their institution will remember the painstaking effort that goes into making sure that everything goes smoothly. This is all in addition to actually designing the test, and producing the form to be used on the day. It includes everything from having enough copies of the test paper and answer sheets, ensuring that not a single copy is 'misplaced', and transporting the materials to a test venue that has been cleaned the evening before and set out according to written regulations so that desks are a set distance apart. Then there is arranging the correct number of invigilators/proctors for the number of test takers expected, ensuring that doors are unlocked, equipment (including lights, heating, air conditioning) is working properly, and that candidate identity can be checked and registered against a number that allows the matching of scores (following blind marking) to individuals. This means that databases have been adequately set up in advance, and candidates informed what they should bring to the test with them. In short, it is a complex planning process. When dealing with the administration of tests, it is always good practice to have a group of teachers working on these matters, each with their own particular responsibility, reporting to a group leader who will monitor task completion.

This is testing life. But why? The first thing that most of us think about is security. The purpose of all the care is to stop cheating. There is a great deal of truth in this, but it is not the only reason. The *Standards for Educational and Psychological Testing* (AERA, 1999: 61) state:

> *The usefulness and interpretability of test scores require that a test be administered and scored according to the developer's instructions. When directions to examinees, testing conditions, and scoring procedures follow the same detailed procedures, the test is said to be standardized. Without such standardization, the accuracy and comparability of score interpretations would be reduced. For tests designed to assess the examinee's knowledge, skills, or abilities, standardization helps to ensure that all examinees have the same opportunity to demonstrate their competencies. Maintaining test security also helps to ensure that no one has an unfair advantage.*

In other words, getting the administration right is also about fairness to the test takers. The quotation really masks two separate issues. The first is replicating the precise conditions that the test designers set out in the delivery specifications. These are the conditions under which the test was originally piloted and field tested. So what we know about score meaning from the research holds so far as the data is collected under identical or very similar circumstances. The second issue is ensuring that these conditions are replicated for all test takers, so that no one experiences taking the test in a condition that provides either advantages or disadvantages. The final sentence of the quotation relates to security and the possibility that a test taker has seen a copy of the test in advance. If one test taker had got hold of a copy of the test, the condition under which he or she took the test has changed. They take the test with prior knowledge of the content, which we would all agree is highly likely to change their score for construct-irrelevant reasons. It is a threat to score meaning, and therefore to validity.

Doing things 'by the book' isn't just about bureaucratic dogma, but about trying our best to protect score meaning, validity, and the fairness of the outcome of the test and any decisions that might be associated with the results.

▶ 2. Controlling extraneous variables

A much better way to think about test administration is to conceptualise it in terms of the control of extraneous (construct irrelevant) variables. These variables are simply any factors that affect test scores which are not related to what the test is intended to measure. Carroll (1961: 319) helpfully put it like this:

> In some ways, a good test is like an experiment, in the sense that it must eliminate or at least keep constant all extraneous sources of variation. We want our tests to reflect only the particular kind of variation in knowledge or skill that we are interested in at the moment.

Notice in this quotation the two key phrases 'eliminate' and 'keep constant'. In fact, we can't eliminate all extraneous sources of variation, because we cannot hold tests in no environment whatsoever. The best we can do is keep them constant. This maximises the opportunities for test takers to perform to the best of their abilities, and mini-mises the opportunities for distraction or cheating. Standardising the conditions to what we assume is the optimal for data collection is therefore the goal.

Also notice the analogy with an experiment in the natural sciences. We may recall from Chapter 2 the constant comparisons that testing makes with natural sciences. To make this analogy more concrete, I will give a particular example. Between 1886 and 1888, Heinrich Rudolf Hertz was experimenting with radio waves in an attempt to prove the electromagnet theories of James Clerk Maxwell. He constructed a primitive radio system in a laboratory to observe the action of radio waves. His experiments led to two major steps forward. Firstly, he showed that he could measure the speed of the waves (one cycle per second is a Hertz), and secondly he created the electromagnetic fields necessary for the waves to travel without wires. Theory predicted that radio waves should travel at the speed of light, whether through the air or along wires; but in his early experiments Hertz found that the waves travelled faster through the air. Through further experimentation, Hertz discovered that the data he was collecting was reliable, but was not valid. The room in which the experiments were being conducted was too small and the radio waves were bouncing off the walls. What he needed to do was conduct the experiment in a larger laboratory so that longer waves could develop.

In other words, the environment had a direct effect on the results. Once the environment was changed (using a larger room), longer wave lengths could be created. The experimental results changed and came into line with the predictions made by Maxwell's theory. As Chalmers (1990: 63) points out, the problem with the experimental results 'stems neither from inadequacies in his observations nor from any lack of repeatability, but rather from the inadequacy of the experimental set-up'. In order to collect data that adequately reflects the construct of interest the 'set-up' should not interfere with measurement.

Language testing, like all educational measurement, assumes that the conditions should be standardised and optimal, just as in Hertz's later experiments. The *Standards for Educational and Psychological Testing* (AERA, 1999: 63) codifies this in Standard 5.4, which reads: 'The testing environment should furnish reasonable comfort with minimal distractions.' The associated comment reads: 'In general, the testing conditions should be equivalent to those that prevailed when norms and other interpretive data were obtained.' That is, the conditions under which subsequent tests are held should be as similar as possible to those that were in place during the experimental development of the test. In Chapter 1, for example, we considered how noise can adversely affect test takers and saw the extent to which some countries go to reduce noise around test sites during examination times. Cohen and Wollack (2006: 357) say:

> It is reasonable to expect that administration conditions have a nonnegligible effect on examinee performance. If it is too hot or too cold in the testing room, performances of some examinees are likely to be negatively affected. Similarly, if it is too noisy, some examinees may be distracted and perform below their potential.

These are sources of systematic error that distort results, just as the conditions in Hertz's small room distorted the results of his experiment. Prior to each administration of a test or assessment it is essential that someone is given responsibility for standardising the physical environment to reduce the possibility of any such systematic effects. If there are variations across testing conditions, they should also be investigated afterwards.

We can be sure that if there are perceived changes in test taking conditions, students will complain. If air conditioning breaks down in one examination room when two are being used it is almost inevitable that students in the hot room will complain that they have been put at a disadvantage. Where there is one or more cut scores on the test, there is one fairly simple way for teachers to check if this is the case, by using a chi-square test of significance (X^2). Firstly, let us assume in the case of the failed air conditioning that the test has a pass/fail cut score. (If the test were norm-referenced or did not have a cut score, a t-test could be used instead.) We can create a table like the following, which represents conditions and outcomes.

	Outcomes		
Conditions	**Pass**	**Fail**	**Totals**
Air conditioning	32	8	40
No air conditioning	27	13	40
Totals	59	21	80

Table 9.1 Observed values by conditions and outcomes on a language test

On the face of it, it looks as though the students may have a case. Five more students failed the test in the hot room than did in the air-conditioned room. Assuming that the students were assigned to the rooms randomly, or that there is no reason to suspect that the students in one group are more able than the other, we need to ask whether this amount of variation between the two groups could have occurred by chance. If it could have occurred by chance the complaint is unfounded. If it could not, it would appear that the institution has to give those who failed another chance to take the test, with all the cost that this entails. The formula for X^2 is:

$$X^2 = \Sigma \; \frac{(\text{Observed} - \text{Expected})^2}{\text{Expected}}$$

In Table 9.1 we have all the observed cases. Each case falls uniquely into one cell. This is known as nominal, or categorical, data. What we need to know next is what the expected values are for each cell, that we would expect by chance. To do this we multiply the row total by the column total and divide by the grand total. These values are set out in Table 9.2.

	Outcomes		
Conditions	**Pass**	**Fail**	**Totals**
Air conditioning	29.5	10.5	40
No air conditioning	29.5	10.5	40
Totals	59	21	80

Table 9.2 Expected values by outcomes on a language test

There is one more thing to do. If (and only if) a X^2 table has four cells (a 2 × 2 grid), we have to make a small correction for a distribution problem. If the observed value is higher than the expected value, we deducted .5 from the observed value. Similarly, if it is lower, we add .5 to the observed value. In our example, this gives observed values as: 31.5, 8.5, 27.5 and 12.5. If we had had three outcomes (e.g. 'advanced', 'proficient' and 'basic'), this correction would not have been necessary.

We can now plug the numbers into the formula. For the first cell (air conditioning + pass) we have:

$$\frac{(31.5 - 29.5)^2}{29.5}$$

We then produce the same sum for the other three cells:

$$\frac{(8.5 - 10.5)^2}{10.5} + \frac{(27.5 - 29.5)^2}{29.5} + \frac{(12.5 - 10.5)^2}{10.5}$$

This gives:

$$\frac{4}{29.5} + \frac{4}{10.5} + \frac{4}{29.5} + \frac{4}{10.5} =$$

$$.14 + .38 + .14 + .38 = 1.04$$

The next step is to determine the degrees of freedom (df) of the X^2 test. This is easily calculated as the number of rows – 1 multiplied by the number of columns – 1. In our example we only have two rows and two columns, which gives 1 degree of freedom.

In order to tell if this result means that the outcomes could have occurred by chance we now check the value of X^2 with the table of critical values, in Table 9.3.

df	P = .05	P = .01	P = .001
1	3.84	6.64	10.83
2	5.99	9.21	13.82
3	7.82	11.35	16.27
4	9.49	13.28	18.47
5	11.07	15.09	20.52
6	12.59	16.81	22.46
7	14.07	18.48	24.32
8	15.51	20.09	26.13
9	16.92	21.67	27.88
10	18.31	23.21	29.59

Table 9.3 Critical values of chi-square

The degrees of freedom are listed in the left-hand column. We go down to 1. Across the top row we have the p-values, or the level of probability that we wish to associate with the test. It is normal practice to use values of .05 in most educational research, unless the stakes are very high indeed. This means that we are testing the hypothesis that there is no association between the conditions under which the students took the test, and the outcomes (pass or fail). When we hypothesise that there is no association, we say that the hypothesis is null. If the data is consistent with the null hypothesis, the value of X^2 will be lower than the value in the relevant cell of the table, and the result is said to be non-significant. From Table 9.3 we can see that the critical value of X^2 with 1df at the .05 level is 3.84. The value of X^2 in our example is 1.04, which is not significant. The observed differences between the two conditions that we observe in Table 9.1 are therefore well within the chance fluctuations that we would expect, with no failure rates apparently due to heat. We would be fairly safe in rejecting the claim of some students that the breakdown in the air conditioning led to them being classified as failing unfairly.

3. Rituals revisited

If we ask 'why is it done in this way?' and the response is 'because that's how it's always been done', in the field of testing and assessment, it's likely to be a fairly good reason. Of course, it does not mean that things never change, because they do. However, each change to the test or the way it is administered has to be shown not to change score meaning. This is why Fulcher and Davidson (2009) liken changing a test, its delivery method, or administration, to making architectural changes to buildings. It requires careful planning, and often alterations to test specifications. Tests and their administration will always evolve to suit changing circumstances, but we must always be alert to the possibility that changes in administration – in the way the data is collected – may also change the meaning of the score.

It is not unfair to say that administering the test is a ritual, just as we described it in Section 3 of Chapter 1. Now we can explain the deeper reason for the ritual. It follows the directions laid down by the test developers to the letter and used in the first field trials. It is as if we wished to replicate the experiments of Hertz, and so had to copy the experimental conditions precisely. This principle goes back to administration of the earliest tests. In his 1922 text on school tests, Burt says:

> *Whenever it is proposed to use the tests for an examination by the Binet-Simon method the examiner should adhere with meticulous exactitude to the procedure described for every test. In no way should he alter the wording of the instructions to be repeated to the child. The formulae may seem as arbitrary as the rules and rigmaroles of heraldry; but conventions are inevitable for uniformity; and without uniformity comparison becomes invalid. The novice is apt to presume that the test involves doing the tasks as he himself would understand it from the directions, and is accordingly beguiled into improving supplementary aids and explanations.*
> (1922: 15)

All those involved in testing need to be trained not to innovate! For teachers this is often hard. As we have seen in assessment for learning, teachers respond to learners to help them do better; in dynamic assessment the key element is to intervene to provide the bridge between what the learner can do now, and what they wish to achieve next. In more formal testing this is not allowed. Burt continues:

During a test neither teach nor criticize. These are the two lapses which, by sheer force of professional habit, the teacher most inclines. Criticism diminishes candour and destroys self-confidence. Instruction transforms the examinee's entire attitude toward the remainder of the tests.
(1922: 15)

Not only can such interventions change the outcome of the test, they also send an indication to the test taker about how well they are doing. In the modern environment it is possible for a test taker who has been led to believe that they have done well to take legal action against the institution giving the test if the scores are not what they had been led to expect.

The ritual extends to all aspects of the testing activity, including the manner of the person who registers the test takers, checks their identity, and the invigilators/proctors who will direct the test. If their behaviour upsets the test takers in any way, test outcomes may be compromised. In supermarkets the checkout staff are trained to be both friendly and professional because marketing experts know that this is the most important factor affecting customer loyalty. The training of test administrators should be conducted just as carefully. Burt again, says

Avoid all pomp and circumstance. By a tactful use of the customary civilities – a compliment, a handshake, or a smile – court and keep that atmosphere of intimacy which psychological testing presupposes. It was said of Mirabeau that, alike in private intercourse and on public occasions, he possessed le don terrible de familiarité. This 'formidable gift' is one which the psychologist must possess and cultivate until it is formidable no longer. The test-room manner should be as proverbial for its tone of sympathy as the 'bedside manner' for its urbanity and ease.
(1922: 16)

The advice has changed little over the decades. Neither be unwelcoming nor too friendly, uncaring nor too helpful. All must behave in the same way, and teachers must avoid their natural tendencies to intervene. It may go against the grain, as Burt clearly recognised, but that is just the way formal testing is.

4. Standardised conditions and training

We have already intimated that the way to achieve standardisation in testing is to train those involved to follow the set procedures. Training invigilators/proctors usually involves simulating test conditions and watching them deal with a variety of 'test takers' who have been prepared to act out roles from the extremely anxious to the downright rude. The test administrators are given advice on how to deal with each type of test taker, how to advise them and when they should ask someone to leave the test venue for unacceptable behaviour that might impact upon the performance of others. The conditions that may trigger such actions, and the precise procedures to follow, should be written down in a training manual. All incidents, whether before or during the test, should be logged in an incident book and brought to the attention of supervisory staff afterwards in case any further action is required.

Interlocutor training in speaking tests is probably one of the most difficult and time-consuming training activities for any testing programme. Sometimes the interlocutor and the rater are the same person, but increasingly two examiners are present during speaking tests. The rater is free to make judgements about the quality of the performance, while the interlocutor concentrates on managing the interaction with a single candidate, or a pair of candidates. A growing body of research has shown that the outcome of a speaking test can depend upon the interlocutor as well as the ability of the test takers. While this could be argued to be a part of interactional competence (see Chapter 4), it is most often seen as an extraneous variable that needs to be controlled through training and placing restrictions upon what the interlocutor may say. Ross (1992, 1998b) and Ross and Berwick (1992) have shown that interlocutors tend to vary their discourse in speaking tests to accommodate to the abilities of the test taker. This has the effect of scaffolding the speech of the test taker through grammatical or lexical simplification, slowing down speech or checking for comprehension. Similarly, Lazaraton (1996) has shown that 'teacher talk', such as modelling language, supplying words, rephrasing questions, or providing corrective and evaluative responses, supports the test taker's performance. And Brown (2003) has shown that such features make the test easier and inflate the scores of those who are helped through interlocutor accommodations.

Apart from training interlocutors not to provide too much help, the most frequently used technique to control variation is the 'interlocutor frame' (Lazaraton, 2002: 124–151). This is not at all dissimilar to the interlocutor guidance that Burt provides for his picture description oral literacy test that we discuss in Chapter 5, for an interlocutor frame is basically a list of acceptable questions and utterances that the interlocutor may use to manage the test and guide the candidate(s) through the test tasks. If additional prompts are required to get them talking, these are specified, so that all interlocutors are following the same procedures and using the same language, whoever is taking part, and wherever the test is taking place.

As you can imagine, interlocutor frames are kept very secret. If teachers or test takers have access to interlocutor frames, they know a great deal about the content of a test and this increases the likelihood that some may score well simply because they have had the chance to rehearse their response to the prompts. However, the Ministry of National Education in Greece has released the interlocutor frames for its 2008 English Language Certificates, which are modelled on those pioneered by the University of Cambridge. In Figure 9.1, we show the interlocutor frame for the introduction and first activity, along with the fixed questions that the interlocutor is allowed to ask.

This is highly scripted. It looks like a 'slot and filler' exercise, where only limited variability is allowed to the interlocutor. Nevertheless, there is evidence that, even with such tightly scripted frames, interlocutors will start to vary the interaction (Lazaraton, 2002). It is therefore essential that in training the interlocutors use the frames in simulations, and are periodically retrained, to ensure that nothing unwanted creeps into the test.

INTERLOCUTOR FRAME-ACTIVITY 1
Introducing ourselves (about 1 minute for both candidates) [NOT MARKED]

Examine	Good afternoon. Welcome. Can I have your evaluation forms, please? (*Take them and give them to your co-assessor, making sure you don't mix up who is who.*)
	Thank you, please take a seat.
	My name is .... (and) this is my co-assessor .... (and this is an observer...........). S/he (They) will be observing us.
	Please speak in English, loudly and clearly, throughout the test. You may ask me to repeat task instructions or give any other clarifications, but only in English. So... What is your name? (*Write it down.*) And yours? (*Write it down.*)
Examine	(*Addressing candidate A*) So... , *his/her NAME*, what do you do ...?/where do you live?/what are your plans for the future? etc. (*any general questions to break the ice and get to know the candidate.*)
Examine	(*Addressing candidate B*) And what about you, *His/her NAME*, what do you do ...?/where do you live?/what are your plans for the future? etc. (*Any general questions to break the ice and get to know the candidate.*)

Activity1 (3–4 minutes for both candidates)	
Examine	Ok. Let's start with Activity 1. I will ask each of you some questions.
Start with candidate A. Choose 2–4 questions from the ones given in the <u>Examiner Pack</u> and ask him/her.	
Examine	(*When the candidate has finished.*) Thank you.
Examine	Now, let's go on with *candidate's B NAME*.
Choose 2–4 DIFFERENT (from the ones you asked candidate A) questions from the ones given in the <u>Examiner Pack</u> and ask him/her.	
Examine	(*When the candidate has finished.*) Thank you.

ACTIVITY 1: INTERVIEW

Questions about themselves and their immediate environment
1. When you are under a lot of pressure, what do you do? Why?
2. What kind of clothes do you prefer wearing? Why?
3. What would you choose as a birthday present for your best friend? Why?
4. Who do you tell your problems and secrets to? Why?

Questions about free time or preferences
5. Do you exercise regularly? Why or why not?
6. What do you like to read? Why?
7. Do you prefer watching a movie at home or going to the cinema? Why or why not?
8. Do you prefer to travel by boat, by train or by plane? Explain why?

Questions about school life, studies or work
9. What do you plan to do when you finish your education or training? Tell us about your plans.
10. Do you study better alone or with the help of someone else? Why?
11. Do you dress differently at school and when you go to a party? Why or why not?
12. What do you think will be very different in 20 years time?

Questions about holidays and places
13. What is the best trip you've ever been on? Why?
14. What do you like most/least about the city/town you live in?
15. How would you like to spend your summer holidays? Talk to us about your plans.
16. If you had the choice, would you prefer to go on holiday with your family or with your friends? Why?

Fig. 9.1. An interlocutor frame

There is always the question about what to do if a test taker does get into serious trouble during the interactions, and communication becomes extremely difficult or simply breaks down. In this case, the frame provides a 'problem–solution' approach that guides the interlocutor through the difficulty. For example:

Problem: The candidate is very hesitant, pauses for too long and produces little output.
Solution: 1. Repeat the candidate's last phrase with rising intonation; 2. Ask a few prompting questions (Is there anything else you would like to add?); 3. Try to break down the task into simpler questions.

Problem: The candidate is nervous and has difficulty speaking.
Solution: 1. Smile, use body language, facial expressions and intonation to make the candidate feel more comfortable; 2. If you asked the nervous candidate to begin first, switch to the other candidate and then come back to the nervous candidate.

Problem: The candidate draws a blank and seems unable to answer.
Solution: 1. Repeat the question/task; 2. If the candidate still hesitates, change the task but stick to the same visual prompt/text.

These variations are listed as permissible, but using them is taken into account in scoring, and in this particular test can incur a penalty. Both the restrictions on what is possible, and the penalties incurred when there is variation, are there to ensure that all test takers have the same experience, under the same conditions and with equality of opportunity to show what they know and can do.

5. Planned variation: accommodations

As soon as it looks as if we have established a rule, we have to break it. Administering the test in exactly the same way, under precisely the same conditions, is simply not possible for everyone. Standard 5.1 of the *Standards for Educational and Psychological Testing* (AERA, 1999: 63) states: 'Test administration should follow carefully the standardized procedures for administration and scoring specified by the test developer, unless the situation or a test taker's disability dictates that an exception should be made.'

There is always an 'unless' and an 'exception'. This is not only true of large-scale tests; it is also true of tests that we give in our institutions. When planning tests, teachers should take into account these exceptions. Referring once again to Burt, it is clear that it has long been recognised that there are going to be cases where some test takers will need additional help or alternative test delivery mechanisms. Although he did not specify the factors that might have to be taken into account, the advice is clear:

> To overcome these difficulties, and to meet these special cases, I suggest the following principles. Distinguish scrupulously between an unmodified and a modified procedure; and admit the latter only so far as it will not invalidate the former.
> (Burt, 1922: 18)

This statement encapsulates the current position with regard to test accommodations, or modifications of test delivery or administration, to meet the needs of specific test takers with special needs or disabilities. Cohen and Wollack (2006: 359) translate the same position into modern English:

> Accommodations are designed to remove or mitigate as much as possible the effects of the disabling condition(s) from the measurement of the ability of interest … the exception is that it is not necessary to grant accommodations that will compromise the fundamental interpretation of the test.

Two principles are at stake, and can often pull in the opposite direction. The first is that if a test taker has a disability that could affect his or her test score, the score may not reflect their true ability, but the existence or degree of their disability. In many countries legislation requires test designers to provide accommodations that can be shown to reduce the impact of the disability on outcomes. Even if it is not legislated for, if a test taker with a disability is in some way disadvantaged as a result of taking a test without appropriate accommodations there is the possibility that successful litigation may follow (see Fulcher and Bamford, 1996; Pitoniak and Royer, 2001). The provision of accommodations is therefore driven by the concern for validity.

Pulling in the opposite direction is any question that the accommodation itself puts validity in question by altering the meaning of the score. For example, students with visual impairment may be accommodated in a number of ways, including providing large-print text, screen magnification, Braille versions of input materials, Braille response, or audio materials (Allman, 2005, 2006). These are all extremely good methods of mitigating the disability. However, if we assume that a blind student is taking a reading test in which the text is read, or presented in audio, it is arguably the case that it is no longer a test of reading (Cohen and Wollack, 2006: 359). In this case the accommodation itself changes the construct being measured, and therefore the meaning of the score is no longer the same as it is for other test takers.

This is a balancing act. While every effort must be made to avoid any disability impacting upon test performance, whatever we do should not change score meaning so that the link between performance and score interpretation is broken (see Hansen *et al.*, 2005).

All disabilities should be taken into consideration, but the most common are visual and hearing impairments (see Cawthon, 2009), dyslexia, attention deficit hyperactivity disorder and physical disabilities. Typical accommodations that may be allowed include:

- additional testing time
- additional rest breaks
- reader (to read text or instructions)
- audio
- amanuensis (provision of a person to write answers)
- sign language interpreter
- Braille test/writer
- printed copy of spoken instructions
- large print/screen magnifier
- additional space or special furniture
- omission of one or more parts of the test
- small group or single test administration.

All teachers should be aware that accommodations are available from reputable large-scale test providers. Booklets describing accommodations and how to apply for them are available from test websites, and should be consulted well in advance. The real problem arises when these accommodations have to be provided for in-house tests. There is no doubt that it creates a great deal of additional work, and cost. Nevertheless, all test administrators are obliged to provide an accommodation even if it is for a single student, if that student would otherwise be put at a disadvantage. When it comes to cost, it is worthwhile remembering that the cost of discrimination is much higher, should the institution be taken to court.

There are essentially two ways that teachers can approach the issue of accommodations. The first is to wait until a student with a disability needs an accommodation and then it can be retrofitted to an existing test. This is potentially a great deal of hard work that would have to be done in a short period of time. In addition, there is no guarantee that the accommodation would result in the desired outcome. The alternative approach is to consider the range of potential disabilities that we might come across in the student population and consider how these might be catered for when the test is being designed. If this is done, it is possible to create a flexible system that can adapt fairly easily if the need arises. Considering accommodations at the outset is known as 'universal design' (Ketterlin-Geller, 2008). Drawing on architectural principles for ease of access and use for the disabled in buildings, the aim is to create a test delivery system that already incorporates the flexibility that might be required later, such as enlargement features for text, and text to speech synthesis. Even if such variable features are difficult to implement, thought can be given to issues such as font size, the use of colour, clarity of graphics, and the provision of audio. One step further might be to consider multiple ways of tapping the same construct, leading to different task types that can be empirically tested for similar outcomes with disabled and non-disabled test takers (Ketterlin-Geller, 2008: 6).

Giving thought to accommodations is important because of the accessibility issues that they raise for students with disability, and because it is where practical considerations in how to deliver a test meet the theoretical validity concerns that drive test design. This is the point at which the practical, the ethical, the legal and the theoretical meet.

▶ 6. Unplanned variation: cheating

While accommodations represent the one extreme of planned variation to the conditions under which tests are taken, cheating represents the opposite of unplanned variation. It hardly needs to be stated that cheating directly threatens validity as the score of the successful cheater is much higher than it otherwise would have been. Standard 5.6 in the *Standards for Educational and Psychological Testing* (AERA, 1999: 64) states: 'Reasonable efforts should be made to ensure the integrity of test scores by eliminating opportunities for test takers to attain scores by fraudulent means.' This includes preparing seating charts, checking candidate identity properly, spacing seats to avoid copying, and the appropriate monitoring of test takers during the test. In most of this section we will deal with cheating in formal large-scale tests, as there is little incentive to cheat in classroom assessment. However, if institutions hold formal examinations where the outcome impacts upon the future of the student, teachers responsible for the tests should consider the possible scale of the problem they may face and take appropriate action to reduce the likelihood of cheating.

The study of cheating is fascinating. Why do people do it? In Chapter 1 we considered the use of tests to open up opportunities for those from less socially advantaged backgrounds, and the answer to our question lies in what happened during the assessment reforms of the mid-nineteenth century. Reformers like Lord Macaulay used tests to remove patronage and nepotism in appointments in favour of merit. By this point in the industrial revolution the new self-made middle classes valued education and opportunity. It was no longer acceptable for the sons of the aristocracy to be given choice government positions because of their birth. Testing evolved as a means of social engineering (Roach, 1971: 9). Then, as now, those who did better on the tests tended to be those from more privileged backgrounds. The tests in themselves did not create equality, only equality of opportunity at the moment of taking the test. This gave great advantages to the new middle classes. The tests were but the vehicles for a new form of motivation. The test – or a certificate showing a pass at the set standard – now acquired a market value. Reflecting the new values, Latham (1877: 23) says:

> *Parents want something to shew for education; a place in an examination list seems to gauge the advantage which they have paid for, and besides it frequently has a positive market value as opening the door to some emolument or profession.*

Latham (1877: 44) repeats that 'some market value must be attached to the certificate.' This sounds terrifyingly modern. He goes on to consider the possible expenditure incurred by families in acquiring education and test preparation measured against the potential future income that success is likely to generate (1877: 52–55).

This provides the answer: test scores are constantly being given a market value in different ways. In Chapter 8 we saw some of the effects of the market value of test scores that are linked to 'standards' for immigration, and the effects that it can have. What is most desired is the life that the test score makes possible, not the test score itself. If achieving the test score is problematic, many will turn to other means to achieve their goals, like the sham marriages we considered in Activity 8.4. Cheating is just a much more common method. And, like many of the practices that we have discussed in this book, cheating is not new. Miyazaki (1981: 119–120) discusses the cost incurred by families to provide an education for their sons that might lead to success in the Imperial Chinese tests, which brought posts in the civil service, the incentives of test takers to cheat and of officials to use their posts to earn large amounts of money:

> *They brought miniature books to the examinations, or wrote classical texts over an entire undergarment. Still worse was the hiring of substitutes to take the examinations. Some substitutes were so well paid that they easily set themselves up in business.*

Miyazaki reports on one instance of collusion of the examiners to ensure that certain test takers received high scores in 1699. This resulted in public unrest and street protests against favouritism. The examiners were arrested, charged and sent to prison. The controls to stop cheating, both by test officials and test takers, are still in use today. On the day of the test an independent supervisor oversaw the test administration. Test takers were subjected to physical searches (both personal and bags) for crib sheets (1981: 44) and money that could be used to bribe officials. Entrance and exit to the test rooms were controlled at all times, and early departure was not permitted. Test papers were also sealed until the beginning of the examination, at which point each individual candidate opened the seal (1981: 27). At the grading stage test papers were graded anonymously by up to eight raters; the final grade was arrived at by averaging the scores (1981: 80).

Cases of officials selling test content prior to tests and altering the papers of test takers immediately after a test still take place today, despite all the security measures in place. For example, the *Sydney Morning Herald* for 26 July 2009, reported:

> *A source in the Sydney Indian community said education agents had been selling copies of the May International English Language Testing System exam for between $12,000 and $18,000. He said advance copies of the exam had come from inside IDP Australia, a company owned by 38 Australian universities in partnership with the job site Seek, and were being sold throughout Sydney 'These have been leaking out for months,' he said. 'It's like a chain of command. It came from the official service who gives it out and takes his cut.'*

Although the cheating methods recorded by Miyazaki are still widely used, cheating has also become much more sophisticated. Videos teaching students how to cheat are also widely circulated on social networking sites and posted on sites like YouTube. But the reasons for cheating have changed little since Victorian times.

It would appear that cheating is not only as old as testing itself, but that it has always been an 'entrepreneurial enterprise' (Cohen and Wollack, 2006: 361). Countermeasures against cheating still include those used in the ancient Chinese tests, but electronic countermeasures such as video surveillance, screening for electronic and metal devices, and the use of electronic signal scramblers, are in common use. The incentives to cheat should not be underestimated whenever the stakes are fairly high.

Entrepreneurship also inspires another form of cheating, which is driven by the test preparation industry. Although there is very little literature documenting the practice, it is known that test preparation organisations pay students to take high-stakes tests, remember a subset of questions, and record them as soon as they leave the test venue (Tsagari, 2009). 'A few examinees can essentially reproduce an entire test by assigning different parts of the test to each co-conspirator' (Cohen and Wollack, 2006: 362). The reconstructed test is then used in test preparation classes by the company funding the activity, or made available on a pay-per-view basis on the internet. This form of cheating is much more difficult to detect or combat as no cheating technically takes place during the test. However, the test form is insecure as soon as it is used, and the next group of test takers will already have prepared their answers.

For many years it had been argued that *computer adaptive tests* (CATs) avoided this reconstruction problem. However, as we saw in Chapter 7, we now know that computer adaptive tests are just as susceptible to item disclosure as other tests. The only realistic way to combat this is to ensure that the item pool is both extremely large and regularly repopulated with new items. This is often prohibitively expensive even for very large testing companies. With off-the-peg computer adaptive software within the price of many institutional programmes, teachers sometimes think that using a CAT might be the answer to their many administrative and security problems. It has been estimated that to run a CAT securely it is necessary to have enough items in the pool at any one time to administer at least twelve forms without the repetition of any single item. This requires a huge initial investment of item writing effort, and an ongoing effort to replenish the pool at frequent intervals. This effort might be disproportionate to any advantages gained over linear testing, whether computer based or on paper.

7. Scoring and moderation

Although we discussed scoring tests in Chapter 7, we did not consider how to train raters to score constructed response or performance items. Once a test has been operationalised it is in the interests of the institution and all the test takers that raters judge the quality of performances equitably. In Chapter 2 we introduced the concept of inter-rater reliability as a measure of rater agreement when judging the same sample of speech, or piece of writing. We also need to ensure *intra-rater reliability*, or the extent to which a single rater agrees with him- or herself over a period of time. To increase the reliability of rating, most institutions introduce rater training sessions, although may (rather confusingly) refer to them as 'standardisation meetings'.

The procedures are not dissimilar from the familiarisation and benchmarking activities that we described in Chapter 8. The first stage in the process is to ensure that all raters are familiar with the tasks used in the assessment, and the rating scales. Discussion of the meaning of each descriptor in a rating scale should highlight potential misunderstandings, so that a common interpretation emerges. The second phase is for the leader to present samples of writing or speech from previous administrations or field tests that are deemed to be particularly clear examples of what is expected at a particular level. The samples can be studied in relation to the level descriptors, with particular performance features highlighted. The third phase is to present new samples that the raters mark, and agreement levels calculated. If raters show significantly different marking patterns to others, are particularly harsh or lenient, they should be excluded from the current round of rating until they are able to retrain. Something similar to this kind of process operates in most educational institutions. When raters are working for testing agencies operating large-scale tests, they are frequently recertified on a regular basis to ensure that the marking does not drift over time.

The second quality assurance procedure that is put into place is *moderation*, although the term for this activity differs from country to country. Following a test, moderation is the process of randomly sampling from written scripts or recordings of speaking tests to check that the grades awarded appear to be reasonable, according to the scoring plan. This is usually done by a senior member of the rating team who has oversight of the process, possibly with the help of other senior raters. If it is found that a particular rater routinely awards a grade lower than would be expected, it is possible to re-grade at this stage in order to correct for unexpected variation.

8. Data handling and policy

If your test is computer based, it should be possible for the computer to conduct the scoring against a key and automatically record the scores in a database. This ease of scoring, which we discussed in Chapter 7, removes many opportunities for errors to occur in data handling. However, it also removes the use of constructed response items, unless some automated speech or writing scoring software is being used. In most large-scale and local testing contexts, this is neither feasible nor desirable, and so scores for performance tasks may have to be recorded on the database by humans. If scoring machines are not available for closed response items, clerical staff are frequently used to count the number of correct responses (often using a scoring template) and to transfer the totals to a database.

There will inevitably be errors in the data if it is handled by humans. Counting responses, adding up and noting the totals on paper, then transferring to computer, opens up the possibility for mistakes to be made. When fatigue sets in, the probability of an error occurring increases exponentially. The eye can slip across columns or rows, a number may be entered twice, or a number left out. A column may be totalled incorrectly. An additional digit may appear because of a slip of the finger. While efficiency is important, it can never be achieved at the expense of accuracy. When dealing with large data sets the operators should take frequent breaks, and make random checks on accuracy. When a set of data has been entered onto the database someone else should start to debug it. One useful procedure is simply to 'eyeball' the data file to ensure that all numbers are within expected ranges and have the expected number of digits. If the descriptive statistics do not fluctuate a great deal between administrations, these may be calculated as a check that there are no extremely high or low numbers that have crept into the data set by chance. Looking at scatterplots can also be informative. In short, all aspects of data handling from scoring to recording should be carefully planned, well in advance (Davidson, 1996). And data handlers should always be reminded to back up all files every fifteen minutes.

While the data is stored it should be kept entirely secure and not made available to any third party without the permission of the test taker. The only exception to this is if a data set is made available for the purposes of research, but all personal identifiers should have been removed. Nevertheless, it may be advisable to inform test takers that their scores may be used for regular research and quality control procedures.

In many large-scale language tests the computer-generated certificate that is issued with the results has a lifespan of approximately two years. This is because, as the *Standards for Educational and Psychological Testing* (AERA, 1999: 66) say, test scores 'become obsolete over time'. This is not surprising. If a student continues to study the language or moves to a country where the language is the medium of communication, they would be expected to have made significant improvement within this time period. Alternatively, if they had ceased to learn the language and had little contact with it, significant attrition may have taken place. The certificate therefore expires, and the data upon which it is based becomes worthless for the individual concerned. While the score data may be retained for research purposes, all personal identifiers should be removed at this point. Most countries also have data protection legislation. This affects the large test providers and educational institutions alike.

For regulations governing the storage and deletion of test data with personal identifiers, it is highly advisable that anyone responsible for data collected from test takers become familiar with the legislation affecting their own country, and produce a data storage and usage policy.

▶ 9. Reporting outcomes to stakeholders

The basic assumption made in the discussion of data handling is that a database has been set up with all the relevant variables to be able to process outcomes in the way intended. This means that you should know precisely what you wish to do with the data, and how you wish it to be displayed, before the database is set up. This includes variables for candidate name and identification number, any demographic variables that are regularly recorded, and scores by item, sub-test and test total. If the structure of the database is not considered in advance, it is possible that it will not be able to generate the reports required for test analysis or for announcing results to individuals or the public.

Decisions about the structure of a database are not merely dry administrative decisions. For example, if a test contains three sub-tests of reading for gist, reading for detail and reading for inference, it may be that the correlation between the sub-tests are moderate. Indeed, we may hope that this is the case. Although we would expect them to correlate because they all involve reading, if they are designed to measure different aspects of the reading construct we would hope that the correlations were not very high. Further, our purpose in designing the test this way may have been to provide diagnostic feedback to teachers and learners on reading progress. The theoretical considerations relating to test purpose and the intended constructs of measurement, and the empirical evidence about how the sub-tests relate to each other, impact on how we intend to report scores, and hence the structure of the database. In this hypothetical example we would probably wish to produce a score report with three sub-test scores, and a test total score.

Planning the database and score reporting in advance helps us to meet Standard 5.10 in the *Standards for Educational and Psychological Testing* (AERA, 1999: 65), which reads:

> *When test score information is released to students, parents, legal representatives, teachers, clients, or the media, those responsible for testing programs should provide*

appropriate interpretations. The interpretations should describe in simple language what the test covers, what scores mean, the precision of the scores, common misinterpretations of test scores, and how scores will be used.

As always, there is sometimes a conflict between theory, and what is possible. The clearest example of this is in the practice of *flagging* test scores. In Section 5 we looked at a range of test accommodations for students with disabilities. If an accommodation changes the nature of the test in a way that may impact upon the meaning of the score, until recently it was common practice to 'flag' the score with a note to say that the test had been taken under a particular accommodation, together with an interpretation of what the score may mean. This had been common practice since large-scale tests were introduced. For example, Burt (1922: 18) recommends that 'The scores respectively obtained "without assistance" and "with assistance" should be kept distinct, and denominated as such'. Sireci (2005: 4) refers to accommodations as 'the ultimate psychometric oxymoron', in the sense that standardisation in testing is designed to limit the impact of test-taking conditions on the score, whereas the accommodations are changes to the conditions that are also designed to limit the impact of conditions on score meaning. Knowing precisely whether score meaning is affected is often very difficult, which is why flagging occurs. However, there may be social consequences for the test taker whose score is flagged. In the 1985 edition of the *Standards for Educational and Psychological Testing*, Standard 14.4 reads:

> *Interpretive information that accompanies modified tests should include a careful statement of the steps taken to modify tests in order to alert users to changes that are likely to alter the validity of the measure.*
> (APA, 1985: 79)

In the 1999 issue, the comparable Standard 10.11 reads:

> *When there is credible evidence of score comparability across regular and modified administrations, no flag should be attached to a score. When such evidence is lacking, specific information about the nature of the modification should be provided, if permitted by law, to assist users properly to interpret and act on test scores.*
> (AERA, 1999: 108)

The changes to this standard are far from trivial. The first is that a flag should only be attached if there is no evidence of 'comparability' of scores. The second is that legal considerations now come into play. Immediately after the last issue of the *Standards* was issued, a student took Educational Testing Service to court (*Breimhorst v. Educational Testing Service*, 2000). Breimhorst was a disabled student who took a computerised test with extended time, using a computer trackball. This was flagged on his results, and Breimhorst sued ETS on the grounds that this revealed the fact that he was disabled to the colleges to which he was applying. He claimed that this was likely to bias the admissions tutors against him. ETS settled the case out of court and stopped flagging scores on its tests, including the Test of English as a Foreign Language (TOEFL).

Leong (2005: 21–22) argues that, while this settlement may have satisfied those who believe that flagging stigmatises and disadvantages the disabled, it 'creates an untenable situation' as 'simply removing the flags without modifying the format impairs the validity of the test and creates undesirable incentives for fraud'. Leong reports on the sudden upsurge of candidates wishing to register disabilities simply in order to gain the accommodation of additional time now that they know it will not be flagged. She raises an important issue: the tests are not designed to measure 'speed', as it is not part of the construct. Timing studies, in which the test is given to groups of students under different time conditions also show that additional time does not have any impact on average scores (Bridgeman, McBride and Monaghan, 2004). The answer to the problem, Leong suggests, is to make the test time longer for everyone. This removes the requirement for a time accommodation, without threatening test validity. Why this solution has not been implemented is a question we address in the final section of this chapter.

But before we do, we turn to the question of how scores are released to test takers. This is not a major issue for large-scale test providers. They are made available on an individual basis, either as a paper report or an electronic download. However, if the report is also being provided to a receiving institution, such as a college or university, they do have to ensure that the institution receives it directly from the provider rather than the test taker, in order to avoid the possibility of fraud. In schools and universities, the issue is not always quite so straightforward, as the method of release depends upon what effect the institution wishes to achieve. The tendency is to give results to individuals and not make any information public apart from summary statistics. However, some institutions still 'post' the outcomes of tests and assessments for public view, especially at the end of an academic year. This was in fact the practice in most institutions until very recently, when the 'competitiveness' of examinations became something that was considered demoralising for those who were in the lower tail of the distribution. Miyazaki (1981: 22) describes the public posting of test results in China, which is not dissimilar to what happened with university examination results in the not too distant past:

> With the grading of the answer sheets finished, the results were announced. The dramatic production the authorities made of this important event was a special feature of the system. For the district examinations the names of successful candidates were written on sheets of paper large enough to hold fifty names. The name of the best candidate was placed at the top, in the twelve o'clock position, and the names of the rest were written counter-clockwise, in order of descending rank. Then the men in charge checked each name with a mark in black ink, distinguished it with a red dot, wrote 'successful' (chung) in the empty space at the center of the list, and, lining up all the sheets, posted them in front of the yamen gates. In consequence of this elaborate procedure, the successful candidates were all the more exalted, while the failures became more and more despondent.

Miyazaki's final sentence highlights the heart of the matter for modern political sensibilities. In an age where the concept of 'failure' in education has largely become unacceptable, practices like these have, for the most part, been consigned to history.

10. The expense of it all

All teachers know that testing and assessment is expensive in terms of their time. Writing tests takes a long time. Marking loads are frequently quite onerous, eating into evenings and weekends. The administrative arrangements, training and moderation seem to take forever. There is never enough clerical or technical support, either. It is not surprising that in many cases the resources are not available for a properly planned programme of test development, or for preparing and studying test reports after the event to investigate how everything went. Or to put plans in place for ongoing test validation and improvement. Fred Davidson is fond of saying that there are three factors that drive testing activities: '(1) money, (2) money and (3) money' (Fulcher and Davidson, 2007: 294). For some reason those who control the purse strings often do not think that testing needs proper resourcing and funding in the way that multimedia facilities or libraries might. This is a mistake. Testing always impacts upon students and the institution in ways that demand the task be done as well as possible, and this requires time and resources.

Money has, and always will be, a problem. Latham (1877: 377) is clear about why many examinations do not contain an oral test, and why written tests are as short as possible:

> When candidates have to go to a particular place for an examination the expense is great, and increases with the length of the examination; hence the tendency to drop viva voce, and otherwise to shorten examinations, which diminishes their trustworthiness.

Why do testing agencies not wish to extend testing time to solve the accommodation problem and the validity problem in one simple administrative move? They 'typically cite[s] a desire to minimize expenses associated with test administrations, such as hourly fees for proctors' (Leong, 2005: 31). We might also add the rental of testing venues, the hire of equipment, and all the other variable expenses that come with flexible testing time.

Speaking tests have always been particularly problematic. But cost factors impinge on all test issues. Despite a realisation that performance testing can tap rich constructs that give valuable information, large-scale tests have seen the tendency to go back to the use of multiple choice at the expense of constructed response formats. Koretz and Hamilton (2006: 536) are under no illusion why this is the case in the United States:

> states are facing heavy testing demands and severe budget costs. The problem of high costs may be the most important factor contributing to states' reliance on multiple-choice testing. The magnitude of the problem is evident in a study by the U.S. General Accounting Office, which estimated states' costs for implementing large-scale testing. The total estimated cost for states using only multiple-choice tests was approximately $1.9 billion, whereas the cost if states also included a small number of hand-scored open-response items such as essays was estimated to be about $5.3 billion.

These are exceptionally large sums of money. Barton (2009: 9) questions whether it is possible to genuinely provide information for politicians and educators on whether learners have reached desired standards on many of the more complex constructs that we may wish to assess. He is aware that this is difficult, 'given the nation's unwillingness to invest in high-quality assessments that go beyond filling in the bubbles'. This is not only true for nations, it is true for schools, colleges, universities, and all other institutions that develop and administer tests. The quality of the information that tests provide, and the fairness of the decisions that are made, are dependent upon the resources that are made available to do the job well.

Activities

○ 9.1 Share your experiences

At the beginning of the chapter we make some attempt to list all the tasks that teachers are required to undertake to arrange institutional testing. In your experience, what are the most difficult and frustrating aspects of test administration? Share your experiences with colleagues. Are they similar? Or do you find that there are different problems across institutions?

○ 9.2 Practising your calculation skills VI

You book two large rooms for the end-of-module listening test. One is at the front of the building, the other at the back. Students are assigned to rooms and chairs randomly by candidate number. Just as the test starts, workmen and vehicles arrive on the street at the front of the building and start digging up the road to repair a water pipe. Pneumatic drills and a bulldozer are used to break up the road and remove the rubble.

  The students complain bitterly, so you decide to analyse the outcome of the test.

	Outcomes		
Conditions	**Pass**	**Fail**	**Totals**
No noise	35	15	50
Noise	18	32	50
Totals	53	47	100

Will you:

(a) Reject the claim of the students and let the scores stand?
(b) Cancel the scores and hold the test again using a different form?
(c) Let anyone who was in the noisy room take the test again?
(d) Let only those who failed the test and were in the noisy room take the test again?
(e) Let everyone who failed the test take it again?

Provide a rationale for your answer.

○ 9.3 Identifying disabilities and modifications

What kinds of disabilities might your own students suffer from? Make a list. For each, what kind of accommodations (a) does your institution provide, and (b) should your institution provide, but doesn't. What do you think are the relative cost–benefit trade-offs for your institution in providing more accommodations?

◯ 9.4 Reviewing accommodations

Gallaudet University hosts the National Task Force on Equity in Testing the Deaf and Hard of Hearing. Visit their website: http://gri.gallaudet.edu/TestEquity/accommodations.html. Write a brief review of the issues surrounding testing the deaf and hard of hearing, including a summary of recommended accommodations. Can you identify any tensions between using the accommodations and changing score meaning on language tests?

◯ 9.5 Testing the testers!

Visit the websites of *two* or *three* of the major test providers. You can make a selection from those listed at the following website if you wish: http://languagetesting.info/links2.html.

Search for information on test accommodations.

- What range of accommodations do they provide?
- Is the information on how to apply for accommodations clear?
- Do you think that they are offering a good service?

If no information is provided on accommodations, you may wish to contact the testing agency to ask for their policy on providing accommodations.

Write a short evaluation of the provision each testing agency makes for the disabled.

◯ 9.6 When is it cheating?

It is often very clear when something is cheating, and when it isn't. But sometimes there is a grey area, especially when it comes to test preparation. Go to this website: http://languagetesting.info/features/testprep/testprep.html. Listen to the radio programme. With colleagues, discuss whether the practices described are 'cheating' or acceptable test preparation practices.

If you are working in a larger group, be prepared to express and defend your views.

◯ 9.7 On the Tube

Visit YouTube and do a search on 'cheating on tests'. What 'advice' do you get? How sophisticated are the methods recommended? What administrative procedures would you have to put in place to detect cheating by these methods?

◯ 9.8 Money, money, money

If it hadn't already been done (at least twice), it would be a good title for a song. What resources does your institution put into testing and assessment? Are they enough to do the job well? Once you have reflected on the question and made notes, share your views with colleagues.

○ 9.9 Project work VII

Time once again to look at your own test, and its purpose. Are you likely to have any test takers who may need accommodations? If you are, what accommodations might you include? Would these be available to anyone who takes the test, or just to those with a particular disability? Do you need to make any alterations to your test specifications?

10 Testing and teaching

 ## 1. The things we do for tests

Much of this book has been concerned with how teachers and testers can develop language tests in professional ways. This chapter looks at the effects that tests can have on classrooms. Teachers, as we have observed, have to respond to the demands made by testing regimes and students' desires to pass tests. It is therefore about evaluating the impact that test use may have on teaching and learning, in the broadest sense. The effects of the use of language tests are the measure of the meaning of the test in practice. If the test has been well designed, with its purpose and effect in mind, we might expect to see many positive practical effects for most stakeholders.

We first discuss washback and related research, and the practice of aligning tests and the curriculum to content standards. We then consider what is probably the most widespread responsibility of teachers: preparing students to take externally mandated tests. We also look at how to select tests when resources aren't available to develop them in house.

 ## 2. Washback

The present concern with washback began with Messick's (1989: 20) introduction of the notion of consequences into his definition of validity. His conception of validity incorporated both the values that the test endorsed, and the impact that the use of the test had on individuals and institutions. Messick (1996: 241) says that 'washback refers to the extent to which the introduction and use of a test influences language teachers and learners to do things that they would not otherwise do that promote or inhibit language learning'. Alderson and Wall (1993) set out a number of questions that they referred to as 'washback hypotheses', many of which have been subsequently investigated. The most important of these are listed below. A test will influence:

- what teachers teach
- how teachers teach
- what learners learn
- how learners learn
- the rate and sequence of teaching
- the rate and sequence of learning
- attitudes to the content, method, etc. of teaching and learning.

While it seems obvious that washback does exist, it is not quite so clear how it works. For example, it does not appear that it is systematic (Tsagari, 2009). It affects some learners more than others, and some teachers more than others. Nor is washback always negative. Washback is mediated by many other factors, such as the nature of the curriculum, the training background of teachers, the culture of an institution, and the quality of the support and resources available in the teaching context (Watanabe, 2004a). Washback studies have therefore not been able to pick any particular classroom teaching or learning activity and unequivocally state that it is 'caused' by the test (Alderson and Hamp-Lyons, 1996; Green, 2007). Evidence from major studies into the introduction of new tests in education systems with the intention of introducing change generally shows that things do not work as intended; there is no simple relationship between the use of a test and its effects (Wall and Alderson, 1993, 1996). Indeed, with reference to their study of the introduction of a new test into the Sri Lankan educational system, Wall and Alderson (1996: 219) conclude that:

> the exam has had impact on the content of the teaching in that teachers are anxious to cover those parts of the textbook which they feel are most likely to be tested. This means that listening and speaking are not receiving the attention they should receive, because of the attention that teachers feel they must pay to reading. There is no indication that the exam is affecting the methodology of the classroom or that teachers have yet understood or been able to implement the methodology of the text books.

Although empirical studies show that the deliberate use of high-stakes tests to modify teacher behaviours is usually not effective, even over time (Qi, 2004), washback remains an important and highly emotive subject. Evidence or not, many teachers feel the pressure of the test. Sometimes, this pressure is internal to an institution, where a test may become entrenched. Sometimes the administration or groups of teachers who are comfortable with the testing status quo accept a situation that places what seems like a straitjacket on newer members of staff. This has led to a trend to look at washback in the small cultures of institutions, rather than those of national or international tests. For example, Nicole (2008) studied the impact of a local test on teaching and learning in Zurich. Using survey and interview techniques to gather teachers' views of the impact of the test, and classroom observations against which to confirm what she was told, Nicole discovered that the test appeared to encourage greater coverage of skills and content. She also reported evidence of an improvement in teaching methodology. In this case, the participatory teacher-researcher, working with her own colleagues, produced evidence to suggest that the test appeared to have positive washback on teaching.

Teachers can and should study washback in their own professional contexts. Studies of the kind conducted by Nicole can provide washback evidence to militate for change, or to support positive developments. This is professionally valuable at a local level, and can be empowering for teachers in shaping their own testing world. There is little point in spending all the time and resources available to produce an excellent test, following the practical advice in books like this, if the effect on those who matter is not evaluated.

Researching washback requires careful thought, especially if you are investigating washback within a context with which you are extremely familiar, like Nicole. This is mainly because it is very easy not to notice key features of the context that are important to arrive at an informed interpretation. Familiarity can desensitise us to important features of the context (Watanabe, 2004b: 25). The first requirement is, therefore, an attempt to distance yourself from the familiar; to make it unfamiliar, and to find it curious. The next step is to consider the scale of the investigation. Should it be limited to the context of a particular classroom, a particular school, a school district, or an educational system? This is important, because it determines not only the size of any sample you will need to study, but also the kinds of data that might be collected. For example, if an educational system is to be evaluated it is reasonable to look at press reports, curriculum documents, teacher training systems, and so on. This is a matter of focus. Descriptive work is important. This will include the test itself, the institution(s) in which the washback study is taking place, the participants, the intended purpose of the test, and all facets of the teaching environment such as materials, syllabus and learning objectives.

It is also important to describe those aspects of washback in which you are interested. This is similar to construct definition, as discussed in Chapter 4, but it is guided towards answering this question: what would washback look like in my context? This was the question asked by Wall and Alderson (1996: 197–201) when they began looking at changes to the examination system in Sri Lanka. As the introduction of a new test was meant to be 'a lever for change', one of the expected effects was an increase in the time devoted to speaking and listening in the classroom. This therefore became a key focus of their study.

Next, it is important to consider what kind of data would provide the evidence you need to decide whether the washback is working as intended (see Wall, 2005). In the case of the Sri Lankan project, classroom observations in which observers recorded the percentage of time devoted to different skills would generate the evidence needed to make an evaluation. Typical data sources, depending upon the questions asked, include surveys of teachers, supervisors, managers or policy makers; these are often followed up by interviews with selected participants in order to get more fine-grained views that cannot be elicited in questionnaires. The same may be undertaken with language learners. Classroom observations are frequently an important part of washback studies, as what teachers and learners report happens in classrooms does not always tally with reality. Before conducting classroom observations it is important to decide what is going to be observed. Checklists need to be drawn up in advance. If audio recording is an option, pilot studies can be conducted to see whether or not check-lists need to be altered or expanded with new categories before a main study takes place. Follow-up interviews might be conducted with teachers or learners, either with or without playing back a recording, to ask them to reflect on how particular classroom activities are related to their understanding of the test.

Documentary evidence is always important. Teacher-prepared lesson plans, teacher-prepared activities, selected textbooks and other resources, can be analysed to detect washback. Focus groups may be used to discover whether materials are deliberately developed to teach the skills that teachers think the test measures, or how they adapt published materials to meet their own teaching goals.

Two issues concerning data need to be raised at this point. Firstly, it is always unwise to rely entirely upon one source of evidence in washback studies. Using multiple sources of evidence is termed *triangulation*. When data can be presented from multiple sources and used in a coherent interpretative argument, it gives more weight to the usefulness of the emerging understanding of how washback operates in the context. Secondly, if at all possible, data should be collected before the introduction of a new test, and again after its introduction, using the same methods, and ideally the same teachers in the same institutions. It is not always clear that a particular practice might be followed irrespective of whether a test is used or not, even if teachers claim that it is. It could be that these practices are part of the culture of the institution, or are used because of the content of teacher training programmes. If data is collected before the introduction of a test – in a *baseline study* – it is possible to compare the results of the baseline study with those of a post-introduction study to see what changes come about. Of course, in complex environments like educational systems and schools, it is always possible that changes occur for other reasons. Perhaps there is staff turnover, a syllabus is changed, a new textbook is introduced. But baseline studies do provide another anchor that allows us to try to see which practices may be caused by the use of a test, and which are incidental to it.

This was the practice adopted in what is perhaps the largest language testing washback study conducted to date, which is reported in Wall and Horák (2006, 2008). In the first study Wall and Horák (2006: 3) note that one of the intended effects of the introduction of the TOEFL iBT over 2005–06 was a positive impact upon classroom teaching and learning. The previous pencil-and-paper test had been criticised for encouraging the use of multiple-choice items in classroom teaching, and a neglect of speaking and writing. In order to study whether the test designers' intentions were realised, they conducted a baseline study in a number of institutions in Eastern and Central Europe. Description is central to their study, as they argue that the impact from innovation is determined 'by the interaction of features in the antecedent situation (the context into which the innovation is being introduced) and a number of factors that work together (or against one another) during the process period (the time that the innovation is introduced and being tried out by the users)' (2006: 4–5). Only by undertaking this description can the consequences – the adoption, adaption or rejection of an innovation – be understood. They described existing test preparation classes (materials, methodology and assessment) and the institutional context (policies, practices, resourcing), in preparation for a second study to take place after the innovation (the new test) had been introduced. Wall and Horák also studied the washback intentions of the test designers.

One example in relation to writing is the following:

> **Writing**
>
> *Innovation*: introduction of multiple writing tasks that include both independent and content-dependent tasks.
>
> *Intended effect*: move beyond the single independent essay model to a writing model that is more reflective of writing in an academic environment.
>
> *Washback intention*: specific to the teaching of writing, and positive.

With such specific intentions it is possible to use interviews, observations and analysis of writing materials to chart the impact of the innovation in the classroom. Using a similar approach in a specific institution would allow teachers to consider how they wish to change teaching, and to co-ordinate this with changes in assessment practices.

As part of the data collection it is important to design or adapt appropriate questionnaires or observation schedules. It is not within the scope of this book to discuss questionnaire design, for which the reader is directed to the relevant literature (Brown, 2001; Dörnyei, 2003). However, Wall and Horák (2006, 2008) reproduce all their survey and observation schedules in the appendices to their reports, which the reader is encouraged to study. With regard to collecting data on the changes to the writing test that we considered above, Wall and Horák (2006: 173) used the following classroom observation schedule when visiting writing classes during the baseline study, and to collect data in the follow-up study after the new test had been introduced.

This observation schedule is designed to direct the attention of classroom observers to the key lesson features that are related to an existing test, and which are expected to change when the new test is introduced. Every instrument needs to be sensitive to the context. However, these schedules can be adapted to suit new contexts.

Start time:	End time:	S work mode: I P G C	Medium: Com PP	Language: LI L	Atmosphere:	Skill focus: Int Sing
		WRITING			✓	
Activities:				Notes:		
						Generating ideas
						Organizing ideas
						Developing ideas
						Supporting ideas with examples/evidence
						Selecting appropriate vocabulary
						Developing sentence structure
						Writing essays
						Writing an essay–no time limit
						Writing an essay in time limit
						Writing essays–no word limits
						Writing essays with word limits (NT)
						Writing essay based on a listening (NT)
						Writing an essay based on reading (NT)
						Organizing ideas from listening/ reading before writing (NT)
						Writing on topics from ETS pool
						Writing on topics selected by teacher
						Writing on topics selected by student(s)
						Examining ETS scoring scale
						Synthesizing data from 2 or more texts

Fig. 10.1. An observation schedule for writing classes

Investigating washback is primarily qualitative research which involves the careful interpretation of data generated from a number of methodologies. They may also be quite time-consuming to conduct. Nevertheless, washback is critical to the evaluation of the extent to which testing policies have been successful in terms of their intended effect.

▶ 3. Washback and content alignment

It has long been argued that tests should be totally independent of any method of instruction, or the content of instruction (Latham, 1877: 46). While tests may be aligned to standards (Chapter 8) for reporting purposes, the traditional view has been that success in the test should not be correlated with attending any particular educational institution or programme. There is merit in this position. It holds that the test taps a construct, but the test does not dictate to teachers or learners how this construct is acquired. The role of the teacher is to plan a curriculum that enables the acquisition of the tested abilities. The methodologies and materials may therefore look very different depending upon the people and institutions, even if the learners ultimately take the same test. Some even go so far as to claim that any attempt to abandon this 'separation of power' is to undermine the validity of a test on the grounds that test content and classroom teaching are confounded (Haladyna, Nolen and Haas, 1991). The 'separationists' would argue that classroom teaching should take priority and the test is an independent measure of the achievement of the learners.

The alternative point of view is that tests can drive curriculum change. This argument holds that, when test content and instructional content are closely aligned, there is an opportunity to claim that teachers are covering the necessary material to achieve desired educational goals. This is frequently referred to as curriculum alignment. Koretz and Hamilton (2006: 555) describe this alignment as having taken place when 'the knowledge, skills and other constructs measured by the tests will be consistent with those specified in the [content] standards'. Of course, it has always been the case that test designers should take content into account. Defining the universe of possible content and then sampling from that content is part of defining the test purpose and the domains to which the test scores are relevant. What is different in curriculum alignment is the attempt to completely specify all the content that learners are supposed to cover, and replicate this as far as possible in the assessments. The intention is to use the test to control curriculum, removing it from the professional control of teachers. The 'integrationists' argue that the closer the alignment between test and curriculum, the better the teaching, and the more valid the measurement. For example, Gottlieb (2006: 36) argues:

> In today's classroom, standards are the cornerstone for accountability. Content standards are the starting point, anchor, and reference for teaching and learning. English language proficiency standards lead to instruction and assessment of English language proficiency, and academic content standards are geared to instruction and assessment of academic achievement.

The 'integrationists', as I have called them, see the process of aligning content standards, curriculum and tests as the means to measure educational success, and in the process to make teachers and institutions accountable for the learning outcomes. Teachers are therefore increasingly being asked not only to align their tests to performance standards (Chapter 8), but also align both their curriculum and their tests to content standards.

The first point to make about this approach for language testing is that, while 'content' in mathematics or history can contain specific topics, in language they generally do not. Rather, they resemble fairly complex performance standards – indeed, the example we will consider is actually called 'performance standards' rather than 'content standards'. In language standards, the content arranged within a performance level is frequently described in terms of tasks that are considered to be of the right level of difficulty. Thus, for example, the McREL Content Knowledge Standards (2009) contains 24 topics, each with sub-standards set out under five general standards, with entries by grade level. If this complexity were not enough, each sub-standard is broken down into 'benchmarks' – or sub-skills within sub-standards. The matrix created by this classification system is extremely large. To illustrate, within the standard 'writing' for topic 'writing for audience and purpose', at the level of grades 9–12, benchmarks 2 and 3 read:

> *Drafting and revising: uses a variety of strategies to draft and revise written work (e.g., highlights individual voice; rethinks content, organization, and style; checks accuracy and depth of information; redrafts for readability and needs of readers; reviews writing to ensure that content and linguistic structures are consistent with purpose.*

> *Editing and publishing: Uses a variety of strategies to edit and publish written work e.g., uses a checklist to guide proofreading; edits for grammar, punctuation, capitalization, and spelling at a developmentally appropriate level; refines selected pieces to publish for general and specific audiences; uses available technology, such as publishing software or graphics programs, to publish written work.*

Teachers are required to create a curriculum that covers all the necessary skills and abilities within each standard at the class level, and construct tests that will assess whether the learners have met the requirements for that level. Alternatively, the creation of the tests is outsourced to a specialist testing agency.

One of the most widely used sets of standards is produced by the WIDA consortium in the United States (WIDA, 2007). Produced for both Spanish and English language learners (and other subject areas), WIDA creates the standards used by many states to comply with accountability legislation. All documentation relating to the consortium and its standards can be downloaded at its website (www.wida.us). The content standards are organised within two frameworks: formative (the process of learning) and summative (the outcomes of learning). They reflect both social and academic aspects of language learning in schools according to sets of proficiency standards (see Chapter 8) for subject areas, and are presented in hierarchical clusters for school grades Pre-K, Grades 1–2, 3–5, 6–8 and 9–12.

As the entire set of standards may be downloaded from the website, we will select a small sample for discussion. This is taken from the academic area of language arts, and relates to the teaching and assessment of writing in grades 9–12. There are further standards for other academic and social areas, and for other skills (listening, reading and writing).

	Level 1: Entering	Level 2: Beginning	Level 3: Developing	Level 4: Expanding	Level 5: Bridging
Example Genre: Critical Commentary	Reproduce comments on various topics from visually supported sentences from newspapers or websites	Produce comments on various topics from visually supported paragraphs from newspapers or websites	Summarize critical commentaries from visually supported newspaper, website or magazine articles	Respond to critical commentaries by offering claims and counterclaims from visually supported newspaper, website or magazine articles	Provide critical commentary commensurate with proficient peers on a wide range of topics and sources
Example topic: Note taking	Take notes on key symbols, words of phrases from visuals pertaining to discussions	List key phrases or sentences from discussions and models (e.g. on the board or from overhead projector)	Produce sentence outlines from discussions, lectures or readings	Summarize notes from lectures or readings in paragraph form	Produce essays based on notes from lectures or readings
Example Topic: Conventions and Mechanics	Copy key points about language learning (e.g. use of capital letters for days of week and months of year) and check with a partner	Check use of newly acquired language (e.g. through spell or grammar check or dictionaries) and share with a partner	Reflect on use of newly acquired language or language patterns (e.g. through self-assessment checklists and share with a partner)	Revise of rephrase written language based on feedback from teachers, peers and rubrics	Expand, elaborate and correct written language as directed

Table 10.1 Standards for formative writing, language arts, grades 9–12 (WIDA, 2007: 59)

	Level 1: Entering	Level 2: Beginning	Level 3: Developing	Level 4: Expanding	Level 5: Bridging
Example genre: Critical commentary	Reproduce critical statements on various topics from illustrated models or outlines	Produce critical comments on various topics from illustrated models or outlines	Summarize critical commentaries on issues from illustrated models or outlines	Respond to critical commentaries by offering claims and counter-claims on a range of issues from illustrated models or outlines	Provide critical commentary on a wide range of issues commensurate with proficient peers
Example topic: Literal and figurative language	Produce literal words or phrases from illustrations or cartoons and word/phrase banks	Express ideas using literal language from illustrations or cartoons and word/phrase banks	Use examples of literal and figurative language in context from illustrations or cartoons and word/phrase banks	Elaborate on examples of literal and figurative language with or without illustrations	Compose narratives using literal and figurative language

Table 10.2 Standards for summative writing, language arts, grades 9–12 (WIDA, 2007: 61)

Even at a particular grade level (9–12) it is assumed that there are five levels of progression (the actual performance standards), and in the left-hand column we are given example genres and topics, with particular abilities in cells. Once again, the entire matrix to cover all content, by age range and ability level, is mind-blowingly large.

One of the problems with language content standards is that they are not targeted at performance in particular domains (for example, whether there is sufficient language to act as a tour guide in a defined context), but whether test takers have acquired 'language' without reference to any domain at all, across all skills, genres, domains and contexts. This is cross-referenced with other skills, such as use of software for publishing and the ability to work in a team (check performance with partners). However, in defence of the approach, it must be said that most content standards are designed for use in schools. It is arguably the case that language learning in this context is much more general, and less targeted, than adult language learning for specific purpose.

Nevertheless, the scale and complexity of content standards raise the question of the relationship between them and any form of a test. By definition, any form will sample from content standards rather than contain everything, and so the link between score meaning and the claim that learners have 'mastered' the content standards are tenuous at best. If the claim is from a test to score the content standards as a whole, a key validity claim is that from a tiny sample the score meaning can be generalised to a very large universe of potential content. This is the enduring fundamental problem with any content-based approach to considering the validity of score meaning (Fulcher, 1999) that we discussed in Chapter 4. In other words, in any content alignment study there will be a question over whether the content standards are comprehensive enough at all performance levels, and even if there is agreement that they are generally useful for purpose, any form of a test will always be found to under-represent the content.

Before progressing to methodology, it is important to highlight a point of contrast with the content standards discussed here, and the Common European Framework of Reference. While the *Manual* (Council of Europe, 2009) recommends the analysis of content between the CEFR and tests, the CEFR does not contain much in the way of content and, where it does, it is not organised according to levels. This makes content comparison purely arbitrary in a way which it is not with models like WIDA. The CEFR invitation for readers to 'consider' what content might occur at each level is an invitation for invention, not comparison. Perhaps the lesson to be drawn is that under-specification of content is as much of a problem as over-specification for integrationists. I would argue that the cause of both problems is a lack of specific purpose for language use, and for intended score meaning. In short, they are models, not frameworks.

This aside, we turn to the methodology of content alignment. As with alignment to proficiency standards and setting cut scores, all methodologies rely upon expert judgement. Content standards can be used directly in developing curriculum, and 'check-lists' can be developed to ensure that curriculum content and teaching materials map on to content standards.

'Horizontal alignment' is the process of mapping tests and assessments to content standards. As we have argued, no single assessment can measure everything in a set of content standards. The first part of the process is to develop a test specification (see Chapter 5) drawing on the content standards as the domain of interest.

When a test form is compiled, the aim is to include at least one item for every content standard, although this is frequently not possible. The test specifications represent the first piece of alignment evidence. The next stage in the process is for a team of subject experts to compare the content of a number of test forms to the content standards, using a framework for the analysis. The most widely used methods are those of Achieve (www.achieve.org) and Webb (1999). We will describe the Achieve method below, as variants can be used by teachers in their own institutions, whereas the Webb method is more complex.

Before starting the alignment study, teachers are familiarised with the standards contents and the tests, using methods similar to those described in Chapter 8. Ideally, they should also take the test forms which are being used in the alignment study. Once they are fully familiar with all the documentation, the alignment study is conducted in three steps. (Note that the terms 'standard' and 'objective' are used interchangeably, although in some content standards one or the other is used as a superordinate, and the other to describe clusters of related target behaviours.)

Step One. Looking at each item/task individually, each teacher identifies the content standard objective(s) that the item measures, and applies a content standard code to the item (this is sometimes called 'categorical concurrence'). The question that is being asked is whether the test items measure objectives in the content standards, and only objectives in the content standards. The aim is to ensure that learners are only being tested on what they will be covering in the curriculum. In the Achieve method, three judgements are made: firstly, confirmation that the item measures an objective within the content standards (code each item with the appropriate code(s) from the content standards); secondly, estimate content centrality; and thirdly, estimate performance centrality. Content centrality is whether the item clearly and explicitly measures the standard. Performance centrality is a judgement about whether the cognitive complexity of the item is similar to the cognitive complexity of the objective required in the content standards. This usually requires the judges to focus on functions of the standards, such as 'describe', 'compare' or 'analyse'. For both of these a grading system like the following is adopted:

0 = inconsistent

1A = not specific enough (standard or objective is too broad to be assured of item's strong alignment)

1B = somewhat consistent (item assesses only part, and the less central part, of a compound objective)

2 = clearly consistent.

The following example is taken from Rothman *et al.* (2002: 13):

[Passage read is 'When I Heard the Learn'd Astronomer' by Walt Whitman]

This poem is best classified as which of the following?

A. A sonnet
B. Epic poetry
C. Lyric poetry
D. A ballad

Relevant standard: 'The learner will analyze, synthesize, and organize information and discover related ideas, concepts, or generalizations.'

As knowledge of literary types does not appear to be a central part of this standard, the item received 1A for content centrality. The item received 0 for performance centrality as it only requires learners to identify the type of poem, whereas the function words of the standard are 'analyze', 'synthesize' and 'organize'.

Step Two. For each item, each teacher makes a judgement about how difficult or challenging the item is. This is in fact two judgements – one about the source of the difficulty, and the second about the level of difficulty. Source of difficulty is coded as 0 = inappropriate source, or 1 = appropriate source. An inappropriate source of difficulty is anything that is not construct relevant, such as a problem with the item, or a failure on the part of the item writer to produce a good item. The level of difficulty is a simple yes/no decision for each item, assessed as to whether it is of a suitable level for the target learners in terms of the concepts the item employs, and how cognitively demanding it is thought to be.

Step Three. The balance and range of the test are considered. Balance is a judgement about whether groups of items that measure a particular standard focus upon the most important aspects of that standard, rather than on peripheral abilities. Range is not a judgement at all, but is the proportion of total standards/objectives from the content standards that are measured by at least one item, as calculated in step one. Rothman *et al.* (2002: 20) argue that a result of .67 or higher is considered to be a good range, while values of .5 and higher are acceptable.

Reports based upon such content alignment studies provide the evidence with which schools can show that they have adequately taken into account content standards in their curriculum, and that the achievement tests they have devised to measure student outcomes measure the same content. In this way, accountability is imposed through the alignment of both teaching and assessment to the external standards. It is a complex and time-consuming task, which is frequently outsourced to professional testing companies. But perhaps this is an intentional effect of the desire to construct an independent accountability machinery?

4. Preparing learners for tests

It is important to distinguish between two types of preparation (Popham, 1991). The first type is designed to familiarise learners with the item types on the test, the kinds of instructions they will encounter, and give them practice in working within time constraints. If it is a computer-based test, preparation will also include becoming familiar with the interface and navigating through the test. The purpose of this kind of test preparation is to ensure that the learners do not spend time and effort having to work out what they should be doing during the test. Relating this to the ever-present question of validity, this type of preparation reduces the chance that scores will be affected by their unfamiliarity with any aspect of the test; it therefore increases the validity of score meaning by removing a potential source of construct-irrelevant variance. The second kind of test preparation is designed to increase the score of the test taker by instilling test-taking techniques that focus upon the test items, rather than improving the learner's ability on the constructs in question. For example, by spending time looking at the options in multiple-choice items to discover how frequently the longest option is likely to be the correct response, or attempting to match lexical items in the stem to synonyms in the key (see Chapter 6). Haladyna *et al.* (1991: 4) refer to the effects of such preparation as 'test score pollution', and claim that these practices are unethical.

It is not surprising that Haladyna *et al.* also consider it to be unethical to base a curriculum on a test, and to align standards, curriculum and assessments. The reason they give for their separatist stance is that tests are developed and piloted using samples drawn from populations who are not given targeted training in the test content. It is claimed that increasing curriculum alignment results in excessive test preparation that changes the meaning of test scores, and hence reduces validity (Shepard, 1990). Basically, the argument is that if you know what's on the test and you teach to it, it is hardly surprising that the learners get higher scores. But this undermines the validity of the score interpretation. Hamp-Lyons (1998) also questions the ethicality of test preparation practices that focus upon using past test papers (other than for test familiarisation), criticising particularly the production of teaching materials that merely copy test content.

This is most troubling for language teachers who have learners in their classes who wish to pass a test, and have a clear idea of what they should be doing in order to achieve this goal – even if they are mistaken. The dilemma arises from what we have observed in previous chapters; namely, that language testing has become a high-stakes, high-value activity. Test scores and test certificates provide access to many of the good things in life, and so teachers are expected to secure examination passes.

Although it may not make our lives easier, at least we can find some consolation in the fact that it has always been so. Miyazaki (1981) tells us of the long years of test preparation required in ancient China, starting in the home at around the age of 3, with formal education beginning at the age of 7. Much of the learning consisted of recitation and memorisation. From these very early times we also learn that the test results were treated not only as a measure of the success of the test taker, but also the skill of the teacher: 'If education is not strict, it shows that the teacher is lazy' (1981: 15). This provides us with the other part of the test preparation dilemma. The accountability agenda of politicians holds teachers responsible for outcomes, and as we have seen above, alignment to standards is part of this agenda. And so questionable test preparation practices emerge, as we saw in Chapter 9. In ancient China there were also 'quick fixes' to get higher scores. Miyazaki (1981: 17) says:

> Despite repeated official and private injunctions to study the Four Books and Five Classics honestly, rapid-study methods were devised for the sole purpose of preparing candidates for the examinations. Because not very many places in the classics were suitable as subjects for examination questions, similar passages and problems were often repeated. Aware of this, publishers compiled collections of examination answers, and a candidate who, relying on these publications, guessed successfully during the course of his own examination could obtain a good rating without having worked very hard … Reports from perturbed officials caused the government to issue frequent prohibitions of the publication of such collections of model answers, but since it was a profitable business with a steady demand, ways of issuing them surreptitiously were arranged, and time and again the prohibitions rapidly became mere empty formalities.

History repeats itself, and policy makers do not learn. Curriculum alignment leads to teaching to the test, and as soon as test preparation practices and materials focus upon the test, teachers are rounded upon for doing precisely what they have been encouraged to do. Similarly, accountability leads to the publication of 'league tables' for schools, most of which are tied to rewards and sanctions of some kind. The public now enjoy looking up particular schools to see where they are in the hierarchy of performance. Teachers respond to this by trying to increase test scores by any means possible, given limited time and resources.

The term 'cramming' for test preparation introduced in the nineteenth century, and survives to this day:

> *Those who afford this kind of preparation are often called crammers. Now so far as this term implies any opprobrium it is unjustly applied; a market has been opened for a particular kind of fabric, the stouter and costlier stuffs are thereby rendered less saleable, and the mill owners must meet the popular demand or close his mills. People are hardly aware of how thoroughly the educational world is governed by the ordinary economical rules. While employing the motives of gain and advancement most profusely, the public seems to find fault with teachers and pupils for being influenced by these considerations … they make learning a marketable commodity and then complain that it is grown for the market.*
> (Latham, 1877: 6–7)

These market forces compel teachers to devise the test preparation practices to meet demand. And thus,

> *The tutor must consider not what studies or what kind of teaching will do him [the learner] most good, but what studies will yield the highest aggregate in the given time, and he must teach his pupil each subject not with a view to call out his intelligence, but with a view to producing the greatest show on a stated day; for instance he must teach him a language by some sort of Ollendorff process, which shall address itself to the ear and the memory, rather than by a method which involves any grammatical analysis.*
> (Latham, 1877: 5–6)

It was also acknowledged from the earliest times that test preparation was pretty boring, and distracted learners from the real task of learning. The famous statistician Karl Pearson wrote a biography of Sir Francis Galton, who was one of the first 'scientific' testers. He reports that in 1889 Galton had argued the best way to avoid learners cramming for tests is to have lots of different kinds of tests and assessments, to vary the content as much as possible, and to ensure that what is tested cannot be easily memorised. This is still good advice in the twenty-first century, and one which many test developers try to follow. Cognitively demanding questions that require the application of knowledge and problem solving are particularly desirable.

One way of reducing the amount of test preparation is, of course, not to use tests for teacher and institutional accountability as well as learner achievement. While decoupling the two is not likely to happen for political reasons, there are excellent educational reasons for doing this when possible. Mansell (2007) provides an excellent account of what happens to education when the testing system is used by policy makers for the 'hyper-accountability' that we briefly discussed in Chapter 1. The tests are used for more purposes than they can reasonably bear, and the pressure to find short cuts is increased immensely. It leads not only to poor test preparation practices, but also encourages cheating on coursework, such as dictating answers, and allowing copying from the internet without sanction. With particular reference to language test preparation, Mansell cites practices such as teaching set phrases that can be reproduced in multiple contexts (speaking or writing) without thought (the burglar's 'swag bag' technique; 2007: 85), and the memorisation and scripting of written and oral work (2007: 89–93). He reports a senior official from an examination board as saying that without these techniques teachers simply won't be able to get the 'grim kids' to pass any tests.

This is where the unethical side of test preparation begins to get very sad indeed. While testing is primarily meant to be about meritocracy and giving people the chance to make the best of themselves, hyper-accountability can reduce real learning opportunities and damage equality of opportunity. The 'grim kids' mentality is a symptom of just how damaging the unintended consequences of some testing practices have become. Some politicians do understand this, however. I was struck by this passage from Obama (2006: 163):

> While I was talking to some of the teachers about the challenges they faced, one young teacher mentioned what she called the 'These Kids Syndrome' – the willingness of society to find a million excuses for why 'these kinds' can't learn; how 'these kids come from tough backgrounds' or 'these kids are too far behind.' 'When I hear that term, it drives me nuts,' the teacher told me. 'They're not "these kinds". They're our kids'. How America's economy performs in the years to come may depend largely on how well we take such wisdom to heart.

A narrow focus on test preparation therefore not only threatens the validity of the assessment, it undermines the entire rationale for having tests: providing genuine opportunity, and meritocratic access to education and employment. It actively disadvantages those who are already disadvantaged. In addition, there is no evidence to suggest that test preparation (other than as familiarisation) has any positive impact on test scores at all. When it comes to language learning, quick fixes have always been expensive delusions. The research evidence suggests that learner success in tests depends on the quality of the teaching, teacher training and factors associated with the educational system and resources (e.g. Alderson and Hamp-Lyons, 1996). A study by Robb and Ercanbrack (1999) using TOEIC showed that most gains when undertaking test preparation came from using English, rather than the test preparation *per se*. Similarly, investigating IELTS preparation, Comber (1998) and Bialy (2003) studied the effect of test preparation programmes in China, and discovered that, while test preparation did have a marginal impact on scores, this was not as high as teaching the language. Among other studies of the effect of test preparation on language test scores the findings are remarkably similar (Read and Hayes, 2003; Elder and O'Loughlin, 2003; Zhengdong, 2009). While Brown (1998) found that test preparation did increase test scores on the IELTS writing sub-test, the 'preparation' turned out to consist of a course in writing skills with timed writing practice. This kind of preparation is much closer to teaching than the kinds of activities normally associated with construct-irrelevant test preparation. Similarly, in a meta-analysis of studies looking at the impact of test preparation on the US SAT test scores, Powers (1993) found no significant impact.

From theoretical, ethical and practical points of view, we can therefore say that test preparation, other than for familiarisation, is not only a waste of time, but actively detrimental to learners and the educational system. I doubt, however, that the argument and evidence will have a significant impact upon the test preparation industry, which will always seek to find the quick, easy, ways to improve scores even if there is no significant change in competence. Latham (1877: 149) sums up the damage that this practice has to learners and society:

> If we damage the general standard of truthfulness by leading young men to glory in having outwitted Examiners, and seemed to be what they are not ... then we lose far more morally than we gain in any other way.

The best advice to teachers whose role is to prepare students for tests is therefore to teach the language using the most appropriate methodologies and materials to achieve communicative competence for the learners to be able to function in the target domains and contexts. Looking at tests and test items should be a minor part of any course, with the goal of familiarisation so that learners know what to do. Once this has been achieved, using test materials has no further value.

▶ 5. Selecting and using tests

Teachers and other language professionals are also frequently required to select 'off the peg' tests to use in their institutions. This is frequently the case where the time and resources to develop a local test are not available. This is almost always a second-best solution for local assessment needs where external certification is not required, as it is very difficult to find a test that does precisely what you wish it to do.

The criteria for selecting a test should be drawn up before starting the search. These will differ according to the purpose for which you need the test. However, we are able to generate a number of generic criteria that can be used as a starting point.

A. Test purpose
What decisions do you wish to make?
These may be very specific, or you may wish to classify them more generally as placement, achievement, proficiency, diagnostic or aptitude testing.
Was the test designed to make these decisions?
What evidence is provided by the test developer to justify the use of the test for this purpose?

B. Test taker characteristics
What are the key characteristics of the population to whom you will give the test?

These may include age, gender, educational level, language proficiency, first language background, particular educational or career goals, and so on.

Was the test designed for this population?

Is the test at the right level of difficulty?

What evidence is provided by the test developer to show that the test was piloted using a sample of learners similar to those with whom you are working?

C. Domain of interest

Do you wish to predict performance in a particular domain, such as a particular occupational field?

Is the test content relevant to the domain of prediction?

What evidence is provided by the test developer that the domain has been adequately defined and sampled?

D. Constructs of interest

What particular constructs do you wish to assess?

Does the test assess these constructs?

What evidence is provided by the test developer that these constructs have been included in the test specifications?

E. Reliability

How reliable do you wish the results to be?

How is the test scored?

How are scores reported?

What evidence is provided by the test developer regarding reliability, including information on the standard error of measurement or other estimates of potential sources of error?

F. Validity

What evidence is there that we can correctly make inferences about constructs from the scores?

Does the test provider make research reports available?

Does the test provider make claims about the usefulness of scores to constructs or domains that are not part of test purpose?

G. Parallel or equated forms

Do you need multiple forms of a test in order to maintain security?

Are multiple forms available?

What evidence is provided by the test developer that forms have been developed to ensure that scores do not vary significantly across forms?

H. Test administration and practicality

What resources, including time and budget, do you have available?

Can the test be administered and scored using available resources?

Do you have the funds to purchase the test and continue using it over the projected time scale?

I. Impact

What impact or washback do you expect the use of the test to have on your institution, and on classroom teaching and learning?

Is the format and content of the test likely to produce the intended impact?

What evidence is provided by the test developer to suggest that the intended impact is likely?

Many more criteria may be established. For example, if you wish scores to be reported on a particular set of standards, you will need to select a test for which a standard-setting exercise has been undertaken. You would then need to know how sensitive the test was to the standard, how many cut scores had been established, how dependable these were, which standard-setting technique had been used, and how well the standard-setting study had been undertaken. The more criteria you establish, the more effort will be needed to come to a conclusion. However, all the effort you put in will be rewarded.

The second step is amassing the information you will need to make the necessary judgements against each of the criteria. This will include descriptions of the tests, samples, descriptions of the test purpose and design processes, summaries or full texts of relevant research, and information on administration and cost. These are usually freely available from the websites of professional test development agencies.

The third step is trawling through the information to get the answers to the key questions, and to evaluate each test against the established criteria. This is best done by a small study group rather than individuals, so that different views on the quality of information and studies are taken into account. It is advisable for a short report that sets out questions, answers, and evidence to support decisions. If the selected test does not work as expected, this document may form the basis for a review of the decision, and the selection of a new test.

If you have difficulty finding a test for your particular purpose, two popular tools are available to help you.

Tool 1: The Foreign Language Assessment Directory (Center for Applied Linguistics, 2007)

Available at: http://www.cal.org/CalWebDB/FLAD/

Description: A searchable database of tests that allows you to search by name of test, language, US grade level, proficiency level (on the ACTFL scale), intended test uses, and skills to be tested. The Center for Applied Linguistics also provides an online tutorial (Center for Applied Linguistics, 2009) that guides language professionals in the selection and use of language tests using the database.

Tool 2: ETS TestLink

Available at: http://204.50.92.130/ETS_Test_Collection/Portal.aspx

Description: A searchable database of more than 2500 tests, only some of which are language tests. It is possible to search by test title, language or skill. The database provides a summary description of each test, information on the author (where available) and the test provider. This information can be used to trace availability and further information.

The general question we are trying to address is: Is the use of this test valid for the intended purpose? The validation of a testing procedure is concerned with ensuring that the test score means what it claims, and that this meaning is both relevant and useful for any decision we intend to make about the test takers. Validation is never an 'all or nothing' affair. What we need to know is whether the evidence is good enough to support the use of the test, and whether it provides us with the necessary warnings about the inevitable uncertainty that comes with any test.

In short, it is about the test producer constructing an argument for the use of the test for a specific purpose, and our evaluation of whether the argument is a good one (Kane, 1992, 2006). An argument involves a claim about the meaning of a score. Evidence (or data) is amassed in support of this claim. The reason why the evidence supports the claim is provided in a warrant or justification that argues why the two are linked. The argument can be supported by evidence from other research studies or theoretical arguments, and this is often called the 'backing' for the argument. Finally, good arguments usually take into account alternative explanations – or show that the test score is not affected by construct irrelevant variance (Fulcher and Davidson, 2007: 164–166). Some large-scale testing activities directly address the question of the argument for score meaning and test use (Chapelle, Enright and Jamieson, 2008), but this is the exception rather than the rule. One of the important points to recognise is that the more convincing the argument for the use of a test for a particular purpose, the less convincing the argument becomes for other purposes.

We therefore come full circle in our discussion. No test is good for any purpose at all, as Carroll (1961) stated in his groundbreaking contribution. Teachers and language professionals must still be vigilant against tests that have been designed for one purpose being used for another. Tests cannot be 'reused' or 'repurposed' unless there is a clear retrofit argument to show why the test is relevant to its new purpose, or how it has been adapted to suit the new purpose (Fulcher and Davidson, 2009). Some testing organisations tackle this problem head on, recognising the financial advantages that are gained (Wendler and Powers, 2009), but charge the clients with the primary responsibility to review the test or employ 'experts who best know the new test-taking population or the needs of the score users' (2009: 3) to review the suitability of the test. When selecting an 'off-the-peg' solution, beware of taking the easy option without taking due care.

▶ 6. The gold standard

As this final chapter is about tests and their impact upon the classroom, I intend to conclude with a brief consideration of the teacher as an assessor. Testing and assessment theory, and *psychometrics* in particular, have always had what can only be called a 'love-hate' relationship with teachers, as Shepard (1991, 1995, 2000) has noted. One rationale for the use of tests is that teachers are either unreliable, or just downright capricious, in how they grade students. On the other hand, when a criterion is needed for the evaluation of new scoring mechanisms or test tasks, the scores are correlated with teacher assessments. Human ratings remain the 'gold standard' against which other scores are assessed (Chodorow and Burstein, 2004). This dilemma is not going to go away, and so perhaps it is important to set it out as clearly as possible, and learn to live with it.

In his classic treatment, Ruch (1924: 2), with reference to a previous work by Caldwell and Courtis (1923), lists the reasons why a formal test is to be preferred to teacher assessments as:

1. It is impartial.
2. It is just to the pupils.
3. It is more thorough than older forms of examination.
4. It prevents the 'officious interference' of the teacher.
5. It 'determines, beyond appeal of gainsaying, whether the pupils have been faithfully and competently taught'.
6. It takes away 'all possibility of favoritism'.
7. It makes the information obtained available to all.
8. It enables all to appraise the ease or difficulty of the questions.

The assumption underlying this list is that some teachers are not capable of impartiality, and that some teacher assessment is open to unreliable fluctuation that is influenced by construct-irrelevant factors, such as whether a pupil is 'liked'. Two other themes emerge. If tests are used, they can be made available for others to judge how well the assessment has been carried out, whereas a teacher's judgements are not open to such investigation. The other is that tests present the opportunity to judge not only the learner, but the pedagogical abilities and efforts of the teacher.

But how do we know if a test is a good measure of a construct? We have looked at many ways to look at the validation of test scores and how we interpret them. One of the earliest methods, and one that is still very widespread today, is the comparison of test scores with the expert judgments. And who are the best possible judges? Burt (1923: 199) was in no doubt:

> *There is no standard of comparison which can surpass or supersede the considered estimate of an observant teacher, working daily with the individual children over a period of several months or years. This is the criterion I have used.*

As we saw in Chapter 7, the argument about whether machines are capable of scoring constructed responses – either written or spoken – largely hangs on the degree to which they can show agreement with expert human judges, most of whom are classroom teachers. Many studies seek high correlations with teacher judgements as a source of evidence to justify a validity claim for a test. As Kane (2006) argues, teachers are able to refine their views of a student's ability over time and have access to much more complex data than the language test can collect. While this does not guarantee a fair outcome, Kane (2006: 49) believes:

If a qualified teacher applies appropriate criteria to a student's performance, the results would have a strong presumptive claim on our confidence. This is the kind of evaluation that might well serve as a criterion in validating some standardized test.

Teachers are sometimes seen as part of the problem, and then as part of the solution. Perhaps the answer lies somewhere between the two extremes. It has always been intuitively obvious that sensitive teachers with a deep and extensive knowledge of learners over a period of time have an ability to make valid and reliable estimations of their capacities and abilities. That teachers can make fair and dependable decisions (see Chapter 3) is an assumption upon which all classroom assessment is based, and it can be investigated by teachers themselves within the context of professional development and team working. Teacher assessments can be used in place of, or in conjunction with, more formal assessments (Fulcher, 1991). This is the basis of marking coursework and other alternative forms of assessment. Nevertheless, in high-stakes assessment it is not always fair to place the burden of making judgements upon teachers, especially when they have worked with the learners for a long period of time and have come to care deeply about their progress and future careers. Even when a learner clearly does not meet a standard, it is not appropriate to ask a caring teacher to make this decision and communicate it to the learner. It is much better if difficult decisions are taken out of the teacher's hands. The teacher's role is to do the best for the learner, but not to take the blame if the learner ultimately does not meet a required standard.

In a sense, therefore, the teacher is the 'gold standard'. But it is a standard that can always be improved and monitored through the range of techniques that we have described in this book, from designing test specifications to monitoring dependability of judgements. Tests and assessments of all kinds have a legitimate place. The different types of assessment should not be seen as competing with each other. Each fulfils a different function. Some of these are frustrating for teachers – and always have been. But once we can appreciate the conflicting rationales for the varieties of language tests, when we understand their purpose and history, we are much more able to negotiate their use, and control their impact on our lives.

Activities

○ 10.1 Project work VIII

When we design a test we imagine what effect we wish it to have. The intended effect drives design decisions. Now that you have considered washback, and the effects that test use can have on teaching and learning, what type of washback would you expect your test to have if it were to be used as defined in your test framework and specification?

This is your washback hypothesis. How would you go about investigating whether your intention is translated into reality? Outline your plan for a research study.

○ 10.2 When testers are trainers …

Look at the extract from an article published in the *Times of India* (17 September 2009).

> The IELTS officials warn candidates against joining coaching centres that lack quality. 'We guide students on what they need to look for in terms of preparation for IELTS. The students should preferably join institutes where the trainers are trained by IELTS officials. This will ensure credibility,' said [the head of] English and Exams, British Council.
>
> British Council/IELTS combined also launched a partnership programme to train IELTS trainers in the city. 'The programme is set to teach the trainer to give out accurate information on how to crack IELTS,' [a spokesperson] said.'

With colleagues, decide whether you think the advice and practices described in this article are acceptable, or harmful. Give your reasons.

○ 10.3 The big debate: which side of the fence are you on?

Decide whether you are a 'separatist' or an 'integrationist'. Prepare to argue your case in a debate with your colleagues. You may wish to devise a formal proposal, beginning 'This House believes that …'

○ 10.4 Content standards and the classroom

WIDA provides online support for teachers to prepare lessons that are linked to WIDA content standards: http://www.doe.virginia.gov/VDOE/Instruction/ESL/elp_videos.html#. Watch the videos.

Select *one* video and write a critical review of the value of the approach for the ESL classroom.

⭕ 10.5 Achieve!

Visit the Achieve website: http://www.achieve.org/node/278. Write a short review of the work of Achieve, which indicates the impact you think an organisation like this might have on teaching and learning in ordinary schools.

⭕ 10.6 In a league of your own

Accountability and league tables usually go together. Countries are placed into league tables by the PISA tests, and institutions are placed into league tables by national tests. Proponents of league tables claim that they drive teachers and schools to higher levels of performance. Opponents claim that they lead to test preparation and a narrowing of the curriculum.

If you could decide whether to keep or abolish league tables, what would you do? Come to an agreement with your colleagues and be prepared to share your views.

⭕ 10.7 Test preparation practices

In Activity 9.6 we looked at test preparation practices that may border on 'cheating'. Make a list of the test preparation practices that are used in the institution where you teach, or an institution with which you are familiar.

- How much time is devoted to test preparation?
- Which of the practices you list are 'useful'?
- What pressures are teachers under to engage in these practices?

⭕ 10.8 Take your pick

Imagine that you work in a language school that does not have either (a) a suitable placement test, or (b) a suitable achievement test, for intermediate learners. First, describe the learners and their purpose for learning the language. The description may be purely imaginative, or it may be a description of actual learners known to you.

Establish the criteria you will use to select a suitable test.

Use the two tools discussed in this chapter, and internet search engines, to see if you can identify a test that may be useful in your context.

Epilogue

This book was planned as a journey. The expedition began with the use of tests in society. We then wandered through the history and technology of standardised testing, and into approaches to classroom assessment and criterion-referenced testing. We then travelled through the process of designing, creating, trying out, scoring, evaluating, administering and using language tests; not forgetting alignment and accountability. Along the way we stopped to take in the sights, marvel at great achievements and question some of the more dubious test uses and consequences.

The end was in sight from the beginning. In the conclusion to the first chapter we argued that if we can see the effect we wish our tests to have, we have a guiding principle for all test design decisions we make. In a sense, the end is the beginning.

Or, as Latham (1877: 122) put it so much more eloquently,

> Here we come to the truth on which we must rest. If we can frame an examination in which that which will enable the candidate to do the best is that which it is best for him to learn, and to learn in the best way, then we shall have constructed a perfect educational instrument.

Perfection, like certainty, will always elude us. But it should not stop us from trying to build the best tests we possibly can, and ensuring that they are used responsibly.

Appendices

	0.00	0.01	0.02	0.03	0.04	0.05	0.06	0.07	0.08	0.09
0.0	0.0000	0.0040	0.0080	0.0120	0.0160	0.0199	0.0239	0.0279	0.0319	0.0359
0.1	0.0398	0.0438	0.0478	0.0517	0.0557	0.0596	0.0636	0.0675	0.0714	0.0753
0.2	0.0793	0.0832	0.0871	0.0910	0.0948	0.0987	0.1026	0.1064	0.1103	0.1141
0.3	0.1179	0.1217	0.1255	0.1293	0.1331	0.1368	0.1406	0.1443	0.1480	0.1517
0.4	0.1554	0.1591	0.1628	0.1664	0.1700	0.1736	0.1772	0.1808	0.1844	0.1879
0.5	0.1915	0.1950	0.1985	0.2019	0.2054	0.2088	0.2123	0.2157	0.2190	0.2224
0.6	0.2257	0.2291	0.2324	0.2357	0.2389	0.2422	0.2454	0.2486	0.2517	0.2549
0.7	0.2580	0.2611	0.2642	0.2673	0.2704	0.2734	0.2764	0.2794	0.2823	0.2852
0.8	0.2881	0.2910	0.2939	0.2967	0.2995	0.3023	0.3051	0.3078	0.3106	0.3133
0.9	0.3159	0.3186	0.3212	0.3238	0.3264	0.3289	0.3315	0.3340	0.3365	0.3389
1.0	0.3413	0.3438	0.3461	0.3485	0.3508	0.3531	0.3554	0.3577	0.3599	0.3621
1.1	0.3643	0.3665	0.3686	0.3708	0.3729	0.3749	0.3770	0.3790	0.3810	0.3830
1.2	0.3849	0.3869	0.3888	0.3907	0.3925	0.3944	0.3962	0.3980	0.3997	0.4015
1.3	0.4032	0.4049	0.4066	0.4082	0.4099	0.4115	0.4131	0.4147	0.4162	0.4177
1.4	0.4192	0.4207	0.4222	0.4236	0.4251	0.4265	0.4279	0.4292	0.4306	0.4319
1.5	0.4332	0.4345	0.4357	0.4370	0.4382	0.4394	0.4406	0.4418	0.4429	0.4441
1.6	0.4452	0.4463	0.4474	0.4484	0.4495	0.4505	0.4515	0.4525	0.4535	0.4545
1.7	0.4554	0.4564	0.4573	0.4582	0.4591	0.4599	0.4608	0.4616	0.4625	0.4633
1.8	0.4641	0.4649	0.4656	0.4664	0.4671	0.4678	0.4686	0.4693	0.4699	0.4706
1.9	0.4713	0.4719	0.4726	0.4732	0.4738	0.4744	0.4750	0.4756	0.4761	0.4767
2.0	0.4772	0.4778	0.4783	0.4788	0.4793	0.4798	0.4803	0.4808	0.4812	0.4817
2.1	0.4821	0.4826	0.4830	0.4834	0.4838	0.4842	0.4846	0.4850	0.4854	0.4857
2.2	0.4861	0.4864	0.4868	0.4871	0.4875	0.4878	0.4881	0.4884	0.4887	0.4890
2.3	0.4893	0.4896	0.4898	0.4901	0.4904	0.4906	0.4909	0.4911	0.4913	0.4916
2.4	0.4918	0.4920	0.4922	0.4925	0.4927	0.4929	0.4931	0.4932	0.4934	0.4936
2.5	0.4938	0.4940	0.4941	0.4943	0.4945	0.4946	0.4948	0.4949	0.4951	0.4952
2.6	0.4953	0.4955	0.4956	0.4957	0.4959	0.4960	0.4961	0.4962	0.4963	0.4964
2.7	0.4965	0.4966	0.4967	0.4968	0.4969	0.4970	0.4971	0.4972	0.4973	0.4974
2.8	0.4974	0.4975	0.4976	0.4977	0.4977	0.4978	0.4979	0.4979	0.4980	0.4981
2.9	0.4981	0.4982	0.4982	0.4983	0.4984	0.4984	0.4985	0.4985	0.4986	0.4986
3.0	0.4987	0.4987	0.4987	0.4988	0.4988	0.4989	0.4989	0.4989	0.4990	0.4990

Appendix 1 Table of z-scores

T	0	1	2	3	4
500	50000000	50400001	50800002	51200002	51599997
510	53979999	54380000	54780000	55170000	55570000
520	57929999	58319998	58710003	59100002	59480000
530	61790001	62169999	62550002	62930000	63309997
540	65539998	65910000	66280001	66640002	67000002
550	69150001	69499999	69849998	70190001	70539999
560	72570002	72909999	73240000	73570001	73890001
570	75800002	76109999	76419997	76730001	77029997
580	78810000	79100001	79390001	79670000	79949999
590	80590003	81860000	82120001	82380003	82639998
600	84130001	84380001	84609997	84850001	85079998
610	86430001	86650002	86860001	87080002	87290001
620	88489997	88690001	88880002	89069998	89249998
630	90319997	90490001	90657997	90824002	90987998
640	91924000	92072999	92220002	92364001	92506999
650	93318999	93448001	93573999	93699002	93822002
660	94520003	94630003	94738001	94845003	94950002
670	95542997	95637000	95727998	95818001	95907003
680	96407002	96485001	96561998	96638000	96711999
690	97127998	97193003	97257000	97320002	97381002
700	97724998	97777998	97830999	97882003	97931999
710	98214000	98256999	98299998	98341000	98382002
720	98610002	98645002	98679000	98712999	98745000
730	98927999	98956001	98983002	99009699	99035800
740	99180198	99202400	99224001	99245101	99265599
750	99378997	99396300	99413198	99429703	99445701
760	99533898	99547303	99560398	99573100	99585497
770	99653298	99663597	99673599	99683303	99692798
780	99744499	99752301	99759901	99767298	99774402
790	99813402	99819303	99825001	99830502	99835902
800	99865001	99869400	99873602	99877697	99881703
810	99903238	99906462	99909568	99912602	99915528
820	99931288	99933630	99935901	99938101	99940240
830	99951661	99953347	99954993	99956578	99958110
840	99966311	99967521	99968690	99969822	99970913
850	99976742	99977589	99978417	99979222	99979991
860	99984092	99984688	99985272	99985832	99986368
870	99989218	99989641	99990040	99990427	99990797
880	99992764	99993050	99993324	99993593	99993849
890	99995190	99995387	99995571	99995750	99995923
	1.00000000				

Appendix 2 The Gaokao conversion table

T	5	6	7	8	9
500	51990002	52389997	52789998	53189999	53590000
510	55960000	56360000	56750000	57139999	57529998
520	59869999	60259998	60640001	61030000	61409998
530	63679999	64060003	64429998	64800000	65170002
540	67360002	67720002	68080002	68440002	68790001
550	70880002	71230000	71569997	71899998	72240001
560	74220002	74540001	74860001	75169998	75489998
570	77340001	77640003	77939999	78230000	78520000
580	80229998	80510002	80779999	81059998	81330001
590	82889998	83149999	83399999	83649999	83890003
600	85310000	85540003	85769999	85990000	86210001
610	87489998	87699997	87900001	88099998	88300002
620	89440000	89620000	89800000	89969999	90147001
630	91149002	91308999	91465998	91621000	91773999
640	92646998	92785001	92922002	93055999	93189001
650	93943000	94062001	94178998	94295001	94408000
660	95052999	95153999	95253998	95352000	95449001
670	95994002	96079999	96164000	96245998	96327001
680	96784002	96855998	96925998	96995002	97061998
690	97441000	97500002	97557998	97614998	97670001
700	97982001	98030001	98076999	98123997	98168999
710	98422003	98461002	98500001	98536998	98574001
720	98777997	98808998	98839998	98869997	98899001
730	99061298	99086303	99110597	99134099	99157602
740	99285698	99305302	99324399	99343097	99361300
750	99461401	99476600	99491501	99506003	99520099
760	99597502	99609298	99620700	99631900	99642700
770	99702001	99711001	99719697	99728203	99736500
780	99781400	99788201	99794799	99801201	99807400
790	99841100	99846202	99851102	99855900	99860501
800	99885601	99889302	99892998	99896502	99899900
810	99918360	99921119	99923778	99926358	99928862
820	99942303	99944288	99946231	99948102	99949908
830	99959588	99961030	99962419	99963760	99965048
840	99971968	99972987	99973983	99974930	99975848
850	99980742	99981463	99982148	99982822	99983472
860	99986893	99987388	99987870	99988341	99988788
870	99991161	99991506	99991840	99992156	99992466
880	99994093	99994332	99994558	99994779	99994987
890	99996090	99996251	99996406	99996555	99996698

1. The individual linguality test

Verbal	Performance
E	
What is your name? (Help) How old are you? (Help) How long have you been in camp? (Help) Where is your home? (Help) What did you do (work at) before you came into the army? (Help)	Sit down. (Help) Put your hat on the table. (Help) Stand up. (Help)
D	
What is your name? (No help) How long have you been in camp? (No help) How old are you? (No help) Where is your home? (No help) What did you do (work at) before you came (got) into the army? (No help)	Sit down. (No help) Stand up. (No help) Turn around. (No help) Put your hat on the table. (No help) Fold your arms. (No help) Turn around. (No help)
C	
When the sergeant tells you to keep your eyes to the front, what does he mean? What does it mean to 'keep your eyes to the front'? What kind of shoes should a soldier wear? (No help) What does it mean when you are told that you are 'required to remain in your barracks'?	Take two steps forward. (No help) Turn your eyes to the right. (No help) Put your hands on your shoulders. (No help) Carry the right foot 6 inches straight to the rear. (No help). Extend the fingers of the left hand. (No help)
B	
What does this mean: 'Do not enter the Captain's office without the sergeant's permission'? What does it mean when you are told to 'keep always on the alert'? If an officer told you to remain in the 'immediate vicinity', what would you do? Just what does it mean 'to quit your post'? What is a 'violation of orders'? What is meant by the 'strength of an organisation'?	Fold your arms. (No help) Place your feet at an angle of 30 degrees. (No help) Rise on the toes and inhale deeply. (No help) Bring the elbows to the side and clench the fists. (No help) Raise the arms laterally until horizontal. (No help) Raise the arms vertically, palms to the front. (No help)

A

What does it mean for one man to 'conform to the gait of another'?

Explain the meaning of this sentence: 'The moment to charge is when you have broken the enemy's resistance and destroyed his morale.'

Explain the meaning of this sentence: 'Cavalry cannot always prevent sudden incursions of the enemy.'

Explain the meaning of this sentence: 'The rate of advance is dependent upon the nature of the terrain.'

What does it mean when two soldiers are said to be 'mutually visible'?

Explain the meaning of this sentence: 'A converging fire is more efficacious than a diverging.'

Appendix 3 The linguality test

2. The group linguality test

Preliminary demonstration

Preliminary demonstration with blackboard and orderly is used to teach the meaning of what it is to 'put a cross on' something. The blackboard has a shovel, a pitcher, a boy, a flower, and a doorway with an open door. The demonstration is arranged to teach the subjects what a cross is, what it is to put it on a part, that it must be exactly on the part called for and not so large as to extend over the greater part of the picture. The shovel, the boy's foot, the handle of the pitcher, and the open door are finally crossed; the orderly makes two mistakes which are corrected.

Group examination

The examiner then picks up a paper and pointing to the men says, 'Now, you take up your pencils; look here – number one on top here – see these pictures here – not the same as these (pointing to the blackboard); you do pictures here, Number 1, top.'

'Now, listen. You (pointing to men), make cross (drawing an X in the air) on the hat.'

'Now, look. On top again. These pictures. See the dog? Make a cross on the dog.'

During these two tests the orderlies move quickly and quietly among the men, making sure that they get started and saying, 'You know hat (or dog) – make a cross on the hat (dog).'

For these tests and the following ones the examiner must depend upon his judgment of the group as to how long each test should take, but in no instance should more than 10 seconds be allowed.

'Now, look here, Number 2. A boy – see – that's a boy.' (Make sure by repetition that the men have found the right place.) 'Make a cross on the boy's head.'

'Now, look, Number 3. A house.' (Repeat and point, if necessary.) 'Make a cross on the roof of the house.'

'Now, look, Number 4. A hand.' (Holds up hand.) 'Make a cross on the thumb.'

'Now, Number 5 – here. Make a cross on the envelope.'

'Number 6 – here. Make a cross on the girl's eyelash.'

'Number 7. What is it? Make a cross on the muzzle of the gun.'

'Number 8. Make a cross above the pig's back.'

'Number 9. Make a cross at the entrance to this house.'

'Number 10. Make a cross on the rear wheel of the automobile.'

'Number 11. Make a cross on the spout of the kettle.'

'Number 12. Make a cross beneath the horizontal line.'

'Number 13. Make a cross at the base of the tower.'

'Now turn your papers over so – Number 14 – the letter – see.'

'Number 14. Make a cross on the signature of the letter.'

'Number 15. Make a cross on the pendulum of the clock.'

'Number 16. The box. Make a cross on the partition.'

'Number 17. Make a cross on the flange of the wheel.'

'Number 18. Make a cross on the mosaic pattern.'

'Number 19. See the two drawings? Make a cross at the point of conjunction.'

'Number 20. Make a cross on the barb of the hook.'

'Number 21. Make a cross on one of the tines.'

'Number 22. Make a cross at the apex of the cone.'

'Number 23. Make a cross on the filial descendant of the mare.'

'Number 24. Make a cross on the caudal appendage of the squirrel.'

'Number 25. Make a cross at the orifice of the jug.'

'Number 26. Make a cross on the superior aspect of the pulpit.'

'Number 27. Make a cross on the major protuberance of the bludgeon.'

'Number 28. Make a cross on the sinister extension of the swastika.'

'Number 29. Make a cross on the cephalic extremity of the homunculus.'

Linguality test page 1

Linguality test page 2

	Transactions to obtain goods and services
C2	As B2
C1	As B2
B2	Can cope linguistically to negotiate a solution to a dispute like an undeserved traffic ticket, financial responsibility for damage in a flat, for blame regarding an accident. Can outline a case for compensation, using persuasive language to demand satisfaction and state clearly the limits of any concession he/she is prepared to make.
	Can explain a problem which has arisen and make it clear that the provider of the service/customer must make a concession.
B1	Can deal with most transactions likely to arise whilst travelling, arranging travel or accommodation, or dealing with authorities during a foreign visit. Can cope with less routine situations in shops, post offices, banks, e.g. returning an unsatisfactory purchase. Can make a complaint. Can deal with most situations likely to arise when making travel arrangements through an agent or when actually travelling, e.g. asking passenger where to get off for an unfamiliar destination.
A2	Can deal with common aspects of everyday living such as travel, lodgings, eating and shopping. Can get all the information needed from a tourist office, as long as it is of a straightforward, non-specialised nature.
	Can ask for and provide everyday goods and services. Can get simple information about travel, use public transport (buses, trains and taxis) and give directions and buy tickets. Can ask about things and make simple transactions in shops, post offices or banks. Can give and receive information about quantities, numbers, prices, etc. Can make simple purchases by stating what is wanted and asking the price. Can order a meal.
A1	Can ask people for things and give people things. Can handle numbers, quantities, cost and time.

Appendix 4 Service encounters in the CEFR

Band 0

Candidates in band 0 do not reach the required standard to be placed in band 1.

Band 1

The candidate frequently pauses in speech before completing the propositional intention of the utterance, causing the interviewer to ask additional questions and/or make comments in order to continue the conversation. (Utterances tend to be short), and there is little evidence of candidates taking time to plan the content of the utterance in advance of speaking. However, hesitation is frequently evident when the candidate has to plan the utterance grammatically. This often involves the repetition of items, long pauses, and the reformulation of sentences.

Misunderstanding of the interviewer's questions or comments is fairly frequent, and the candidate sometimes cannot respond at all, or dries up part way through the answer [categories 1 and 8]. (Single word responses followed by pauses are common), forcing the interviewer to encourage further contribution. It is rare for a band 1 candidate to be able to give examples, counterexamples or reasons, to support a view expressed.

Pausing for grammatical and lexical repair is evident i.e., selection of a new word or structure when it is realised that an utterance is not accurate or cannot be completed accurately.

Candidates at band 1 may pause because of difficulty in retrieving a word, but when this happens will usually abandon the message rather than attempt to circumlocute. It is rare for a band 1 candidate to express uncertainty regarding choice of lexis or the propositional content of the message. (The message itself is often simple.)

Band 2

A band 2 candidate will almost always be able to complete the propositional intention of an utterance once started, causing no strain on the interviewer by expecting him/her to maintain the interaction. However, just like a band 1 candidate, a band 2 candidate will frequently misunderstand the interviewer's question or be completely unable to respond to the interviewer's question, requiring the interviewer to repeat the question or clarify what he/she wishes the candidate to do. Similarly (single word responses are common), forcing the interviewer to encourage further contribution.

Although the candidate will spend less time pausing to plan the grammar of an utterance, it will be observed that there are many occasions on which the candidate will reformulate an utterance having begun using one grammatical pattern and conclude with a different form. Similarly, with lexis, there will be evidence that the candidate pauses to search for an appropriate lexical item and, if it is not available, will make some attempt to circumlocute even if this is not very successful. From time to time a band 2 candidate may pause to consider giving an example, counterexample, or reason for a point of view. However, this will be infrequent and when it does occur, the example or reason may be expressed in very simplistic terms and may lack relevance to the topic.

Band 3

A candidate in band 3 will hardly ever misunderstand a question or be unable to respond to a question from the interviewer. On the odd occasion when it does happen, a band 3 candidate will almost always ask for clarification from the interviewer.

Most pauses in the speech of a band 3 candidate will occur when they require 'thinking time' in order to provide a propositionally appropriate utterance. Time is sometimes needed to plan a sentence grammatically in advance, especially after making an error which the candidate then rephrases.

A band 3 candidate is very conscious of his/her use of lexis, and often pauses to think about the word which has been used, or to select another which they consider to be better in the context. The candidate may even question the interviewer overtly regarding the appropriacy of the word which has been chosen.

Often candidates in this band will give examples, counterexamples or reasons to support their point of view.

(At band 3 and above there is an increasing tendency for candidates to use 'backchanneling' – the use of 'hm' or 'yeah' – when the interviewer is talking, giving the interview a greater sense of normal conversation, although many better candidates still do not use this device).

Band 4

A band 4 candidate will only very rarely misunderstand a question of the interviewer, fail to respond, or dry up in the middle of an utterance.

A candidate in this band will exhibit a much greater tendency than candidates in any other band to express doubt about what they are saying. They will often use words such as 'maybe' and 'perhaps' when presenting their own point of view or opinion. More often than not, they will back up their opinion with examples or provide reasons for holding a certain belief. They will pause frequently to consider exactly how to express the content of what they wish to say and how they will present their views. (They will only rarely respond with a single word unless asked a polar question by the interviewer.)

There will be far fewer pauses to consider the grammatical structure of an utterance and pausing to consider the appropriacy of a lexical item chosen is rare. A candidate in this band will reformulate a sentence from time to time if it is considered to be inaccurate or the grammar does not allow the candidate to complete the proposition which he/she wishes to express.

Band 5

A candidate at band 5 almost never misunderstands the interviewer, fails to respond, or dries up when speaking. The majority of pauses or hesitations which occur will be when the candidate is considering how to express a point of view or opinion, or how to support a point of view or opinion by providing appropriate examples or reasons. However, a candidate at band 5 will not express uncertainty regarding these views or opinions as frequently as a candidate at band 4, and so there are fewer hesitations when introducing new propositions.

Very rarely does a band 5 candidate have to pause to consider the grammatical structure of an utterance and almost never hesitates regarding choice of lexis. Band 5 candidates demonstrate a confidence in their ability to get things right the first time. Whilst they do sometimes pause to reformulate sentences this is always because they cannot put across the propositional content of their utterance without changing grammatical form.

It may be noticed by the interviewer that the candidate responds to questions and prompts so quickly and efficiently that the next question or prompt has not been prepared, resulting in a pause in the interview while the interviewer plans his/her next utterance.

Band 6

Candidates in band 6 reach a standard higher than that described in band 5.

Appendix 5 Fluency rating scale

Appendix 6 Suggested answers for selected activities

Activity 2.4 Practising your calculation skills I

a. Here are 25 scores on the individual linguality test, which has a possible range of 0 to 45. Calculate the mean and standard deviation. State which raw scores would be found at exactly −1 and +1 standard deviations (z-scores of −1.0 and +1.0).

The completed table:

Scores	$\overline{X}$	$X - \overline{X}$	$(X - \overline{X})^2$
11	27.44	−16.44	270.27
12	27.44	−15.44	238.39
17	27.44	−10.44	108.99
18	27.44	−9.44	89.11
21	27.44	−6.44	41.47
22	27.44	−5.44	29.59
24	27.44	−3.44	11.83
24	27.44	−3.44	11.83
24	27.44	−3.44	11.83
26	27.44	−1.44	2.07
27	27.44	−0.44	0.19
27	27.44	−0.44	0.19
27	27.44	−0.44	0.19
28	27.44	0.56	0.31
29	27.44	1.56	2.43
30	27.44	2.56	6.55
30	27.44	2.56	6.55
31	27.44	3.56	12.67
32	27.44	4.56	20.79
33	27.44	5.56	30.91
33	27.44	5.56	30.91
35	27.44	7.56	57.15
36	27.44	8.56	73.27
44	27.44	16.56	274.23
45	27.44	17.56	308.35
$\Sigma = 686$		$\Sigma = 0$	$\Sigma = 1640.07$
$\overline{X} = 27.44$			
$N = 25$			

$$Sd = \sqrt{\frac{1640.07}{25 - 1}}$$

$$Sd = 8.27$$

A score at +1 standard deviation would be $27.44 + 8.27 = 35.71$
A score at −1 standard deviation would be $27.44 - 8.27 = 19.17$

b. Next, calculate Cronbach's alpha, and then use it to calculate the 95 per cent confidence interval.

The completed table:

Item	p	q	pq	Item	p	q	pq
				23	.02	.98	.02
1	1.0	.00	.00	24	.02	.98	.02
2	.97	.03	.03	25	.01	.99	.01
3	.98	.02	.02	26	1.0	.00	.00
4	.98	.02	.02	27	.99	.01	.01
5	.97	.03	.03	28	.99	.01	.01
6	.97	.03	.03	29	.97	.03	.03
7	.92	.08	.07	30	.95	.05	.05
8	.90	.10	.09	31	.94	.06	.06
9	.85	.15	.13	32	.93	.07	.07
10	.85	.15	.13	33	.91	.09	.08
11	.63	.37	.23	34	.82	.18	.15
12	.48	.52	.25	35	.73	.27	.20
13	.23	.77	.18	36	.71	.29	.21
14	.26	.74	.19	37	.64	.36	.23
15	.21	.79	.17	38	.55	.45	.25
16	.08	.92	.07	39	.54	.46	.25
17	.09	.91	.08	40	.39	.61	.24
18	.12	.88	.11	41	.21	.79	.17
19	.08	.92	.07	42	.14	.86	.12
20	.03	.97	.03	43	.11	.89	.10
21	.03	.97	.03	44	.09	.91	.08
22	.03	.97	.03	45	.09	.91	.08
$\Sigma pq = 4.43$							

$$r = \frac{45}{44} \left\{ 1 - \frac{4.43}{68.39} \right\}$$

$$R = 1.02 \times .94 = .96$$

$$Se = 8.27 \sqrt{1 - .96} = 8.27 \times .2 = 1.65$$

The 95 per cent confidence interval is therefore: $1.65 \times 1.96 = 3.23$

In practical terms, this would mean that if a test taker received an observed score of 27, we could be 95 per cent certain that the true score would fall in the range $24 < 27 < 30$.

The 99 per cent confidence interval would be $1.65 \times 2.58 = 4.26$. We could therefore be 99 per cent confident that the true score of a test taker who received an observed score of 27 would fall in the range $23 < 27 < 31$.

c. What does this tell us about the reliability and usability of this test?

Although the reliability of the test is high, the standard error gives a fairly wide confidence interval around the score for a test of this length. This demonstrates the level of uncertainty we face when interpreting observed scores from a single test administration.

Activity 2.5 Practising your calculation skills II

$$R = 0.9617, r2 = .92$$

This is an exceptionally high correlation. We cannot conclude from this that the two tests are definitely measuring the same construct. However, it does mean that it does not really matter which form of the test any test taker is given. We can predict with a great deal of accuracy what score a test taker would get in the other test from the one that he or she has taken. We can be fairly confident that the two forms of the test are interchangeable. We may also suspect that the correlation has been calculated using (N) in the denominator, rather than the unbiased population estimate (N − 1). The latter would reduce the correlation by approximately .03 to .04.

Activity 3.5 Practising your calculation skills III

$$P_o = .8$$
$$P_{chance} = .62$$
$$\text{Kappa} = .47$$

The results show a moderate level of classification agreement between the two forms of the test. However, we do not know where the source of misclassification comes from. It could be that the two forms of the test are not parallel – perhaps one is more difficult than the other, or is actually assessing something quite different. Perhaps it is eliciting a different genre altogether! On the other hand, it could be that the raters are not applying the criteria in the same way for responses to each of the prompts, or simply do not understand the criteria in the same way. Worst of all, it could be a combination of all these factors (or others that you may have thought of). Statistics do not provide us with answers to problems, but with information that helps us look for the sources of problems, and potential solutions.

Activity 3.6 Practising your calculation skills IV

$$\Phi\lambda = .98$$
$$CI = .03$$

The confidence interval tells us that we can expect a 3 per cent variation around the cut score, which means that we should further investigate any student scoring between 66 and 74 before deciding whether they progress to the new class or stay in general language studies. Tests like this are usually used when it is impractical to give large numbers of students speaking and writing tests. Perhaps a speaking test could be used with just those scoring within this range to make a final decision? These two statistics do not tell us anything about the suitability of the test in terms of content, but in terms of measurement this is about as good as it gets for a 100-item test.

Activity 6.5 Practising your calculation skills V

Student	Item 1	Item 2	Item 3	Item 4	Item 5	Total
1	C1	B1	A1	D1	D1	28
2	C1	B1	A1	D1	A0	27
3	C1	D0	A1	B0	A0	25
4	C1	B1	A1	D1	A0	25
5	A0	C0	A1	D1	A0	20
6	C1	D0	A1	D1	A0	19
7	C1	B1	A1	D1	B0	19
8	C1	B1	B0	C0	B0	17
9	C1	D0	C0	C0	D1	15
10	C1	D0	D0	D1	D1	15
11	C1	D0	D0	C0	A0	13
12	B0	B1	C0	C0	D1	12
13	C1	D0	D0	D1	B0	12
14	C1	D0	C0	C0	D1	11
15	C1	D0	C0	C0	D1	10
FI	.87	.40	.47	.53	.40	
FI Top	.8	.6	1	.8	.2	
FI Bottom	.8	.2	0	.2	.6	
DI	.0	.4	1	.6	–.4	

Activity 6.6 Item review

Item 1

The clue to the key is in Tony's utterance, not Linda's; however, the item is supposed to be testing the ability to understand implicature in Linda's response.

As the focus is on Linda's utterance, the use of the complex 'at this pace' in Tony's utterance is an unnecessary distraction.

The key is the longest option.

The key contains more complex language than the distractors.

(c) and (d) are possible keys from Linda's utterance alone.

Item 2

The topic is unsuitable for teenagers.

The topic potentially offensive to sub-groups of the test taking population for cultural reasons, and may therefore introduce bias.

The item makes value judgements about the lifestyle of British teenagers and alcohol use.

Tom's response appears unrelated to the topic.

Tom's language is exceptionally colloquial, and pronominal reference is so complex as to be a problem at this level.

Item 3

Grammatical and spelling mistakes (invite and loft). The latter is particularly serious, as it is in the key, meaning that more able students are less likely to select the keyed option.

(a) is a potential key.

(c) is the only negative item and so stands out, potentially making this distractor more popular.

The answer may depend too heavily on intonation.

Both speakers are female and may be difficult to distinguish.

The exchange is unnatural.

Item 4

The input text is too difficult for the test takers, both in terms of lexis and sentence construction/length.

The input text requires significant background knowledge to understand.

'forcing more and small to medium-sized businesses' should read either: 'forcing more and more small to medium-sized businesses' or 'forcing more small to medium-sized businesses'. 'Excessively tighter' is ungrammatical.

Medium-sized

Options (b) and (d) have little connection with the text and may not distract.

The item is related to a news story that may give it a very limited lifespan.

Glossary

This glossary has been compiled with the sole purpose of helping the reader acquire the basic 'jargon' of language testing that will make progress through the book easier. If a technical word in the book is in *italics*, it will in all probability have an entry in the glossary. However, I have deliberately omitted terms that are fully explained within the text itself, and so it should not be treated as an exhaustive list. Nor is any entry definitive. For a comprehensive dictionary of language testing, the reader is directed to Davies *et al.* (1999).

Alignment. The process of linking the meaning of a score to some external criterion, or definition of a level of language ability required for a specific purpose. Content alignment is the process of matching the content of the test, and sometimes the content of the curriculum, to a set of content standards that state what should be studied and mastered at a particular level of educational achievement. (See *standard.*)

Baseline study. The description of a teaching context before a new test is introduced. This may include an analysis of the syllabus, teaching methods and materials, and learning activities. It usually involves document analysis, observations and interviews. After a new test is introduced, the same features are studied again to investigate any possible effects.

Bias. Unfair treatment which comes about when test content or format results in lower scores than would be normally expected for identifiable groups of test takers. This may happen if, for example, some test items are insensitive to cultural taboos, or deal with topics that are unfamiliar to some test takers.

Classical Test Theory. Usually shortened to 'CTT', the theory holds that an observed test score is made up of the 'true' score of the test taker, and error. CTT uses reliability coefficients and measurements of standard error to estimate the true score.

Computer Adaptive Test (CAT). In a CAT the items or tasks presented to the test taker may change depending upon the current estimate of the test taker's ability. If a string of correct responses are given, the computer algorithm will select more difficult items. Vice versa, it will select easier items as a test taker answers items incorrectly. The test comes to an end when the software has pinpointed the ability of the test taker within a pre-specified level of error.

Confidence interval. The distance from an observed test score within which we can be reasonably sure the 'true score' lies.

Consequential validity. A term that is used to refer to the effect that the use of a test has on test takers, teachers, institutions and society at large. Messick (1989) did not use this term, but the concept dates from this work and is usually attributed to Messick. Issues of test fairness also fall within the boundaries of consequential validity, as do questions of who is responsible for negative consequences, which are usually unintended.

Consistency. Test scores are likely to change over time, and over different administration conditions. However, test designers do not wish them to fluctuate too much, and try to ensure that scores obtained in different administrations are as similar as possible.

Construct. A construct is an abstract concept that is defined in such a way that it can be observed, and can be measured. Constructs are usually labelled with abstract nouns, such as 'motivation' or 'achievement'. It is one of the tasks of the applied linguist and the test designer to create theories that state which observable variables can be used to measure the degree or presence or absence of a construct.

Construct irrelevant variance. Test takers get different scores, which should reflect the degree of presence or absence of a construct. If two test takers get a different score, but they have the same ability, it is clear that one got a lower or higher score for some other reason than what the test intends to measure. The reason may be that the second person did not interact well with an interlocutor on a speaking test, or was ill at the time of the test. Any change in a score for reasons unrelated to the construct is termed 'construct irrelevant'.

Construct under-representation. Any single test can only test so many constructs. However, many constructs may be relevant to an ability to perform a task using language in the real world. The extent to which a test does not measure the relevant constructs is the degree to which it under-represents the constructs that are genuinely required.

Convergent validity. Usually calculated using correlational techniques, convergent validity is the degree to which two or more independent measures of the same ability agree with each other. (See *divergent validity*.)

Counterbalanced design. If students take two forms of a test, one after the other, it is highly likely that they will get a slightly higher mean score on the second test because of a practice effect. If the purpose is to discover if the two tests are interchangeable forms, it is better if half the students take one test first, and the other half take the other test first. This counterbalances for a potential order effect.

Criterion-referenced testing. Interpreting test scores in relation to 'absolute' performance criteria, rather than in relation to other scores on a scale.

Criterion-related evidence. The relationship between one test and others that are thought to measure the same (or similar) abilities.

Cut score. The score on a test which marks a boundary between two classification decisions, such as 'pass' and 'fail', or 'intermediate' and 'advanced'. A test can have multiple cut scores.

Dependability. Similar to 'reliability' for norm-referenced tests, dependability is the degree of consistency in making classification decisions using criterion-referenced tests.

Descriptor. A prose description of a level of performance on a scale. Scales for rating performance tests have multiple 'bands' or 'levels', each of which normally has a descriptor.

Design chaos. A situation in which a test designer does not have a clear idea of what purpose the test is to be used for. As a result there are no grounds for preferring any one design decision over another.

Dichotomous item. Any test item that can be scored 'right' or 'wrong', 1 or 0. (See *polytomous item* and *partial credit*.)

Direct test. An older term, popular in the communicative language testing movement, to describe a performance test that was said to 'directly' measure the construct of interest. (See *indirect test*.)

Discrimination. Separating test takers who are at different levels of ability.

Discrimination index (DI). A statistic that tells us how well a test item is capable of separating high scoring test takers from low scoring test takers.

Distractor analysis. In the evaluation of multiple-choice test items, the analysis of how well the distractors succeed in tempting lower scoring students away from the correct answer (key).

Distribution. The spread of test scores across the possible range available.

Divergent validity. Usually calculated using correlational techniques, divergent validity is the degree to which two or more measures of different abilities result in different patterns of scores. (See *convergent validity*.)

Effect-driven testing. Documenting the intended effect of the test before it is designed, in order to make design decisions that are more likely to produce the intended effect. The procedure also requires a precise statement of test purpose, which acts as a limitation on future unintended test use.

Extraneous variables. Any factors that affect test scores which are not related to what the test is intended to measure. (See also *construct irrelevant variance*.)

Facility index. A measure of how difficult a test item is.

Flagging. The practice of adding a note to the results of tests to tell users if the test taker has taken the test under non-standard administration conditions, such as being allowed additional time.

Formative assessment. The use of tests or assessment procedures to inform learning and teaching, rather than assess achievement, or award certificates. A major feature of formative assessment is the provision of useful feedback to learners on how they can improve. (See *summative assessment*.)

Gatekeeping. The use of tests to restrict access to education or employment, or to limit international mobility.

Generalisability. The degree to which a test score reflects what a test taker would be able to do on tasks that are not present in the test. It is often assumed that a test score indicates an ability to use language in contexts that are not directly modelled in the test, if they are proficient in the constructs that enable such language use.

Halo effect. The tendency of judges to give the same score across multiple ratings. The initial judgement tends to 'contaminate' all the others, making it difficult to produce profiles.

High-stakes testing. Any test context in which the outcome has significant consequences for the test takers, institutions or society. (See *low-stakes testing*.)

Independent tasks/items. Questions that do not require the use of other language knowledge or skills to answer. Essay questions that have a single prompt are examples of independent writing tasks. (See *integrated tasks/items*.)

Indirect test. A test in which the items do not require performance, but from which an ability to perform is inferred. (See *direct test*.)

Integrated tasks/items. Tasks that require the use of other language knowledge or skills to answer. This is most evident in questions that require a test taker to read a text, and perhaps listen to information, before writing or speaking about the topic. (See *independent tasks/items*.)

Interface design. Designing the format, layout and style of what the test taker will see when taking a computer-based test.

Inter-rater reliability. The degree to which two judges or raters agree with each other, when rating the same performances.

Intra-rater reliability. The degree to which any individual judge or rater agrees with him- or herself, when rating the same performances on different occasions.

Invigilation. An administrative role during an examination, primarily concerned with ensuring that the test is conducted according to set rules, and that no cheating is possible. Also known as proctoring.

Item. Individual test questions. In this text, 'item' and 'task' are generally used interchangeably; however, in some texts an 'item' is one that is dichotomous, whereas a 'task' involves performance.

Item homogeneity. Items are said to be homogeneous when they are highly correlated, so that the responses (right or wrong) can be added together to create a total scores. (See *dichotomous items*.)

Item difficulty. The proportion of test takers who answer an item correctly.

Item shells. A template used to write test items.

Item–spec congruence. The degree to which a particular test item mirrors the item specification from which it was written.

League tables. Lists of schools or other institutions, ranked according to the performance of students on tests (and sometimes other measures).

Low-stakes testing. Any test context in which the outcome has few or no consequences for the test takers, institutions or society. (See *high-stakes testing*.)

Method effect. The impact on test scores of the method of testing. Some test designers argue that it is important to test a construct using at least two methods in order to be certain that the score is not particularly sensitive to the method being used.

Models. General descriptions of what it means to know, and be able to use, a language for communicative purposes. These may be very abstract, or attempt to be encyclopedic.

Moderation. Randomly sampling from test papers or recorded performances to check on the performance of raters.

Negatively skewed distribution. When the spread of scores on a test is not normally distributed, but most test takers score very highly. (See *positively skewed distribution*.)

Norm-referenced testing. The use of Classical Test Theory to produce scores that are distributed on a normal curve; the meaning of the score is its position on a scale in relation to other scores.

Partial credit. If an answer to an item can be partially right (or partially wrong), it may be given a score that represents 'half right'. The score may be 2 for 'completely correct', but 1 for 'half right' and 0 for 'wrong'. Score ranges may be as wide as 0 to 6 if so many levels can be discerned and described. (See *dichotomous item*.)

Performance conditions. The task conditions under which a performance test is conducted.

Performance tests. Tests in which test takers are required to perform tasks that are modelled on similar tasks in education or employment; the tasks usually require the test takers to speak or write.

Piloting. Also referred to as 'pre-testing', a pilot tries out items or tests on a sample drawn from the intended test-taking population. Its purpose is to evaluate the quality of the items and tests, and make adjustments as necessary, before a test is used operationally. It is at this stage in the test development process that item statistics can be calculated and examined.

Point-biserial correlation. A correlation coefficient that calculates the relationship between a dichotomous test item and the test total score, which is a continuous variable. It is a measure of item discrimination.

Polytomous item. A test item that is not scored dichotomously, but is given partial credit. (See *dichotomous item* and *partial credit*.)

Portfolio assessment. An assessment technique that requires a test taker to undertake a variety of tasks, the outcome of which are assembled into a compendium of work that demonstrates the range and depth of learning. The teacher usually holds portfolio conferences to give feedback on performance that informs future learning. Assessment of a portfolio often includes self- and peer-assessment.

Positively skewed distribution. When the spread of scores on a test is not normally distributed, but when most test takers get very low scores. (See *negatively skewed distribution*.)

Pre-testing. See *piloting*.

Proctoring. See *invigilation*.

Prototyping. Initial item 'try-outs' with small groups of test takers.

Psychometrics. The measurement of psychological constructs.

Rater. A judge who is asked to score the quality of a piece of writing, or a speech performance.

Rating scale. A scoring instrument used by a rater to judge the quality of a piece of writing, or a speech performance.

Raw score. The total of all the 'points' or 'marks' on a test when they are added up, before anything else is done to change the number.

Reliability. Reliability is the degree of score consistency in norm-referenced tests. (See *dependability*.)

Retrofit. Upgrading a test, or redesigning test specifications and the test itself, so that it may fulfil a new purpose for which it was not originally designed.

Reverse engineering. The analysis of test items or tasks to reconstruct the specification that might have generated them.

Rubric. The term 'rubric' is also used in the United Kingdom to refer to the instructions given to test takers on how to answer items. (See *descriptor*.)

Scorability. The ease with which an item can be scored. This is an administrative and technical matter that should not be confused with reliability.

Stakeholders. Everyone who has an interest in the test, its use and its effects. These will include the test takers, teachers and educators, and educational policy makers. The list of stakeholders may be very extensive when high-stakes decisions are being made.

Standard. The term 'standard' is used with many different meanings in language testing and educational assessment more generally. It is important to establish precisely which meaning is being used in each context. It can mean (at least) the following:

- a code of practice, or guidelines, designed to guide test development and use
- a set of hierarchical descriptors of levels of achievement
- a level of performance required to pass a test, be classed as a 'master', or receive certification
- a comprehensive list of content standards for what it is expected learners will master at specific educational levels
- 'standard-setting' or 'aligning tests to standards' – establishing cut scores against performance standards, or aligning test content to content standards
- a non-technical expression indicating the role of tests in improving educational progress, as in the phrase 'raise standards'.

Standard deviation. The most commonly used measure of score distribution.

Standard error of measurement. The statistic that tells us by how much a true score might differ from an observed score.

Standardised test. A test is standardised 'when the directions, conditions of administration and scoring are clearly defined and fixed for all examinees, administrations and forms'.

Standards-based testing. The assessment of learners in relation to absolutely standards, or criteria, which are often listed in a 'standards document'.

Stochastic independence. A test item is said to be stochastically independent if getting the correct answer is not dependent upon the answer to any other item on the test.

Sub-tests. If a test has many parts designed to test different constructs, and each part is scored separately, the parts are referred to as sub-tests.

Summative assessment. Testing at the end of a programme of study to measure achievement or proficiency, often with the intention of certification (See *formative assessment*.)

Tasks. See *items*.

Test battery. A test that is constructed of a number of sub-tests. (See *sub-tests.*)

Test criterion. The 'real-world' performance, in which the test is trying to predict ability to succeed.

Test framework. A document (or part of a document) that establishes test purpose, the constructs that are relevant to the purpose, the decisions which are going to be made on the basis of test scores, and any other relevant research or information which provides the basis upon which design decisions can be made.

Test specifications. The 'blueprints', or design documents of a test. The test specifications tell item writers and test assemblers how to write items and construct new forms of the test.

Triangulation. The practice of collecting data about the same subject using two or more methods.

Usability testing. Asking test takers to try out a computer-based test to discover whether they have problems with aspects of the design, such as the colour scheme, use of icons, or navigation.

Validity. The degree to which the inferences drawn from test scores to test taker abilities are sound. Establishing a validation argument is an ongoing process of showing that scores are relevant to, and useful for, the kinds of decisions for which they are used. (See Messick, 1989 for the most comprehensive discussion of validity, which is difficult to replicate in a glossary.)

Validity chaos. A situation in which it is almost impossible to design validation studies for a test because it has not been constructed with a specific purpose in mind. Researchers do not know which questions to ask to discover if the test is 'fit for purpose'.

Washback. The effect that a test has on teaching and learning in the classroom.

References

Adams, R. J. Q. (1978). *Arms and the Wizard: Lloyd George and the Ministry of Munitions, 1915–1916*. London: Cassell.

Alderson, J. C. (1988). Testing English for specific purposes – how specific can we get? In Hughes, A. (ed.), *Testing English for University Study*. London: Modern English Publications and the British Council, 16–18.

Alderson, J. C. (2009). Air safety, language assessment policy, and policy implementation: the case of aviation English. *Annual Review of Applied Linguistics* 29, 168–187.

Alderson, J. C., Clapham, C. and Wall, D. (1995). *Language Test Construction and Evaluation*. Cambridge: Cambridge University Press.

Alderson, J. C. and Hamp-Lyons, L. (1996). TOEFL preparation courses: a study of washback. *Language Testing* 13, 3, 280–297.

Alderson, J. C., Percsich, R. and Szabo, G. (2000). Sequencing as an item type. *Language Testing* 17, 4, 423–447.

Alderson, J. C. and Wall, D. (1993). Does washback exist? *Applied Linguistics* 14, 2, 115–129.

Allman, C. (2005). *Building Assessment Inititatives for Schools: An Accommodations Guide for Parents and Students with Visual Impairments*. American Foundation for the Blind. Available online: http://www.afb.org/Section.asp?SectionID=58&TopicID=264&DocumentID=2762.

Allman, C. (2006). *Position Paper: Accommodations for Testing Students with Visual Impairments*. American Printing House for the Blind. Available online: http://www.aph.org/tests/accomodations.html.

American Educational Research Association (AERA), American Psychological Association (APA) and National Council on Measurement in Education (NCME) (1999). *Standards for Educational and HorPsychological Testing*. Washington, DC: AERA.

American Psychological Association (APA), American Educational Research Association (AERA) and National Council on Measurement in Education (NCME) (1985). *Standards for Educational and Psychological Testing*. Washington, DC: APA.

Assessment Reform Group (1999). Assessment for Learning: 10 principles. Retrieved from http://www.qca.org.uk/qca_4336.aspx, 12 May 2009.

Atali, Y. (2007). *Construct Validity of e-Rater in Scoring TOEFL Essays*. Research Report 07-21. Princeton, NJ: Educational Testing Service. Available online: http://www.ets.org/Media/Research/pdf/RR-07-21.pdf.

Austin, J. L. (1962). *How to Do Things with Words*. Oxford: Clarendon Press.

Babbage, C. (1857). *On Tables of the Constants of Nature and Art. Annual Report of the Board of Regents of the Smithsonian Institution, Showing the Operations, Expenditures and Condition of the Institution, for the Year of 1856, and the Proceedings of the Board up to January 28, 1857.* Washington, DC: House of Representatives.

Bachman, L. F. (1990). *Fundamental Considerations in Language Testing*. Oxford: Oxford University Press.

Bachman, L. F. (1998). Language testing–SLA research interfaces. In Bachman, L. F. and Cohen, A. D. (eds), *Interfaces Between Second Language Acquisition and Language Testing Research*. Cambridge: Cambridge University Press, 177–195.

Bachman, L. F. (2004). *Statistical Analyses for Language Assessment*. Cambridge: Cambridge University Press.

Bachman, L. F. and Palmer, A. S. (1996). *Language Testing in Practice*. Oxford: Oxford University Press.

Bachman, L. F. and Savignon, S. J. (1986). The evaluation of communicative language proficiency: a critique of the ACTFL oral Interview. *Modern Language Journal* 70, 4, 380–390.

Barton, P. E. (2009). *National Education Standards: Getting Beneath the Surface*. Policy Information Center, Princeton, NJ: Educational Testing Service. Available online: http://www.ets.org/Media/Research/pdf/PICNATEDSTAND.pdf.

Bechger, T. M., Kuijper, H. and Maris, G. (2009). Standard setting in relation to the Common European Framework of Reference for languages: the case of the state examination of Dutch as a second language. *Language Assessment Quarterly* 6, 2, 126–150.

Bentham, J. (1787). *The Panopticon Writings*. Ed. M. Bozovic (1995). London: Verso. Available online: http://www.cartome.org/panopticon2.htm.

Berk, R. A. (1986). A consumer's guide to setting performance standards on criterion-referenced tests. *Review of Educational Research* 56, 1, 137–172.

Bernstein, J. (1999a). *PhonePass™ Testing: Structure and construct*. Menlo Park, CA: Ordinate.

Bernstein, J. (1999b). *Validation Summary for PhonePass SET-10*. Menlo Park, CA: Ordinate.

Bernstein, J., de Jong, J., Pisoni, D. and Townshend, B. (2000). Two experiments on automatic scoring of spoken language proficiency. In Delcloque, P. (ed.), *Integrating Speech Technology in Learning*. Dundee: University of Abertay, 57–61. Available online: http://www.pearsonpte.com/research/Documents/Bernstein_DeJong_Pisoni_and_Townshend_2000.pdf.

Bialy, J. M. (2003). IELTS speaking test preparation in the People's Republic of China: communicative approaches and rote-memorization compared. Unpublished MA dissertation, University of Surrey. Available online: http://www.surrey.ac.uk/ALRG/dissertations/pdf/Bialy_J_2003.pdf.

Bishop, S. (2004). Thinking about professional ethics. *Language Assessment Quarterly* 1, 2/3, 109–122.

Black, E. (2003). *War Against the Weak: Eugenics and America's Campaign to Create a Master Race*. New York: Four Walls Eight Windows.

Black, P., Harrison, C., Lee, C., Marshall, B. and Wiliam, D. (2003). *Assessment for Learning: Putting it into Practice*. Buckingham, UK: Open University Press.

Black, P., Harrison, C., Lee, C., Marshall, B. and Wiliam, D. (2004). Working inside the black box: Assessment for Learning in the classroom. *Phi Delta Kappan*, 86.

Black, P. and Wiliam, D. (1998). Inside the black box: raising standards through classroom assessment. *Phi Delta Kappan*, 80.

Blastland, M. and Dilnot, A. (2008). *The Tiger that Isn't: Seeing through a World of Numbers*. London: Profile Books.

Bond, T. G. and Fox, C. M. (2007). *Applying the Rasch Model: Fundamental Measurement in the Human Sciences*. 2nd edition. Mahwah, NJ: Lawrence Erlbaum.

Bonnet, G. (2007). The CEFR and education policies in Europe. *Modern Language Journal* 91, 4, 669–672.

Breimhorst vs. Educational Testing Service (2000), C-99-3387 WHO (N.D. Cal, March 27, 2000).

Brennan, R. L. (1984). Estimating the dependability of scores. In Berk, R. A. (ed.), *A Guide to Criterion-Referenced Test Construction*. Baltimore, MD: Johns Hopkins University Press.

Bridgeman, B. McBride, A. and Monaghan, W. (2004). *Testing and Time Limits. R&D Connections*. Princeton, NJ: Educational Testing Service. Available online: http://www.ets.org/Media/Research/pdf/RD_Connections1.pdf.

Brindley, G. (1998). Outcomes-based assessment and reporting in language-programs: a review of the issues. *Language Testing* 15, 3, 45–85.

Brindley, G. (2001). Outcomes-based assessment in practice: some examples and emerging insights. *Language Testing* 18, 4, 393–408.

Brooks, L. (2009). Interacting in pairs in a test of oral proficiency: co-constructing a better performance. *Language Testing* 26, 3, 341–366.

Brown, A. (2003). Interviewer variation and the co-construction of speaking proficiency. *Language Testing* 20, 1, 1–25.

Brown, J. (1992). *The Definition of a Profession: The Authority of Metaphor in the History of Intelligence Testing, 1890–1930*. Princeton, NJ: Princeton University Press. Original in *Camplife Chickamauga,* April 1918.

Brown, J. D. (1998). An investigation into approaches to IELTS preparation, with particular focus on the academic writing component of the test. In Wood, S. (ed.), *IELTS Research Reports,* vol. 1. Sydney: ELICOS Association/Canberra: IELTS Australia, 20–37.

Brown, J. D. (2001). *Using Surveys in Language Programs*. Cambridge: Cambridge University Press.

Brown, J. D. and Hudson, T. (2002). *Criterion-Referenced Language Testing*. Cambridge: Cambridge University Press.

Buck, G. (1991). The testing of listening comprehension: an introspective study. *Language Testing* 8, 1, 67–91.

Buck, G. (2001). *Assessing Listening*. Cambridge: Cambridge University Press.

Burstein, J. (2003). The e-rater® scoring engine: automated essay scoring with natural language processing. In Shermis, M. D. and Burstein, J. C. (eds), *Automated Essay Scoring: A Cross-disciplinary Perspective*. Mahwah, NJ: Lawrence Erlbaum, 113–121.

Burstein, J., Frase, L., Ginther, A. and Grant, L. (1996). Technologies for language assessment. *Annual Review of Applied Linguistics* 16, 240–260.

Burt, C. (1922). *Mental and Scholastic Tests*. London: P. S. King and Son Ltd.

Burt, C. (1923). *Handbook of Tests for Use in Schools*. 2nd Edition. London: Staples Press.

Burton, R. F. (2001). Quantifying the effects of chance in multiple choice and true/false tests: question selection and guessing of answers. *Assessment and Evaluation in Higher Education*, 26, 1, 41–50.

Bygate, M., Skehan, P. and Swain, M. (2001). *Researching Pedagogic Tasks: Second Language Learning, Teaching and Testing*. London: Longman.

Byram, M. (2000). Assessing intercultural competence in language teaching. *Sprogforum* 6, 18, 8–13. Available online: http://inet.dpb.dpu.dk/infodok/sprogforum/Espr18/byram.html.

Caldwell, O. W. and Courtis, S. A. (1923). *Then and Now in Education, 1845–1923*. Yonkers on Hudson, NY: World Book Company.

Canadian Language Benchmarks (2006). *Companion Tables to the Canadian Language Benchmarks 2000*. Canada: Centre for Canadian Language Benchmarks. Available online: http://www.language.ca/cclb_files/doc_viewer_dex.asp?doc_id=247&page_id=550.

Canale, M. (1983a) From communicative competence to communicative language pedagogy. In Richards, C. and Schmidt, R. W. (eds), *Language and Communication*. London: Longman, 2–27.

Canale, M. (1983b) On some dimensions of language proficiency. In Oller, J. W. (ed.), *Issues in Language Testing Research*. Rowley, MA: Newbury House, 333–342.

Canale, M. and Swain, M. (1980). Theoretical bases of communicative approaches to second language teaching and testing. *Applied Linguistics* 1, 1, 1–47.

Carnevale, A. P., Fry, R. A. and Lowell, L. (2001). Understanding, speaking, reading, writing, and earnings in the immigrant labor market. *American Economic Review*, 91, 2, 159–163.

Carroll, J. B. (1958). *Notes on the Measurement of Achievement in Foreign Languages*. Mimeograph: Library of the Iowa State University of Science and Technology.

Carroll, J. B. (1961). Fundamental considerations in testing for English language proficiency of foreign students. Reprinted in Allen, H. B. and Campbell, R. N. (eds) (1965), *Teaching English as a Second Language: A Book of Readings*. New York: McGraw Hill, 313–330.

Carroll, J. B. (1967). The foreign language attainments of language majors in the senior year: a survey conducted in US colleges and universities. *Foreign Language Annals* 1, 2, 131–151.

Cattell, J. M. (1893). Mental measurement. *The Philosophical Review* 2, 3, 316–332.

Cattell, J. M. and Galton, F. (1890). Mental tests and measurements. *Mind*, 15, 59, 373–381.

Cattell, R. B. (1937). *The Fight for Our National Intelligence*. London: P. S. King and Son.

Cawthon, S. W. (2009). Accommodations for students who are deaf or hard of hearing in large-scale, standardized assessments: surveying the landscape and charting a new direction. *Educational Measurement: Issues and Practice* 28, 2, 41–49.

Cecil, R. (1971). *Education and Elitism in Nazi Germany*. ICR Monograph Series No. 5. London: Institute for Cultural Research.

Center for Applied Linguistics. (2007). *Foreign Language Assessment Directory*. Retrieved 3 July 2009, from http://www.cal.org/CALWebDB/FLAD

Center for Applied Linguistics. (2009). *Understanding Assessment: A Guide for Foreign Language Educators*. Retrieved 3 August 2009, from http://www.cal.org/flad/tutorial/

Chalhoub-Deville, M. (1997). Theoretical models, assessment frameworks and test construction. *Language Testing* 20, 4, 369–383.

Chalhoub-Deville, M. (ed.) (1999). *Issues in Computer-Adaptive Testing of Reading Proficiency*. Cambridge: Cambridge University Press.

Chalhoub-Deville, M. and Deville, C. (2008). Nationally mandated testing for accountability: English language learners in the US. In Spolsky, B. and Hult, F. (eds), *The Handbook of Educational Linguistics*. London: Blackwell, 510–522.

Chalhoub-Deville, M. and Fulcher, G. (2003). The oral proficiency interview and the ACTFL Guidelines: a research agenda. *Foreign Language Annals* 36, 4, 498–506.

Chalmers, A. (1990). *Science and its Fabrication*. Milton Keynes: Open University Press.

Chapelle, C. and Douglas, D. (2006). *Assessing Language through Computer Technology*. Cambridge: Cambridge University Press.

Chapelle, C. A., Enright, M. K. and Jamieson, J. M. (eds) (2008). *Building a Validity Argument for the Test of English as a Foreign Language*. New York: Routledge.

Chiswick, B. R., Lee, Y. L. and Miller, P. W. (2006). Immigrants' language skills and visa category. *International Migration Review* 40, 2, 419–450.

Chiswick, B. R. and Miller, P. W. (1999). Language skills and earnings among legalized aliens. *Journal of Population Economics*, 12, 1, 63–89.

Chodorow, M. and Burstein, J. (2004). *Beyond Essay Length: Evaluating e-Rater®'s Performance on TOEFL® Essays*. TOEFL Research Report 73, Princeton, NJ: ETS.

Chomsky, N. (1965). *Aspects of the Theory of Syntax*. Cambridge, MA: MIT Press.

Cizek, G. J. (1996). Standard-setting guidelines. *Educational Measurement: Issues and Practice* 15, 1, 13–21.

Cizek, G. J. and Bunch, M. B. (2007). *Standard Setting. A Guide to Establishing and Evaluating Performance Standards on Tests*. Thousand Oaks, CA: Sage.

Clark, J. L. D. (1975). Theoretical and technical considerations in oral proficiency testing. In Jones, R. L. and Spolsky, B. (eds), *Testing Language Proficiency*. Arlington, VA: Center for Applied Linguistics, 10–28.

Clark, J. L. D. (1977). *The Performance of Native Speakers of English on the TOEFL Test*. TOEFL Research Report 01. Princeton, NJ: Educational Testing Service.

Cohen, A., Kane, M. and Crooks, T. (1999). A generalized examinee-centred method for setting standards on achievement tests. *Applied Measurement in Education*, 14, 343–336.

Cohen, A. S. and Wollack, J. A. (2006). Test administration, security, scoring and reporting. In Brennan, R. L. (ed.), *Educational Measurement*. 4th edition. New York: American Council on Education/Praeger, 355–386.

College English Test. (2005). *CET-4*. Shanghai: Foreign Language Education Press.

Comber, J. (1998). Are test preparation programs really effective? Evaluating an IELTS preparation course? Unpublished MA dissertation, University of Surrey. Available online: http://www.surrey.ac.uk/ALRG/dissertations/pdf/Coomber_J_1998.pdf

Coniam, D. (2008). Investigating the quality of teacher-produced tests for EFL students and the effects of training in test development principles and practices on improving test quality. *System* 37, 226–242.

Council of Europe (2001). *Common European Framework of Reference for Languages: Learning, Teaching, Assessment*. Cambridge: Cambridge University Press. Available online: http://www.coe.int/t/dg4/linguistic/Source/Framework_EN.pdf.

Council of Europe (2009). *Relating Language Examinations to the Common European Framework of Reference for Languages: Learning, Teaching, Assessment (CEFR): A Manual*. Strasbourg: Council of Europe Language Policy Division. Available online: http://www.coe.int/t/dg4/linguistic/Manuel1_EN.asp#TopOfPage.

Crocker, L. and Algina, J. (1986). *Introduction to Classical and Modern Test Theory*. Orlando, FL: Holt, Rinehart and Winston.

Cronbach, L. J. (1984). *Essentials of Psychological Testing*. 4th edition. New York: Harper and Row.

Cumming, A. (2009). Language assessment in education: tests, curricula, and teaching. *Annual Review of Applied Linguistics*, 29: 90–100.

Cumming, A., Kantor, R., Baba, K., Eouanzoui, K., Erdosy, U. and James, M. (2006). *Analysis of Discourse Features and Verification of Scoring Levels for Independent and Integrated Prototype Written Tasks for the New TOEFL*. Princeton, NJ: Educational Testing Service. Available online: http://www.ets.org/Media/Research/pdf/RR-05-13.pdf.

Dandonolli, P. and Henning, G. (1990). An investigation of the construct validity of the ACTFL proficiency guidelines and oral interview procedure. *Foreign Language Annals* 23, 1, 11–22.

Davidson, F. (1996). *Principles of Statistical Data Handling*. Thousand Oaks, CA: Sage.

Davidson, F. and Fulcher, G. (2007). The Common European Framework of Reference (CEFR) and the design of language tests: a matter of effect. *Language Teaching* 40, 3, 231–241.

Davidson, F. and Lynch, B. K. (2002) *Testcraft: A Teacher's Guide to Writing and Using Language Test Specifications*. New Haven, CT: Yale University Press.

Davies, A. (1997). Demands of being professional in language testing. *Language Testing* 14, 3, 328–339.

Davies, A. (2003). *The Native Speaker: Myth and Reality*. London: Multilingual Matters.

Davies, A. (2008a). Textbook trends in teaching language testing. *Language Testing* 25, 3, 327–348.

Davies, A. (2008b). Ethics and professionalism. In Shohamy, E. (ed.), *Language Testing and Assessment*, vol. 7, *Encyclopedia of Language and Education*. New York: Springer, 429–443.

Davies A., Brown, A., Elder, C., Hill, K., Lumley, T. and McNamara, T. (1999). *Dictionary of Language Testing*. Cambridge: Cambridge University Press.

de Jong, J. H. A. L. and Stevenson, D. K. (eds) (1990). *Individualizing the Assessment of Language Abilities*. London: Multilingual Matters.

Dewey, J. (1916). *Democracy and Education*. London: Macmillan. Available online: http://www.ilt.columbia.edu/publications/dewey.html.

Dikli, S. (2006). An overview of automated scoring of essays. *Journal of Technology, Learning and Assessment*, 5, 1, 1–36. Available online: http://escholarship.bc.edu/cgi/viewcontent.cgi?article=1044&context=jtla.

Dörnyei, Z. (2003). *Questionnaires in Second Language Research*. Mahwah, NJ: Lawrence Erlbaum.

Dörnyei, Z. and Ushioda, E. (eds) (2009). *Motivation, Language Identity and the L2 Self*. Bristol: Multilingual Matters.

Dunkel, P. (1999). Considerations in developing or using second/foreign language proficiency computer-adaptive tests. *Language Learning and Technology*, 2, 2, 77–93. Available online: http://llt.msu.edu/vol2num2/article4/.

Edgeworth, F. Y. (1888). The statistics of examinations. *Journal of the Royal Statistical Society*, 51, 599–635.

Educational Testing Service (2005). *TOEFL iBT Tips. How to Prepare for the Next Generation TOEFL Test and Communicate with Confidence*. Princeton, NJ: Educational Testing Service.

Elder, C. and O'Loughlin, K. (2003). Investigating the relationship between intensive EAP training and band score gain on IELTS. In Tulloh, R. (ed.), *IELTS Research Reports*, vol. 4, Canberra: IELTA Australia, 207–254.

Engineers Australia (2008). *Visa Subclass 457 Integrity Review: English Language Requirements. Submission to the Department of Immigration and Citizenship*. Canberra: Engineers Australia. Available online: http://www.engineersaustralia.org.au/shadomx/apps/fms/fmsdownload.cfm?file_uuid=2109ED4F-A559-F9CA-2F75-CDFEDD09DCF6&siteName=ieaust

Evans, B. and Waites, B. (1981). *IQ and Mental Testing: An Unnatural Science and its Social History*. London: Macmillan.

Foucault, M. (1975). *Discipline and Punish: The Birth of the Prison*. London: Penguin.

Frederiksen, J. R. and Collins, A. (1989). A systems approach to educational testing. *Educational Researcher* 18, 27–32.

Frederiksen, N. (1984). The real test bias. *American Psychologist*, 39, 193–202.

Fulcher, G. (1987). Test of oral performance: the need for data-based criteria. *English Language Teaching Journal* 41, 4, 287–291.

Fulcher, G. (1991). The role of assessment by teachers in schools. In Caudery, T. (ed.), *New Thinking in TEFL*. Aarhus: Aarhus University Press, 138–158.

Fulcher, G. (1993). The construction and validation of rating scales for oral tests in English as a foreign language. Unpublished Ph.D. dissertation, University of Lancaster.

Fulcher, G. (1995). Variable competence in second language acquisition: a problem for research methodology? *System* 23, 1, 25–33.

Fulcher, G. (1996a). Does thick description lead to smart tests? A data-based approach to rating scale construction. *Language Testing* 13, 2, 208–238.

Fulcher, G. (1996b). Invalidating validity claims for the ACTFL oral rating scale. *System* 24, 2, 163–172.

Fulcher, G. (1997). An English language placement test: issues in reliability and validity. *Language Testing* 14, 2, 113–139.

Fulcher, G. (1998a). Testing speaking. In Clapham, C. (ed.), *Language Testing and Assessment*, vol. 7, *Encyclopaedia of Language and Education*. Amsterdam: Kluwer Academic Publishers, 75–86.

Fulcher, G. (1998b). Widdowson's model of communicative competence and the testing of reading: an exploratory study. *System* 26, 281–302.

Fulcher, G. (1999). Assessment in English for academic purposes: putting content validity in its place. *Applied Linguistics* 20, 2, 221–236.

Fulcher, G. (2000a). The 'communicative' legacy in language testing. *System* 28, 483–497.

Fulcher, G. (2000b). Computers in language testing. In Brett, P. and Motteram, G. (eds), *A Special Interest in Computers: Learning and Teaching with Information and Communications Technologies*. Manchester: IATEFL, 93–107. Available online: http://languagetesting.info/articles/Computers.html.

Fulcher, G. (2003a). *Testing Second Language Speaking*. London: Longman/Pearson Education.

Fulcher, G. (2003b). Interface design in computer based language testing. *Language Testing* 20, 4, 384–408.

Fulcher, G. (2004). Deluded by artifices? The Common European Framework and harmonization. *Language Assessment Quarterly* 1, 4, 253–266.

Fulcher, G. (2005). Better communications test will silence critics. *Guardian Weekly*, 18 November. Available online: http://www.guardian.co.uk/education/2005/nov/18/tefl3.

Fulcher, G. (2006). Test architecture. *Foreign Language Education Research*, 9, 1–22.

Fulcher, G. (2008a). Criteria for evaluating language quality. In Shohamy, E. and Hornberger, N. (eds), *Encyclopedia of Language and Education*, 2nd edition, vol. 7, *Language Testing and Assessment*. New York: Springer, 157–176.

Fulcher, G. (2008b). Testing times ahead? *Liaison* 1, 20–24.

Fulcher, G. (2009). Test use and political philosophy. *Annual Review of Applied Linguistics*, 29, 3–20.

Fulcher, G. (2010). Communicative language testing. In de Bot, K. (ed.), *The Mouton Handbook of Teaching English as a Foreign Language*. The Hague: Mouton.

Fulcher, G. and Bamford, R. (1996). I didn't get the grade I need. Where's my solicitor? *System* 24, 4, 437–448.

Fulcher, G. and Davidson, F. (2007). *Language Testing and Assessment: An Advanced Resource Book*. London and New York: Routledge.

Fulcher, G. and Davidson, F. (2009). Test architecture, test retrofit. *Language Testing* 26, 1, 123–144.

Fulcher, G., Davidson, F. and Kemp, J. (2011). Effective rating scale development for speaking tests: performance decision trees. *Language Testing*.

Gabbott, M. and Hogg, G. (2000). An empirical investigation of the impact of non-verbal communication on service evaluation. *European Journal of Marketing*, 34, 3/4, 384–398.

Gardner, R. C. and Lambert, W. E. (1972). *Attitudes and Motivation in Second Language Learning*. Rowley, MA: Newbury House.

Gass, S. M. and Mackey, A. (2000). *Stimulated Recall Methodology in Second Language Research*. Mahwah, NJ: Lawrence Erlbaum.

Geisinger, K. F. (1991). Using standard-setting data to establish cutoff scores. *Educational Measurement: Issues and Practice* 10, 2, 17–22.

Genesee, F. and Upshur, J. A. (1996). *Classroom-Based Evaluation in Second Language Education*. Cambridge: Cambridge University Press.

Ginther, A. (2001). *Effects of the Presence and Absence of Visuals on Performance on TOEFL CBT Listening-Comprehension Stimuli*. Research Report 01-16. Princeton, NJ: Educational Testing Service. Available online: http://www.ets.org/Media/Research/pdf/RR-01-16.pdf.

Ginther, A. (2002). Context and content visuals and performance on listening comprehension stimuli. *Language Testing*, 19, 2, 133–168.

Glaser, R. (1963). Instructional technology and the measurement of learning outcomes. *American Psychologist*, 18, 519-521.

Glaser, R. (1994a). Criterion-referenced tests: part I. Origins. *Educational Measurement: Issues and Practice* 13, 4, 9–11.

Glaser, R. (1994b). Criterion-referenced tests: part II. Unfinished business. *Educational Measurement: Issues and Practice* 13, 4, 27–30.

Glass, G. V. (1978). Standards and criteria. *Journal of Educational Measurement* 15, 4, 237–261. Available online: http://glass.ed.asu.edu/gene/papers/standards/.

Gottlieb, M. (2006). *Assessing English Language Learners: Bridges from Language Proficiency to Academic Achievement*. Thousand Oaks, CA: Corwin Press.

Gottlieb, M., Cranley, M. E. and Cammilleri, A. (2008). *Understanding the WIDA English Language Proficiency Standards*. Madison, WI: University of Wisconsin Board of Regents. Available online: http://www.wida.us/standards/Resource_Guide_web.pdf

Gould, S. J. (1997). *The Mismeasure of Man*. London: Penguin.

Grabe, W. (1999). Developments in reading research and their implications for computer-adaptive reading assessment. In Chalhoub-Deville, M. (ed.), *Issues in Computer-Adaptive Testing of Reading Proficiency*. Cambridge: Cambridge University Press, 11–47.

Grabe, W. and Stoller, F. L. (2002). *Teaching and Researching Reading*. London: Longman/Pearson Education.

Green, A. (1998). *Verbal Protocol Analysis in Language Testing Research: A Handbook*. Cambridge: Cambridge University Press.

Green, A. (2007). *IELTS Washback in Context: Preparation for Academic Writing in Higher Education*. Cambridge: Cambridge University Press.

Green, D. R., Trimble, C. S. and Lewis, D. M. (2003). Interpreting the results of three different standard-setting procedures. *Educational Measurement: Issues and Practice* 22, 1, 22–32.

Greenwood, M. (1919). Problems of industrial organisation. *Journal of the Royal Statistical Society*, 82, 2, 186–221.

Gremler, D. D. and Gwinner, K. P. (2000). Customer–employee rapport in service relationships. *Journal of Service Research*, 3, 1, 82–104.

Haines, M. M., Stansfeld, S. A., Head, J. and Job, R. F. S. (2002). Multilevel modelling of aircraft noise on performance tests in schools around Heathrow Airport London. *Journal of Epidemiology and Community Health*, 56, 139–144.

Haladyna, T. M. (1999). *Developing and Validating Multiple Choice Test Items*. Mahwah, NJ: Lawrence Erlbaum.

Haladyna, T. M., Downing, S. M. and Rodriguez, M. C. (2002). A review of multiple-choice item-writing guidelines for classroom assessment. *Applied Measurement in Education*, 15, 209–334.

Haladyna, T. M., Nolen, S. B. and Haas, N. S. (1991). Raising standardized achievement test scores and the origins of test score pollution. *Educational Research* 29, 5, 2–7.

Halliday, M. A. K. (1973). Relevant models of language. In Halliday, M. A. K., *Explorations in the Functions of Language*. New York: Elsevier North-Holland.

Hambleton, R. K. (1994). The rise and fall of criterion referenced measurement? *Educational Measurement: Issues and Practice* 13, 4, 21–26.

Hambleton, R. K. (2001). Setting performance standards on educational assessment and criteria for evaluating the process. In Cizek, G. J. (ed.), *Setting Performance Standards: Concepts, Methods, and Perspectives*. Mahwah, NJ: Lawrence Erlbaum, 80–116.

Hambleton, R. K. and Pitoniak, M. (2006). Setting performance standards. In Brennan, R. L. (ed.), *Educational Measurement*. 4th edition. Westport, CT: American Council on Education/Praeger.

Hambleton, R. K. and Rodgers, J. (1995). Item bias review. *Practical Assessment, Research & Evaluation*, 4, 6. Available online: http://edresearch.org/pare/getvn.asp?v=4&n=6.

Hamp-Lyons, L. (1991). Scoring procedures for ESL contexts. In Hamp-Lyons, L. (ed.), *Assessing Second Language Writing in Academic Contexts*. Norwood, NJ: Ablex, 241–276.

Hamp-Lyons, L. (1998). Ethical test preparation practice: the case of TOEFL. *TESOL Quarterly* 32, 2, 329–337.

Hansen, E. G., Mislevy, R. J., Steinberg, L. S., Lee, M. J. and Forer, D. C. (2005). Accessibility of tests for individuals with disabilities within a validity framework. *System* 33, 1, 107–133.

Harper, C. A., de Jong, E. J. and Platt, E. J. (2007). Marginalizing English as a second language teacher expertise: the exclusionary consequence of No Child Left Behind. *Language Policy* 7, 267–284.

Harris, D. and Bell, C. (1994). *Evaluating and Assessing for Learning*. 2nd edition. London: Kogan Page.

Hart, B. and Spearman, C. (1912). General ability, its existence and nature. *British Journal of Psychology* 5, 51–84.

Hasan, R. (1985). The structure of a text. In Halliday, M. A. K. and Hasan, R., *Language, Context, and Text: Aspects of Language in a Social-Semiotic Perspective*. Victoria, Australia: Deakin University Press, 52–69.

Haswell, R. H. (2006). Automatons and automated scoring: drudges, black boxes, and dei ex machina. In Ericsson, P. and Haswell, R. H. (eds), *Machine Scoring of Student Essays: Truth and Consequences*. Logan, UT: Utah State University Press, 57–78.

He, A. W. and Young, R. (1998). Language proficiency interviews: a discourse approach. In Young, R. and He, A. W. (eds), *Talking and Testing: Discourse Approaches to the Assessment of Oral Proficiency*. Amsterdam: John Benjamins, 1–24.

Henning, G. (1992). The ACTFL oral proficiency interview: validity evidence. *System* 20, 3, 365–372.

Hoey, M. (1983). *On the Surface of Discourse*. London: Allen and Unwin.

Hulstijn, J. A. (2007). The shaky ground beneath the CEFR: quantitative and qualitative dimensions of language proficiency. *Modern Language Journal*. 91, 4, 663–667.

Humboldt, W. von (1854). *The Limits of State Action*. Indianapolis: Liberty Press.

Hymes, D. (1972). On communicative competence. In Pride, J. B. and Holmes, J. (eds), *Sociolinguistics*. Harmondsworth: Penguin Books. Reprinted in Brumfit, C. J. and Johnson, K. (1979) (eds), *The Communicative Approach to Language Teaching*. Oxford: Oxford University Press, 5–26.

Inbar, O. (2008). Constructing a language assessment knowledge base: a focus on language assessment courses. *Language Testing* 25, 3, 385–402.

Ingram, E. (1968). Attainment and diagnostic testing. In Davies, A. (ed.), *Language Testing Symposium: A Psycholinguistic Approach*. Oxford: Oxford University Press.

Jaeger, R. M. (1989). Certification of student competence. In Linn, R. L. (ed.), *Educational Measurement*. 3rd edition. New York: American Council on Education/Macmillan.

Johnson, M. (2001). *The Art of Non-conversation*. New Haven, CT: Yale University Press.

Johnstone, C. J., Thompson, S. J., Bottsford-Miller, N. A. and Thurlow, M. L. (2008). Universal design and multimethod approaches to item review. *Educational Measurement: Issues and Practice* 27, 1, 25–36.

Jones, C. W. (1963). An early medieval licensing examination. *History of Education Quarterly* 3, 1, 19–29.

Kaftandjieva, F. (2007). Quantifying the quality of linkage between language examinations and the CEF. In Carlsen, C. and Moe, E. (eds), *A Human Touch to Language Testing*. Oslo: Novus Press, 33–43.

Kane, M. T. (1992) An argument-based approach to validity. *Psychological Bulletin* 112, 3, 527–535.

Kane, M. T. (1994). Validating the performance standards associated with passing scores. *Review of Educational Research* 64, 3, 425–461.

Kane, M. T. (2006). Validation. In Brennan, R. L. (ed.), *Educational Measurement*. 4th edition. New York: American Council on Education/Praeger, 17–64.

Kaulfers, W. V. (1944). War-time developments in modern language achievement tests. *Modern Language Journal*, 28, 136–150.

Kefalides, P. T. (1999). Illiteracy: the silent barrier to health care. *Annals of Internal Medicine* 130, 4/1, 333–336.

Kelves, D. J. (1968). Testing the army's intelligence: psychologists and the military in World War I. *Journal of American History*, 35, 3, 565–581.

Kerlinger, F. and Lee, H. B. (2000). *Foundations of Behavioral Research*. Fort Worth, TX: Harcourt College Publishers.

Ketterlin-Geller, L. R. (2008). Testing students with special needs: a model for understanding interaction between assessment and student characteristics in a universally designed environment. *Educational Measurement: Issues and Practice* 27, 3, 3–16.

Kirsch, I., Jamieson, J., Taylor, C. and Eignor, D. (1998). *Computer Familiarity Among TOEFL Examinees*. TOEFL Research Report 59, Princeton, NJ: Educational Testing Service.

Koretz, D. M. and Hamilton, L. A. (2006). Testing for accountability in K-12. In Brennan, R. L. (ed.), *Educational Measurement*. 4th edition. Westport, CT: American Council on Education/Praeger, 531–578.

Kramsch, C. J. (1986). From language proficiency to interactional competence. *Modern Language Journal* 70, 4, 366–372.

Krashen, S. (1981). *Second Language Acquisition and Second Language Learning*. London: Pergamon.

Labardo, J. C. (2007). From Fulcher to PLEVALEX: issues in interface design, validity and reliability in internet based language testing. *CALL-EJ* 9, 1. Available online: http://www.tell.is.ritsumei.ac.jp/callejonline/journal/9-1/laborda.html.

Lado, R. (1961). *Language Testing*. London: Longman.

Lamb, M. (2004). Integrative motivation in a globalizing world. *System* 32, 1, 3–19.

Lantolf, J. P. (2000). *Sociocultural Theory and Second Language Learning*. Oxford: Oxford University Press.

Lantolf, J. P. (2002). Sociocultural theory and second language acquistion. In Kaplan, R. B. (ed.), *The Oxford Handbook of Applied Linguistics*. Oxford: Oxford University Press, 104–114.

Lantolf, J. P. (2009). Dynamic Assessment: the dialectic integration of instruction and assessment. *Language Teaching*, 42, 3, 355–368.

Lantolf, J. P. and Frawley, W. (1985). Oral proficiency testing: a critical analysis. *Modern Language Journal* 69, 4, 337–345.

Lantolf, J. P. and Poehner, M. E. (2007). *Dynamic Assessment in the Foreign Language Classroom: A Teacher's Guide*. Pennsylvania: Calper Publications.

Lantolf, J. P. and Poehner, M. E. (2008a). Dynamic Assessment. In Shohamy, E. and Hornberger, N. H. (eds), *Encyclopedia of Language and Education*, vol. 7, *Language Testing and Assessment*. New York: Springer, 273–284.

Lantolf, J. P. and Poehner, M. (2008b). *Sociocultural Theory and the Teaching of Second Languages*. London: Equinox.

Lantolf, J. P. and Thorne, S. L. (2006). *Sociocultural Theory and the Genesis of Second Language Development*. Oxford: Oxford University Press.

Larsen-Freeman, D. and Long, M. H. (1991). *An Introduction to Second Language Acquisition Research*. London: Longman.

Latham, H. (1877). *On the Action of Examinations Considered as a Means of Selection*. Cambridge: Dighton, Bell and Company.

Lawn, S. and Abramowitz, S. K. (2008) *Statistics Using SPSS: An Integrative Approach*. Cambridge: Cambridge University Press.

Lazaraton, A. (1996). Interlocutor support in oral proficiency interviews. The case of CASE. *Language Testing* 13, 2, 151–172.

Lazaraton, A. (2002). *A Qualitative Approach to the Validation of Oral Language Tests*. Cambridge: Cambridge University Press.

Lee, J. (2008). Is test-driven external accountability effective? Synthesizing the evidence from cross-state causal-comparative and correlational studies. *Review of Educational Research*, 78, 3, 608–644.

Lee, Y. W., Gentile, C. and Kantor, R. (2008). *Analytic Scoring of TOEFL CBT Essays: Scores from Humans and E-rater*. Research Report 08-01. Princeton, NJ: Educational Testing Service. Available online: http://www.ets.org/Media/Research/pdf/RR-08-01.pdf.

Leech, D. and Campos, E. (2003). Is comprehensive education really free? A case study of the effects of secondary school admissions policies on house prices in one local area. *Journal of the Royal Statistical Society: Series A (Statistics in Society)*, 166, 1, 135–154.

Leong, N. (2005). Beyond Breimhorst: appropriate accommodation of students with learning disabilities on the SAT. *Stanford Law Review* 57, 6, 21–35.

Leung, C. and Scott, C. (2009). Formative assessment in language education policies: emerging lessons from Wales and Scotland. *Annual Review of Applied Linguistics* 29, 64–79.

Lipman, W. (1922). The mental age of Americans, *New Republic* 32, 412 (25 October), 213–215; 413 (1 November), 246–248; 414 (8 November), 275–277; 415 (15 November), 297–298; 416 (22 November), 328–330; 417 (29 November), 9–11. Available online: http://historymatters.gmu.edu/d/5172/.

Liskin-Gasparro, J. (2003). The ACTFL proficiency guidelines and the oral proficiency interview: a brief history and analysis of their survival. *Foreign Language Annals* 36, 4, 483–490.

Little. D. (2006). The Common European Framework of Reference for languages: content, purpose, origin, reception and impact. *Language Teaching* 39, 167–190.

Livingston, S. A. and Zieky, M. J. (1982). *Passing Scores: A Manual for Setting Standards of Performance on Educational and Occupational Tests*. Princeton, NJ: Educational Testing Service.

Long, M. H. and Robinson, P. (1998). Focus on form: theory, research and practice. In Doughty, C. and Williams J. (eds), *Focus on Form in Classroom Second Language Acquisition*. Cambridge: Cambridge University Press, 15–41.

Lowe, P. (1986). Proficiency: panacea, framework, process? A reply to Kramsch, Schulz, and particularly Bachman and Savignon. *Modern Language Journal* 70, 4, 391–397.

Luria, A. R. (1979). *The Making of Mind: A Personal Account of Soviet Psychology*. Cambridge, MA: Harvard University Press.

Mansell, W. (2007). *Education by Numbers: The Tyranny of Testing*. London: Politico's Publishing.

Matsuno, S. (2009). Self-, peer- and teacher-assessments in Japanese university EFL writing classrooms. *Language Testing* 26, 1, 75–100.

May, L. (2009). Co-constructed interaction in a paired speaking test: the rater's perspective. *Language Testing* 26, 3, 397–421.

McEldowney, P. L. (1982). A place for visuals in language testing. In Heaton, J. B. (ed.), *Language Testing*. London: Modern English Publications, 86–91.

McNamara, T. (2001). Language assessment as social practice: challenges for research. *Language Testing* 18, 4, 333–349.

McNamara, T. (2005). 21st century shibboleth: language tests, identity and intergroup conflict. *Language Policy* 4, 4, 351–370.

McNamara, T. and Roever, C. (2006). *Language Testing: The Social Dimension*. London: Blackwell.

McREL (2009). *Content Knowledge Standards*. Denver, CO: McREL. Available online: http://www.mcrel.org/standards-benchmarks/.

Menken, K. (2008a). High-stakes tests as de facto language policies. In Shohamy, E. and Hornberger, N. H. (eds), *Encyclopedia of Language and Education*. 2nd edition, vol. 7, *Language Testing and Assessment*. New York: Springer, 401–413.

Menken, K. (2008b). Editorial. Introduction to the thematic issue. *Language Policy* 7, 191–199.

Menken, K. (2009). No Child Left Behind and its effects on language policy. *Annual Review of Applied Linguistics* 29, 103–117.

Messick, S. (1989). Validity. In Linn, R. L. (ed.), *Educational Measurement*. New York: American Council on Education/Macmillan, 13–103.

Messick, S. (1996). Validity and washback in language testing. *Language Testing* 13, 3, 241–256.

Milanovic, M., Saville, N., Pollitt, A. and Cook, A. (1996). Developing rating scales for CASE:

theoretical concerns and analyses. In Cumming, A. and Berwick, R. (eds), *Validation in Language Testing*. London: Multilingual Matters, 15–38.

Mill, J. S. (1859). *On Liberty*. In J. Gray (ed.), *John Stuart Mill on Liberty and Other Essays*. Oxford: Oxford University Press.

Mill. J. S. (1873). *Autobiography*. London: Longmans, Green, Reader and Dyer.

Mills, S. (2009). An evaluation of a paired format oral test for Korean learners of english for hotel and tourism. Unpublished MA dissertation, University of Leicester.

Ministry of National Education and Religious Affairs. (2008). *English Language Certification Examiner Pack*. Athens: Ministry of National Education and Religious Affairs. Available online: http://www.ypepth.gr/docs/b2_m4_may08_080513.pdf.

Mislevy, R. J., Almond, R. G. and Lukas, J. F. (2003). *A Brief Introduction to Evidence-Centred Design*. Research Report RR-03–16. Princeton, NJ: Educational Testing Service.

Miyazaki, I. (1981). *China's Examination Hell: The Civil Service Examinations of Imperial China*. New Haven, CT: Yale University Press.

Morrow, K. (1979). Communicative language testing: revolution or evolution? In Brumfit, C. K. and Johnson, K. (eds), *The Communicative Approach to Language Teaching*. Oxford: Oxford University Press, 143–159.

Moss, P. (2003). Reconceptualizing validity for classroom assessment. *Educational Measurement: Issues and Practice* 22, 4, 13–25.

Nicole, N. (2008). Washback on classroom practice for teachers and learners. Unpublished MA dissertation, University of Leicester.

Norris, S. P. (1998). *Informal Reasoning Assessment: Using Verbal Reports of Thinking to Improve Multiple-Choice Test Validity*. Washington, DC: Educational Resources Information Center, Technical Report 430. Available online: http://www.eric.ed.gov/ERICDocs/data/ericdocs2sql/content_storage_01/0000019b/80/1c/a7/d7.pdf.

North, B. (1992). Options for scales of proficiency for a European Language Framework. In Scharer, R. and North, B. (eds), *Toward a Common European Framework for Reporting Language Competency*. Washington, DC: National Foreign Language Center, 9–26.

North, B. (1993). *Scales of Language Proficiency: A Survey of Some Existing Systems*. Strasbourg: Council of Europe, Council for Cultural Co-operation, CC-LANG (94) 24.

North, B. (1995). The development of a common framework scale of descriptors of language proficiency based on a theory of measurement. *System* 23, 4, 445–465.

North, B. (2000). *The Development of a Common Framework Scale of Language Proficiency*. New York: Peter Lang.

North, B. (2007). The CEFR illustrative descriptor scales. *Modern Language Journal* 91, 656–659.

North, B. and Schneider, G. (1998). Scaling descriptors for language proficiency scales. *Language Testing* 15, 2, 217–262.

Northwest Lifeguards Certification Test (2008). Available online: http://www.seattle.gov/Parks/Aquatics/LifeguardTest.pdf.

Obama, B. (2006). *The Audacity of Hope: Thoughts on Reclaiming the American Dream*. New York: Three Rivers Press.

OECD. (2006). *PISA Released Items – Reading*. Available online: http://www.pisa.oecd.org/dataoecd/13/34/38709396.pdf.

Oscarson, M. (1989). Self-assessment of language proficiency: rationale and applications. *Language Testing* 6, 1, 1–13.

Patri, M. (2002). The influence of peer feedback on self- and peer-assessment. *Language Testing* 19, 2, 109–132.

Pawlikowska-Smith, G. (2000). *Canadian Language Benchmarks 2000. English as a Second Language for Adults.* Canada: Centre for Canadian Language Benchmarks. Available online: http://www.language.ca/pdfs/clb_adults.pdf.

Pearson, K. (1914, 1924, 1930). *The Life, Letters and Labours of Francis Galton.* Cambridge: Cambridge University Press. Available online: http://www.galton.org/pearson/index.html.

Pearson, K. (1920). Notes on the history of correlation. *Biometrika,* 13, 1, 25–45.

People's Daily Online (2007). *National College Entrance Exam: three decades on.* Available online: http://english.peopledaily.com.cn/200706/04/eng20070604_380679.html.

Perie, M. (2008). A guide to understanding and developing performance-level descriptors. *Educational Measurement: Issues and Practice* 27, 4, 15–29.

Philips, S. (2007). *Automated Essay Scoring: A Literature Review.* Kelowna, BC: Society for the Advancement of Excellence in Education. Available online: http://www.saee.ca/pdfs/036.pdf.

Pienemann, M. and Johnston, M. (1986). An acquisition based procedure for second language assessment (ESL). *Australian Review of Applied Linguistics* 9, 1, 1–27.

Pienemann, M., Johnston, M. and Brindley, G. (1988). Constructing an acquisition-based procedure for second language assessment. *Studies in Second Language Acquisition* 10, 2, 217–245.

Pitoniak, M. J. and Royer, J. M. (2001). Testing accommodations for examinees with disabilities: a review of psychometric, legal, and social policy issues. *Review of Educational Research* 71, 1, 53–104.

Plake, B. S. (2008). Standard setters: stand up and take a stand! *Educational Measurement: Issues and Practice* 27, 1, 3–9.

Plato (1987). *The Republic,* 2nd revised edition. Trans. D. Lee. London: Penguin Classics.

Poehner, M. E. (2008). *Dynamic Assessment and the Problem of Validity in the L2 Classroom.* CALPER Working Paper Series No. 10. Pennsylvania State University: Center for Advanced Language Proficiency Education and Research.

Popham, J. (1978). *Criterion-Referenced Measurement.* Englewood Cliffs, NJ: Prentice-Hall.

Popham, J. (1991). Appropriateness of teachers' test-preparation practices. *Educational Measurement: Issues and Practice* 10, 4, 12–15.

Popham, J. (1992). A tale of two test-specification strategies. *Educational Measurement: Issues and Practice,* 11, 2, 16–17 and 22.

Popham, W. J. and Husek, T. R. (1969). Implications of criterion-referenced measurement. *Journal of Educational Measurement* 6, 1, 1–9.

Popham, W. R. (1994). The instructional consequences of criterion referenced clarity. *Educational Measurement: Issues and Practice* 13, 4, 15–18.

Popper, K. (2002). *The Open Society and Its Enemies.* London: Routledge.

Powers, D. E. (1993). Coaching for the SAT: a summary of the summaries and an update. *Educational Measurement: Issues and Practice* 12, 2, 24–30.

Powers, D. E., Albertson, W., Florek, T., Johnson, K., Malak, J., Nemceff, B., Porzuc, M., Silvester, D., Wang, M., Weston, R., Winner, E. and Zelazny, A. (2002). *Influence of Irrelevant Speech on Standardized Test Performance.* TOEFL Research Report 68. Princeton, NJ: Educational Testing Service.

Purpura, J. E. (2004). *Assessing Grammar.* Cambridge: Cambridge University Press.

Qi, L. (2004). Has a high-stakes test produced the intended changes? In Cheng, L., Watanabe, Y. and Curtis, A. (eds), *Washback in Language Testing*. Mahwah, NJ: Lawrence Erlbaum, 171–190.

Quetelet, A. (1842). *A Treatise on Man and the Development of His Faculties*. English trans. (reprinted 1962). New York: Burt Franklin.

Quinlan, T., Higgins, D. and Wolf, S. (2009). *Evaluating the Construct Coverage of the e-Rater Scoring Engine*. Research Report 09-01. Princeton, NJ: Educational Testing Service. Available online: http://www.ets.org/Media/Research/pdf/RR-09-01.pdf.

Rawls, J. (1973). *A Theory of Justice*. Oxford: Oxford University Press.

Rea-Dickins, P. (2006). Currents and eddies in the discourse of assessment: a learning-focused interpretation. *International Journal of Applied Linguistics* 16, 2, 163–188.

Rea-Dickins, P. (2008). Classroom-based language assessment. In Shohamy, E. and Hornberger, N. H. (eds), *Encyclopedia of Language and Education*, vol. 7, *Language Testing and Assessment*. New York: Springer, 257–271.

Read, J. and Hayes, B. (2003). The impact of the IELTS test on preparation for academic study in New Zealand. *IELTS Research Reports,* vol. 5, Canberra: IELTS Australia, 153–206.

Reckase, M. D. (2000). A survey and evaluation of recently developed procedures for setting standards on educational tests. In Bourquey, M. L. and Byrd, Sh. (eds), *Student Performance Standards on the National Assessment of Educational Progress: Affirmations and Improvement*. Washington, DC: NAEP, 41–70.

Roach, J. (1971). *Public Examinations in England 1850–1900*. Cambridge: Cambridge University Press.

Robb, T. N. and Ercanbrack, J. (1999). A study of the effect of direct test preparation on the TOEIC scores of Japanese university students. *TESOL-EJ*, 3, 4. Available online: http://www.zait.uni-bremen.de/wwwgast/tesl_ej/ej12/a2.html

Ross, J. A. (2006). The reliability, validity, and utility of self-assessment. *Practical Assessment, Research and Evaluation,* 11, 10. Retrieved from http://pareonline.net/pdf/v11n10.pdf, 1 June 2009.

Ross, S. (1992). The discourse of accommodation in oral proficiency interviews. *Studies in Second Language Acquisition* 14, 159–176.

Ross, S. (1998a). Self-assessment in second language testing: a meta-analysis and analysis of experiential factors. *Language Testing* 15, 1, 1–20.

Ross, S. (1998b). Divergent frame interpretations in language proficiency interview interaction. In Young, R. and He, A. W. (eds), *Talking and Testing: Discourse Approaches to the Assessment of Oral Proficiency*. Amsterdam: John Benjamins, 333–353.

Ross, S. and Berwick, R. (1992). The discourse of accommodation in oral proficiency interviews. *Studies in Second Language Acquisition* 14, 159–176.

Rost, M. (2002). *Teaching and Researching Listening*. London: Longman/Pearson Education.

Rothman, R., Slattery, J. B., Vranek, J. L. and Resnick, L. B. (2002). *Benchmarking and Alignment of Standards and Testing*. Los Angeles, CA: Center for the Study of Evaluation, University of California.

Ruch, G. M. (1924). *The Improvement of the Written Examination*. Chicago: Scott, Foresman and Company.

Rudner, L. M. (1998). *Online, Interactive, Computer Adaptive Testing Tutorial*. Available online: http://echo.edres.org:8080/scripts/cat/catdemo.htm.

Russell, M. and Haney, W. (1997). Testing writing on computers: an experiment comparing student performance on tests conducted via computer and via paper-and-pencil. *Educational Policy Archives* 5, 3. Available online: http://epaa.asu.edu/epaa/v5n3.html.

Ryoo, H.-K. (2005). Achieving friendly interactions: a study of service encounters between Korean shopkeepers and African-American customers. *Discourse and Society* 16, 1, 79–105.

Saville, N. (2005). An interview with John Trim at 80. *Language Assessment Quarterly.* 2, 4, 263–288.

Sawaki, Y. (2001). Comparability of conventional and computerized tests of reading in a second language. *Language Learning and Technology* 5, 2, 38–59. Available online: http://llt.msu.edu/vol5num2/sawaki/default.html.

Sawaki, Y., Stricker, S. J. and Oranje, A. J., (2009). Factor structure of the TOEFL internet-based test. *Language Testing* 26, 1, 5–30.

Scharber, C., Dexter, S. and Riedel, E. (2008). Students' experiences with an automated essay scorer. *Journal of Technology, Learning, and Assessment,* 7, 1. Available online: http://escholarship.bc.edu/cgi/viewcontent.cgi?article=1116&context=jtla.

Schmitt, N., Schmitt, D. and Clapham, C. (2001). Two versions of the vocabulary levels test. *Language Testing,* 18, 1, 55–88.

Schulz, R. A. (1986). From achievement through proficiency through classroom instruction: some caveats. *Modern Language Journal* 70, 4, 373–379.

Segalowitz, N. and Hulstijn, J. (2005). Automaticity in bilingualism and second language learning. In Kroll, J. F. and De Groot, A. M. B. (eds), *Handbook of Bilingualism: Psycholinguistic Approaches.* Oxford: Oxford University Press.

Semmel, B. (1960). *Imperialism and Social Reform: English Social-Imperial Thought 1895–1914.* London: Allen and Unwin.

Shepard, L. (1990). *Inflated Test Scores Gains: Is It Old Norms or Teaching to the Test?* CSE Technical Report 307. Los Angeles, CA: University of California at Los Angeles.

Shepard, L. (1991). Psychometricians' beliefs about learning. *Educational Researcher* 20, 6, 2–16.

Shepard, L. (1995). Using assessment to improve learning. *Educational Leadership* 52, 5, 38–43.

Shepard, L. (2000). The role of assessment in a learning culture. *Educational Researcher* 29, 7, 4–14.

Shohamy, E. (1996). Competence and performance in language testing. In Brown, G., Malmkjaer, K. and Williams, J. (eds), *Performance and Competence in Second Language Acquisition.* Cambridge: Cambridge University Press.

Shohamy, E. (2001a). *The Power of Tests: A Critical Perspective on the Uses of Language Tests.* London: Longman/Pearson Education.

Shohamy, E. (2001b). Democratic assessment as an alternative. *Language Testing* 18, 4, 373–392.

Sinclair, J. McH. and Brazil, D. (1982). *Teacher Talk.* Oxford: Oxford University Press.

Sireci, S. G. (2005). Unlabeling the disabled: a perspective on flagging scores from accommodated test administrations. *Educational Researcher* 34, 1, 3–12.

Spolsky, B. (1968). Preliminary studies in the development of techniques for testing overall second language proficiency. *Language Learning* 3, 79–101.

Spolsky, B. (1995). *Measured Words.* Oxford: Oxford University Press.

Stiggins, R. J. (2001). The unfulfilled promise of classroom assessment. *Educational Measurement: Issues and Practice* 20, 3, 5–15.

Stricker, L. J. (2002). *The Performance of Native Speakers of English and ESL Speakers on the TOEFL CBT and FRE General Test.* TOEFL Research Report 69. Princeton, NJ: Educational Testing Service.

Swain, M. (2000). The output hypothesis and beyond: mediating acquisition through collaborative dialogue. In Lantolf, J. (ed.), *Sociocultural Theory and Second Language Learning*, Oxford: Oxford University Press, 97–114.

Taylor, C. S. and Nolan, S. B. (1996). What does the psychometrician's classroom look like? Reframing assessment concepts in the context of learning. *Educational Policy Analysis Archives*, 4, 17. Available online: http://epaa.asu.edu/epaa/v4n17.html.

Taylor, D. A. (1996). *Introduction to Marine Engineering*. 2nd edition. New York: Butterworth-Heinemann.

Taylor, L. (2009). Developing assessment literacy. *Annual Review of Applied Linguistics* 29, 21–36.

Teasedale, A. and Leung, C. (2000). Teacher assessment and psychometric theory: a case of paradigm crossing? *Language Testing* 17, 2, 163–184.

Terman, L. M. (1919). *The Measurement of Intelligence*. London: Harrap.

Terman, L. M. (1922). The great conspiracy or the impulse imperious of intelligence testers, psychoanalyzed and exposed by Mr Lippmann, *New Republic* 33 (27 December), 116–120. Available online: http://historymatters.gmu.edu/d/4960/.

Thorndike, E. L. (1920). A constant error in psychological ratings. *Journal of Applied Psychology* 4, 469–477.

Tsagari, D. (2009). *The Complexity of Test Washback: An Empirical Study*. Frankfurt: Peter Lang.

Underhill, N. (1987). *Testing Spoken Language*. Cambridge: Cambridge University Press.

Upshur, J. and Turner, C. (1995). Constructing rating scales for second language tests. *English Language Teaching Journal*, 49, 1, 3–12.

van Ek, J. A. (1975). *The Threshold Level in a European Unit/Credit System for Modern Language Learning by Adults*. Strasbourg: Council of Europe.

van Ek, J. A. and Trim, J. L. M. (1990). *Threshold Level 1990: Modern Languages*. Strasbourg: Council of Europe.

van Lier, L. (1989). Reeling, writing, drawling, stretching, and fainting in coils: oral proficiency interviews as conversation. *TESOL Quarterly* 23, 3, 489–508.

Wainer, H. (1986). Can a test be too reliable? *Journal of Educational Measurement* 23, 2, 171–173.

Wall, D. (2005). *The Impact of High-Stakes Examinations on Classroom Teaching: A Case Study Using Insights from Testing and Innovation Theory*. Cambridge: Cambridge University Press.

Wall, D. and Alderson, J. C. (1993). Examining washback: the Sri Lankan impact study. *Language Testing* 10, 1, 41–69.

Wall. D. and Alderson, J. C. (1996). Examining washback: the Sri Lankan impact study. In Cumming, A. and Berwick, R. (eds), *Validation in Language Testing*. Clevedon: Multilingual Matters, 194–221.

Wall, D. and Horák, T. (2006). *The Impact of Changes in the TOEFL Examination on Teaching and Learning in Central and Eastern Europe. Phase 1: The Baseline Study*. TOEFL Monograph No. MS-34. Princeton, NJ: Educational Testing Service. Available online: http://www.ets.org/Media/Research/pdf/RR-06-18.pdf.

Wall, D. and Horák, T. (2008). *The Impact of Changes in the TOEFL Examination on Teaching and Learning in Central and Eastern Europe. Phase 2: Coping with Change*. TOEFL iBT Report iBT-05. Princeton, NJ: Educational Testing Service. Available online: http://www.ets.org/Media/Research/pdf/RR-08-37.pdf.

Watanabe, Y. (2004a). Teacher factors mediating washback. In Cheng, L., Watanabe, Y. and Curtis, A. (eds), *Washback in Language Testing*. Mahwah, NJ: Lawrence Erlbaum, 129–146.

Watanabe, Y. (2004b). Methodology in washback studies. In Cheng, L., Watanabe, Y. and Curtis, A. (eds), *Washback in Language Testing*. Mahwah, NJ: Lawrence Erlbaum, 19–36.

Watters, E. K. (2003). Literacy for health: an interdisciplinary model. *Journal of Transcultural Nursing* 14, 1, 48–53.

Webb, N. L. (1999). *Criteria for Alignment of Expectations and Assessments in Mathematics and Science Education. Council of Chief State School Officers and National Institute for Science Education Research Monograph No. 6.* Madison, WI: University of Wisconsin, Wisconsin Center for Education Research.

Weber, M. (1947). *The Theory of Social and Economic Organization.* Trans. A. M. Henderson and T. Parsons. Oxford: Oxford University Press.

Weigle, S. C. (2002). *Assessing Writing.* Cambridge: Cambridge University Press.

Weir, C. (2005). *Language Testing and Validation.* London: Palgrave Macmillan.

Wendler, C. and Powers, D. (2009). What does it mean to repurpose a test? *R&D Connections* 9. Princeton, NJ: Educational Testing Service. Available online: http://www.ets.org/Media/Research/pdf/RD_Connections9.pdf.

WIDA. (2007). *ELP Standards.* University of Wisconsin: Board of Regents of the University of Wisconsin System, on behalf of the WIDA Consortium. Available online: http://www.wida.us/standards/elp.aspx.

Widdowson, H. G. (1978). *Teaching Language as Communication.* Oxford: Oxford University Press.

Wilds, C. (1975). The oral interview test. In Jones, R. L. and Spolsky, B. (eds), *Testing Language Proficiency.* Arlington, VA: Center for Applied Linguistics, 29–44.

Wiliam, D. (1996). Meanings and consequences in standard setting. *Assessment in Education: Principles, Policy and Practice* 3, 3, 287–308.

Winter, E. (1977). A clause-relational approach to English texts: a study of some predictive lexical items in written discourse. *Instructional Science* 6, 1, 1–92.

Wresch, W. (1993). The imminence of grading essays by computer – 25 years later. *Computers and Composition* 10, 2, 45-58.

Wright, B. (1996). Reliability and separation. *Rasch Measurement Transactions* 9, 4, 472. Available online: http://www.rasch.org/rmt/rmt94n.htm.

Xi, X., Higgins, D., Zechner, K. and Williamson, D. M. (2008). *Automated Scoring of Spontaneous Speech Using SpeechRater v1.0.* Research Report RR-08-62. Princeton, NJ: Educational Testing Service.

Yerkes, R. M. (1921). *Psychological Examining in the United States Army.* Memoirs of the National Academy of Sciences 15. Washington, DC: Government Printing Office.

Yerkes, R. M. (1941). *The Role of Psychology in the War.* Reprinted from the *New World of Science* (1920), 351–380. Mimeograph.

Ylänne-McEwen, V. (2004). Shifting alignment and negotiating sociality in travel agency discourse. *Discourse Studies* 6, 4, 517–536.

Yoakum, C. S. and Yerkes, R. M. (1920). *Army Mental Tests.* New York: Henry Holt and Co.

Young, R. (2008). *Language and Interaction.* London and New York: Routledge.

Zeithaml, V. A. (2000). Service quality, profitability, and the economic worth of customers: what we know and what we need to learn. *Journal of the Academy of Marketing Science* 28, 1, 67–85.

Zhengdong, G. (2009). IELTS preparation course and student IELTS performance. A case study in Hong Kong. *RELC Journal* 40, 1, 23–41.

Index